JUNGLE CHRONICLES

AND OTHER WRITINGS
RECOLLECTIONS OF A SOUTH SUDANESE

ATEM YAAK ATEM

© 2017 Atem Yaak Atem
ISBN 978 0 98761441 8 6

All rights reserved. No part of this publication may be reproduced, stored in any information storage system or distributed by photocopying, email, or online without the prior written consent of the author, except in the case of brief quotations with proper reference, for study or research purposes or embodied in critical articles and reviews.

All quotations remain the intellectual properties of their originators. All use of quotations is performed under the fair use copyright principle.

Editor: Rachel Kear.
Typesetting and layout: All in One Book Design, Perth, Western Australia

Dedication

To the memories of my parents
Yaak Atem Achuoth Yaak and Nyanluak Bior Aguek Bior,
who were some of the most hardworking, honest,
and caring persons I have known

About the Author

Atem Yaak Atem is a South Sudanese journalist and translator. He has written and commented on his country's political and social issues for more than four decades.

After receiving a BA in English and Philosophy from the University of Khartoum in 1974, Atem worked for the Regional Ministry of Culture and Information, where he was deployed on the weekly newspaper, the *Nile Mirror*, as features editor and Arabic-English translator.

In 1977, after obtaining a Diploma in Communication from Khartoum Institute of Mass Communication he was appointed founding editor of *Southern Sudan*, a government monthly news and cultural magazine.

In 1978, Atem attended an advanced course in journalism in West Berlin's International Institute for Journalism, which awarded him a further diploma in journalism.

He left the periodical *Southern Sudan* to study printing in Britain in 1981. In 1982 he enrolled for a postgraduate study in journalism at the University of Wales in Cardiff, where he obtained an M. Ed in 1984. The area of research covered by his dissertation was "The Role and Problems of Broadcasting by Radio with Special Reference to the Sudan".

In 1984, Atem was the founding director of the clandestine Radio SPLA. The station was a mouthpiece for the Sudan People's Liberation Movement, SPLM, campaigning for the creation of a democratic Sudan with justice and equality for all of its citizens, irrespective of their ethnic, religious, cultural or geographic affiliations. Besides serving as a forum for public education, recruitment and morale boosting for the SPLA fighters, the broadcaster succeeded in allaying the fears of liberal Northern Sudanese elite. Some members of the elite joined the insurgency that began in Southern Sudan in 1983, fighting the central government in Khartoum to change the system of rule. As head of the broadcaster, Atem persuaded the leadership of the rebel movement to adopt a policy that would make field commanders spare the lives of POWs. The request was accepted and became an official policy of the insurgents. Soon after, the SPLA had hundreds of POWs, most of whom were later released to their families. The Government of Sudan held none of the rebel captives.

About the Author

In addition to his media responsibilities Atem was a speechwriter for the SPLM/A leader, Dr John Garang. Atem also took part – as a member of the SPLM/A delegations – in various peace talks- in Ethiopia, Kenya, Abuja in Nigeria- with the Government of Sudan and other Sudanese political parties and opposition groups.

For six months while based in Accra, the capital of Ghana, he was also part of a team to outline an SPLM peace plan to the leaders of West African countries, among them Nigeria, Ivory Coast, Senegal, Mali, Burkina Faso and Togo.

In 1988 Atem was appointed member of the SPLM/A's humanitarian branch, Sudan Relief and Rehabilitation Association, SRRA, and took part in the launch of the UN Operation Lifeline Sudan, the first ever programme devised by the world body to allow the flow of relief supplies to areas controlled by a state and a non-state actor, respectively. OLS-Sudan was launched in April 1989 at Panyagoor by the UN's director general of Unicef, James Grant and the rebel leader, John Garang. Atem served at Panyagoor- not far from his home village- and was later transferred to Bor and Torit where he directed the SRRA operations- in conjunction with leading international humanitarian bodies- for two years before being recalled to the SPLM/A headquarters for a foreign mission.

After the change of regime in Ethiopia in 1991, the SPLM/A relocated its offices to Kenya. From 1993 to 1994, Atem worked as an editorial consultant at the African Development Bank, Abidjan, Ivory Coast.

After reunion in 1994 with his family who had been "stranded" at Nasir in Southern Sudan since 1991, Atem settled in western Kenya where he taught English at Lodwar Secondary. While there he began writing articles, for Kenyan newspapers as well as the weekly newsletter, the *SPLM Update*, in which he maintained a weekly column, 'Far Away from War'.

In 1997, Atem became the founding editor of the *Horn of Africa Vision*, a monthly magazine published by the Horn of Africa Centre for Democracy and Development, an advocacy NGO for social justice and women's rights based in Nairobi, Kenya.

From 2003, he was a regular contributing columnist for the *Sudan Mirror*, a Nairobi-based weekly newspaper.

In 2005 Atem co-chaired a committee to select young Southern Sudanese to be trained as reporters for the United Nations peace advocacy FM radio station, *Miraya*, based in Juba, South Sudan, following the end of an armed conflict in that country. Before that he had participated in the training of young Southern Sudanese journalists living in Kenya.

On returning to Australia in 2006 (in 2000 he joined his family who had gone there in 1997 for resettlement), Atem taught English at the University of Newcastle, NSW. He was one of the teaching staff nominated for the 2009 TAFE (Technical and Further Education) NSW, South Western Sydney Institute's Staff Excellence and Innovation in Teaching and Learning Awards. During the previous year Atem had taught methodology and ethics of interpreting and translation at Granville TAFE, Sydney.

Atem is fluent in English, Dinka and Arabic and understands basics of Shilluk and Nuer, languages. He has worked as a translator for SBS, Special Broadcasting Service, Australia, Language Professionals, and the former Sydney West Area Health Service, among others.

On return to Southern Sudan in December 2009, he edited *The Pioneer* weekly English language newspaper in Juba. After the outbreak of the civil war in December 2013, a development that has curtailed freedom of expression in general and the press in particular, Atem returned to Australia. He is now a full time writer and is self-employed as English-Dinka translator. As an active member of South Sudanese community in Australia, Atem is a tireless advocate of unity, social cohesion and integration of his compatriots among themselves as well as with the wider Australian community. Since the outbreak of armed conflict in South Sudan in 2013, Atem has consistently distanced himself from all the warring parties of the ruling and divided SPLM of which he is a lifelong member.

He is also an occasional lecturer in Modern History of South Sudan and Media at the Rift Valley Institute, an independent, non-profit research and education organisation working in seven Eastern and Central African countries, with offices in Nairobi, Kenya and London.

Before the outbreak of the civil war in his country in December 2013, Atem had made arrangements to settle for good in Pakuoor, his home of birth in rural Kongor area, South Sudan. The plan consisted of taking up teaching at the nearby Dr John Garang Secondary School; contributing to environmental awareness, planting trees and other activities aimed at conserving nature; listen and record oral history and traditional literature from the now

About the Author

diminishing older generation, in addition to writing full time. Once stability returns to the land, he says he will return home immediately.

He is married to Anna Abul Malual who is a professional interpreter and they have five adult children. Atem currently lives on the NSW Central Coast, family home since 1997. *Jungle Chronicles* is his first book. He is currently preparing for publication his three-volume memoir, and three drafts in Dinka, one of them a translation of selected tales from Aesop's Fables.

Contents

About the Author	4
Abbreviations and Acronyms	10
Preface	11
Introduction	15

Society And Culture

Neologisms for popular sub-culture of South Sudan	26
A spectrum of meanings	32
The dangers of conformity, prejudice and stereotyping	35
At the crossroads: Southern Sudanese losing their identity	41
Of pens and books	47
When food becomes a killer	49
Innocent Abroad : A black man and a black dog in rural Wales	53
The night I became an Arab	63
Breaking with customs is hard to do	68
Erosion of some social values (1)	71
Erosion of some social values (2)	74
Erosion of some social values (3)	76
Are we the leading exporters of rudeness worldwide?	80
Other uses for dogs	94
Paweer, or The Years of Dispersion	96
The Agamlöng: An unacknowledged entertainer	101
Imagery of night in rural lore	104
The Arab-Muslim community in Kongor of the old days	108
When Juba reeled under Ebola	127
After all radio is a luxury	132
Sudanese Supermodel Alek Wek sparks African beauty debate	137
'Comrade' is neither a name nor an honorific	140
'Romancing' Sudan	143
Is complaining becoming our national pastime?	147
Is setting the standards too high the cause of disillusionment?	152
The Civil Service delivery fiasco	158
All patriots? Count me out	163

Of corrupt governments and persons	169
Criteria for Selection for Public Office Holders	174
Why chiefs are still relevant	179
Democracy in an Ethnically Diverse Society	185
A move away from cities	188
South Sudan: An unknown country without an identity	193
A long journey to authorship	198

War and Peace

The Origins of 'Far Away from War'	226
When Gaddafi and SPLM/A played a game of wits	231
The speech that John Garang rejected	247
Yousif Kuwa: Back to his roots	252
Kerubino Kuanyin Bol as I knew him	261
Martyrs: We shall not forget them	293
Assassinations of leaders and mass murders	295
Conversation with Mansour Khaled	302
The origins of Garang-Mirghani summit of 1988	311
Why some people dread peace	319
Of unity and independence	323
Garang, Taha deserve sympathy	328
South Sudan tragedy: Choice of words for waging peace, reconciliation	337
Reform should begin from the SPLM Extraordinary Convention itself	347
The dawn of the Addis Ababa Agreement of 1972: a recollection (1)	352
The dawn of the Addis Ababa Agreement (2)	355
The dawn of the Addis Ababa Agreement (3)	359
The dawn of Addis Ababa Agreement: a recollection (4)	363
The dawn of the Addis Ababa Agreement: a recollection (5)	366
The role of the media in peace and reconciliation	372
Current national tragedy: A possible satirist version	376

Acknowledgements	382

Abbreviations and Acronyms

AAA	Addis Ababa Agreement (of 1972)
CPA	Comprehensive Peace Agreement
DUP	Democratic Unionist Party
GoSS	Government of Southern Sudan
Igad/IGAD	Igad Intergovernmenta/Authority on Development
SAF	Sudan Armed Forces
Sanu	Sudan African National Union
SPLA	Sudan People's Liberation Army
SPLM	Sudan People's Liberation Movement
SPLM/SPLA	Sudan People's Liberation Movement/Sudan People's Liberation Army
SPLM/A	Shortened form of the above
SOUTHERN SUDAN	The name of the Sudan before its independence in July 2011
SOUTH SUDAN	The name taken by the former Southern Sudan after independence
Unesco	United Nations Educational Scientific and Cultural Organisation
Unicef	United Nations International Children's Emergency Fund

Preface

A real journalist must serve the truth, even if that means becoming unpopular or inviting hatred from those related by blood, political or ideological bonds.
Atem Yaak Atem, 2003

South Sudan which split from Sudan in 2011 has been known for its years of political and social upheaval even before the end of colonial rule in 1956. The two countries are so intimately linked to one another by their history that anyone writing about what has become known as the two Sudans cannot hope to provide meaningful context without reference to that shared past. This is what the author has done in this volume of his memoir. From time to time, the stories here refer to Sudan, Southern Sudan, Southern Region and finally South Sudan, names of territories likely to cause confusion to a general reader. The first two were used to designate the third southern part of Sudan – known during colonial days as the Sudan- before the partition of the country in 2011 into the now independent republics of Sudan and South Sudan, respectively.

Over the ensuing six decades, the country was embroiled in two bloody civil wars. Because the peripheral regions, among them Southern Sudan, lagged behind the North especially in education, the British authorities handed political, economic and security instruments of control over to the Northern intelligentsia who went on to exclude the rest of the Sudanese from share of power and wealth – with most of the country's natural resources in the South. When the representatives of the neglected regions demanded a constitutional setup that would safeguard the interests of their people, the Northern ruling elite ignored that. Instead they further alienated the regions by declaring at independence Sudan as an Arab nation that had to be built on the basis Arab culture with Arabic as the official language of country and Islam as the source of legislation.

As the country had – both Sudan and South Sudan are still multicultural societies and home to an estimated 100 mainly African languages and dialects – a bewildering cultural, religious and ethnic diversity, those policies further alienated the rest of the Sudanese. The South in particular rejected what its leaders regarded as Khartoum's drive for a total assimilation and making other Sudanese second class citizens in their country. The stage was set for a chronic disagreement over the constitutional status of the country. That led to the loss of trust between the two regions which in later years developed into an armed resistance. For its part, the central government resorted to military- using the rebellion as a pretext- as a means to intimidate and bring the region under control. Violence spawned violence. Occasionally, Southern Sudanese insurgents turned their guns against one another for control and direction of the rebellion against authorities in Khartoum. This was the genesis of the two bloody civil wars, famine, massive community displacement, destruction of the environment and ecosystem and near-constant political strife and instability.

With a searing honesty characteristic of the world's premier journalists, Atem Yaak Atem examines the attempts of various political interest groups to find a mutually acceptable and lasting peaceful solution to the armed conflict over the years. As an active participant in his country's second civil war of 1983-2005- as the founding director of Radio SPLA, rebel movement's main mouthpiece, and speechwriter for the SPLM/A, Dr John Garang- Atem recalls historic events of the time and his interactions with prominent members of the insurgency, such as the moment's former deputy leader, Kerubino Kuanyin Bol, Yousif Kuwa Mekki, among others. Atem's close proximity to the SPLM/A top hierarchy often brought him into contacts with some of African heads of state, local and international journalists, and not surprisingly, spies posing as diplomats as was the case with an Egyptian official who claimed he was a special envoy from the former Egyptian President, Hosni Mubarak. The author narrates in this volume the account of that fiction-like encounter.

In this collection, the author also examines a host of societal topics about South Sudan whether during the war or when the region was experiencing interludes of tranquillity.

Although he strongly advocates social changes and modernisation of system of governance that incorporates models that have worked elsewhere in the world, he nevertheless, argues a case for the preservation of some elements from social mores that have served rural communities of his South Sudanese society well over millennia. Among those norms and practices is the special care traditional society gives to its vulnerable members. During lean times, for instance, able-bodied members would forego their share of food to be served to children, the sick, women in general and lactating mothers in particular. Another value system he supports is the old-age long culture which does not only criminalise theft but also stigmatises thieves, a practice that was more effective as a deterrence than the penalties meted out by customary courts.

Despite acknowledging positive aspects of traditions and customs, the pieces are not a work of praise-singer of ideas or personalities; in some pieces he is vitriolic and impatient with some conducts by some urban South Sudanese either at home or in the diaspora. As a member of South Sudan's educated and ruling elite, he readily accepts his share of their shortcomings, a responsibility he admits no member can escape whether one is personally involved or not. He has singled out for criticism the widespread, perennial and irritating "Sudan's Time Syndrome", as disregard for punctuality is popularly known. "Virtually all South Sudanese at home and abroad turn up for work and classes on time. But come scheduled social functions or meetings they organise, they are more likely to turn up very late, sometimes as late as four hours at a stretch. This is not only inconvenient to invited non-South Sudanese guests; it is absolutely embarrassing to say the least", he laments in an article contained in this book.

This does not mean that the author seeks to criticise or ridicule everything and everyone in his own society. He remembers with great fondness several people – mostly former teachers, academics and current writers- many of whom he regards as role models for inspiring and teaching him to become a writer. These individuals- as diverse in background as they are in their fields of respective expertise- include the distinguished historian Dr Douglas H. Johnson, creative writer Professor Taban lo Liyong, the peerless authority on Dinka people and cultures, Dr Francis M. Deng, late British journalist and trainer, Frank Burton; and last but not least the former law lecturer and politician, Natale Olwak Akolawin, who first introduced the then-young journalist to the craft of editing on the job.

At once strident, courageous and enlightening, *Jungle Chronicles* is a fascinating and ultimately uplifting snapshot created by a highly-experienced and skilled journalist who has tremendous confidence in his country and its people to forge their own pathway to cohesive and productive nationhood.

Atem creates a blueprint for the revitalised South Sudan to progress as a cohesive, unified nation. He stresses the need to retain the traditional in the face of progress, highlighting the continuing role of rural people who constitute over 90 percent of the country's population- the sole producers of food for urban dwellers- and that at this transitional phase of nation building, the educate elites can't afford to side-line chiefs and their custom-based systems. For the time being, traditional leaders can't be simply wished away; only time will determine their relevance and role in when the new institutions of governance become well established and are effective, efficient and in tune with modernity.

In regard to the development and maintenance of strong international relations, Atem emphasises that these relationships should never be merely paternalistic or co-dependent, but help the South Sudanese to help themselves.

Atem Yaak Atem has covered – and commented on- the affairs of his country, Sudan and later, South Sudan, for four decades, including his role as a senior journalist. Some of those writings appear in this collection; they capture the essence of his non-chronological, four- volume memoir, of which *Jungle Chronicle* (which he considers a "starter" is the first instalment).

Jungle Chronicles is required reading for anyone interested in politics, societal South Sudan and for anyone following the rebirth of this vibrant nation, which, far from defeated and helpless, is going to rise like the phoenix from decades of turmoil.

Rachel Kear
Brisbane, Australia
2017

Introduction

The pieces that form this book come from several sources. March 2017 marked my 42nd year as a journalist, both in print and broadcast media. During these four decades, I have written on many subjects, ranging from events of the day, reportage and features, society in general and culture in particular. With the exception of the Ebola story reproduced here, material from 1975 to the late 1980s is not included in the collection. Copies of those journals some of which I edited –were destroyed during the civil war of 1983-2005. I have not been able to access copies of those publications kept in archives and libraries in the UK, Italy, Norway and US and which contain my writings and photos of those days including occasional fiction and poetry.

Most of the writings in this collection have been selected from articles which were published by newspapers in Kenya such as the *EastAfrican* weekly which is read all over the region; the *Daily Nation* and the now defunct *Sudan Mirror*, a weekly newspaper owned by a former Irish priest, Dan Eiffe. The *Mirror*, like the *SPLM Update* newsletter were edited and produced in the Kenyan capital city, Nairobi. These papers had a wide readership consisting of foreign missions, employees of international organisations based in Nairobi as well as the Kenyan middle class and ruling elites.

My writings in those periodicals were mainly on culture. The rebel SPLM/A newsletter was embarrassingly propagandistic and never pretended to be anything other than a mouthpiece for the former Sudanese rebels. Interestingly, it was the abhorrence in which the cosmopolitan readership held the propaganda sheet- talking about war, enemy casualties, abusive language and other gory reports – that led me to embark on something not remotely connected to Sudan's armed conflict and the accompanying war of words, as well as the shooting war in the battlefield. Thus the "Far Away from War" column was born. My weekly contribution to the paper dealt with cultural matters especially within the rural setting of the Southern Sudan of the past. To the surprise of the editor of the *Update* who was a long-time colleague, those pieces attracted huge readership among non-SPLM members who had grown bored stiff by the war coverage and the propaganda nuisance. Although my articles on culture were/are not work of research, they introduce non-Sudanese and the youth in that part of the world, to a world that is almost on the verge of extinction. For example, one of the pieces from the column and which is included here is the strict division of labour between Dinka males and females in domestic chores: men never milk cows; cook food; never go anywhere near a kitchen or try to know the amount of food a family has in store as that is the wife/mother's domain, and so forth. Very strict taboos governed the way of life of the rural Dinka people right through to the recent past.

However, slowly but inescapably, times are changing. These changes are inevitably affecting the younger generation, especially the millennials to whom those customs do not only appear as outdated but also irrational. For an appreciation of this social change, I have written extensively on the subject from the perspective of someone within the intergenerational border between the old and the modern. When Alek Wek, the former Dinka refugee girl in England made the headlines in late 1990s as a world class model in the West, I wrote an article in the *EastAfrican*. In "Sudanese Supermodel Alek Wek sparks beauty debate", I wrote that her Dinka society never used talents, physical graces included, for material gain.

As expected, the encroachment of modernity into an otherwise conservative society such as that of the Dinka people is bound to face some resistance; it becomes an arena for potential conflict. On that subject, "If rudeness were a commodity, South Sudan would be its leading exporter", looks – in a light-hearted manner – at that kind of cultural clash. Two of the issues discussed in that piece are the discernible lack of politeness, for example, by receptionists in public offices and organisations operating in the country's capital, Juba. Queuing for service in public makes little sense to many South Sudanese used to queue jumping.

Politics as a way of life and the way its practitioners go about it, is a domain that puts off many people who prefer to be left alone to go about their daily lives. Even for the few enthusiasts, political commentariat is a genre that has little value, as its subject matter is essentially ephemeral. Despite my awareness of the problem with opinion pieces, I have added some of my personal viewpoints on some selected issues.

Some of the topics were transient while others addressed problems that still confront the South Sudanese society of today. "All Patriots? Count me out" was published by *Sudan Mirror* on the eve of the signing of the peace agreement between the Government of Sudan and the former rebels of the SPLM/A that ended Sudan's civil war in early 2005. As the reader will appreciate later, my comment drew vitriol, anger and denunciation from nearly all spectrums of Sudanese political groupings including my own colleagues in the then rebel movement, the SPLM. For a long time, my views expressed in that article almost made me a pariah, politically and socially. (More often than not, I am not the darling of the establishment because of such views on public matters).

What is important for the reader, however, is that comments- prickly or mild in tone- written and read years after the issue they tried to address no longer exists, and whose relevance has waned, is that they reveal the mood of the day when they were published.

Opinion articles on perennial issues – and which refuse to go away – such as abuse of power by public servants or "tribalism", as Africans call racism when applied to favouring of clan members and nephews over others who are not related to the persons doling out job opportunities for instance, may not be the stuff entertainment is made of. However, since such behaviours are part of the human condition, talking or writing about them becomes unavoidable. South Sudan as an emerging nation is in the grip of the problems that militate against nation building projects. "The Problem of Conformity, Stereotype…" is my attempt in that direction. I wasn't sure I had made the point convincingly until a stranger wrote me a very brief but flattering note informing me that they had quoted the piece in what they called "Peace Journalism". That email is published unedited after the opinion.

Except in movies, war and war stories are an unpleasant experience; probably the heroic aspect may appear admirable to some people. However, since armed conflicts and the violence and suffering they cause to the affected people horrify many, even those outside the orbit of the warring parties always welcome attempts aimed at ending bloodshed. War stories and the roles of principal actors in the Sudan's civil war are recorded in this collection under the section allotted to war, peace and some of the principal protagonists. Incidentally, my role in that armed conflict and the efforts exerted locally and internationally to resolve the rebellion through peaceful means, meant that I was both an eyewitness and a participant rolled into one.

In these war stories, "Jungle Chronicle", I have documented some of the events in which I took an active part as well as witnessing the developments and the leaders who played their part at work. In some cases, I worked with those leaders as part of a team. The objective of these narratives is to record them for history. Much of what is available in print on the last war in Sudan is typically geared towards two main goals: self-glorification of the narrator and demonisation of rivals, real or perceived. In that case, objective reporting is lost. I am not laying claim to be one hundred percent objective; even innocently unintended amnesia may sometimes play a role in undermining impartiality and fair reporting on one's opponents, for example.

I have selected some of the stories dealing with war and peace in order to remind South Sudan's warring camps to look into the previous conflicts and how they were resolved. Although some of the methods used to achieve and maintain peace in past may not be valid today, there is no harm if parties in a conflict can borrow some of the approaches that eventually worked.

As recollections, these tales don't build a complete picture of the society of South Sudan of the past or present; nor do they constitute an overall body of my memoirs of the war in which I played a leading role of media campaigner as head of the rebels' clandestine radio station, Radio SPLA. (Although my job in that capacity was essentially propaganda, I am always unwilling to accept the label, which obviously has a stigma attached to it). The full account of that assignment and the role the clandestine radio played during the 22 year-long Sudan's war will follow immediately after the publication of this book.

The stories and opinions that now form the substance of this work, in short, are the observations of an ordinary person whom fate had placed in a situation in which powerful leaders, whether they were state or non-state actors, were grappling with gigantic problems of war and peace, some which were a matter of life and death and affecting the lives of millions of human beings and their future.

During the past years, I have written press articles, edited newspapers and magazines, besides other activities that were related to writing. From the mid-1980s to the present, I edited a dozen books including ones written by established authors such as Dr Mansour Khaled and Dr Peter Adwok Nyaba. I was once a speechwriter for the late SPLM/A leader, Dr John Garang.

Introduction

Friends and colleagues have often wondered why I have not been able to write and publish a book-length material of my own, given that they believe I have what it takes to write a book – necessary experience in public life and stories to share.

The problem has always been – and still is – the feeling of inadequacy. I can't blame that crippling thought on others; the victim is also the perpetrator. I once belonged to a group of university graduates – most of them of the Khartoum and Makerere (in Uganda) universities of the 1970s. Most of those young men and women gained notoriety for their hair-splitting criticism of ideas, books and their authors. The common words for describing anyone who dared to write or speak publicly was "mediocre" or "trash". That description was used to label ideas, books, individuals and their level of thinking. As far as I can recall, only one of those critics came out with books, for example, to show the meritocracy they claimed put them ahead of the pack.

This attitude – negative as it was – however, directly or indirectly, tended to instill fear of exposed to be wanting in anyone trying to produce, for instance, a work of art or factual material. Paradoxically, that numbing self-doubt became so pervasive and destructive to the extent that the critics themselves became victims of their own dose of their inflated self-importance and questionable claim to all-encompassing knowledge. I got the virus while running with the pack.

In fairness, ideas made available to the public in form of opinion on public affairs; political philosophy; work of art or any form of discourse, should be subject to comment and scrutiny that would put the subject in question under the microscope and – if necessary – be torn to shreds by those holding contrary views. Ideas on public affairs are not private matters and shouldn't escape judgement by others. Experts have a right to comment on what is on public display – a novel, a biography dealing with public matters, a history book and the like. Furthermore, persons who engage in self-appraisal are actually being honest when that assessment convinces them they are not up to the task to undertake a project that will require an immense intellectual input. In this aspect, humility shouldn't be judged as a weakness but as a trait that should be appreciated. But since perfection is a rare and an elusive goal, idealists must break free and try to do what is within their ability. This is the position I reached several years ago after finding irresistible pressures from family, friends and colleagues that it was time I wrote and published my experiences in public life.

I joined my family in Australia in 2000. The family of five at that time were among Southern Sudanese refugees in Kenya accepted by Australia for resettlement in 1997. My wife, Anna Abul Malual and several of my colleagues and friends believed the environment in Australia would provide me with an ideal environment for writing. They were right. But other factors at the time constrained me from writing and publishing. So I dithered, arguing that, whether it was a memoir or a book on current affairs I was going to publish, to write candidly – warts and all about the then-ongoing war – was not a prudent idea.

Alternatively, if I were going to expunge unpleasant facts – omissions, misguided policies and deeds or erring leaders, then the best course of action was just to write and sit on the material until a better time. Regrettable as the decision sounds now, I was justified to do that: suspending publication. Any one baring everything about the SPLM and its leaders – in the hope that by exposing mistakes would lead to their correction and reform – was unwittingly playing into the hands of the opposing camp, the Government of Sudan.

When Dr Peter Adwok Nyaba –x a friend of many years- published his award winning book, *The Politics of Liberation: An Insider's View*, in 1998, the Embassy of Sudan in the UK immediately published a booklet which used Adwok's criticisms of his own organisation as "proof" of the rebels' unsuitability to govern or to champion the rights of the people of Southern Sudan. Gloating that the Government of Sudan had been vindicated of frequent allegations against (all manner of wickedness including allegation of inhumanity) of the SPLM/A, the authors of the pamphlet produced by the Sudan Embassy in London extensively quoted *The Politics of Liberation*. I am not saying Adwok deliberately set out to destroy the SPLM/A by means of his frank portrayal of the rebel movement's shortcomings; his intention was presumably – I guess – to jolt its leadership to reform both the organisation itself and the manner in which it was being managed.

Whatever the case may be, I had learned a good lesson: that not only was public criticism of the SPLM/A during the struggle branded a no-go sphere; it boomeranged as the opponents –mainly the Government of Sudan – used such barbs against the insurgency and its cause. The result of that situation was that I, like some of my colleagues who were critical of the direction of the struggle, decided to embrace uneasy self-restraint in order to deny the adversary any fodder for destroying the organisation of which I was – and remain – a member.

The advent of South Sudan independence in July 2011 would have meant the fear of Khartoum's exploiting any dirty laundry was no longer a factor. However, it didn't take long for some important observers within the international community to voice their fear that the new nation was heading towards a failed-state status. I was one within the ruling SPLM crowd to contradict what many wiser people saw as wishful thinking by prophets of doom, but which has unfortunately proved a prescient observation.

By rejecting and actually refuting the claim that South Sudan was a stillborn child was not a product of nationalism; far from it. My argument that we – South Sudanese – *have* what it takes as a ruling elite to manage *effectively* and *efficiently* a modern state. I usually take refuge in our recent past experience with governance which, I believe, can serve as a proof of the ability of the people of South Sudan to run a modern state in a proper manner. I haven't changed that conviction.

The country's experiment with governance during the eleven years of self-rule from 1972 to 1983, proved that despite the dearth of human and financial resources at the time, the Southern Regional executive and legislative organs surprised the world as well as roused the envy and anger of Khartoum – by proving that its native bureaucrats were competent, conscientious and were adhering to the rule of law most of the time, with few aberrations here and there, nevertheless.

In that short time, Southern Sudanese evolved and consolidated institutions of governance. And they used those organs for satisfactory management of the affairs of their society. Examples abound but few are mentioned to support these claims. The People's Regional Assembly was investigating government functionaries over cases of corruption. The speaker tried to obstruct the investigation as an attempt to protect the government; MPs voted out the speaker for being partisan; in the election of 1978, a sitting president was defeated in a free and fair vote. Virtually all of African governments of the day were either one-party state system or military-one-man dictatorship or both.

My argument was and continues to be: if we were able to behave reasonably and decently then although there were "a few "hooligans" there, to quote Dr Mansour Khaled when he was referring to Southern Sudanese serving in Khartoum as ministers in the 1950s whom he said were generally honest men, why can't we do the same now?

Anyone refuting accusations against independent South Sudan rulers of incompetence or running weak and dysfunctional institutions was defending the indefensible after a power struggle within the SPLM led to violent confrontation and a full blown civil war in December 2013. South Sudanese leaders by their behaviour have proved their critics right and citizens like me have no choice but to swallow our pride. Again, for me that was a reason for me not to rush and publish those unflattering recollections made over the last three decades – the life of the SPLM/A.

There is another problem with memoirs whose author witnessed and experienced the good, the bad, the ugly and of course the indifferent. When most of the actors are dead, writing negative things about them is definitely mean and in bad taste since they are no longer alive to answer back. Another problem often posed by an attribution of an act or statement by a deceased person is that the authenticity of quotations- mainly undocumented- could be questionable especially when no living witness is mentioned or when the stated deed, omission or statement, sounds unlikely or probably out of character with the source.

So, should one conclude that there has never been and there will never be a suitable time for me to publish the myriad experiences – some tumultuous and of game changer nature – I have gone through over the years as an eyewitness and, at times, as participant? At times I was almost taking that position. But four factors have goaded me to go public. The first of these is my deference to friends who have consistently asked me to write.

The second and most important is provocation. Since the end of Sudan's second civil war in 2005 and the subsequent attainment of sovereign status by South Sudan, barely six years ago, there have been spirited and conscious attempts by some political activists within the deniers' circles, to rewrite the history of the struggle. It has become commonplace these days that one reads about events in which a narrator speaks – based mostly on hearsay or guesswork – with authority on events in which they were neither witness nor a participant. If one, for example, were at the centre of the story in question, one's natural reaction would be to take to a computer and come up with the version of what really happened. One doesn't necessarily need to personally witness events to come out with an objective historical account, otherwise we would not have recorded and reliable history as it exists now and taken as credible.

A third reason why I strongly feel I should make a contribution is that some of the books that have been published or statements being constantly put out by rival political and military leaders are virtually about glorifying themselves and their roles while at the same time demonising opponents and debunking *their* role. That is to be expected but history is being lost to the mists of time.

Finally, because of this attitude, there is little or no recognition in the writings on the liberation struggle published so far, of the role played by some groups of South Sudanese society during the war of liberation. In those works, there is usually only passing mention of the rural population.

These are the people who bore the heaviest brunt of the war: they sent their sons and daughters to train and fight; accommodated and fed recruits going to training centres and did the same on their return as soldiers; often targeted in factional quarrels. Women took care of children while husbands went to fight and for those whose fathers fell, mothers took care of the orphans. Women had *Katiba Banat* (girls' battalion in Arabic). Their role is almost being forgotten, marginal in the works of foreign researchers. In the spirit of liberation theology many prominent church leaders added their voice in supporting a movement that was fighting for justice. SPLM's secret cells operating in government controlled areas and in various parts of the world took risks by providing information, advice and money to advance the cause of liberation. While confining to generalities what the last group did, acknowledging the contributions of those faceless and anonymous citizens has to be made for the record now before their role is forgotten forever.

Despite the existence of a plethora of books on the SPLM/A, the former rebel movement is one of the least documented organisations of the modern times. For example, the famous Koka Dam Conference, which brought together major Sudanese political groupings and the SPLM, has a tiny amount of its minutes. Much of the documents are in private hands and there is little hope they will be made available to the public. And almost none of the SPLM's participants are aware of this fact nor why it happened.

Most observers of South Sudan's political scene conclude that the power struggle within the SPLM that led to the bloody armed conflict in 2013, was a recent phenomenon. The roots of the crisis in governance and lack of effective institutions, the emasculation and the dysfunction of existing ones, should be traced to the beginning of the rebel movement whose leadership shunned building the party and instead concentrated attention on the military at the expense of the political component of the movement. In the memoirs – with the exception of *Atar School Days* – these are the issues I have addressed from time to time.

This book is general in nature. The books that will follow I have tackled the topics in detail and chronologically.

Most of the articles published in this book have appeared in many newspapers in Kenya and South Sudan over a long period beginning in the 1990s and ending just last year. Some are reproduced with specific dates or just a year or month of publication. This was done because there has been confusion over the exact dates. What is reproduced is a copy of what I sent. Some editors in Juba were and are in the habit of receiving my writings, publish them the day they reach them but rarely send me acknowledgement or an electronic copy of the published piece. This is the case especially with the articles which were carried by newspapers in Juba. Some articles don't even have the names of the publication in which they appear because of the same reason. I apologise for that and ask. I am therefore asking the proprietors of those newspapers so that in the next editions they are acknowledged by name.

Notes on names

Written forms of many Dinka personal names leave a lot to be desired. Names with long vowels, for example, are given short versions. I begin with the names of my family members. Acuoth, Bior and Nyanluak: when each of them is pronounced, the vowel in the second syllable is long, namely Acuööth (Achuooth), Biöör (Bioor) and Nyanluaak, respectivel. In this work I have retained- for convenience sake- the conventional spellings. See the dedication.

Atem Yaak Atem
Gosford City, Australia, 2017

Society & Culture

Neologisms for Popular Sub-culture of South Sudan

Almost any statement made about Southern Sudan and its inhabitants is bound to be generalised and therefore controversial. Nevertheless, there is one exception to the rule: the region and its people are not stagnant; change, although sometimes imperceptible, is taking place in all aspects of life. One of these spheres is the growth of a popular sub-culture that manifests itself in the emergence of new concepts, which in their wake produce neologisms and their nuances or expressions, or change in the shades of meaning of existing vocabulary.

Invariably, the producers of new terminologies or slang are from various ethnic and linguistic groups found in major towns such as Juba, Wau, and Malakal and in Khartoum in Northern Sudan.

It appears that the biggest output of – and contribution to – the coinage come from Upper Nile Province, and particularly from its capital, Malakal. This is not surprising when one considers that the region is home to some of the Nilotic peoples, who speak a family of related languages and whom constitute over 90 percent of the population of that territory. In this region, Collo or Shilluk language, used to rank second after Arabic as a medium of communication inside Makal town, the Shilluk name for Malakal. Government officials, members of the police force, business people and students in the town and in neighbouring Obel and Atar intermediate schools (and later Malakal Secondary School and Teachers' Training Institute) to whom Shilluk was not a mother tongue, learned and spoke some Shilluk of various levels. This type of medium made it possible for slang, jargons and other idioms originally invented and used by native Shilluk speakers to gain widespread acceptance and usage among non-Shilluk persons. To support this assertion, the writer has cited three examples of Shilluk words below.

Jaldwong in Shilluk literally means "big man". It can also be a form of address for a chief, notable or any senior public figure. Jaldwong, which is easy to pronounce by even those to whom Shilluk may be Greek, was widely used as a form of address inside and outside its home of origin. In the mid-1970s, there was an unofficial discussion in Juba, the capital of the South for the adoption of "Jaldwong" to replace the value-loaded Arabic "*Sayed*", equivalent of the English "Mister" or "Mr" ("Sayed" in Arabic means "master". In the understanding of some Southern Sudanese, the presence of a master implies the existence of servant or slave). Since nobody took the suggestion to a public forum for discussion or recommendation for adoption, the talk remained academic.

Not all words with the prefix "jal" are sweet or polite, however. For example, "*jalpac*" means a man of homestead or village or something similar to that. In its pejorative usage, it means among other things, a rustic, uncouth, vulgar or unsophisticated person from a rural area who is not conversant or at home with the ways of the "civilised" town folks. In general, the word is abusive. Both members of Shilluk and *dh* (dhong) – Shilluk for a stranger or alien – communities use "jalpac" in that sense. The honorific for teacher is *"jalpwuonyo"* while *"Jalyath"* rather deceptively is understood to mean "man of medicine" or "herbalist" or a witch doctor, although the word mostly refers to a witch doctor and is evidently rude.

Words or expressions uttered or written to denigrate or belittle other people or things in Shilluk do not necessarily have their roots in "jal". In content, *nya ara* (nyangara) is both indifferent and negative, as with jalpac. In both senses, *nyangara* is a modifier and noun, depending on the context. Nyangara is a person, or his or her quality, denoting severe deficiency in refined manners; of inferior and inadequate social graces and decorum. A person with these attributes is described as a nya ara of a man or woman. In real life, Nyangara is a hamlet in the Shilluk country, several kilometres south west of Malakal. It is true to say that the people of this village have not committed any crime to earn them such an unpalatable appellation, but one can only conjecture: in the eyes of their compatriots next door to east bank of the White Nile at Malakal they may not measure up to the standards of Westernised or Arabised Southern Sudanese.

Juba, the provincial capital of Equatoria, later in the early 1970s became the seat of regional government and legislature of Southern Sudan. At that stage, the principal Southern city was a melting pot. The integration of the people of Southern Sudan that followed led, among other facets of social change, to the spread of expressions, national in scope and usage, but which before that time were peculiar to some parts of Equatoria. In that city, Juba

Arabic, a blend of the Semitic and African languages, and a form of pidgin that dispenses with grammar, as experts say, proliferated and gained wide acceptance and use as a lingua franca among Southern Sudanese. A few such words are mentioned here in passing.

In colloquial Arabic, *kasir el beit* means burglary. Over the years, the concept has moved from one category of crime to another as defined by customary law. Lower courts in Juba and nearly all the towns and villages in Equatoria brand cases of elopement or pregnancy – what Western societies call birth out of wedlock – kasir el beit. Outside Equatoria, where customary law applies and courts use Arabic, kasir el beit is the word which describes some sexual offences, including rape and adultery. Until recently, such offences used to be settled through payment of fines to aggrieved parties.

The lighter side of life has coined its share of idioms in Juba. *Igliimi*, is derived from *igliim*, Arabic for region. This word in its new shade first appeared in the early 1970s. It means pot-belly. The word has its root in class division. When the international community donated money, clothes, cooking utensils and so on, to the people of Southern Sudan for resettlement after the end of the first civil war, some of the senior officials who managed these resources were suspected to have been more generous in allocating the aid assistance to themselves than to the majority of the needy persons. It was widely believed that the persons misappropriating relief supplies were leading a comfortable lifestyle, eating good food, hence bulging tummies. Regional ministers and senior civil servants were later to be given the nickname –behind their backs, of course. It is ironic that the majority of those office holders and supposed sole beneficiaries from the regional-self-rule did not exhibit features that are associated with luxurious living, whether from legitimate or ill-gotten means.

There are words said to have been borrowed from Arabic but later corrupted beyond recognition. One of these is *samblah*. Depending on the context in which it is used, the adverb suggests a status or something that is haphazard, unplanned, random. One prominent politician with a streak of demagoguery once advised the people of Southern Sudan that since the war that had killed many people had ended, they must produce *samblah* to restore demographic balance.

Nyarkuk, which means a child, is rarely used these days. It must have its origin in African languages of the South, given that Arabic does not have a

/ny/ (similar to Italian /gn/) sound or an equivalent. Similar to nyarkuk is *banjos*, whose origin is not known but has most likely been borrowed from one of African languages spoken in the North where the word used to be common especially among manual workers from western Sudan and the South. Banjos means lad.

Besides the influence of Arabic in popular usage, indigenous African words and idioms have crept into every day speech in Equatoria in recent years. *Kurju*, or "tilling the land" is said to be of Bari origin. This word was popularised by the politicians and officials of the then Regional Ministry of Agriculture. When the Regional Government declared that the working class should report to their small farms during the rainy season instead of offices and other workplaces, Saturdays became known as kurju days.

Not all the loan words have the same meaning for all who use them. For instance, *kokora*, from one of the dialects of Bari speaking people, is said to mean "divide", or "cut into parts". This word entered political and social lexicography in the early 1980s when most people from Equatoria demanded that the Southern Region should be sub-divided into three- Equatoria, Bahr el Ghazal and Upper Nile, respectively – and that each of these regions should be responsible to the central government in Khartoum. To the proponents, kokora stood for decentralisation of powers. To the opponents the movement meant mutual exclusivity, a rejection of unity and cooperation among the people of Southern Sudan in their opposition to ruling circles in Northern Sudan. Because of the resultant tension, ethnic rivalry and animosity, and the concept and the debate it generated, kokora was – and remains – a highly emotive word which to the understanding of some people could mean "be content with what you have and leave me alone with what is mine."

Sudan's two civil wars, the first from 1955-1972, and the current one, which broke out in 1983, have made their contributions towards the growth of this vocabulary.

In the 1960s, Southern Sudanese who informed government on elements sympathetic with Anya Nya guerrillas were simply known as CID, shortened form of the Police Criminal Investigation Department. The Nilotic people, especially Nuer and Dinka, whose languages do not have an equivalent of the English sibilants (/ch/, /s/ or /z/) sounds turned the abbreviation to *thiaidït*, or big informer. Thiaidït is more than a government spy. Dinka speakers verbalise it when they say "so and so *acï thiai*" or he or she has "become a *thiai*". Thiaidït in popular usage also means a tale-teller or one who secretly reports the conduct, utterances and minor misdemeanours of colleagues to higher authorities, usually in exchange for favour and confidence, or to satisfy spite.

The SPLA as a sub-culture has not put an end to the invention of words. Instead, its members have added more to the corpus of word-creation. The first of these was *nyagat*.

There is disagreement over the origin and specific meaning of nyagat. Some people claim that the word is of Amharic origin while others contend that it is Nuer. One of my former elementary teachers, Henry Lul Lual who hailed from Akobo, not far from the Ethiopian border, told me in 1984 at the SPLA headquarters in Bilpam where he was a senior officer, that the word was from Amharic. As to the meaning, the position of the user makes the difference. In the first armed conflict, nyagat was a generic name for those insurgents who defected from Anya Nya command to operate on their own in the countryside where they often looted, raped and terrorised civilian populations. In other words, nyagat were renegades operating outside the mainstream rebel fighters under specific command. Others, especially some among speakers of Dinka, pronounce it as *nyïgät*.

With the conflict raging between Anya Nya Two and the SPLA between 1983 and 1987, the former referred to their enemies as nyagat. Anya Nya Two hurled the same at the SPLA. In broad terms, nyagat has come to be a label for someone on the other side of ideological or political, and in some rare cases, ethnic divide. The differences between nyagat and their enemies, being settled always by force of arms. In short nyagat is a compatriot and possibly a former colleague who is not with us in our struggle against one who should be a common enemy. In rare cases, nyagat can be used in jocular tone, the way some speakers of English would use the expression "Don't be such a fool" to a friend. Late Cdr William Nyuon, formerly SPLA chief of general staff, was fond of using the word when joking with junior officers.

Another old word given a new meaning by the SPLA during its infancy was *bourgeois* (and its derivative *bourgeoisie*). The adjective and noun were applied to explain the relations between exploiters and the exploited in accordance with socialist ideology and its interpretation of class struggle. The Arabic version is *burjuazi*. To the Nuer and Dinka speakers, this was *burjuath*, which means more than exploitation as it stands for someone as the Nuer speakers would say of someone engaged in *cam nyin naath*, meaning literally, someone "eating [other] people's things". Or what the former Tanzanian President Julius Nyerere called a society where "man eats man", when he was referring to the ruthlessness of capitalist societies. Cannibalism, almost.

Literary works, songs, dictionaries of archaic words and the like serve as depositories of words in any language. For South Sudan, words which were coined during their wars of liberation have been immortalised in war songs. "Burjuath" appears in several war songs composed by SPLA fighters in the early 1980s.

It is natural that a military and political organisation like the SPLM/A's communication should be essentially rhetorical and propagandistic. The rebel movement, however, in addition to that has created a dialect of its own, much of it which is "neutral." When the going is tough, the SPLA members describe the situation as one in which their "eye has become small". The split in August 1991 was the time when the "eyes" of the members of what became to be known invariably as Torit Faction or Mainstream, had shrunk to the smallest possible size. The converse was the period between 1988 and 1990 when its forces over-ran the whole east bank of the White Nile south of Sobat river and virtually the whole of western Equatoria. It was the time when the "eye became very big" or *acï nyin dït arëët* in Dinka language.

Regarding titles, the SPLA has had an aversion to the use of Arabic *Sayed* and His Excellency or HE as a military organisation the SPLA members address one another as "Comrade". In that context there is no problem as what is meant is comrade in arms. When the word is associated with the socialist ideology, some eyebrows are raised especially by the civilian members or those who were uncomfortable with anything associated with Marxism-Leninism. *Hakuma* soon replaced comrade. The substitute is curious. It is an Arabic word for government but with the SPLA it is a shortened form of *Bäny de Akuma*, which is a Dinka expression for the chief or officer of the government. This elaboration was seen to be necessary to differentiate a senior office holder from the traditional chief.

Borrowing, coining or giving meanings to familiar words and expressions are a never-ending process; some concepts and their expressions peter out, while others endure and take their place in people's thought-processes and everyday speech. It is not easy for anyone to speculate about which of these are going to wither and disappear forever and which will remain, or what new words and expressions will emerge from nowhere and capture people's imagination. Perhaps the right custodians of the ingredients of the popular sub-culture are the poets, short story writers and novelists, historians of social trends and fashion or linguists with interest in etymology, neology and semantics.

First published in the SPLM/A Update *newsletter in early 1990s.*

A Spectrum of Meanings

In the first part of this article, we examined the inaccurate labels such as "animists" that many among non-Sudanese writers and journalists often attach to Southern Sudanese. This final section sheds light on how Northern Sudanese – always interchangeable with the central government and the ruling class in that part of the country, and the Sudan as a whole – describe and address their compatriots from the South. The last portion of this piece touches on how Southern Sudanese view fellow Southern Sudanese.

Mass media such as radio and TV, owned and run by either the government of the day in Sudan, or by Northern Sudanese businessmen, have been, for years, paternalistic, treating Southern Sudanese and their region in a manner similar to that used by a parent dealing with a petulant child who is quietened with offer of candies and a lullaby or, sometimes, spanking. Of course there are exceptions from past decades, such as *Al Ayyam* daily under Beshir Mohammed Saeed and Mahjoub Mohammed Salih, and *Es Sahafa* headed by Abdurrahman Mukhtar.

From the turbulent days of the early 1950s, when nationalism against British rule had boiled to fever pitch, and especially after the August 1955 mutiny at Torit by soldiers from the South, this condescending, insulting and, often, intimidating attitude towards Southern Sudan persists to this day, regardless of whether the regime in power is "democratic" or a military dictatorship.

The Arabic name for "south" is *janoub*. As an attempt at coaxing and pleasing Southern Sudanese, Northern mass media and most politicians talk of *janoub el watan* or south of the nation, and *el janoub el habiib* or beloved south, absurd concepts since countries (geography), not people (nation) are the compass point in this context.

The inhabitants of this part of the country are *el Ikhwa el Janoubyiin* or our Southern Brothers (I am sure they would be reluctant to use "brethren". The northern, western and eastern parts of Sudan which the ruling elite consider as components of Northern Sudan do not share in this sentiment of feigned brotherhood.

Chauvinistic reference by the North to the South is translated into abusive language when the Southern Sudanese take up arms as a means to assert themselves as a last resort. Governments of the day brand members of armed groups such as Anya Nya and the present SPLA *khawarij*. "Khawarij" is short form of *kharijiin 'ala ganuun*. This simply means law breakers. Behind this thinking is the fact that any person questioning or rejecting the *status quo* has broken the law. The milder but yet value-loaded version is *el mutamarid*, the rebel, and *harakat et tamarud*, for their organisation, rebel movement. Northern press which opposed to the SPLM/A dubbed it *harakat Garang*, that is [John] Garang's movement.

Infasaal is the Arabic word for secession. Those who advocate separation therefore become *infasaaliyiin*. In the context of North–South conflict, secession does not only denote separation; it means among other things, disloyalty to the state and its authority, absence of patriotism and incitement to anarchy and lawlessness. In the 1960s, for a Southern Sudanese to be labelled a "separatist" invariably meant that the suspect could be arrested, detained without trial and tortured, and was at the mercy of the security forces that were free to physically liquidate the alleged rebel, whose guilt was treason.

For more than five decades now, though the number of progressives and liberals among Northern Sudanese has increased greatly, the official Northern attitude towards Southern Sudanese and the rebellion has hardly changed for the better.

On the other hand, Southern Sudanese are not exempt from prejudice against their Northern compatriots. Concept and words which hardly square with reality have been and still are being used in reference to Northern Sudanese of Arab stock. For instance, *jallaba*, which was a name for the itinerant traders from Northern Sudan is now applied to all including politicians, members of intelligentsia; in short all Northern Sudanese who claim Arab lineage are called jallaba. In Arabic, "jallaba" simply means procurers, particularly of merchandise. Predictably, almost all Northern Sudanese detest and protest being called by such a name, which they believe is not only inaccurate but downright offensive, as it has acquired negative connotation over the years.

Here and in my other writings on this subject, some people may believe I emphasise the point that the Southern Sudanese have always been at the receiving end of distorted portrayal, created by the Western news media, and from their fellow citizens at the north of the border making them a laughing stock. That is neither correct nor the objective of my writing. Indeed, that behaviour is grossly unfair and should be stopped by people being objective rather than just paying back in kind, namely stereotyping. However, I assert that the Southern Sudanese have received and continue to receive a disproportionate amount of negative and sometime deliberately misleading and bad profiling.

Although they present themselves as being more sinned against than sinning themselves, some members of the elite from Southern Sudan are not free from prejudice against their fellow Southern Sudanese as well as those from the North. For example, when the British colonial administrators lorded over all the Sudanese, with few formally educated, Southern Sudanese who could not write or read were referred to simply as natives, while high and middle ranking civil servants such as intermediate and secondary school teachers and junior administrators enjoyed the flattering title of "Effendi," a Turkish equivalent of Mr, alongside "Sayed" which eventually replaced the Turkish rank.

This attitude smacks of double standards all the way. This is unacceptable; anyone yearning to be accorded justice, respect and dignity must give the same to others.

This article was published under the title of "Inappropriate Usages"
SPLM/A Update newsletter in early 1990s.

The dangers of conformity, prejudice and stereotyping

Recently, a colleague told me that when the shooting war in the Sudan ends, the media war for the hearts and minds of the Sudanese people – waged by conflicting political and interest groups – would begin.

According to him there are now three competing camps. The first consists of the unionists or the advocates of the *status quo*, the second are the reformists who are ready to make some concessions but not at the expense of Sudan's territorial integrity. Almost all Northern Sudanese can be found in this camp.

The anti-thesis of unity is secession, an option favoured by many Southern Sudanese.

The third group clusters around "New Sudanism" whose author, Dr John Garang, posits that the Sudan can remain united if and when the country becomes secular, non-Arab and non-African, racially speaking, and with a system of rule that is fair and just to all the citizens in the share of power and resources.

These three political trends are fairly represented in the media. The war of words will be waged on those bases.

I agreed with my friend, who has a wide and deep experience of mass media and their uses and abuses. However, I quickly reminded him that in his classification he had forgotten to include the most important and perhaps the largest group: the conformists whose members are spread over the three spectra already listed. The conformists fear two things: first, going against the fiction known as conventional wisdom and second, social ostracism. Therefore, they prefer to keep their views to themselves sharing them only with trusted friends and like-minded persons.

Many of these work in newsrooms as reporters, editors, producers, managers and in some case own the newspapers, TV and radio stations and other communication outlets.

Conforming with and to what is seen as received wisdom, self-evident "truth", religious tenets, communal values or majority opinion is not a new thing, nor is it peculiar to Sudan and the Sudanese.

As recently as seven hundred years ago, Europe was in the grip of a ruthless form of conformity known as censorship, exercised by the Church. Free thinkers risked being burnt alive; the Church believed that the world was flat like the top of a table and woe to those who simply believed that the earth was round, not to mention the extreme cases of atheists and agnostics.

In that climate it was prudent for people who held unorthodox views and ideas to keep them within the confines of their craniums.

In Sudan, conformity is found across social, political, religious, divides; in the North, in the South, in the East, and in the West and down to the village and clan level.

Stereotyping, gross generalisation and prejudice are constant companions of conformity. I will give a few examples to illustrate the point.

When the SPLA captured the strategic Northern garrison of Kurmuk in 1987, Prime Minister Sadiq el-Mahdi's government called for general mobilisation. The result was a huge upsurge of emotions among Northern Sudanese; women donated jewellery, businessmen gave money and the youth volunteered to undergo military training and participate in the retaking of the town.

Fatima Ahmed Ibrahim, a respected female politician and a senior member of the Sudan Communist Party, SCP, lent her voice in supporting the mobilisation. I was stunned at this and wrote a commentary, broadcast over the Radio SPLA which then had a huge audience in Khartoum as well as in the South. In that opinion I questioned her rationale for supporting the government headed by an ultra-conservative and Islamic-based Ummah Party. Furthermore, Fatima's party, the SCP, was ostensibly an ally of the then "socialist" SPLM/A. I never received a personal response although some of her comrades later told me my criticism touched most of them and that some members were concerned that something was not in order. However, a former member of the SCP from the North, who was an officer in the SPLM/A told me I was being unreasonable for attacking the stand of the veteran woman activist and leader. He warned me also that anyone in Khartoum at the time of the mobilisation and who did not join the bandwagon was in danger of being lynched.

Since everyone – including political groups – who did not support mass mobilisation were accused of being fifth columnists, Fatima Ahmed Ibrahim's support for the government on behalf of the Communist Party was to be a token expression of Northern solidarity. The party's constituency has always been the central Sudan, the capital Khartoum and Atbara, the headquarters of the Sudan Railways, whose workers were loyal supporters or sympathisers of the left wing organisation.

Many Northern Sudanese hold the Nuba of the Nuba Mountains, the Southern Sudanese and the Funj inhabiting the Southern Blue Nile, in contempt and often refer to them as *abiid* or slaves. This is not a mere allegation or a fabrication by this writer. During the colonial rule, it was an offence to call someone a slave. But laws are enacted to meet the need of the time. The law punishing persons calling others slave must have been made to address what must have been a widespread practice, viewing and treating others- mostly people of non-Arab descent as slaves.

But the most important documentary evidence of how widespread this attitude was, comes from a recently released statement made many years ago by Sayed Abdurrahman el-Mahdi, Sadiq's grandfather. In that document, the Ummah leader is reported to have referred to Ali Abdel Latif, a half-Nuba, half-Southerner, as a slave. (Johnson: *Sudan Civil Wars*, 2003). Paradoxically, most Northern Sudanese cite the case Ali Abdel Latif, an ardent nationalist, as proof that the South has always advocated a united Sudan.

If such leading personalities such as the son of Mahdi could descend to such levels, calling as bondsman, another important public figure – Ali Abdel Latif was an officer in the Sudan Defence Force and led a mutiny against his British officers in 1924 – then what could be expected of ordinary Northern Sudanese?

Although this attitude is expressed discreetly, it persists to this day in Sudan. It is obviously declining among most of the educated, especially among those who have travelled and lived abroad and might have been victims of racial discrimination or of derogatory remarks on account of their colour.

Unsurprisingly, Southern Sudanese, because of this or other reasons are not immune to making gross generalisations, prejudice and looking down on their Northern compatriots, who they call Arabs. Strictly speaking, very few Northern Sudanese can qualify as such when rigid racial criteria are applied.

It is not uncommon to listen to a conversation among Southern Sudanese, usually members of the elite, making unflattering statements about Northern Sudanese whom they refer to as Arabs or *Mundukuru*. Incidentally, *jallaba* is a neutral word. Originally, jallaba meant "procurers", a reference to itinerant traders who used to import goods such as beads, salt, soap and cloth from the North to the South. Since most Northern traders in the South were not universally liked because of their close ties with, and their influence on, the Northern administrators and security personnel, especially the army who were themselves feared and hated, the word *jallaba* began to acquire insulting connotations. *Mundukuru*, said to be a word from one of the languages from Equatoria and whose meaning is not clear, is pejorative in the extreme.

I have an associate who, when people discuss politics, is in the habit of interjecting, "I don't like Arabs. I don't trust Arabs. Arabs are bad". And each time I remind him that he himself is a racist because it is wrong to generalise, he would hit back with, "All Arabs are bad".

"Including Ushari[1] and those who are fighting alongside the SPLM/A against their own brothers in power in Khartoum?" I would suggest, to wake him up.

"All Arabs are bad," he would never tire of repeating his creed.

And are all Southern Sudanese good? To answer with yes is pure

---

1 Dr Ushari Mahmud is a Northern Sudanese academic who, together with fellow scholar and fellow Northerner Dr Suleiman Ali Baldo, documented and published in 1987 *Dhein Massacres,* a shocking revelation of how the government authorities in the town of Dhein in Western Sudan encouraged the killing and enslavement of thousands of Southern Sudanese.

hypocrisy. Some Southern Sudanese hate and despise each other, on ethnic, regional and political grounds, as intensely – and possibly worse – than the Northerners. Some of them also bear morbid grudges and ill-feeling towards one another, in just the same way as they behave and think about Northern Sudanese.

There is a joke, and a serious one at that, to the effect that the Dinka love power so much that if one of them is told to sit on a chair – symbolising authority – in a blazing sun he would accept the furnace seat with relish.

Some people among Southern Sudanese portray the Dinka as brutal, avaricious and primitive, people who do not love their homeland but, instead, covet other people's lands.

The demand by the people of Equatoria in the early 1980s, that the South should be sub-divided, was largely triggered by a desire on the part of the inhabitants of that region to end what was perceived as Dinka domination of public life in the South.

It is true that the administration of the South headed by a Dinka politician, committed some inexcusable mistakes, such as appointment and protection of some unqualified and corrupt Dinka officials at the expense of their more experienced and more competent non-Dinka civil servants. But mistakes by a few Dinka were enough for most non-Dinka to lump the community with the label of DAB – (All) Dinka Are Bad.

For their part, chauvinists among the Dinka think that non-Dinka peoples, especially from Equatoria, are irrational, over-demanding positions and rights they do not deserve and that they are full of hatred; always complaining about petty things.

Interestingly, a Dinka who follows a non-Dinka leader and vice versa is treated by most members of their community as a traitor and someone who has been "bought"; that is, bribed with money or position of power.

These beliefs and practices, although they sometimes arise out of an actual situation, are extremely harmful and reactionary. They militate against rational thinking, sober judgement and logical conclusion.

It is a moral responsibility for the political leaders, media people and the members of civil society and their organisations to fight these dangerous ideas by adopting a moderate, objective and realistic approach in which each case is judged individually and which avoids attributing crime or condemnation to others who are innocent by association.

A real journalist must serve the truth, even if that means becoming unpopular or inviting hatred from those related by blood, political or ideological bonds.

Sudan Mirror, October 6-19, 2003

Postscript

Upon reading this article, someone based in the United Kingdom sent this email, which remains unedited, to the writer:
From: sd81@kent.ac.uk
To: wundut@yahoo.com
Subject: Comment on 2003 article: "Dangers of Prejudice..."
Date: Mon, 15 Aug 2005 05: 26: 33+0100

Mr Atem,
I have been reading an article you wrote in 2003 about the dangers of prejudice and encouragement for balance in journalism.
I admire your brand of "peace journalism", or however one wishes to refer to it, and praise you for putting your neck on the line.
My current research is on Peace Education in the Sudan and I have referenced your work several times. I feel obliged to let you know, that before reading your work, I was almost convinced that we had no leadership on just media issues.
Best regards,
Sama.

Despite having corresponded with the writer, she or he remains someone I don't know personally.

At the Crossroads: Southern Sudanese Losing Their Identity

On the surface it would appear that Southern Sudan and its people are not African and as such have to be converted to qualify for that epithet. Far from it; there is no argument about the African-ness of Southern Sudanese as race, beliefs, values and practices go.

The reasoning is that this part of Sudan and its people have over the years lost substantial aspects of their identity, either through conscious attempts by non-Southern Sudanese to change the names of people and places and substitute them with foreign or corrupted versions, or by the indigenous people accepting them without question or even aping the foreigners.

When foreigners first came into contact with the local peoples, they either gave them invented names – to replace those the aliens considered too difficult to pronounce – or distorted retained names beyond recognition. The result is that several people have lost the names by which they were known before the coming of foreigners.

For example, the people known today to the rest of the world as Dinka can swear that that is not what they call themselves. From time immemorial to the present, these people have been referring to themselves as *Jiëëng* and their language as *Thong e Jiëëng*, literally the mouth of Jiëëng. The non-Jiëëng speakers, especially the Baggara Arabs and most people from Equatoria, call them *Jengge*, which at times used to give offence to most Jiëëng people, particularly the urban dwellers. But this "offensive" version can be attributed to quirks in phonetics such as the Bantu speakers pronouncing "*shiringi*" instead of "shilling".

Shilluk, too, is a foreign name for the *Collo*, or black people. To this day, members of this nationality use the foreign version when talking with people. As a result, people have been led to believe this is the name of these Southern Sudanese, known for their institution of *Reth*, their spiritual and temporal leader.

The people known to the outsiders as *Nuer* call themselves *Naath* and their language as *Thok Naath*. Though popularised by anthropologists such as Evans Pritchard, epitomising what they describe as acephalous people, the students of these Nilotic peoples seem fixated on their customs and much less to what their name is.

It is inconceivable that a given people living on a river or near a mountain would not have a local name for such natural landmarks. Yet this is exactly what aliens have implied when, on their arrival in Africa, they started christening these features as if they did not exist before. For example, the Bari-speaking people's name for the White Nile is *Supiri*. Neither the British explorers nor the Arabs, it appears, thought that the name was "civilised" enough to be used. So Supiri went down into history as White Nile or *Bahr el Jebel* (river of the mountain), respectively.

Kiir and *ciir* – both alternative pronunciations are dialect-based – mean "river" in Jiëëng (Dinka) language. But neither the Europeans nor the Arabs would accept this indigenous appellation. What appears in world maps today as Bahr el Arab, meaning, the Arab sea or lake is, in fact, Kiir River. Because of these changes, native names of what are *Bahr el Zeraf* (river of giraffe), *Mashra er Req* (slave swamp), *Bahr el Ghazal* (river of gazelle), and so on, have gone into oblivion especially for the younger generation.

As if to honour their "pioneers" in the South, the Northern ruling class in Khartoum gave the names of such adventurers, who were often slave traders, to villages and camps in that part of the country. Deim Zubeir in Bahr el Ghazal carries the name of Zubeir Rahma Mansour, the notorious Northern Sudanese slave catcher and dealer, who lived in the last half of the 19th century and the beginning of the 20th century.

Kuachlualthuon, an Anyuak village, and a name given by *Naath* after they had evicted the original inhabitants, was renamed Nasir after a certain Donglawi (a man from Dongola in Northern Sudan) at the end of the last century. (Source: Douglas H. Johnson).

When the African name of a place or river was not abolished altogether, a blend of the local and Arab name was the result. *Khor* is the Arabic word for a stream. Upper Nile Province has more place names with khor prefixes than any other region in Southern Sudan. In south east of Malakal, there are Khor Fullus (corruption of Dinka *Pul Luth* or the pond of the mud fish) and Khor Atar. To the north of the provincial capital there are Khor Adar, and Khor Shammam near Renk, while in the east one finds Khor Machar.

In cases where outright change or a blend was not possible, the local name was corrupted. For example: Fashoda instead of Pacota, or hornless bull, in Shilluk (Douglas H. Johnson); Fanjak instead of Pan-gak or crow's home in Dinka; Fashalla instead of Pachalla or Pochalla or home of Challa[1]; Bibor for Pibor; Waath for Waat; Aliab for Aliap; Bantiu for Bentiu; Renk for Areng; Thumbura for Tembura; Nagachoth for Nagachot. The list is long.

The attempts at such changes by cultural chauvinists in Sudan have not stopped. When the authorities in Khartoum and of the former Regional Government in Juba decided in 1976, for easy administration of the territory and for enhanced local involvement and participation, to divide the then three provinces of Bahr el Ghazal, Equatoria ad Upper Nile, each into two, Tonj, Rumbek and Yirol districts were hived out of the greater Bahr el Ghazal to form Lakes Province. Khartoum did not hesitate to exploit this development. Seeing that there was nothing indigenous in the new name of Lakes, officialdom and the Arabic language media came up with Buheirat. It is now on official maps in English, so is Jungli- in Upper Nile- for Jonglei, an African name.

The change of people and place names, complete or partial, has been wholly attributed to outsiders. But in fairness, the natives have consciously or unwittingly contributed to the process. After "nationalisation" and Arabicisation of the educational system in the Sudan in 1957, the Arabic language became increasingly encouraged by the government of the day. Teaching Arabic became mandatory in schools which used English as a medium of instruction, while the so-called national pattern schools – those offering all subjects in Arabic – began to proliferate in the South. Southern Sudanese students from the latter began to look down on their counter-parts because of their lack of fluency and literacy in Arabic. By a twist of irony, girls from the South who read and wrote in Arabic openly despised male students with little or no grasp of the language. At that time, it was fashionable for young people to conduct romance, especially poetry and billet doux, in Arabic. With that attitude, knowledge of Arabic began to be equated with being trendy, even civilised, while its lack was seen as a mark of *ahli* or cast one as a member of ignorant rural folk, who according to the prevailing attitudes, were considered a bunch of ignoramuses, not far from savages.

Under those circumstances, upstarts strove to imitate many Arabic phrases, notably pronunciation of African names, such as the one given earlier: Waath, Thumbura and the like. Saying things as the locals did, meant "going native".

After the establishment of the Regional Government of Southern Sudan in 1972, some voices began to be heard among the region's ruling elite who wanted place names that reminded people of their painful past. (In Bor town for example, there is a market place called Abiith, which serves as one of these reminders. Obviously this is corruption of Arabic *abiid* or slaves because the very spot was a slave market during the second half of the 19th century. The sellers of human commodity were Arab traders whose customers were the Turkish and Egyptian businessmen whose cousins were also the rulers of the country.

The place and personal names that have been imposed on Southern Sudanese by outsiders must be dropped and old indigenous ones revived, especially when they still exist in parallel usage by the locals or are being remembered by the old people now in their twilight years.

This change from foreign to native names has been effected in several African countries after the attainment of political independence. In 1957, the former British colony of Gold Coast became sovereign as Ghana, a powerfully, culturally and economically rich ancient West African kingdom that flourished before the European conquest. Similarly, what was Southern Rhodesia took the name of Zimbabwe, once a civilisation of note in Southern Africa before the era of Western imperialism in Africa.

But no matter how desirable and appropriate this return to the roots may be, the objectives, approach and steps leading to that have to be rational and relevant. There have been cosmetic and politically-inspired name changes in Africa in recent years. In the 1980s, for instance, the former West African nation of Upper Volta dropped the name of the river for which the country had been known under the French rule and after independence in 1960. The rechristening changed the country to Burkina Faso or the Land of the Upright People. Others added modifiers such as "People's Republic", "Democratic Republic" and suchlike.

Common sense, however, suggests that people do not become decent or democratic merely because an emotive adjective is attached to the name of a country. Sudan was a case in point. The Sudanese people did not enjoy democratic governance during the dictatorial regime of Jaafar Nimeiri who, on assuming power in 1969, named the country the Democratic Republic of Sudan. Similarly, there was no proof to show that, in the countries known as People's Republics, the masses had more say in public affairs because of the epithet.

This reasoning leads us to the current debate over the internet about a suitable (African) name to be given to a future state in Southern Sudan. The issue reminds an African reader of parents naming an unborn child, an act which is a taboo in many African societies including some in Southern Sudan. The belief claims that by giving a name to an unborn child, the parents are alerting evil spirits to the existence of a human being; demons would harm the child before birth. One is not giving credence to this piece of superstition; the message is: get the child first and choosing a proper name would not be a problem since certain guidelines are followed parents in such situations.

At any rate, I appreciate the concern expressed by those Southern Sudanese. But my view on this is that as long as the proposed name is not foreign or divisive (such selecting and applying a name of one of ethnic groups for the whole nation or using the group's language as an official one), there would be no cause for grousing. In this context, a word of caution would be necessary: change for its own sake can be futile and redundant if it does not define or influence the content of desired objectives. Such goals include factors such as the prevalence and provision of basic freedoms, justice for all, participation of as many people as possible in decision-making processes and decent living conditions for all citizens.

Some countries such as Liberia (land of the free) or Burkina Faso have been living under sweet sounding names for themselves. It is questionable that the Liberians have not been free from despotic rulers for more than a century, nor has the name set the Liberians free from poverty or disease since the founding of their republic. Similarly, it is doubtful that all the Burkinabe suddenly found themselves conscientious, honest and hardworking after their country became Burkina Faso.

In fact, some forms of name-change could be negative. For the sake of argument, let us assume that the name of my native village Pakuoor, one of the satellite villages circling Kongor, the headquarters of what used to be known as Kongor Rural Council, were to be dropped and a new name substituted. To me that would amount to a declaration of war. I would resist and fight by all means. The reasons are not difficult to fathom.

First, the village's name has been in use for hundreds of years; it has become part and parcel of the local history, embodied in epic songs and legends, names of past great warriors and leaders, their deeds and so forth. Second, boyhood memories, especially happy ones, would be negatively affected as recollections exist in space and time. Finally, as identification and other legal documents must include the name of birthplace, the removal of the village's name would contradict what is in passport, ID or birth assessment of age certificates, rendering the bearer of such documents a fraudster; in fact, a forger.

What then would be the most suitable name for Southern Sudan reflecting its African identity? African Republic of Something? No way! Africa, Arab or whatever racially-loaded adjective attached to a name of a country excludes people of different racial groups and communities, who are nevertheless full citizens, only of different race from the rest of their compatriots.

I think what really matters in this context is how a country is ordered and managed, not necessarily what name is used. For example, South Africa is undoubtedly a neutral name, yet its post-apartheid constitution, and how the people of all races strive to live in harmony with one another, all make the republic not necessarily a paradise but certainly a relatively good place to live in and for its citizens to be proud of. In Asia, the Republic of South Korea is a rising economic and technological giant. Frankly speaking, I would be a proud citizen of Southern Sudan and as a Southern Sudanese as long as I am secure – from discrimination, oppression or fear of physical elimination on account of race, creed or political beliefs – and a free citizen of a democratic and prosperous country.

*The EastAfrican**, Nairobi, Kenya, June 1-7 1998

*The name of the weekly is written as one word, *The EastAfrican,* not *The East African* as one might expect.

Of Pens and Books

The other day I went to one of Nairobi's bookshops to pick up my copy of London *Sunday Times*. In addition to books, dailies and magazines, the bookshop sells a variety of pens, some expensive while other are cheap. One of the fountain pens I saw on display cost Ksh 25,000. Converted into American dollars – the major international exchange currency in Kenya and other countries around the world – this is roughly $500. To further translate this amount into the living conditions in the Kenyan capital, this would be equivalent to a five months' rent for a house in the working class residential areas.

At this point, the translation and conversion end.

On my way back home while travelling in a bus, I kept asking myself why someone should throw away such an amount for an article of writing when pens as cheap as Ksh10 would do. In the course of my reasoning with myself, it became clear to me that such outrageous prices were not peculiar to pens as there are strong reasons behind the exorbitant costs. First, the value of the item, especially durability, is one of the justifications. Recently, a friend informed me of a primary school teacher who went to England in the 1950s. On his return to Southern Sudan he brought a pen called Cross. The teacher had been using that pen daily all these years until he passed it on to his son recently. One can conclude that the teacher had the value for his money.

The second reason is prestige. The wealthy of the world buy watches for two million pounds sterling, just to give an example. (This is from a newspaper report that a European prince wore a watch costing that amount). Well, the watch is made of gold, so he is wearing money. Prestige and taste scorn function; a cheaper watch or suit would still perform the same purpose as a costly suit off the peg from London's Harrods department store.

The majority of us are slaves to pursuit of status, to be recognised. This is summed up by the adage that a pauper dreams to be a prince. Pens, cheap or expensive, are status symbols; anyone wearing a pen in their breast pocket is taken for granted to be literate; that they write. This is a subtle advertisement. But here lies the greatest deception. It is common knowledge that semi-literate and sometimes the illiterate who cannot write even their own names, love to exhibit pens. Some of these people carry up to three pens in their pockets and they make sure that these tools are conspicuously displayed for everyone to see.

Notwithstanding this self-promotion by those who cannot read or write, most of them victims of their societies which failed to provide formal education for all, the pen is one of the best inventions the word has been blessed with; it is the midwife of civilisation. Its role can be likened to that of middlemen in the world of merchandise. Scientists, sages, novelists, and so on, transfer their ideas from their heads to paper – previously to wall and sheepskin – and later books through the medium of the pen. This tier gave birth to the axiom that the pen is mightier than the sword.

This brings us to the role of books. One cannot conceive a world without writing and, therefore, books. The Bible, the Quran and the writings of great men and women have not only changed the world; they are the foundation of the moral, political and legal systems of the present world.

But what are books? This was the question put to prominent British historian, A.J.P. Taylor, some years ago. Professor Taylor said books were tools, like equipment used by carpenters, articles of work. This means you own or borrow a book to read and get knowledge or entertainment from it. Modern research heavily depends on the use of references, usually books written by people who are authorities in specific disciplines. Even works of fiction have come to rely upon research. British novelist Frederic Forsyth's thrillers, *The Day of the Jackal* and *The Odessa Files* utilised research on the subjects the novels are based on, just to cite one example.

For these reasons, buying books and owning a library are imperative to the life of a writer, to a cultured person and also for enjoyment. But, in the same way as pens have been abused as mentioned earlier on, books, too, have suffered.

In my Juba days, I knew a man of modest academic background who spent a fortune buying books from a local bookshop in town. Whenever he heard of a bestseller not available locally, he would not hesitate to order it from Khartoum, Nairobi or even London. In the process he acquired a big library, which he strategically placed in the sitting room for any visitor to see.

Although he never ceased talking about his collections and the latest purchase, he believed that once a book had been hyped as a bestseller, the product must be genuinely good, not knowing this was a commercial stunt to make books sell to unsuspecting and indiscriminate buyers and readers. The man did not read them. Each time a book and its contents came to be discussed, his remarks were invariably, "This is a good book" or, "this is a very good writer", no mention of contents or how the author had handled the subject were ever made.

Buying and maintaining status and status symbols can be very expensive indeed.

SPLM/A Update newsletter 1994.

When food becomes a killer

While hundreds or thousands of Sudanese often starve to death because they have no food to eat, a small number of their compatriots with sufficient material means become sick or die because of too much food or as a result of sharp taste and appetite, wrong or harmful diet.

At the height of the severe famine that hit Bahr el Ghazal region in 1998, during which many victims died, foreign relief workers were scandalised to discover young men undergoing *tëëc* (teec), or literally "lying down" in Dinka. This is a practice in which young people go on what would be called a fattening programme. It is an old culture practised by some sections of the Dinka community of South Sudan. The main objective of this custom is for the young men to show the wealth of their family.

The fattening scheme takes this form: participants, mostly young men and from families which were rich in cattle came together in a homestead or cattle camp. The youths who do nothing else except constant drinking of large quantities of milk and most of the time lying down. This is a sport, and as such, victors and failures emerge at the end of the exercise. The "winner" who had to be the fattest of all and a survivor of *rëët* (reet) *e yic* or bursting of the stomach. The idea behind this competition is that a top winner becomes the pride of his family: exhibition of riches. Though not very common, some young men die while undergoing this form of self-inflicted torture. But those who finish the process re-join the society with grotesque, zombie-like bodies, some weighing twice or more their original weight.

Many people, Sudanese and foreigners, do not hesitate to condemn this outdated practice. It is a waste of resources in a society where not everyone can afford three meals a day. It is also risky to the lives of those being fed. But are some of the Sudanese living in urban centres aware of the dangerous lives they lead, in the way they eat or what they consume?

To appreciate why most Sudanese town dwellers, engage in risky eating habits, we need to look to the past for explanation. For Sudanese in all four corners of their country, through physical interaction and mutual cultural borrowing, their diet has become increasingly uniform.

An article carried by the *British Financial Times* in the early 1980s reported that in the consumption of sugar, Sudan led the world. Why? Love of all things sweet probably came to Sudan from the Middle East through poetry and tales of how the rich of the ancient world lived the good life. Romantic poets and singers wrote and sang – and still do – using *sukar* (sugar) '*assel,* or honey, as similes for a lover.

A beautiful girl and a lover is just that, or *helwa,* sweet. Anyone working in the advertising industry will readily agree that for one to sing praise of anything is a promotion. In many parts of the world, governments ban advertising tobacco product precisely because it makes tobacco and smoking attractive and cool especially to young people.

In Sudan, sugar is found in everything one eats or drinks: heavily sweetened tea; homemade *kerkede* (hibiscus); orange squash; cake, you name it. Date trees do well in desert or semi-desert lands such as Northern Sudan and most of the Arab lands. *Balah* or dates contain a lot of sugar. No wonder that wherever you travel in the world you will find confectioners preparing and selling their sugary wares. For example, in Sydney, the capital of New South Wales, Australia, there is a big retail and wholesale shop that carries an advert in Arabic, which goes *haluyat baledna* or sweets of our homeland. There one can buy all types of sweets from the Middle East and Sudan. *Tahniya,* sesame paste, with a very heavy dose of sugar is on sale there.

But why should anyone complain about people who consume sweet things and not poison? Sugar – unlike cigarettes – has yet to be criminalised, but opinion suggests that sugar and its by-products contribute, especially in adults over 40, to unhealthy increase in consumers' bodyweight. (In the Western culture, the less offensive expression is "gaining weight" which most of us in Sudan proudly describe as being fat. Whether we call the condition as that of one putting on weight or getting fat, the medics tell us too much of that at a certain age carries with it dangers affecting health for the worse.

Sudanese cuisine may not be at the same level as the French or Italian, for example, but many Sudanese including the widely-travelled, boast that their dishes are among the best in the world.

Meat (beef, mutton, goat) is the main component of a Sudanese meal, cooked with vegetables and other greens such as *kudhura, bamiya* or okra.

A typical Sudanese meal is made from some of these and more often than not, contains a lot of oil, fats and table salt. Beef, mutton, fish and chicken are fried in oil. Being rich in livestock, many Sudanese think a meal without meat, broth and stew to go with *kisra*, thin pancake, is incomplete.

In the seventies, Khartoum had two famous food outlets that served the middle-class with dishes of choice. These were El Math'am el Jamhouri and Funduk esh Sharg. The former specialised in boiling chunks of overcooked meat with bones and marrow, and accompanied by tasty stew. Esh Sharg menu combined Sudanese dishes such as *bamiya, khudhara* and assortments of Eastern and Mediterranean cuisine.

During that time, one would observe civil servants, legislators and officials on duty from the South, trooping to these restaurants for late lunch. It is true that at the time in review, there was little medical knowledge available to the public about risks from certain foods and the habits of their consumers. This meant that almost all the Sudanese enjoying their money by means of food either in public eateries or at home were exposing their health to dangers without knowing.

A true story of a rich man
In 1991 while I was at an SPLA base in Kidepo in Eastern Equatoria, someone with whom I used to spend time and while away long and indolent periods, told me how he nearly killed himself by eating the richest foods he could lay his hands on. Incidentally, we were going through rough times after the split within the rebel movement. There was a severe shortage of

food. He did not need to tell me, but I knew the man was one of the richest men in the district we both hail from. Being so, why should he not live in comfort, he reasoned. His morning tea, he would have with milk and a lot of sugar. One hour later, his breakfast would consist of fried meat, dripping with oil, porridge from sorghum flour mixed with sesame paste, oil, honey and again a lot of sugar.

Between meals, the man would go out to sip fresh orange juice, also full of sugar. Lunch varied but whatever dish he ordered contained red meat with plenty of fats, oil and salt. Supper at home was usually *asida* sunk in a bowl of milk, and, of course, full of sugar. At weekends, he would go out to eat with friends. His favourites were fried tilapia and *basim* or boiled lamb's head. Whenever he invited friends to his house for a meal, he made sure that a ram was slaughtered. He saw no reason not to join the guests in attacking ram's tail – a bundle of fatty tissues.

His job was a sedentary one and he never went for an evening walk, nor did he play any sport. He put on very heavy weight. And he loved it. That was what it meant to be a man of means. And he felt and thought he was hale and as fit as a fiddle.

One evening, he collapsed and was rushed to hospital. Hours later he woke up to realise that he had been unconscious while on the way to hospital. Three days later he was discharged after treatment and a lecture consisting of "don't eat this" or "take that in moderation". Now in his early sixties, the man who since leaving hospital has been living a frugal life and is a symbol of good health which guards jealously by eating frugally.

Now eating healthy foods is no longer what people used to associate with girls' dieting to be slim or beautiful according to Western standards, but a way of reducing health risks such as hypertension and heart diseases directly or indirectly resulting from consumption of certain diets and lifestyles.

But do many people take such warnings seriously? Prove me wrong by walking into one of Nairobi's restaurants serving *nyama choma*, or roast meat, in Kiswahili.

Innocent Abroad: A black man and a black dog in rural Wales

I

When I went to England for the first time in 1981, to do a diploma in printing at the London College of Printing at Elephant and Castle, being black was not a problem. The metropolitan London had known peoples of different races for centuries. With many foreign diplomatic missions, students, tourists and businesspeople from nearly all corners of the world staying and mixing with the inhabitants of the capital, the sight of a black, brown or yellow person was commonplace.

After moving a year later to Cardiff, the capital of Wales, I never encountered staring looks from anyone. Cardiff being a city and seat of two universities – the University of Wales and the University of Cardiff – with a large number of foreign students, persons from different racial and cultural outlooks did not attract curiosity from the locals.

At the Centre for Journalism Studies – later to become Media and Cultural Studies – I was rather a rarity, however. At the start of the academic year in September 1982, I was one of the five foreign students who had registered for a master's degree research in media. These were: two young men from South Korea, a girl from Peking (as the Chinese capital city, Beijing, was then known), one girl from Finland, and me.

All of us were studying pure research, no taught courses. At different stages during that academic year, my four colleagues dropped out, leaving me as the only non-British student at the centre. As the only African student and journalist, I attracted interest – in a positive way – from diploma students, all of whom were graduates from British universities studying for an advanced diploma in journalism. Most of those young people developed an interest in me for a good reason: as students of journalism they naturally wanted to know how the mass media operated in the developing world and how journalists there were coping with the dictatorial regimes in power in many countries, including my own, Sudan at the time.

Being a Sudanese also meant that one of the students was keen for me to meet her father –who had been to Sudan decades earlier – wanted me to meet him as he was said to be nostalgic about the country, its people and his time there. The student was the daughter of M. K. Barbour, a retired educationalist who had taught and taken part in designing the syllabus at Sudan's prestigious Bakht er Ruda Institute of Education. Mr Barbour was a household name in Sudan in the years before and following independence of Sudan in 1956. He was remembered by generations of Sudanese teachers and students for his book, *Sudan: A Regional Geography* which was published in 1961. The hardcover instantly became a favourite textbook with teachers of geography and their students all over the country. Because of those factors I became a friend to several of the diploma students, some of whom invited me out on weekends from time to time. I immensely enjoyed my time in Cardiff in general and at the Centre for Journalism Studies in particular, despite the fact that my studies were very demanding and sometimes stressful at the beginning. The Welsh used to boast of being friendly people, although at the time I was in their capital city, Welsh nationalism said otherwise, regarding the attitudes of some members of the youth who agitated against the English. For instance, my supervisor, a veteran journalist and a Briton who was not Welsh, told me he once received a letter from some individuals affiliated to a nationalist organisation. This letter, he said, was written in Welsh. The author had created a dilemma for him, as was the case with other non-Welsh speakers: if he told the authors that the contents were Greek to him he would play into their hands: what business was he doing in the principality whose language he didn't understand? The journalist-turned-academic further told me that less than 18 percent of the region's population spoke and wrote Welsh. Generally, throughout my two-year sojourn in Wales, I neither experienced any form of discrimination on account of my colour nor did I learn of any other foreigner getting a hint they were unwelcome because they were different.

A day trip to rural Wales

One day, some of the diploma students organised a day trip to rural Wales. When they invited me to join them, I readily jumped at the offer. I didn't want to repeat the mistake I had made while in London: not venturing outside of the city to see the countryside that should have included Stratford-upon-Avon, Shakespeare's birthplace and resting place. Despite the nature of my career (journalism), I have not always been a keen traveller; visits for pleasure to me are frankly an activity I reluctantly undertake, partly not to disappoint a friend or a family member, or because – as often happens in my type of work – business colleagues or an employer plan them and, like the rest of the team members, I am required to comply. Trips I undertake are, invariably, out of necessity.

The students had hired a minivan to be driven by the students themselves. The places of interest we were going to visit were Laugharne Castle and the boathouse where the famous Welsh poet, Dylan Thomas lived. The house "on a cliff overlooking the Taf Estuary" (the Boathouse website) where Thomas wrote much of his poetry is preserved as a museum and a tourist attraction in Swansea area. More about that later in the piece.

We drove through the beautiful Welsh landscape crisscrossed by verdant valleys and dotted with tree shrub-covered hills. On arrival in Swansea city, the team decided that we should have some snacks at a café on the beach. The van was parked some distance from the pier. As we were walking towards the café, we caught up with an elderly lady who was walking her dog. The dog was soot dark. She was holding the dog on a leash and he was walking alongside her, as well as other people who were heading in the same direction.

Without warning of any sort, all hell broke loose. At seeing me, the dog rushed towards me, growling madly. And since the dog had got free, he was approaching me, ready for an attack. Although I put out appearances of being unruffled, the opposite was the case. The owner repeatedly, in a voice devoid of authority, called out "Come on … come on…" (I failed to capture the dog's name). Despite the fact that my family owned a friendly dog that was popular in the neighbourhood of my rural home, I always have felt uncomfortable with dogs, without a reason. Perhaps this is a phobia I have yet to acknowledge.

The "pleadings" the dog's owner was making were ineffectual – her pet doggedly pursued me as if he was out to settle a long-held grudge. A few steps away from me the dog began to jump at me. When it became clear that he meant to hurt me, the students formed a cordon around me and began to wave him off with their bare hands. But this preventive measure emboldened the dog as he was trying at every turn – and barking – to break into the human shield around me. The dog followed us in that way until we reached the café. On reaching the café's door, the students gently pushed me ahead, almost shoving me into the building, and closed the door once I was safely inside. Surprised, and apparently frustrated, the dog stopped, and wagged his tail before he slowly returned to his owner.

Sombre mood
The unprovoked and unpleasant drama triggered by the dog undoubtedly spoiled the mood among us; for me, I was both upset and left wondering. For me to ask why the dog had picked me out of a dozen people in the company was essentially rhetorical – if not outright nonsensical: why me? If something was wrong with the black colour – so I reasoned – then the dog should be the last creature to mock and terrorise me on that account, being black as he was. My friends on the other hand were genuinely sorry for me and were constantly saying "Sorry" as if they had a hand in what had happened. None of them could hide their sympathy for me. This was in sharp contrast to the old woman, who appeared to see nothing wrong with her dog's attempt to express himself: probably it was his first time to see a black human being. Seen objectively, the dog was absolutely innocent. Since non-human animals such as dogs act on instincts rather than on contrived deception called diplomacy or euphemism, we members of the human race tend to condemn this form of sincerity at work.

II
White child seeing a black person for the first time
It was late afternoon when we had a brief stopover in a rural homestead at the foot of a hill. After enjoying some snacks, we left for the Laugharne Castle. Not far from this Medieval edifice we called at a house in the valley, where a man in his fifties met us. As we were approaching the family house, he came out of his compound to welcome us. He was a congenial soul who talked fast and with little restraint concerning what he was saying. A moment later, his daughter, a chubby and excited child aged about eight years, joined us. After welcoming us to his village, the man lurched into a talk that left me uncomfortable. "You see", the man addressed me in person, "that hill over there. Many years ago, the English would come from

the south to attack us. But we gave them a bloody nose", he said, as he obviously relished the memories of the era of warfare between the Welsh and their southern neighbours and rivals to the southeast, the English. For my benefit, he said the castle was a symbol of things martial from the distant past. Paradoxically, the students – most of them English – just chuckled, and appeared to take no offence from his boast, irrelevant in these changed times.

It was not long before the child approached me to grab and hold my left forearm. I tried to pull it back but she wouldn't let go, and began to gently stroke it as she shouted out "This is the first time to see a black person. His skin is smooth! I see black people only on telly!"

My colleagues were uneasy, presuming that she was annoying me. For my part, I was fully aware of the fact that she was driven by innocent curiosity; she had to be forgiven. Furthermore, one should appreciate the child's peculiar environment. In the valley in which she and her family lived, there was no way they could have come face to face with a black person of flesh and blood.

My colleagues had apparently failed to take note of that fact. Perhaps they were upset by the failure of the child's father to rebuke and pull her away from me. To my companions, the child was being ill-disciplined and childish, a tautology. If I had accurately read what was possibly going in my companions' mind, then they were wrong: those were the feelings of an innocent child who spoke her mind truthfully. This was not the first time I had encountered such a situation, as will be shown by the previous and similar incidents involving me, one in Germany and the other back home in Sudan when I myself was a child.

III

A precedent in Germany

In 1978, I was attending a training course in journalism in what was then known as West Berlin, with a group of journalists from sub-Saharan Africa. With the exception of a fellow Sudanese colleague, Fatima – a girl of Arab descent with a lighter skin – and two copper-brown Somali journalists, all of us (drawn from Kenya, Tanzania, Zambia, Nigeria, Somalia Liberia, Malawi and Cameroon) were black. One day we boarded an autobahn taking us to a function in another suburb of Berlin. We became a spectacle to those inside but most of them controlled their curiosity, preferring to steal swift stares. Of course, I noticed two or three adults in discreet non-verbal communication about us. In the same compartment there was a young mother with her child of about three to four years old. On seeing us, the child released a piercing shriek accompanied by *"Schwatzer! Schwatzer!"*. He was wailing as loudly as he could. Although I was the only member of the group to grasp what the child was saying – I understood some German, having several years earlier privately learned the language, at the centre run by the embassy of the Germany Democratic Republic, GDR, in Khartoum – I decided to withhold what I had heard until our return to the hostel where most of us lived.

The child's mother was a sensible person. Her reaction to the drama her child had created was to leave the compartment for the next. It was after we had arrived at our destination that I told my colleagues that the child was calling us blacks or dark ones. A somewhat shocked colleague responded with "What?" Generally, no one among us expressed hard feelings towards the child; he was just curious, although it would have been impossible for a child living in the Berlin of the time not to have seen a black person at all; there were many black Africans all over Germany, including both in East and West Berlin. Boney M, the four-member music band which was at the height of their popularity all over the world at the time and who began their career in Munich, Germany, were blacks from the West Indies.

IV

'The First Time I Saw a White Man'

When I was a student at Atar Intermediate School, teachers of English language used to give students topics for composition writing.

Composition writing was one of the ways to test student's understanding of the rules of grammar – especially tenses and concord between pronouns and verbs and the correct application of the vocabulary at their disposal. Such writings, often between 250 to 1000 words at most, were also meant to develop a student's ability to reason logically.

Some topics I remember were very common. These included topics such as "The Day When Everything Went Wrong", and "The first time I Saw a

White Man". (I think in our age of political correctness; the subject would be re-paraphrased as "The First Time I Saw a White Person". My class was once asked to write on the first topic although I don't recall the gist of my own story which I submitted to the teacher. The second topic, however, had been attempted by previous classes before us. In fact, the subject had been on the school curriculum almost from its establishment in 1946. The majority of the teachers at the time were drawn from England and from the American missionaries of the Presbyterian Church; they were also white. The school's first headmaster was a Mr Williams, a Briton. His wife taught English. It was at this time that the students, most of them hailing from the various districts in Upper Nile Province *(source: Durham University Library, Sudan Archives)*. Since virtually all the students at Atar at that phase hailed from rural and traditional communities of Southern Sudan, whose members had little or no contact with the outside world of the day, teachers tried to introduce them- through lessons in geography and history- to peoples and cultures in other parts of the world. In that context, writing about a black person's experience of seeing a white person for the first time began to gain a topicality that ended more than 15 years later. Although I hadn't written on that topic, seeing a white person for the first time was an event that was as memorable as it was exciting.

My personal experience

I know this for a fact. During my childhood, in a rural area of what is South Sudan today, seeing people of a white race was a spectacle to behold. My native homestead is in Pakuoor village. It still stands there today. It takes me 15 minutes to walk to Kongor town[2] and about 40 minutes to Panyagoor, the administrative capital of the former Twï County. Kongor is exactly 100 kilometres northwest of Bor, the principal town of Jonglei State. My native

---

2 Town is used here in the inverted commas because the place would not fit into the conventional attribute of a town. The appropriate name would be what is now called in Kenya a "trading centre". During the colonial days, the lowest units of local government were referred to as court centres where chiefs sat, more often than not, under trees to settle disputes using customary law.

homestead – which lies south of Panyagoor – is just under 150 metres west of the Cape-Cairo dirt "highway".

During my boyhood, this continental land artery was very busy during dry season – early November to mid-March every year. Different types of vehicles, ranging from heavy military trucks to Volkswagen Beetles, motorbikes and even bicycles – most of them northwards bound – were almost a daily sight for people living on both sides of this road. The passengers of those passing strangers were as different as the vehicles they were riding in; there were black people as well as whites and other people with colours in between. Seeing the whites was what fascinated us, the children in the neighbourhood, the most.

As the weather used to be – as it is now – very hot, some of these white people in their cars – men to be specific – would be seen wearing only shorts. In that state their bodies appeared to us, the onlookers – who were just on the edge of the road – like the bodies of hippos out of water, and this increased our inquisitiveness still further. Kongor, then a trading hub officially designated by the colonial authorities as a court centre, used to provide a brief stopover to these strangers. The centre had a well, which supplied clean water. At the station, passers-by would get to fill their water containers, possibly for the use of cars. Sometimes they would come out of their vehicles to exercise their muscles for the long drive ahead. The children, mostly boys, would cluster around to satisfy their burning curiosity.

It was not a free show, however. The court centre had men who looked after a government guesthouse. These men sometimes behaved as if they had the authority to keep public order. Once a convoy of such vehicles had stopped at the centre for whatever reason, these men –who were actually guards responsible for the conservation of government buildings – would drive away youngsters (and a few adults) who had swarmed around the strangers. If the crowd thirsting to watch human species who happened to be of different colour, refused to disperse, the guards would use twigs from trees or sometimes a whip from hippo skin to chase them. One of the guards – who was always ready to send away disobedient boys with the threat of lashing – had his own reason.

Speaking to a handful of men who had gathered around a group of white people – men, women and young children – Deng, as the guard was known, explained that it was prudent to keep away from them for a good reason: they could be carrying contagious diseases, which could be easily passed to the watchers. His fears were confirmed – although not really justified – by a middle-age man in the group who was coughing persistently. All we boys knew about Deng was that he was a servile man who wanted to be known as caring for the welfare of Turuk – the urban dwellers and those who were different from the locals.

From a close look at the uncovered parts of those white people in transit, we thought that their skin was pink, not white, as I would learn years later was the accepted description. We youngsters believed that the pink skin was so delicate that it would be vulnerable to insect bites or could be easily broken by even a blunt object.

Seeing white people up close

The first time I came into very close contact – shaking hands – with some persons who at the time I considered to be white, was at school. After entering Atar Intermediate School, I was among students who sought baptism. The school chaplain was Swalem Sidhom, an Egyptian affiliated to the Presbyterian Church, whose head office was in nearby Malakal. Most of the church leaders were white Americans. Besides catering to the spiritual needs of the students, our chaplains – the other was an Irish Catholic priest, Fr John Slater – taught religious education as a subject.

For catechism classes we had to go every Saturday to Swalem's residence, which was about a kilometre away from school. The priest, who was in his early 40s, was married with two young children. The Egyptian was a very friendly man who allowed us inside his house (catechism classes were held outside under a tree) and lent us books that weren't available in the school library. Soon we got to know his children. Although much younger than we were, some of us became friends and we would play together. We soon realised that the difference in the colour of skin was not a barrier, nor would that create a problem. Swalem Sidhom and his wife – although a reserved lady who rarely spoke – treated us like their own kids. To us, they were just like us in everything except the colour.

Later that year Swalem left for further theological studies in Kenya. We missed him and his family. His temporary replacement was a white American who was very fluent in spoken as well as written Arabic. Like his predecessor, the priest, Rev Dr J. L. Anderson, who was based in Malakal taught us hymns in Arabic. After lessons and church service, the priest would mix with the students, telling stories and joking with them at times. He became one of us. His successor, Rev Bill Adair, another white American priest, was not different in his closeness to the students and the local workers.

The myth of a white person being an object attracting curiosity was cracked by those close contacts with the people who were white. We learned they were just normal human beings like us. It was also their belief that they and members of other races – white, red, yellow, and so forth – all belong to the one large and extended family of humanity.

A white man in the Ituri Rain Forest of the Congo

Many people are at home with what is familiar while the unknown is likely to create suspicion or fear. In the parts the world where white people have not been seen before, their first sight can cause panic. In 1989, Robert C. Bailey, an American researcher travelled to a village in Ituri Forest in the Democratic Republic of the Congo. Part of his experience there goes: "… a child playing in the middle of the dirt track would spot me and run screaming in terror. The villagers, dropping what they were doing, beheld one of the most frightening sights they had seen since the Congolese rebels invaded this area in 1965: a perspiring six-foot-two-inch white male with hairy face and bare legs…". The anthropologist adds that most of the men ran and that those "who remained averted their eyes, their hands trembling, as we took seat". The researcher's reference to his own height is relevant: the adult males among the people he was meeting, previously known pejoratively as pygmies, are under five feet tall.

The explanation for the fright and flight is that the inhabitants of Lese and Efe "firmly believed that the white people eat black people and find their children especially appetizing. Perhaps their view developed from the reputedly brutal treatment that Africans received under the Arabs and then Belgian rule".

Bailey, Robert C., "The Efe: Archers of the African Rain Forrest", *National Geographic*, p. 667, November 1989.

The night I became an Arab

In 1978, the West Berlin based International Institute for Journalism organised a study course for print journalists from Africa. Sudan was one of the countries which had students taking part in the three-month course. On that course Sudan had two journalists, Fatima, not her real name, from a minor Arabic language periodical, and myself. I was the editor of *Southern Sudan*, a monthly magazine owned by the Regional Government of Southern Sudan.

The course included travel to places of interest in the former Federal Republic of Germany and a day trip to East Berlin, then the capital of the Communist German Democratic Republic. During the visit to East Berlin, we had to pass through then infamous – in the word of a travel book – Checkpoint Charlie which was the border crossing between the American and Soviet sectors. In the then divided city, the most visible symbol was the Wall. Security was very strict, which included the people passing through the gate sometimes being searched. We had almost had no problem since our course director, a native of West Berlin, was accompanying us and was handling communications.

On entering, the guards waved us to proceed. But Fatima, was told to get into a nearby cubicle where a prim-looking female guard was sitting. When Fatima later re-joined us she was in an ugly mood; she had been subjected to body search. She was bitterly complaining: why was she singled out? We sympathised with her and wanted to know the reasons. It wasn't long when we later realised that her gender and race might have played a role in what was a humiliating experience. Another female colleague, a Cameroonian, was allowed to go just like the rest of us. Fatima on the hand, was told being an Arab, the security people couldn't take chances.

This was the 1970s, when Palestinians and their sympathisers in other parts of the world were busy hijacking airplanes, among other acts of terrorism. The 1970s were the decade of plane hijackings by angry young people ranging from radical left – from West and even Japan – to the Palestinian members of Front for the Liberation of Palestine or Black September. And there were women among them; of which Leila Khaled, who hijacked the American TWA Transworld Airline, was the most well-known.

■

Three weeks after this incident, we were visiting Bonn, then capital of West Germany, after a tour that took us to the north (where among other places we visited the Airbus Industrie manufacturing plant near Hamburg) and to the south (to Trier, birthplace of Karl Marx and where his house is now a museum). Trier is an important tourist town, not simply because the father of Communism was born there, but because of its stunning historical sites. A bridge over the River Mosel built during Roman time is a wonder of ancient engineering feats, as is the amphitheatre where, we were told, condemned men were thrown to wrestle with lions as the public watched, in much the same way as they enjoy watching soccer in the comfort of modern stadiums today.

A night in a Bonn nightclub

Bonn was the last leg of our tour of this naturally beautiful, albeit highly-industrialised, country. We had to go to Bonn for two reasons. The birthplace of Beethoven is very close to Koln (Cologne) the headquarters of the German international broadcasting station, Deutsche Welle; which hosted us. Second, being the capital city of the FRG, Bonn had many foreign legations. On the second day we were allowed to visit our respective embassies, most of which were in the city suburb of Bad Godesberg. It was Friday. In the Sudan mission, the staff, which consisted of juniors, warmly welcomed us. The ambassador and senior diplomats were away. The staff in charge, mostly middle ranking personnel, appeared to have little or no work to do. Most of them appeared somewhat homesick. There were copies of old newspapers from home, most of them were in Arabic and were more than three days old, but for Fatima and me, their contents were fresh. This was the pre-internet world.

The staff couldn't hide their pleasure with our presence as they seemed to have got tired of each other. We provided them with new and interesting company as we talked about our trips to various parts of the country, which most of these fellows would not manage on their own salaries. Much of our conversation concentrated on our sojourn in West Berlin. I was careful not to mention anything about our visit to East Berlin, lest it bring up Fatima's ordeal. She also did well by saying nothing about it.

One of the staff members was from Nubia, the northernmost part of Sudan, sharing its border with Egypt. The Nubians are among Sudan's ancient people who were among the first Africans to embrace Christianity right from the faith's infancy. Archaeological treasures in the territory are testimony to the glorious past of the Nubians who once conquered and ruled Egypt and established a ruling dynasty there from the 8th -7th century BCE.[3] In Sudan, Nubians of today are known for their pride in their ancient history and its glory. Outsiders sometimes accuse Nubians of being a community whose members always love to bond together where they happen to be and by extension are suspected of being xenophobic, which may be an exaggeration.

My colleague and her fellow Nubian began to warm up to one another. Curiously, they spoke in Arabic instead of what should have been their mother tongue. Perhaps neither knew it, as is the case of the "diasporic" Nubians. None of us was surprised to notice that. Soon, the two of us from Berlin were invited to experience Bonn's life night the following Saturday. Those were the days of youth infatuation with disco.

---

3   Crofton, Ian, World History: 50 key milestones you really need to know, p. 68,
This recollection first appeared in the SPLM/A Update in 1994 in a slightly shorter version.

It was eight in the evening when we enter a nightclub that was popular with foreigners. There are many patrons, mostly young people. We have to stand in a queue to buy tickets, at the entrance to a large structure that looks like a hangar. This is a discotheque. The three men and Fatima and I stand in line, waiting to enter the club. The man at the gate who appears to be a bouncer and doubling as ticket collector, refuses to take the money for the fifth person: me. Some sort of an argument develops between our hosts and the German, who is determined not to allow me into the club. The Sudanese tries to talk quietly to suppress what they don't want to come to the attention of the other party-goers. The gatekeeper is talking loudly in quite good English: "Africans are not allowed into the club". But the Sudanese insist they I should be allowed in; they and I are Africans.

"No, you are Arabs!" argues the German, differentiating my companions from me.

"Fine, if you have problems with Africans and no problems with the Arabs, then he should be allowed to enter", argues one of the Sudanese as he is pointing at me. The diplomats, who have their passports with them, point at me.

"He is an Arab", says the Sudanese.

"Impossible," says the German.

"He is an African, not an Arab".

Because of their passports and their copper-brown skins (of which Fatima was lighter than the rest), the guard doesn't contest that claim. One of the Sudanese is determined that I should be admitted otherwise we all should leave the club and go, he threatens. His argument in support of his claim of my being an Arab goes along these lines: Sudan is an Arab country. He – pointing to me – is a Sudanese citizen. Being a citizen of an Arab country he- meaning me- is therefore an Arab.

"Okay, he can enter, but there has to be an extra fee. And mind you, you will be responsible for his behaviour while inside the disco". That is the fiat from the hard-bargaining German.

We are allowed in. Florescent lights – yellow, green and blue – are flickering above the roof and in the four corners. We find an unoccupied table. Five of us take our places around it. The poles that prop the building are gigantic and look as if they are from a tropical rainforest whose murals are on the wall and roof.

We don't talk for a few moments. There is nothing to talk about. Except later, one of the men throws what is practically a tantrum, without the target getting it. "*Mala'oon!*", he repeats several times. This is the Arabic word for "accursed". He is referring to the German bouncer.

At the table we begin a subdued conversation before we make orders. Despite the loud music, one of our Sudanese hosts, talking in Arabic, tells me the reasons why Africans, which he refers to as *Fallata* – being a derogatory name for people of West Africans, especially Nigerians – were responsible for giving the people from the African continent a bad name. In fact, West Africans come second; the main culprits are the Congolese migrants fleeing Zaire under the rule of Mobutu Sese Seko, he tells me. According to the information he has gathered, those Africans used to enter discos, get into brawls; sometimes they wouldn't pay for what they ordered and consumed. Rule: no admission for all Africans. He studiously refrains from using the adjective, black.

Ironically, this club we are in plays some music from Zaire. It is now time for us to forget the hassles and relax. The Northern Sudanese society – which is overwhelmingly Muslim – tends to be generally conservative and rarely encourages Western lifestyle such as dancing to pop music. Members of the opposite sex rarely mix or dance in public, to cite one example.

Our group draws the discreet attention of other young men and girls sitting next to us: we are an oddity: four men to a woman. Who should dance with her? We all rise and dance, circling around Fatima. it was at that stage that one of the girls sitting with other three female friends and three male companions, asks us in English "Why do you dance with one girl?" As we hesitate, wondering what to tell her, she urges us "Come on, join us at our table over there". I and the other two Sudanese move to their table, leaving Fatima with her fellow Nubian alone. I dance and enjoy my time with a girl who has introduced herself as Bettina, and tells me she is studying science. She informs me she loves Africa and hopes to visit Tanzania after completing her studies in a couple of months. She tells me also that one of her uncles was in that African country when it was known as Tanganyika. She doesn't tell me what he was doing there in those days when the German colonisation of parts of Africa would make people shy to revisit.

We dance until three in the morning when our hosts from the embassy call a taxi to take Fatima and me to the hotel where we are staying with the rest of our journalist colleagues. We leave Bonn for Berlin by plane in the morning. When I narrate to my Somali friends what happened to me the previous night, they find it rather hard to believe. The story tickles them. "So you are now an Arab?", asks Abdi in jest. Ironically, the Somalis, most of whom are not dark and have more semblance to Arabs in features, such as the shape of nose, are often reluctant to consider themselves Arabs despite the fact that former dictator Mohamed Siad Barre single-handedly drove their country into the League of Arab Nations, a short time after taking power in a coup in 1969.

Breaking with Customs is Hard to Do

Recently I overheard a woman boasting to her friend that her husband, a widely travelled man and in his late forties, was an accomplished cook. Decades ago, such talk among members of my ethnic community could surely have been branded indiscreet as it would damage the man's reputation. His wife would have been considered as divulging a secret she and her spouse should guard.

In those days, the gender world of that community, like other societies, was compartmentalised with the role of each sex clearly defined and rigidly observed, leading to the classification of the non-conformists as odd and puerile characters.

Broadly speaking, the world of those people, mostly rural dwellers, consisted of two distinct classes: women and teenage children, and men, each with specific duties and roles. Men had to handle what was regarded as masculine matters pertaining to the protection of the community; of cattle from predators such as lions and hyenas; wrangles involving civil suits; hunting and fishing in rivers and streams – home to crocodiles and hippopotamus. For their part, women had to contend and be content with chores ranging from household administration – preparation of food – to nursing and nurturing of babies and young children.

This division of labour left some areas where roles overlapped. Women practised limited fishing and, for a very small group of them, particularly among widows, engaged in litigation for retrieval of property taken by relatives of their deceased husbands if they did not have brothers-in-law or adult sons.

Once initiated into manhood, young men gave up activities assigned to boys. In the community under discussion, an initiate should not cook, milk cows or goats. Incidentally, it is called *päl de räk,* that is giving up milking, a job for females of all ages, and boys. This taboo was violated only when a group of men had a milking cow – mostly when away from home – but no boy or woman to milk the animal. In such a situation, which was rare anyway, a man would volunteer to milk the cow for the benefit of the rest of the men, and under no circumstances should the volunteer taste the milk.

Although men could be excused to cook or roast fish in an all-male fishing camp, no man was permitted to cook. A male cook, known pejoratively as *dhuthët,* or the one who cooks, carried a stigma that could disqualify him when seeking to marry.

Men had to avoid even casual mention of matters related to the kitchen such as cooking utensils, granary for grains, and raw or cooked food. A man's job was to purely keep the kitchen supplied; what happened to its contents was none of his business. For a man to be slightly associated with this strictly female domain would be to engage in *näp* or *guïk,* literally – search or inspection – the name given to intimate interest in the kitchen, its contents and condition. The idea behind such contempt for a man meddling in what was clearly designated as women's domain, was the assumption that he was usurping his mother's or wife's duties, along with the implied conclusion that he did so because he had no trust in the woman in charge of that division.

These restrictive customs and practices governed the lives of the entire rural population. Townspeople from the same ethnic group judged the effect of the customs as village or "cattle-camp mentality". Paradoxically, these urban dwellers never escaped the long arm of the traditions which embarrassed them as their culture was derived from the same source.

With the spread of formal education and the mingling of these people with others from different cultural backgrounds, most of the old customs have over the years come under critical questioning based on practical considerations. For more than five decades now, some educated young Southern Sudanese have travelled to and lived in foreign countries where pragmatism speaks louder than traditional beliefs and some practices considered outdated. A young Dinka bachelor studying in Europe or North America, for example, has to cook his own food unless he is prepared to spend his entire stipend on the relatively costly meals available in restaurants. He would be committing financial suicide if he did not cook his own meals.

But such experiences and liberal thinking do not always change cultural ways overnight. On return home, the man who has been cooking and perhaps milking cows in foreign land, cannot continue carrying out such practices without meeting strong opposition and condemnation from every corner of his wider society. He therefore stops and avoids cooking in order to conform to the wishes of his community, whose opinion he cannot afford to flout unless he is prepared to be ostracised socially and become the butt of mean jokes behind his back.

Popular opinion about certain beliefs and practices is so strong that those challenging their usefulness find themselves helpless in effecting change or modification of apparently outmoded customs. Take for example a case of a man and his wife, living alone within their community. When the wife gives birth, the man's right to cook, wash and press clothes for his wife and to look after the baby would be denounced as unnatural. The woman who under the circumstance is weak and in need of rest will have to undertake those chores in order to protect her man's standing.

For some people to get out of this situation, a system has been devised by which a couple in a situation like this described above would obtain help from an "idle" hand, commonly a relative, but more likely to be a young cousin or niece.

This solution in itself raises other problems. Assistance from close relatives is solicited, given and accepted gratefully under the premise that kinfolks have a moral obligation to support each other in times of need. Such girls invariably offer their services free of charge, except for occasional gifts and the supply of basic needs such as food, clothes, accommodation or medical care. But a closer look at this kind of arrangement reveals that the girls are seriously disadvantaged. If they are of school age, for instance, their education is being interrupted in exchange for helping kin and kith. For those not attending school and old enough to earn their own livelihood, for example, selling second hand clothes, vegetables and fruits, or learning tailoring and embroidery for self-employment, working for relatives without pay or vocation makes the young women victims of exploitation, in the name of altruism. It may sound far-fetched to consider this system as violating girls' rights to develop their ability to be economically independent. But that is exactly what the custom does.

SPLM/A Update newsletter, 1994.

Erosion of some social values (1)

Several years ago Anna, my wife who is a professional interpreter, and I went to a studio in Sydney, Australia, to record an educational health programme for some members of the South Sudanese migrant community. (The subject was ear infections that affect young schoolchildren, and how it could be prevented or treated). Our hostess, the technician in charge of recording video programmes, was herself a migrant of European extraction, but a full-bloodied Aussie, as they say there. Although a pleasant person, she was clearly naïve and probably held stereotypes about migrants from non-European backgrounds, or didn't appreciate that something different was not necessarily negative or inferior to others.

As she was escorting us to a railway station, the recordist turned to ask us whether, in our society, Sudan (this was before the South had become independent), people observed table manners. I was stung by her question. On the other hand, Anna played down what was an impolite view based on no case, since we had not taken a meal, water or tea, to justify her gratuitous question. However, unlike me, Anna remained calm.

"Yes", we replied in unison. I immediately launched into a lecture, or what almost amounted to a tirade.

"We observe what you call table manners. I am wrong to use that expression; these practices to our community, back home and here, are more than manners or etiquettes. What we have are values that define a proud and dignified person. Those who fail to live according to what I can call "food ethics" are seen as outcasts, uncivilised. Failure to observe them would lead others to brand uncouth and immature any person violating those norms. Such a person would become a subject of ridicule by family, peers and society at large; an embarrassment..."

I had to stop to take a breath. I had also noted that Anna's silence might have been an indication that I had over-reacted to a trifle that should have been attributed to ignorance on the lady's part, in failing to understand – or appreciate – the existence of different cultural and social values. Indeed, her question deserved to have been overlooked and forgotten altogether.

To my surprise, the recordist responded with, "Why don't you write those things? Nobody knows about these things you are saying. Put them in writing for other people from other cultures. They will like to read about them", she told us.

We agreed, however, that there was an urgent need for such customs that are rapidly fading, as globalisation is making slow but sure inroads into the lives of traditional conservative African societies to be documented for people from non-African backgrounds and for the records and posterity.

Eating etiquettes and food ethics

While on the train on our way home we began to recall the way children were brought up to observe several "dos" and "don'ts" in the area of eating in general, and food in particular. In the pre-modern Dinka society, children were severely reprimanded if they sang or talked while eating. One was to sit down properly to eat and any other postures such as lying down while eating was not permitted, neither was gulping, eating noisily, eating in a hurry or picking huge morsels of food, especially when one was sharing with others. Such conducts were condemned as a form of gluttony and greed.

Concepts such as *wäth* or gluttony and *aciwäth/raan ci wäth*, synonyms for a glutton, are decidedly abusive in content. Every self-respecting person, young or old, or even children of five years old, would try very hard to avoid doing what would earn them such labels.

In general, nearly everyone in those days avoided eating food from families or individuals who were not directly related by blood. With the in-laws one would take food from them only after certain ceremonies had been performed. Even with relatives, there were unwritten laws of civility known as *dhëëng*, a value-loaded word that stands for dignity, grace, gentleness, well-fashioned and behaved, nobility, and so forth.

I recall a tall man who called at our homestead to spend the night. I must have been about seven years old at that time. The visitor, who was a complete stranger, had travelled – walking – from a distant place. He was evidently tired, thirsty and probably hungry. His destination was another 70 kilometres away from our home. My parents offered him water and tobacco, which he took and enjoyed. His face radiated happiness. Traditionally, good manners prevented a grateful recipient from saying "thank you" in the face of someone who had done them a favour, whether that person was a relative or a friend. And strangers had to do the thanking and praise behind the giver's back.

When the turn for food came, no amount of persuasion from my father would make him drink the milk or eat the *cuïn/kuïn* (solid porridge made from grain and prepared with fresh butter as condiment) that my mother had prepared and offered him. His word prevailed because my parents respected his sense of self-esteem and the prevailing social norms of the time. It was clear the guest was going to make the day-long trip on an empty stomach, all the way to his destination, just depending on water and tobacco. Even at that tender age, I felt sorry for the visitor, a kindly-looking man of about fifty years old.

My father and the guest spent much of the evening in conversation as they smoked the traditional tobacco. The following morning our hungry but proud guest, who was provided with a comfortable sleeping place, bade the family farewell to continue his journey to the home of his sister at the southern end of the district.

To this day I still wonder about the premium people in that part of the world and that time who so highly valued upholding mores that we today easily dismiss as obsolete and burdensome.

In one of his books, one of the best-known writers – and an undisputed authority on the cultures of Dinka – Francis Mading Deng, has documented a fact that a young man in the habit of moving aimlessly between relatives' homesteads would risk being misunderstood as someone looking for an opportunity to be "invited" to a meal.

Consumption of food in public or in an open place outside the house or in daylight was unthinkable, except for very young children. Some years ago a friend of this writer told a story which had scandalised the narrator. He said that on the previous day he had seen a formerly prominent political figure in Southern Sudan chewing at a roasted maize cob at a crowded Nairobi bus stop. That was during the last war and the former VIP was a destitute refugee there.

Erosion of some social values (2)

Apportioning food
Life in rural South Sudan, through its recent or oral history, has most of the time been a struggle for survival, with periods of prosperity as a rarity rather than the norm. The economy of the rural population in many areas used to be – and continues to be – subsistence due to the nature of agricultural practices that depended largely on hoes and even wooden shovels in the early stages, followed by the hoes. To this day little has changed in that outdated agricultural method. To use those primitive tools was a back-breaking activity, with little output in form of yield. Often, vagaries of nature would affect crop harvest. These included occasional flooding, drought and plant disease as well as pests such as locusts or grain-eating birds, among them sparrows. Livestock diseases such as rinderpest would reduce large herds' numbers, as well as the quantity of milk and milk products. Lean years were not uncommon, as is also the case today.

As a result, food shortages, hunger and even famines were not uncommon. Under such a stressful environment some people would be ready to cut corners to survive. One of the consequences of a person falling to temptation and other inappropriate conduct was the ultimate loss of personal integrity. But overall, people's response to endemic hardships caused by food scarcity or total famines was the evolution of coping strategies and attendant moral codes of conduct in trying times. Some of these norms are cited and examined, in passing, in the following paragraphs.

Not enough food to go round

During times of scarcity, the meagre available food had to be given to the most vulnerable members of the household or surrounding hamlet. Children, elderly persons, the sick and all lactating women, especially those who had just given birth, were always the first to be provided when food was too little to go around everyone. (Even during times of plenty, pregnant women were not encouraged to eat diets likely to "fatten" the foetus, in accordance to the traditional beliefs and practices as it was believed that an oversized baby would result in a difficult if not fatal labour or birth for the two). There were exceptions, though. Able-bodied young men would be given food out of insufficient rations, to give them energy needed for hunting for bush meat or to fish in distant and dangerous places.

Communal meals

There were – and still are – times when some members of a clan, an extended family, and peers of different age groups would gather for special occasions. These events included making sacrifices of domestic animals to clan divinities; celebration of a wedding or "thanksgiving" event after a successful fishing expedition, and hunting game animals.

Men- it always had to be an all-male affair- would sit down to share meat, boiled when at home or roasted if they were in a distant wood or an area such as swampland. Someone would volunteer to serve the multitude that had gathered.

Fairness had to be his guiding principle; everyone present- there were times some portions would be put aside for some people to take to a family with special needs, for example- would be given a piece to consume or take home if they were feasting on fish or game meat.

The man doling out pieces of meat or fish must make sure that there was no preferential treatment or discrimination to be employed in the exercise because he knew very well that his reputation would be called into question. The dispenser should never take even a small piece for himself to eat; his role dictated that his methods had to be transparent and involved self-denial. Being a person who had "forgotten" himself to receive his rightful share, other members of the group he was serving would put aside some – usually by "snatching" a chunk from him – to be kept and given to him after the service was over and everyone had had their share of the communal meal.

Erosion of some social values (3)

Stealing

It is not the concern of this piece to examine whether circumstances force a person to steal or that an irresistible urge in someone to help themselves illegally with what belongs to others is a form of disorder- kleptomania. However, theft in any form has been – and still is – so repugnant in many cultures, and through the ages, that organised religions unequivocally condemn it. Stealing has been and still is one of the vices that is widely condemned by many societies whether on the basis of religion, morality or both. One of the Ten Commandments, the eighth, as is found in the Judaic-Christian faith is clear on the subject of larceny: "Thou shalt not steal". The law criminalises stealing while society – especially one that is deeply steeped in traditional values – stigmatises thieves.

Even the Bible-toting European missionaries, during their first contacts with the African societies, knew they were not telling their converts a new prohibition regarding stealing; nearly every human society holds low opinion on a person who deprives others of their things or rights without explicit authorisation by the rightful owners.

What is a given is that, in virtually every culture, theft is held as a reprehensible act and the thief is openly despised as one driven by selfishness and meanness. In Dinka, a thief is called *cuëër/cuäär* (cueer/cuaar) In Shilluk it is *okwu*. A stigma is attached to such a name, because of the strong social disapproval society expresses about stealing and thieves. Any self-respecting individual shuns any situation or act their society has branded as an abomination.

Independent observation

In their administration of Sudan, British colonial officials were quick to realise that the subject peoples abhorred theft. In the late 1920s a DC posted to Kodok wrote in his report to the provincial governor in Malakal "Theft is practically unknown amongst the tribes, but it is harshly dealt with under native custom when it does occur. A thief is required to repay approximately six times the value of the stolen article".[4] Tribes, in that report refers to all the peoples from different ethnic communities inhabiting the province, namely the Shilluk, the Dinka, the Nuer, the Anyuak, the Murle and others.

Although larceny is a criminal act virtually throughout the world, it is its moral and social aspect that seems to preoccupy most preliterate communities: staying clear of it and to treat persons tainted by its incidence as social outcasts. In those societies, parents warn children as early as the time they begin to talk, about the evil of stealing and disrespect for parents and other adults. Any attempt by a child to eat something – including its own food – without being given permission to do so would result in a severe warning, if not spanking. And so the little one would grow up fearing, without even knowing the reason, that pinching is a very bad thing.

It is worse for adults. In the past decades, persons caught stealing were hauled to customary law courts which were open to the public. The spectacle of the accused being watched on stage before the chiefs acting as judges and a huge crowd of contemptuous onlookers was an excruciating punishment in itself. While a school boy in what was an equivalent of year two, my schoolmates and I watched a scene that has lived with me to this day. We were on a mid-day break when two policemen were passing through- the ungated school compound and therefore a thoroughfare- walking, or rather driving, a man to a nearby customary law court.

We learned that the man had been caught red handed after stealing and slaughtering a ram belonging to a neighbour. The accused was carrying a yellow-looking bundle similar to a huge bar of laundry soap. We were told the object that probably weighed more than two kilograms was a boiled tail of a ram. This was an exhibit. Young as we were, the spectacle shocked us as were

---

4   Willis, C. A. *The Upper Nile Handbook: A Report on Peoples and Government in the Southern Sudan, 1931*, Johnson, D. H. (Editor), p. 226, African World Books, Perth, Australia, 2016.

members of the crowd that was gradually forming and cautiously following behind the police and their quarry as they were walking to the courtroom. The man was later found guilty, convicted and ordered to give the ram's owner a calf as compensation. With the passage of time most of us, the eyewitnesses forgot the drama. Unfortunately, the story refused to die. Decades later, I discovered the "legacy" of the unwholesome conduct was very much alive. Although all the relatives of man who was convicted were known as law abiding and decent persons, some of the people who knew the story, directly or through a third party, would often exchange knowing winks whenever a relative passed by. None was spared including those who were born after the event.

Although it is disputable that punishment acts as a deterrent, a court-case spectacle, such as that described above, often did.

Theft the mother of all vices

That fear of public ridicule helped herd offenders into line. The degree to which thieves were despised is best shown in the following story.

In the distant past, young peasant boys and girls used to play the game of husband-choice. The scene of the fake marriage used to be in the meadow where boys would tend calves during the day. Once a girl – who had to be much older than the boys aged between 10-12 years old – passed by, the boys in their numbers would line up and ask the girl to choose a "husband". Each of these boys would try to be as presentable as possible: a poise like that of beauty pageant contestants; erect; baring the teeth especially one with sparkling white sets, the best being the one with a frontal gap in the upper teeth.

Moving along the row, like a VIP inspecting a guard of honour, the girl would finally pat gently the chest of the boy she "liked most", with the flattering, "This is my husband". As expected, the "chosen" boy would proudly jump up and down with excitement. He was the proud winner. At first everyone – the girl included – would round up the game with laughter. However, part of the game was to "spoil" the happiness of the boy who had been singled out for being the "most suitable" in the group.

Someone within the group would shout *"Acï cuëër lɔi! Acï cuëër lɔi!"*[5] (aci cueer loi! Aci cueer loi!), which in Dinka means she has chosen a thief. The

---

5   2 In other Dinka dialects it is "lɔc" instead of "lɔi".

rest would pick the refrain to dance to its tune. It was all playfulness, brewed and acted out in a cauldron of innocence as far as its objective and content were concerned. The jocular message to the girl was: you have chosen the worst among us, theft being the personification of what was conceivably bad socially. In other words, the import of "charge" was that she had made the worst selection, since anyone known to be a thief was the most contemptible person in existence to be a husband, a friend, a child, a parent or indeed a human being. Although it was not a morality play, one could interpret the play as underlining the worst grades the society of the time gave to stealing or thieves.

Wider social implications of stealing

In the old days – especially before the advent of the monetary economy – everyone, young or old, rich or poor, male or female, aspired to lead an upright life whose principle was avoidance of any act or behaviour that would tarnish not only one's own reputation but that of the entire family or the clan of the person concerned.

An individual's bad name was conceived as potentially damaging to future generations. Similar to family wealth, the stained name was passed on to offspring. In their lifetime, persons living with disgrace had a hard time; if they were young and looking to marry, for example, the likelihood of being rejected on the basis of known weakness of character, such as kleptomania for instance, if learned through whispered communication, would lead to the marriage application being politely turned down; no reasons asked or offered.

A pertinent question then arises: why is it that corruption – embezzlement – is now rampant in say, South Sudan, where those values as shown above are strong?

Without belabouring the point, a possible explanation is partially provided by the Nigerian political scientist, Claude Ake. "Ordinary people see the state as a hostile force to be evaded, cheated or defeated as circumstances allowed".[6] (in Martin Meredith's *The State of Africa: A History of Fifty Years since Independence*, p. 369). Well, one might add that not only the *ordinary* people alone; most of the people involved in looting the state are the educated members of power

---

6   Meredith, Martin, *The State of Africa: A History of Fifty Years since Independence*, p 369, Free Press, 2006.

elite. Perhaps such people are convinced – just as the ordinary people are – that stealing from an individual is wrong as the victim is being derived; in the case of state, there is "no victim", as the warped reasoning goes.

Are we the Leading Exporters of Rudeness Worldwide?

The latest edition of *Oxford Advanced Learner's Dictionary* defines "rude" as "having or showing a lack of respect for other people and their feelings". Both its adjective, "rude", and noun, "rudeness", express a relative value and judgement. A behaviour that is considered impolite in a given society may not be so in others. For example, in many parts of Africa, Asia and Islamic communities, adults take special care in how elders are addressed by younger members. In Sudan, especially in rural areas, children and young people are expected to refer to people of the age of their parents and other close relatives by the use of words that indicate blood relationship such as "mother", "uncle", "untie", even when the addressee is not a biological mother, uncle or aunt and so forth. On the other hand, in Western cultures a five-year-old boy will just call a man old enough to be his grandfather by his first name. No eyebrows are raised as this is normal to both the addressee and the addresser or a bystander.

Elements of politeness
We take the phrase "ladies and gentlemen" without giving it a thought about its origins. Feudal Europe was based on a class system in which everyone knew their station or position in society in general and in life in particular. The rich, men in most cases, who were also politically powerful, enjoyed being addressed as gentlemen while their wives were ladies, as opposed to commoners who formed the majority of any population in any country. A gentleman was expected to conduct himself with dignity and politeness. He thought and believed he embodied those attributes. A gentleman had to be

chivalrous to womenfolk – from their class, of course; he had to open doors for them and so on. Women of good reputation, or "ladies", were expected to behave in certain ways, expressed in a feigned demure demeanour, for instance. Some of these etiquettes have survived to this era despite major social changes, especially those introduced by the feminist revolution, that began in a big way in the 1960s.

Today, whether one is a royal or commoner, a Westerner or from urban centres of the developing world, socially approved correct behaviour is spreading globally. There is no option for one but to conform to be seen as a refined person. Usually, men vacate seats for women, and nearly everyone does the same for elderly people or less mobile individuals riding a train or a public bus. But in many circles in Southern Sudan it is common for one to receive a favour such as an offer of a cup of tea, but not to say, "thank you" to the person providing such an act of kindness or service.

Markers of civilised behaviour: when no one size fits all

When Europeans first came into contacts with Africans within their setting, some of them began to apply their Western standards of behaviour as yardstick for judging the natives' ways and cultures. Typical of that class was Elspeth Huxley whose family settled among the Kikuyu people of central Kenya at the beginning of 20th century. Writing later, in 1959, about the early days of interactions between the British settlers and their African hosts, she recalls "No words for thanking people existed in the Kikuyu's language and Europeans often accused them of ingratitude". In her attempt to explain why the Kikuyu and by extension, the Africans, behaved that way, her attempted conjecture goes this way: "Perhaps gratitude was simply a habit Africans had never acquired towards each other, and therefore could not display towards Europeans; or Europeans were looked upon as beings of another order to whom the ordinary rules did not apply..."[1] Her guesswork misses the mark by a wide margin as will be shown later in the following pages when I will discuss the subject as it relates to the Dinka people of South Sudan.

Context as key to understanding action or omission

Often, if someone accidentally steps on your foot, the chances are that you will be lucky if that person says "Sorry!" For outsiders, such conduct is regarded as an epitome of uncivilised conduct. There is a misconception that when somebody doesn't express words or phrases such as "Sorry", "Thanks", "My apologies", it is because the language of the person in question lacks those expressions. Not so. For instance, in Dinka, "thank you" is *"yïn ca leec"* and *"aca wuɔ̈ɔ̈c"* – literally, "I am mistaken", for "sorry". "Please" may not have an equivalent in Dinka, for example, but anyone trying to show politeness would use other means, including body language. (I recently stumbled on a text translated from English to Dinka. The rendering was a ridiculous *"Yïn läŋ"*, which translates as, "I am praying to you"). Thought-transfer is an area where translators and interpreters blunder badly.

Polite requests that should begin or end with "please" are not in the lexicon of many of our fellow citizens. Many South Sudanese communities do have these words. The problem is not really that those communities consist of uncouth individuals; on the contrary, most of them are pleasant, kind and cultured in their conduct and attitude towards others. In the traditional rural Dinka society, a person receiving favours or an act that is praiseworthy is happy but to thank a giver in person is considered bad manners. Certainly a pleased recipient of goodies, will show their gratitude by facial expression, such as a demure smile and lightening of the facial muscles. Furthermore, friends or relatives doing a favour to one are fulfilling their social obligation, which will be reciprocated in one way or another in future; thanking the giver then becomes redundant.

Concerning minor inconveniences such sneezing or coughing, it is assumed that the person performing those involuntary acts is innocent – and, since they can't control reflexes, they don't need to apologise. Similarly, stepping on another person's toe is understood contextually. Motives and intentions of the actor are judged and conclusions drawn from them: "I know Tom respects me. He can't possibly do that to hurt or make fun of me". If on the other hand one suspects malice in an act committed by someone else against them, context also comes into play for the recipient to respond. The entire stratosphere is situational which in turn deciphers what the doer means.

Having pointed out exceptional situations where outsiders might misread actions or words, it is a fact that rude behaviour is more widespread in the society of South Sudan than one would encounter in many parts of the world. Someone reminded me that wars, which have been raging in South Sudan for more half a century, have played their role in the erosion of polite behaviour. The military as an organisation is a respected system, and soldiers are known for chivalry and acts that used to be called gentlemanly. Unfortunately, in Sudan and South Sudan, some members of the military conclude that since relations within the force – superior vis-a-vis underling – operate through orders, there is no room for polite address such as "please". Consequently, "give me the pen" replaces the nicer form.

Circumstantial rudeness

Rudeness like anger, for instance, is in all of us. The difference is how one manages the behaviour or emotion. People who control vulgar outbursts most of the time are considered polite while those eager to explode with expletives are branded rude, often seen as uncultured and lacking in courtesy and behaviours that distinguish humans from animals in the wild. However, to be rude is human; even very refined and patient persons sometimes can be provoked to utter unpleasant and insolent words.

Many years ago, I attended a political rally in Juba following a failed coup attempt in Khartoum a day earlier. During that emotionally charged condemnation of the unsuccessful plotters who had wanted to overturn the regime of Jaafar Nimeiri and subsequently abolish the Addis Ababa Agreement of 1972, the then head of the Government of Southern Sudan, Abel Alier angrily referred to the National Front, the underground opposition organisation behind the failed coup, "*el jabaha el sheitaniyya*" or the "satanic front". The politician was visibly angry. Abel Alier, is a public figure known even by his detractors to be a cool-headed, refined man. Although some of his listeners were surprised by his apparent loss of control over his emotions, they had forgotten that everyone has their limit. In situation such as this one, context – a provocative situation – can justify a behaviour or an act that would qualify as rude.

Personal encounters with rude people

Insulted, offended or treated disdainfully, most people would retaliate with discourteous rejoinders if not outright invectives. I do not need to go far looking for examples of such cases. A couple of years ago, someone appeared to have a difficulty in recognising me since he and I had last met in Juba several years before. He was sitting with a group of friends, killing their time in a public place in the heart of the city that had gained notoriety as a clubhouse of idlers.

The fellow began to survey me, from foot to head and back again. While doing that he was making faces and sniggering, glancing from time to time at his friends who were seated at the table with him. I was irritated. But the most annoying part was coming: "Are you Atem Yak or someone else resembling him?" he asked as he pouted.

I couldn't take anymore. Pumped up with anger I told him off. Swearing and use of expletives have always been completely alien to me, even as a child and adolescent, but during this time in question I came very close to using coarse language. What displeased me most was the way he pronounced my middle name. Yak and Yaak are as different from one another in pronunciation and their "meanings" as Ahmed is different from Hamed. I always get cross with persons who make no distinction, in writing or in pronunciation, between the two Dinka names. One of his companions who was uneasy with the fellow, known to many as a habitually meddlesome character, rose and moved towards me to express his regrets for what had happened. I accepted the vicarious apology and walked away, breathing heavily as I was suppressing a volcano of rage.

Meet the rude ones

Daily, nearly all of us encounter impolite people or conduct. As we have seen earlier, what constitutes a rude behaviour varies from situation to situation, or person to person, or occasion. Some may be mild while others could be upsetting to the extent that a situation might lead to a brawl or altercation. Some of the less offensive omissions could include someone not saying "Thank you" for being nice or for making a compliment.

But again what offends some people may not cause any problem to others. For example, telephone conversation, now made a staple of daily communication by the advent of mobile handsets, has brought to the fore the kind of behaviour that was rare before: instant termination of conversation by one of the two parties in a conversation. An immediate switch off of the handset, unless the two people engaging in an exchange of words are angry with one another, is definitely rude. The message from the one cutting short the line in a split second is: "you are wasting my time." It is implied that the person doing that is showing disgust, impatience or lack of interest in the talk; in a nutshell, the abrupt end of the communication is a clear signal expressing "good riddance!" Although such a behaviour is definitely offensive, an allowance can be made: some of the persons doing so may be innocent and not aware of the vulgar implications of their action. Or interrupted by an emergency.

But again what offends some people may not cause any problem to others. For example, telephone conversation, now made a staple of daily communication by the advent of mobile handsets, has brought to the fore the kind of behaviour that was rare before: instant termination of talk by one of the two parties in a conversation. An immediate switch off of the handset, unless the two people engaging in an exchange of words are angry with one another, is definitely rude. The message from the one cutting short the line in a split second is: "you are wasting my time". It is implied that the person doing that is showing disgust, impatience or lack of interest in the talk; in a word the abrupt end of the communication is a clear signal expressing "good riddance!" Although such a behaviour is definitely offensive, an allowance can be made: some of the persons doing so may be innocent and not aware of the vulgar implications of their action. Or the "network" may have inadvertently interfered with communication.

Another area in which phone communication can cause offence is when someone rings another person but the call goes unanswered. Unless the intended recipient of the call does not know the caller or is in a meeting or a washroom, for example, lack of response can be understood as an expression of rudeness. Among South Sudanese, there are individuals who have gained notoriety for their habit of ignoring to answer calls made by persons they know including intimate friends. Anyone suspected of habitually engaging in the practice, runs the risk of being suspected of insensitivity or arrogance.

'Rude finger'

Pointing with a finger in some African societies including South Sudan is fairly common but most of the people think that it is an innocuous act; while the Western "rude finger" is an insulting gesture which anyone speaking publicly and gesticulating has to guard against by all means. I once coached a friend who was a minister about the "hazards" of public office. I warned him repeatedly against finger pointing when speaking even in private. He gratefully accepted my "intrusion". He turned out to be a good student.

Health-related hazardous behaviour

The famous Sudanese cartoonist, Izz Ed Din has immortalised in a caricature one of the most disgusting social behaviours in his country: urination in public by some people. The cartoon that appeared in a Khartoum daily in early 1970s was a depiction of man urinating at the corner of a public building, in full view of passers-by. The offender, while in the act as he stands in front of the wall, turns to a European tourist armed with a camera, looks quizzically at him and proudly tells him "We call this [his act] culture".

Although public health authorities are supposed to fight this awful practice, it remains widespread in towns and even in Juba where it is not uncommon to observe someone, always males, performing in broad daylight and on street corners; behind office or residential buildings, what is best reserved for the privacy of a water closet or WC as it was commonly called in the Sudan of the old days. The practice is not only rude; it also carries health risks.

Scientists have found proven evidence linking consumption of tobacco products to lung cancer. Smoking cigarettes therefore is a health hazard to both the smokers and non-smokers (referred to as passive smokers). Yet it is common to see people, including senior public figures who should be providing leadership in the fight against smoking, puffing in public and in closed places. Smokers are also known for their role in soiling the environment, by way of discarding used cigarette butts everywhere.

Spitting in public, sneezing and coughing without covering the nose or mouth can expose others to possible infectious and contagious diseases, and are some other common habits a visitor to South Sudan will not miss even while in the company of persons presumed to be refined. Belching – fortunately a rare and recent import – crept in from an alien culture which used to glorify the act as a way in which a rich man – always men – show off their wealth. The assumption is that burping is an expression of someone who has just consumed a sumptuous meal. Whether for self-advertisement or out of control, it is impolite to do this in public.

Nature does funny things with human bodies. One of these is what I shall refer to by its euphemistic version – breaking wind. Luckily, in virtually all the communities of the two Sudans, any person committing that in the presence of another person is exposing themselves to unmitigated contempt.

Until recent years, Sudanese expressions were free of swear words, especially the "f" word. Sadly, because of exposure of youth to video shows containing material that is in bad taste, this is no longer the case. This ugly form of communication has found its way into websites and social media that are – unfortunately – not subject to editorial control and filtering. People are better off to avoid such offensive words; they don't spice up or strengthen messages being communicated even when one is expressing annoyance or anger. It is not a must that disagreement should be expressed an abusive language or words.

The overly curious type

There is nothing wrong with being eager to know anything, particularly things related to one's surroundings. In real life, curiosity is part of a learning process, especially in children. But when that trait is used by adults who are eager to see, hear or be part of a conversation which does not concern them or is not intended for unauthorised individuals for whatever reasons, that urge amounts to intrusion or the invasion of privacy of others. It is a temptation that is best avoided unless one wouldn't mind being called a Peeping Tom.

A person who has an insatiable appetite for poking their nose into other people's affairs is being indecent. That behaviour easily translates to being rude. Such a person belongs to the class of men, for instance, who can peer with deep concentration into a lady's handbag when she opens it. A person consumed by such tendencies is bound to eavesdrop or gossip. Although these habits are almost universal, people in nearly every culture despise and condemn persons who love meddling in the affairs of others.

Unfortunately, gossips – as the persons who constantly talk negatively about others behind their backs are known – are found in sizeable numbers in every society. Gossiping as a habit cuts across age, gender, ethnic, social and other divides. Some gossipmongers may be people who are uneasy with other people's successes or good reputation. In many instances, backbiters happen to be individuals deficient in self-esteem or confidence, always blaming others for their own failures or lack of advancement in social matters or in careers. Driven by envy and jealousy, such characters can easily dampen the friendly company of polite colleagues.

The insensitive ones

There are activities that some people do for enjoyment, such as listening to music, singing or chatting in a group. As long as persons engaged in these hobbies care about the feelings of other people, mostly neighbours in housing estates, hotels or dormitories, there is no reason for concern about what they do. But when music or laughter, for instance, becomes too loud and is happening at late hours of the night, this is a case of inconvenience, an area where the victims might seek redress through the law if the offenders refuse to listen to request for moderation or cessation of the source of excessive noise. Such activities may prevent others from having a normal sleep or being interrupted from any job of a mental nature requiring concentration.

It is common knowledge that many of our compatriots spend parts of their time in misery for living in a noisy neighbourhood where some persons, mostly youths, play music at home as if they are at a discotheque. This happens either because there is no law to protect the people from intrusive noise pollution, or the sufferers may not be aware of their rights to raise complaints – even to the police – when the culprits are insensitive to the welfare of others, or defy the rules of good neighbourhood and respect for the rights of other people.

Queue jumping

Queuing when many people wait to be served in turn is almost non-existent in South Sudan; instead the physically stronger ones push their way to be served first at the expense of those who had been waiting patiently; some junior officials employed to organise jobs such as meetings of senior staff sometimes show little respect to visitors, especially if they are unknown or –worse – when not dressed in apparel worn by the rich and powerful, or not showing symbols of high office. A very senior public servant once told me she was rudely treated by an office manager of her counterpart in another ministry. In disappointment she left without seeing her colleague. The problem was – and remains –her humility and the simple dress code she prefers to trendy and showy dresses.

As I have mentioned above, there are fellows who put their personal interests above the welfare of other fellow human beings. Taking someone else's chance to be served before others who had come first is called queue jumping. This act is bad manners. It can and does cause quarrels, sometimes fist-fights. A couple of years ago, I was at the centre of a bitter exchange with a receptionist in a foreign-owned financial institution operating in Juba. I had entered the building for a routine business transaction. I took my place on a bench. I looked around to ensure that there was no sign prohibiting use of mobile telephone within the room before I called someone and having seen and heard a non-Sudanese in telephone conversation. I took the cue from that and made my own call to chat with a colleague in another part of the city.

The receptionist, a compatriot of the one who had made a call before me, got up from her desk and shouted at me to stop talking, although my communication was almost a whisper, compared with the loud talk by the previous caller. I obeyed and remained seated although a little upset. However, about ten minutes later and when I was fifth in the waiting line, a young woman, also from the same country as the receptionist, took her place at the tail of the wooden bench. Less than a minute later, the woman at the service desk beckoned to the new arrival to proceed straight to one staffer at one of the tills.

I watched the proceedings with keen interest: the two women seated behind the counter were not talking business; they were in a conversation that went on interminably. I arose and began to shout, "This is impossible. One of the things I will not accept lying down is being discriminated against and worst of all by a foreigner in my own country".

I was deliberately loud so as to be heard, and indirectly I was appealing to base sentiments: rallying fellow South Sudanese against foreigners apparently committing an injustice against one of their own in their homeland. After leaving the building later I regretted that I had allowed myself to go low in an act that bordered on xenophobia.

Time

In many parts of the world, particularly in the West, strict observation of punctuality comes naturally to people. It's taken for granted. In South Sudan, on the other hand, "respecting time", as the saying goes, takes some people by surprise, especially when organisers and invited persons turn up a little before the scheduled time, or on the dot. Barring a few instances, being punctual is an exception rather than the norm by a sizeable number of South Sudanese, whether they are in their native land or abroad. Instead of decrying this habit, we ironically take pride in calling our laziness – disrespecting and inconveniencing others – "Sudan's Time", as if it's a trait – such as our legendary hospitality and generosity – of which one could be proud.

Procrastination or delay (not "delayance" or "delayment" as the speakers of "Juba English" would say) was described by sages of yore as a thief of time. One should add: keeping other people waiting indefinitely without a convincing reason is not only a waste of their precious time; it's rude in the extreme.

Virtually all South Sudanese, wherever they are, turn up for work, classes or appointments with their doctors on time. But come scheduled social functions or meetings they organise, they are more likely to turn up very late, sometimes as late as four hours at a stretch. This is not only inconvenient to the invited non-South Sudanese guests; it's absolutely embarrassing to say the least.

No seat for a visiting head of state

It is not uncommon for functions organised by South Sudanese – to which many people and VIPs are invited – to begin late, way beyond schedule; sometimes by even a couple of hours. Even the ceremony to mark the official declaration of South Sudan as a sovereign nation – to which several African heads of state and government turned up to attend – was marred by naked incompetence on the side of the official organisers. In the chaos that reigned at the grounds of the Dr John Garang Mausoleum, the scene of the celebrations, foreign diplomats and journalists as well as some South Sudanese, watched in disbelief the bungling prelude to nationhood; a prime minister and a minister- from neighbouring African countries were temporarily forced to stand as their seats had been occupied by some local and minor dignitaries who had forced their way to the grandstand.

Besides this searing embarrassment, one of the biggest and probably the most memorable days in the nation's history began late. Is there any form of discourtesy one can think of that is worse than treating dignitaries in that way? Our clumsy handling of the occasion and the seating of the foreign guests later appeared in foreign press. And the report, predictably, was not flattering at all: emergence of the image of a young country in the hands of inept and vulgar bureaucrats – an accusation which no single member of the educated and ruling elite can hope to successfully shake off, whether one was involved in the organisation of that event or not[7].

Outside our national borders, we are doing little to change the perception that all is not well with some of us – in the sphere of social skills and some etiquettes – when dealing with ourselves and the members of other communities we interact with from time to time.

On several occasions I have witnessed alarms being set off to warn – or care takers pleading with – South Sudanese to leave a venue because the allotted time was over. I was one of the guests celebrating a wedding in the Granville suburb of Sydney in 2006 when the participants were literally being evicted after the rent time had expired.

I recall, in 2016, a guard in one of Melbourne's community centres, where members of the Twï community in Australia were electing their leaders. As a guest of honour for the function that night, I was scheduled to speak last (to advise the young leaders on the need to promote unity and friendly relations among themselves, beginning with fellow South Sudanese and to extend that to the rest of the wider world). When I started talking, the guard – an Australian of Caucasian descent and aged about forty – moved menacingly towards me, grabbed the mic from my hand and barked loudly, "We are closing the hall. You have to stop now!" He then proceeded to switch off the lights. It was a little to two in the morning. The event was set to close at midnight. I and the remaining small group

---

[6] Huxley, Elspeth, *The Flame Tree of Thika*, p.106, Vintage Publishing, 2014.

had to leave the venue. Because of the delay, more than half of the crowd – numbering more than a thousand – had begun to leave, one by one, after midnight. The occasion began at 3pm the previous day. Or if the invitation letter which said so was to be believed.

My initial reaction was to come to blows with the guard, as he was demonstrably insolent. But I quickly realised that, despite his ill-mannered conduct, he was simply doing his job. The blame ultimately rested squarely on the shoulders of our own organisers who had paid up to midnight but dragged on as if they owned the centre.

This was not my first encounter with such situations. Nor, regrettably, would it be the last.

I recall – with a deep sense of embarrassment – an evening in 2016, when the South Sudanese community held a function in Blacktown, a suburb of Sydney. A local MP and a senior police officer were among the invited guests, to talk about how to promote mutually beneficial relationships between the local police force and members of the South Sudanese community in New South Wales in general and the wider Australia in particular.

Information on the invitation cards stated that the occasion would kick off at 6 pm. The organisers, the invited legislator and the police officer turned up on time. The guests were politely received by a team of well-dressed South Sudanese community leaders who led them to their seats. Seven, eight, nine, successively came and ticked away quietly… but nothing happened. The expected crowd was coming in at a trickle. Those who were concerned had apparently noted that some South Sudanese living not far from the hall were calling to check whether *everyone* had come and that the hall was *full*. It was only after they had established that fact when they would then start coming to the venue.[8]

8   An investigation into the muddle conducted by the local media, which was not published, later found out that some civil servants who previously worked for the Government of Sudan and known for their sympathies with the ruling Islamist National Congress Party, NCP, were believed to have been behind what was judged as a daring sabotage. Their action, the findings concluded, included attempted interference with the speech of the Ugandan President Yoweri Museveni which like the rest of the proceedings was being broadcast live on the national TV and radio channels.

So they waited, and those who had come earlier continued to wait. We in the hall were fidgety and began to ask rhetorical questions. Finally, the video recorder, a man of Egyptian extraction who covers most of the social events organised South Sudanese for hefty fees, arrived. It was a little to 10pm.

Speeches – and I would say – most of them long and stale, followed the arrival of the cameraman. The MP was invited to talk. His statement about the need for cooperation between the community and the mainstream Australian society lasted about three minutes. He didn't return to his seat; he left the hall immediately, because he had other commitments to attend to. In Australia, unlike South Sudan, one of the main jobs of an elected legislators is to keep in touch with their constituents – with an office located within the constituency, not at the capital. MPs listen to the people they represent.

The police representative also spoke about the readiness of his colleagues and their forces to work together with the Sudanese community, as well as others living in the area, in matters concerning security and maintenance of law and order. His message too, was very brief. He left the hall immediately after reading his last sentence.

I felt very bad about it. I was not alone in that; there were several, if not many, who equally were shamed by this behaviour, which is condemned but nobody seems to have a way of stopping or preventing.

Those are just a few examples out of many occasions when members of the South Sudanese community in Australia have had conflict with the owners of establishments where they conducted their social functions. In one state – which I will not name here – the use of a church and its premises by the South Sudanese congregation has been withdrawn because every time they were allowed to conduct their services there – including social functions – they overstayed and went beyond the allotted time. Warning after warning fell on deaf ears. Finally, a notice of severance was issued. That was it.

These cases I have cited weren't the first nor the last. Because of this unacceptable behaviour, South Sudanese leaders – women, youth and elders – occasionally appeal to their members to learn to adjust some of their practices and to emulate good habits and practices from their new environment and neighbours. However, these pleas for change, in particular understanding the value of time in regard to ourselves and others, and to stick to schedules, have unfortunately – in the opinion of this writer – come to nothing.

Part of this article was published in January 2010 by Citizen *newspaper then based in Khartoum*

Other Uses for Dogs

It is said that the dog is man's – should it not be rephrased to humankind's? – oldest companion. A local folktale credits the dog with the discovery of fire. He gave fire to man as a present, so a Dinka fable says. In all climes and times, man used dogs for hunting and as such the dog through ages has been a breadwinner for hunting communities. This role has almost been taken over by the gun. Both the gun and gunpowder are going to put dog and hunters – using spears, bows and arrows – out of the bloody business.

Fidelity has been and still is the major bond between man and dog. The dog's loyalty made it possible in the old days for man to sleep with doors open: his dog would scare away strangers and wild beasts at night. But the days of dog acting as sentry all night long are about to come to an end, as this job is being taken over by alarms such as electronic devices which chime and bark when potential burglars and thieves try to trespass on your compound or sneak in to fiddle with your vehicles, doors, windows or fruit trees in the backyard garden.

In some lands dogs were – and are still being served as meals. Pets? Yes, a friend whose owner would care as he does for his human friend. That is what most people use dogs for in many parts of the world. In that role, the dog occupies second place between human beings and the rest of the domestic animals. In my village of yesteryear, a dog was not simply a pet; the way the owner treated him spoke louder about the humanity or cruelty of the owner. Generosity or stinginess was manifested by way a well- or poorly-fed dog. Owners' wealth or poverty was advertised by dogs. In my village of those days that are gone, and indeed in the culture of the Dinka people, dogs were adopted in order to be given names as a means of sending out subtle messages to enemies or members of the family one was at loggerheads with. It is true that other races give their dogs names, but that is another story.

Once upon a time, and it was not a very long time ago, I had a childhood friend. This friend – I will here call Tong – was poorly regarded by many, including his elder siblings and cousins. And for good reason. They called him *matil*, a difficult word to translate into any foreign language. In Dinka, it means, among other things, a greedy and self-centred person, an envious and covetous one; very mean when it comes to sharing. Because of those attributes – perceived or real – they did the name-calling in his absence because Tong was such an adept and tough fighter that he would repay his detractors with punches in their noses. It was not long before Tong discovered that his secret and unflattering nickname had spread far and wide in the village. But he was not a fool to fight all and sundry. He had an answer in store for his cowardly backbiters.

One fine November day – as I later discovered the month that followed two months after harvest time was called – and when a cool western breeze would blow over the land, Tong, who was returning from tending the calves, came across a hungry, thin brown dog who had either lost his way or whose owner had discarded him as an economic burden. The dog came home and took up permanent residence at Tong's home. The two stuck together and became inseparable.

The dog's owner fed and cared for him very well, as did the rest of the family members. He was a good and loyal canine. Unknown to all, Tong, who had found an answer to the name-calling, gave his dog the name of *Cïn Tiɛɛl Wun,* which when translated into English would mean, among other things, "no one has the monopoly of *tiɛɛl* (tieel)". Tiɛɛl in Dinka means, among other things, envy, discrimination self-centred-ness, jealousy, vindictiveness, covetousness. A *matil* then is one possessed by these negative attributes.

On a happy note, my friend was simply thrifty and economical in the management of his resources, which he often demonstrated in the way he distributed carcasses of wild animals bagged by his faithful and resourceful dog, Cïn Tiɛɛl Wun.

It was once well known, that thrift was preached as a virtue that people should uphold and practise.

SPLM/A Update newsletter, 1994.

Paweer, or The Years of Dispersion

This is a true story. I hesitated concerning its inclusion, as initially I was not convinced it was entirely relevant to the wider purpose of this collection. However, I have decided to include it to honour the memory of Deng Kur Chien, a close family relative and a memorable figure in my earlier days. In our lives we all encounter individuals who leave impressions (positive or negative) for various reasons. It is to his memory that this piece is dedicated.

Nineteen-sixty-four was a time when much of the area south of Sobat River, east of the White Nile and north of Bor town, the current capital of Jonglei State, came underwater from the overflowing Nile and unseasonably heavy rain. The deluge that went on for about five years in a row wreaked havoc on the inhabitants of the area and their property. The place of my birth and another place where I was at school were at the centre of the cataclysmic events. So in a way the writer was partially a victim and an eyewitness, and a subjective one at that.

After the indefinite closure in December 1964 of all schools in Southern Sudan because of the civil war, my colleagues and I travelled, each to our respective homes all over the region. I, along with some students from my home district, travelled to rural Bor. What we found were deserted villages, still under water and one of the most desolate places on earth at that time, a heartbreaking spectacle whose memories remain fresh in my mind to this day.

At its peak, the flood had raised water levels in some places to over a metre high, leaving marks on tree stems and stumps afterwards. The water invasion had resulted in the mass dispersal of thousands of people from their ancestral homes. The people left their homes, literally with empty hands, abandoning everything – personal items and even foodstuffs.

This was understandable. Children and the infirm – especially among the elderly – and persons with disabilities had to be carried; people who had no means other than transhumance had to take turns in carrying them, splashing through a seemingly endless expanse of land covered mostly by water, and for days, with little or no food at all. Trekking to high grounds to the south or north of the flooded area became an ordeal in itself.

The evacuees contended with more hardships on their way to seek safety, shelter and new means of livelihood. The strong currents, created by massive amounts of water bursting through the dykes, swept away some people, especially the most vulnerable such young children and the elderly. Cattle also got knocked down and carried by swift and strong currents as carcasses.

The slow and painful walk to higher grounds took its toll as some of the sick and sometimes-starving people succumbed to exhaustion, hunger or disease.

The natural catastrophe has now been immortalised; the local people named this time of mass distress as *Run de Awai-thar*, or the year when people became soaked [because of flood water] to the waist.

As for the flood and its consequences, the entire period became known as *Paweer* (paweer), a Dinka word whose loose translation is great dispersal.

This is what we (I was travelling with some fellow students from Atar Intermediate School, who hailed from the northern part of the district) saw on our way to my village at that time.

The whole landscape was still a huge expanse of water throughout much of the terrain we traversed. There was an element of eeriness in the surroundings: everything was deathly quiet as many birds had migrated and insects appeared to have all died. Occasionally, lonely trees several kilometres apart appeared; so did abandoned luaks and tukuls; there was nothing that one could call "ground", as much of the land had been covered by a blue blanket of water extending to the horizon, with only water lilies here and there as the main plants.

When I arrived in my deserted village, a year after it had gone under water, there were some people still living in Kongor, a former court centre for the area and the town where I received my primary education.

These characters who were determined to stay put come what may, had built high and thick mud walls to keep water away. Fish and seeds of water lily were the main sources of food for those people who had taken it upon themselves to remain in their place of birth. Indeed, they believed the disaster would soon be over. The rest of the population had relocated to what is today Duk County and to the southern part of Bor district, which remained less affected by the floods.

They told me that cattle had died *en masse*. About half of the livestock had been lost, mainly to water-borne diseases.

A year later, at the time of my arrival in the area, things had begun to improve, although slowly. Cattle were no longer dying and people began to rebuild their lives, putting up shelters and growing food in the small patches given to them by generous hosts.

Despite this, people could not easily get over the losses of their property and in some cases, of their loved ones. At any rate, it was time for the displaced persons who preferred to consider themselves as victims of *riääk de piny* or "spoliation of the earth", to move on.

This is where our central story begins.

There was a man called Deng Kur Chien. He was a close relative of my family, a cousin of my father on his mother's side. Deng's family and our own had known each other for years. I knew him, his children, his wife and his two brothers who were younger than he.

Everyone loved Deng Kur greatly. He had many cattle and was a hardworking man. His granary used to be full of dura, the staple food crop of the land at the time.

Before the floods, Deng Kur and his family lived about five kilometres away from our homestead. Children and parents from the two families used to exchange visits.

Deng Kur had two distinguishing attributes: first, he loved milk more than any other form of diet, and second, he was totally deaf. Unlike some people in his situation at the time, Deng Kur was a cheerful man; he did not suffer self-pity because of loss of hearing. I do not know what caused his affliction, or how long he had suffered from it. During that time children did not go about asking parents or other adults how Uncle X lost his left eye, or how Auntie Z became a cripple. That kind of nosiness was considered brazen insolence, which at times could lead to corporeal punishment.

Despite the loss of most of his herd, he still had enough cattle including several milking cows to support his family. At the time in question, he was staying in a famous cattle camp belonging to the Nyarweng people of Duk Payuel. The camp is called Gorbek. At the time in question, the Twï people who had moved to settle among the Nyarweng were welcomed as brothers and sisters. The host community even shared the cattle camp with their guests and the groups lived in harmony with one another.

One dry, bright mid-morning April day, 1966, boys released cattle to graze, as usual, in the nearby forest. As was customary, people withdrew to spend the rest of the day under the cool shades of giant leafy trees while others went to neighbouring homesteads for the day.

As the sun began to set, it was time for all to prepare for the return of their beloved animals to be tethered, and for the evening chores, such as milking cows, an activity for uninitiated boys and females of all ages, to begin.

However, that evening seemed jinxed. Deng Kur and others started feeling jittery as the dusk approached with no signs of cattle returning to base. Something unusual must be happening. It was already six o' clock in the evening and no sign of the cattle coming, or mooing in the air.

With the fall of darkness, Deng Kur began to ask – using sign language – but no one had an answer to his questions, which were also preoccupying the minds of everyone in the camp.

By now it was clear something very frightening and unspeakable had gone wrong, but what? While it was common for cattle to get lost after wandering off from the herd, this was usually a group of rogue animals ranging in number from ten to thirty, not the entire herd.

The Gorbek cattle numbered in their hundreds, possibly a couple of thousands, and it looked they had disappeared without a trace. Where had they gone to? Moreover, what had happened to them?

It was time for people to take action. Several young men picked their weapons – spears and clubs – and moved to the forest to search for the herd.

Towards midnight, the youths returned empty-handed. Meanwhile Deng Kur, who had not stopped asking questions about the whereabouts of the cattle all evening, could not go to sleep without knowing what had really happened.

One of my elder brothers, Aruei, was in the camp where our family herd was part of a multi-clan community. Those cattle, too, were all lost.

The following day, the bad news filtered through the cattle camp and the neighbouring villages: cattle rustlers had driven off almost the entire herd; only a few cattle had escaped and returned and several young men who had followed the cattle and the raiders had been shot dead. Among the dead people was one prominent cattle camp leader and champion wrestler. His name was Goi Leek Deng-Akol. Goi, who was from a large family, had many siblings, among them two brothers who were my classmates at school.

Deng Kur, too, got a fragment of the news. He, like the rest of the people around him and in the whole area, was grief-stricken. The deaths of the young men and the loss of cattle threw the entire area into mourning.

Deng, however, refused to be consoled; he withdrew from everyone and spent his time alone, his milk-gourd his only companion. At intervals, he would pull a swig from the gourd, and stare long and hard into the sky. While traditional customs forbade men to cry, except only in a case of a man receiving a humiliating and searing insult, it was considered appropriate in a loss of this magnitude. People who saw Deng later told me the man was suppressing tears. He remained for hours in this state of loss, until someone took hold of his hand to lead him gently to bed. But he hardly slept a wink as his mind was on the unfathomable loss.

When his gourd became empty, he would order a boy to fill the gourd with water, now a substitute for milk. Sipping water from the milk gourd was symbolic. For three days he was taking sips from the container but clearly without relish as each pull brought a furrow to his forehead and his eyes swam with tears. After five days, he went to sleep. For the first time in days, he had a deep sleep, never stirring or even turning. However, the following morning, he was late waking. This raised immediate concern, as Deng Kur was a known early riser. When people went to check, they found him placid and cold, not breathing. No sign of life was evident; he had died peacefully and in the night.

Deng Kur was deeply mourned by his family, all relatives and by anyone who had known him.

The Agamlöng:
An Unacknowledged Entertainer

The adult men of my village of yesteryear devoted much more of their waking time to the affairs of the public than they do today. In between the time of cultivation and weeding, men past youth and the rest of the elders had to attend to court rooms or specifically to the shades of the so called palaver tree for settlement of disputes of all types. Marriages had to be conducted and no one was barred from attending. Matters of public concern such as reconciliation between warring clans, too, were open to all. At the centre of all these were the chiefs, following a hierarchy which stipulated the powers – and limitations – upon them.

The *agamlöng* provided a vital link between the chiefly class and the people. While not a formally recognised office-holder, his role was so instrumental in public rallies or courtrooms that without him the occasion lost its importance and attraction. In Dinka, agamlöng literally means one who consents to or affirms the law or truth. But in practice this is a man who repeats, by paraphrasing the "truth", statements and opinions from the chief speaking in a gathering attended by the members of the public, or the audience in the gallery.

Since agamlöng was not part of the court administration, the manner of his selection was important. A little before proceedings began members of the public would look around for one with suitable qualities of agamlöng; at times a person confident of his power of delivery would come forward, to volunteer. For one to qualify for the job which carried no pay, a man- no woman ever became an agamlöng- had to be gifted with a clear and sonorous voice. It was not surprising that most of those who were picked happened to have been famous singers of the day.

But having an effective and beautiful voice alone was not enough, otherwise an agamlöng would just be just be a human loudspeaker, amplifying statements word for word, inevitably leading to monotony. The task essentially demanded a faithful and honest rendering of substance so that what was said was maintained and transmitted loud and clear, in a humorous style. This entailed that an agamlöng must be a person of wide-ranging knowledge of the affairs, history and culture of his community. As a living, breathing trove of knowledge, an agamlöng had to have a deep grasp of proverbs, allusions, conundrums, similes and other figures of speech for instance, an accurate blend of the mundane with the unexpected, delivered creatively. An agamlöng had to recall these from his own stock for effect, clarification and emphasis. Naturally, this required him to be an exceptionally witty and imaginative person. Below are some hypothetical examples of statements paraphrased or repeated by an agamlöng:

Example One
(Quoting a popular saying):
Chief: So and so has admitted to committing adultery with the wife of another man. For this offence, the court has fined him six herd of cattle.

Agamlöng: The Chief is speaking! Please be quiet. You there, to the left of the tree, you are talking! Silence! *(Pauses before he resumes).* The court has found the accused guilty and the chief has passed the verdict. The fine? Ha! Ha! It was said a long time ago that a man with a wild sex urge brings destitution upon himself. Six head of cattle! (as *aruɔɔk* /aruook) or compensation to the cuckold, according to Dinka and Nuer customary law) Six heads of cattle!

As this example shows, agamlöng used to take liberty to indulge in moralising and passing his own judgement, subtle or crude, depending on the social status of the characters involved in legal duels. When such an approach breached responsible and sophisticated boundaries or tended to pervert the course of justice, the presiding chief or members of the public would interrupt and correct the misleading version. An overly erring agamlöng would be dropped and a substitute picked from the "gallery."

More often than not, an agamlöng preferred presenting rosy and exaggerated sides of drab facts as illustrated below.

Example Two
(sweetened statements):
An elder appealing to parents to send children to school:
Elder: We, all of us including chiefs, have accepted the government's order for children to be taken to school. Education is good for all and all should send their children, including their first-born sons and even daughters to school.

Agamlöng: The elder, full of wisdom as you know, is asking you, all of you, whether any among us has not seen the goodness of education. (*Pauses*). You over there are talking! Stop talking and listen! Who has not seen or heard about the son of so and so driving a car? And right now, look above! That aeroplane buzzing like a tsetse fly above us may be carrying one of those who went to school many years ago. They have become Turuk[9]. But hear me right. I mean an *uncircumcised* Turuk.

Laughter from the audience

But this type of communication was not always conducted for the sake of amusement. Serious matters, discussed by grim-looking and venerated elderly chiefs had to take place in a solemn environment requiring a similarly serious delivery by the agamlöng. For him to treat weighty matters lightly would not only be a slight to the status of the court and the chiefs, but also could cast doubt on his own character and personality. Related to that situation in which an agamlöng wilfully subverted and distorted words and meanings of one of the speakers as shown by this final example.

Example Three

(*subversion*):

Chief: As all of you are aware of the threat posed by the current floods, all young and able-bodied persons should report every morning to build and complete the embankment now under construction. Any person failing to report to work shall be arrested and heavily fined. Everyone must work.

Agamlöng: The chief has said that the floods are a very serious threat. He wonders whether anything could be done about them...

---

9 ¹Turuk: "in some southern Sudanese languages the word *Turuk* came to mean – and still means – a light-skinned foreigner, a uniformed official, or an administrative bureaucrat, even when qualified by a phrase like the *Nuer Turuk*, col, 'black' Turk'" (Johnson, Douglas, *South Sudan: A New History* for a *New Nation*, p 102, 2016, Ohio University Press, Athens). The footnote and the quotation are a new addition to the article which was written more 20 years ago.

Chief: (*interrupting*): What he has said are his own words. I said and I repeat: the flood waters should be prevented from destroying the crops and homesteads. Those who fail to take these words will be punished. (*Turning to traditional policeman standing behind the court to keep order*) Select another agamlöng while this reckless man awaits our decision in jail.

(*A new agamlöng takes over and the court continues with the business of the day*).

SPLM/A Update *newsletter, August 21, 1995.*
The quotation above was added in 2017 while the word "Turuk" was in the story at the time of its publication.

Imagery of Night in Rural Lore

Since I am allergic to the use of words such as "tribe" or "tribal" and their verbal cousins, I have chosen to use "people" to represent what would be perfectly tribal. And so to the story.

In the life of the community of which this writer is a member, a society on the verge of transformation in which the old customs and practices are gradually become distance mirrors and hisses of the past, it is inevitable that the community's way of life along with much of its thought system, is undergoing major changes and modification. This is primarily due to the impact of foreign cultures had. Until the latest 1950s, night was a dominant and recurrent topic in form of myths, legends and songs.

In that community, day begins at dawn and ends with dusk. The other half is night, a time with very few activities except in the old days, reserved for storytelling, conversation and of course, sleeping. But whatever the village folks would be doing, darkness of night gave it a frightening character, which in turn gave rise to some horror stories capable of giving children nightmares.

In the old days when the sky was still generous with rains, which normally fell heavily between early March and October each year, the whole world in the view of the villagers was enveloped in one single seamless and impenetrable garment, from the four corners of the earth. The dark firmament was completed by the virtual silence of all living things except for the occasional whisperings of cicadas and the dirge-like croaking of the frogs. Inside the thatched wattle daub huts, it was pitch dark. The huts had three or four oval-shaped openings for windows, each large enough to admit a closed fist. But at sunset, they were tightly sealed with pieces of clothing either rolled into a ball or totally blocked with solid and wet mud to keep away swarms of mosquitoes. The doors, equally small, could admit entry only when entrants crept in on their knees and elbows. These, too, had to be tightly fitted with a thick, opaque structure made of grass. The reign of night was now supreme.

What was between the inside (of the hut) and the outside? Many untold dangers and unseen but horrifying beings. The dread of the unknown, which was very much alive in the imaginations of the frightened children, often took control of their thinking. The objects of fear did exist outside, except that they were unseen; the predatory creatures or ghosts, circling or moving towards the hut were named *Acïn-yöl*, a shortened form of *wëër cethë acïn-yöl thïn*. This in English would translate as, "the night in which the monster without a tail roams". Another nocturnal companion of this awe-inspiring monster was **Köp-kööp** (Kop-koop), a supposed man-eating beast which was said it craved the flesh of children, especially the naughty ones who would not obey their parents when told not to cry or insist on demanding food late at night.

Like unicorns, the beasts of the night had not been seen by anyone, but for the children of those days, the fiends were of real flesh and blood, except that their sizes, colours, their ferocity and insatiable appetite for human flesh were shaped and dressed by the power of an individual's imagination. While inside the huts, children believed that the monsters were from without, and, while still outside, the carnivorous filled the hut where they were waiting to devour whoever entered first without the company of an adult. The worst act of betrayal a mother could ever commit against her young child was to send them unaccompanied into the dark hut.

In reality, it never happened. A child forced to go inside alone would refuse and scream until they became hoarse. The fear occasioned by belief in the existence of dreadful night animals may have been exaggerated by the children of those days, but there was a very real danger from actual wild beasts. Before the poachers entered the area with their deadly rifles, and when desert and desertification were unheard of, that part of the world was teeming with wildlife.

My village was and still is on the wildlife route from the swamps around Bahr el Jebel on the way to the plain, to the Boma plateau in eastern Upper Nile. Herds of elephants, buffalo, lions, leopards, to name but a few dangerous animals, would pass through our villages as their seasonal migration dictated their search for food and water.

Chilling stories, some of them true, abounded. One of these told of an angry herd of elephants which, for no apparent reason, one night pulled and threw away a roof of a hut where more than 10 members of one family were scooped out; each victim was banged against a nearby giant tree. Despite the wailing that was heard all over the hamlet, the victims and their neighbours were completely helpless against the huge pachyderms.

Lions and hyenas occasionally would carry out daring raids into *luaks* or cattle byres, to kill and carry away goats, sheep and calves, for food. This form of hunting of domesticated animal by their relatives in the wild had been a way of life for hyenas from time immemorial. There is a saying in Dinka attributed to this cat. According to the local folktale, the hyena has Kuir, the goddess of luck as his divinity. Kuir was also the deity women used to pray to during crises such as sickness of their children, her name being invoked as *"Kuir e maa!"*, or Oh Kuir, the goddess of my mother [come to help me out].

According to the folktale, Hyena once requested Kuir to help him in breaking into a stable, telling her that getting out of the building would be his responsibility.

The other group of people of the time who dreaded night's approach, dark or moonlit, were the septuagenarian and octogenarians. These old men, the few survivors of dead and almost extinct age-mates, fled to their huts as soon as darkness set in. Their fears were not of wild animals, however, but of spirits. The old people and others in the village believed that the souls of their departed colleagues were out and about, immediately after sunset. The mission of those spirits was to collect those "cowards" who had remained behind in the world of the mortals. The living old men should be hurried to their deaths so that their souls would join the fraternity of departed.

From these episodes, it would appear that the inhabitants of my village of yesteryears were a faint-hearted or cowardly bunch. Not quite so. The young men of the time, night, no matter how dark it might be, had their duties to perform. Once, when some of the cattle lost their way home, the men had to search and find them before they became meals for lions and hyenas. The search for the prized domestic animals was always a night-time affair.

Travelling to meet young, nubile girls and to spend whole night with them in *gɔk* (gök), the studied and elaborate art of conversation to win the heart of a girl a man loves, as a rule always took place at night. These nocturnal trips and searches involved very serious risks and dangers to young men's lives. During dark nights, travellers would lose their way as footpaths led to cavernous bushes, thorny acacias. When it rained or during flood times, such footpaths would lead to ponds and pools infested with leeches and venomous snakes. Real wild beasts would accidentally cross paths with the nocturnal trekkers and the likelihood that a frightened animal would attack in self-defence. Those youths usually carried spears and clubs which would be useless when used by few in the dark against animals such as a lion, the king of the jungle. But that was what it meant to be a young man, an unofficial soldier of the clan who prided himself in bravery akin to recklessness.

Yesterday's village had its horrors and challenges that satisfied those who measured up to the call of duty. In today's village, inhabitants' fears are not about night beasts but thugs, especially cattle rustlers armed with automatic rifles from neighbouring areas.

SPLM/A Update newsletter, 1995.

The Arab-Muslim Community in Kongor of the old days

Introduction
This is not a work of fiction. Neither is it a distilled piece of academic research. The tract basically belongs to the ethnography genre, and from a historical perspective. The main source of the article is the writer's personal experience and childhood recollections of events, people and customs of times that have gone by. Readers will inevitably be questioning the inordinate amount of space allocated to description and narration of matters pertaining to Dinka of the period being reported. This observation may be correct up to a point. However, if the narrator were to write about the life of members of the Arab and Muslim community in the area at the time, making no mention of the features of the host society that were – and still are – completely different, culturally and in other aspects such as religion, the profile would lack context, point of reference, necessary comparison and contrast.

Another point I should make clear at the outset, is the choice of tenses I have used in the narrative. The story is about the past. In that sense, verbs should be in the past tense. But from sentence to sentence and paragraph to paragraph, present and past tenses appear – haphazardly, as it were. This is likely to be seen as inconsistency. It shouldn't. The idea behind this apparent contradiction is that there were customs, beliefs and practices that are still alive today. An example of this is the importance, verging on adoration, rural Dinka give to cattle. Today, practices such use of cattle as a measure of one's worth or wealth, have almost gone out of currency. These days, Dinka families and particularly members of the Bor community are demanding – and receiving – huge amounts of money, in lieu of cattle, in marriage of their daughters to young men in North America, Europe, Australia and other parts of the developed world.

This sort of concession made about change is, it seems, an act of glossing over issues of transition from a traditionally-based society to a contemporary one. True, at the time under review, there were fewer Christians then than there are today in Kongor town and the surrounding villages. But today's crop of Christians, whether they are nominal, novices or full-bloodied believers, still share some of the indigenous beliefs, such as immortality by means of one begetting a child to continue family name and lineage after the death of a parent. Again, across the spectrum many Dinka Christians still accept and practise polygamy. In a way, the use of present tense throughout this writing would still be in place but still does justice to the concepts and practices in time and space.

A Muslim-Arab island in the heart of an African society

The contacts between the peoples of Southern Sudan and Arabs, Turks and Muslims coming from Northern Sudan, go back to years of incursion and invasion, conquests and slave trade, mainly in the 19th century.

The Arabs and Muslims, whether as hunters of human commodity for sale, or traders bartering salt, beads and cloth for ostrich, ivory or other rare and valued indigenous goods, left footprints in Southern Sudan. Those legacies are there for everyone to witness. I have given the examples of personal and place names- in "At Crossroads: Southern Sudanese losing their identity"- that bear witness to Islamic and Arab influence in the area. That account appears in this book.

As far as the area and people in this story are concerned, one of the traces from the time is preserved by foreign names being applied to the natives, for example. The late John Garang de Bior, pioneer broadcaster and a former Anya Nya fighter who hailed from Kongor, had Jaden as his middle name. Garang- most of his associates frequently called him Garang-Jaadeen- was given that name because at the time of his birth there was a Northern Sudanese paramedic called Jadein. The health worker who was popular with the locals was in charge of the local dispensary. Being a son of a former senior chief of the area, while at secondary school, Garang named himself- in jest- Duke of Pachol, after his village of birth which is next door to Pawel, the town.

At a certain time during the colonial administration, Kongor was second to Duk and later, Bor in administrative hierarchy of the district. When Kongor was under Duk, it was the seat of the Egyptian *mamur*, or an officer next to district commissioner, DC. There are stories about a mamur known by the nickname of Ayɔm-nɔk (Ayom-nok). There were junior government functionaries stationed in the area as policemen, clerks, telegraph operators and so on. Most of these workers were either Muslim or of Arab descent. With the exception of the mamur who is said to have married a local girl, marriage between the "settlers" and the host community didn't happen. Reasons for that weren't racially motivated, but to other factors as I have speculated at the end of this account. One of the hurdles was that non-Dinka people living in the area didn't always own cattle, and those who had, didn't have sufficient number of herd to meet the bride wealth a girl's family would demand.

The profile of the people who were Muslims and persons claiming Arab heritage in Kongor town is about people who operated a largely legitimate business during the boyhood of the writer. The personae in the story consisted of *jallaba* or petty traders, policemen and schoolteachers. The "expatriates" and their host community, for the most part, lived in peace, and, in some cases, the "migrants" almost wholly integrated into the local clans.

The writer lived in Pakuoor village, about a kilometre away from Pawel or Kongor. In colonial days, the government presence in Kongor, like all its counterparts in the district and all over Southern Sudan of the time, was officially designated as court centre. In accordance with the system of Native Administration, chiefs applied customary law in settling cases involving their people. Such court houses were built of mud and grass; in some cases, chiefs sat in judgement under shades of giant trees especially during dry season. At the centre there was a vernacular village school or what was known during the colonial times as bush school.

The stories I am writing about happened when I was a country boy who was fairly familiar with malakiya ways. Strictly speaking, a malakiya or Malaki, for male, person in the context of Southern Sudan refers to a man or woman from African backgrounds in terms of language, culture, customs and sometimes religion but for some reasons is more at home with Arabic, Arab ways and practices. Sometimes that would include profession of Islamic faith. Most of these attributes did not and do not apply to me. Nevertheless, I was closer to belonging to the class of what we used to colloquially call "townese"[10].

---

10 Townese: a colloquial used in the past mostly by Southern Sudanese students to refer to town dwellers and their presumed smartness. "Rogue" was another word which was sometimes used to refer to a boy exhibiting cunningness or being conversant with modern cities and how to survive in them.

Co-existence between diverse lifestyles and cultures

Broadly, the subject of this piece is about three groups of people with different ethnic, socio-economic life, customs, and religious beliefs living in Kongor area of the time. The first consisted of the host community, the Dinka people. The majority of these were rural people who lived in villages surrounding the town and beyond. African by race and culture, the Dinka people share similar customs, value and belief systems, and practices with other communities in Southern Sudan, and in many societies on the African continent.

Mid-way there was this group of Southern Sudanese who had received basic formal education from the mission schools. These were "approved" teachers, clerks, veterinary, medical assistants and the like. Nearly all of them were Christian by creed and had little in common with the Northern traders by way of religion or culture (some of them did not even have sufficient command of Arabic). This group tended to bond together. They ate meals similar to those taken daily by the traders: *kisra* and *mullah*[11], also consumed by other town dwellers such as senior chiefs living with members of their extended families at the court centre.

As a rule, the rural inhabitants practised what some writers refer to as "traditional" religion. The tenets of their faith doesn't require the "believers" to pray at fixed intervals a day. They also don't have a Sabbath, Friday or Sunday as the Day of the Lord. In short, communication between Dinka with *Nhialic* or God is occasional; in other words, a Dinka from this class prays as a response to an emergency, sickness in a family being a case in point. Crises, such as an outbreak of a livestock epidemic, long drawn-out drought, or floods affecting part or the whole area usually require a collective remedy from clan elders. Sacrifices and supplications are made to appease the clan divinity, supposed to have been displeased by human action or omission. Believe it or not, sometimes, the expected "divine" answer was received in form of rain or the mysterious and sudden disappearance of the epidemic.

---

11 *Kisra* and *mullah*: Kisra has been described as a thin pancake made from dura or sorghum dough. It is similar to the Ethiopian injera. Together with mullah, gravy mostly broth, is a staple diet of most Sudanese and South Sudanese. A morsel of kisra is dipped, using fingers for rolling and delivering it to mouth.

The people's representatives report their concern to a spiritual leader – believed and accepted as a mediator between the supernatural being and humans (Dinka prefer the word *acuuk* – the small black ant – in reference to the relationship between human beings and Nhialic. While other faiths have synagogue, mosque, temple or church as places for worship, the Dinka centre for spiritual gathering – when they need help – is a shrine which can be any spot anywhere with a tree or stump, for example, as an emblem, standing alone or within a compound of a spiritual man called *Tiet*. Tiet's role is to interpret whatever, mostly reasons behind tragedies and how Nhialic or family or clan deities can be appeased, mostly through sacrifices of an ox or a ram, to end an illness or other natural calamities.

The Christian and Muslim version of immortality is different from that of Dinka. A Dinka man is dead forever if he leaves no child bearing his name at the time of death. This form of life after death did not speak of a day of judgement. To them divine retribution is instantaneous and doesn't have to wait for "the hereafter".

For their livelihood, the rural population of Dinka rely heavily on livestock, primarily as a source of milk. As the people depended on primordial agricultural methods and tools such as the hoe for food production, the result was insufficient grains – mainly sorghum – that doesn't in most cases last from one harvest to the next, even for the most hard-working of farmers. Other food crops grown, such as beans, pumpkin or maize, which do very well and are not labour-intensive, never receive the interest or the attention they deserve because the community doesn't consider them as staple crops, or part of their daily diet.

Indigenous traders

There were a few traders from Southern Sudan. During this period under review there were three. The oldest was Monychol Deng. A former soldier, Monychol, who all the time wore *jalabiya* and a turban pulled close to his forehead to conceal his scarification, was a shopkeeper for Doka Fadhal Mullah, a rich merchant in Bor town. The shopkeeper was one of the richest in the area; he had a huge herd of cattle. Contrary to expectation Monychol allowed his children to choose their religion and what to do for a living. One son, Deng, went to school and embraced Christianity, becoming Alfred at baptism, while on the other hand, Kiir – later to be known as Mohammed Kheir – went to a Muslim school, before going to study in Egypt and Munich in Germany. Kiir later returned to Bor district, where he operated a *matatu* (minivan) transport business among others. He was an SPLA captain when he was killed, during the fighting before the Government of Sudan forces retook Kapoeta in 1992. The rest of Monychol's sons bred cattle and had always been among the rich families of Kongor, until the split within the SPLA of 1991 when the people in that area lost nearly all their cattle to armed men from neighbouring districts.

Dhebidayo Anyieth Akuei was the second-longest serving indigenous trader. Originally from Pathuyith in central Bor, Dhebidayo owned and operated a modest shop. He was a quiet, and dignified-looking man who enjoyed the conversation of some chiefs who lived next to his shop and residence. Anyieth and his brother in law, Gai Kuot who was a nurse were among active members of the local church congregation. Gai together with some of the local teachers often participated in dances which were staged at the centre. One of his companions at the dance and a fellow nurse was Joseph Kuir Deng. Kuir was a composer and singer of very popular songs, some adopted for public dancing.

The third businessman to open a shop was a pioneer in several things. Probably one of the first in the area to receive formal education – which was high by the standard of the time – William Garang Dut completed intermediate school before he trained in forestry. He was stationed and worked at Kegulu before moving to other areas, including Bor where he introduced several species of trees, which still stand there to this day. Before and after independence from Britain in 1956, William Garang tried his luck at politics by contesting a seat in northern Bor constituency. He lost. The next step was to start a shop which was run by one of his relatives, Duot Gak. The former politician was not a resident businessman and appears to have had no social relations with Northern traders in Kongor. One of the shopkeepers with his nephew, Isaac Kot Goch. Like his uncle, Isaac Kot had attended Loka Intermediate School. I recall the day I went to buy dates from his shop. When I stood behind the shop's counter Isaac was reading a book in English. Before he went to serve me he began to tell me the story he was reading. I was surprised but happy that he was interested to share the story with me. It was about a man, he said, who went out in the rain. He raised his head and to continue. I had just been three months in school, so I didn't understand the story and even the word "rain". He told me the word meant "*deŋ*" (deng) in Dinka. I liked the story but I was in a hurry, so I had to go before the end of what he was reading and retelling to me. Besides buying delicious dates- he gave more than the worth of the *tarifa*, equivalent of a penny, which was the price of roughly 250 grams of dates- I had gained a new English word, rain. Many years later when I reminded late Isaac Kot of that encounter he said he couldn't remember it.

Africanising of Arabic names and words

As is to be expected, the people from Northern Sudan were culturally and linguistically different from their Dinka hosts. The locals had problems with how to pronounce the names of the traders or other outsiders who had come to live and work in the area. There was a Moru policeman whose son was called Tilian. This was a corruption of "Italian", as he said he was born during World War Two. The simplicity of the name saved Dinka friends who would have to struggle with usually difficult patronymic names associated with some people of Moru lineage.

The way around the conundrum was to apply the nearest Dinka equivalents. 'Awad Said, one of the first traders to construct a shop made of a corrugated roof and brick walls in the area was simply known as Awet, the Dinka word for crane, the bird with the gold crown whom dances beautifully. Awad's shopkeeper, al-Amin, was Alɔmin whose nearest equivalent in Dinka is an adjective, for "quiet", the opposite of restless. (In later years I came to learn that Abu Bakr Awad, a popular Sudan TV news reader from late 1960s to 1970s was 'Awad's son).

Another Northern Sudanese trader whose name baffled the customers was 'Omer Habiballah. To make life easier, the Dinka addressed him as Wumer, with the stress on the first syllable or – depending on the addresser's caprice – on the second. *Wum* is Dinka word for nose.

The fasting month of Ramadan was twisted to Arɔk-madhän (Arɔk being a unisex name, given to a child born when a family mourns the death of a close relative; *arɔk* (arok) is a word for a sign of bereavement worn by members of a family that has lost a loved one).

There was nothing predictable in this game of names' or words' corruption. The best escape route was for someone to come up with what students of social anthropology refer to as a "personality ox" name. 'Awad Said was known as Awet Majöng-Yäär, namely a white ox with black spots around forehead or ears. Abdalla or Abdullahi was changed to Adhuläi. Mirghani Marzuk, originally from one of the ethnic communities of Darfur, and who was a medical assistant in the area, settled the matter by introducing himself as Manyang de Dut. Being man past mid-age, he was always referred to as Manyangdït (*dït* being a modifier big or elderly). Thus, Mirghani Marzuk was known to all his patients, friends and the rest of the community by the name his in laws imposed on him. Mirghani was married to two women from Bor and that fact made him a fully integrated settler. When he retired from medical work he set up a shop in Kongor. Like the rest of the members from the North, he sent his children to be educated outside Bor area.

Married to people from the 'earth's end'

There were two other men from the North who had married local girls, one of them, a trader while the other was the headmaster of the then-new Arabic elementary school.

Although several members of the expatriate community would have liked to marry local girls, there were obstacles that had to be overcome. The idea of a girl being married to someone whose home origin was believed to be at *pinythar,* or the earth's end, was one of the main reasons behind the objection or reluctance of many families. At the time, every family insisted on being in regular touch with its members even for those who were married and had gone out of the nest to establish and manage their independent households. Then the huge number of cattle demanded by the families from suitors of their daughters was a further hindrance. And almost none of the girls, or their relatives, of the time could countenance the idea of marriage with circumcised men, although this topic was not discussed at all. (See the second part of this piece towards the end).

Merchandise

The traders were basically retailers meeting the needs of the denizens of the town, as well as the rural inhabitants. The town people's daily household consumption consisted of cooking oil, onion, tea, sugar, salt, soap and so on. Villagers, who were the most numerous buyers, shopped for cloth to be made into loose garments for girls and old women folks, beads, small dance bells (or the head of tsetse fly as these jingle makers were known) and hoes. Country boys living in villages surrounding the centre pestered their parents for a few coins to buy dates, sweets or fishing hooks just like their town cousins. Clothes, mosquito nets, razor blades, needles and salt, to some extent, were the commodities in demand for all the groups. Except for beads, such goods did not bring significant profits to the merchants. Hides and skins from cattle, which were transported to Khartoum first by road to Bor, and then by boats plying the White Nile-Kosti route, and by rail to the capital city, were the real money-spinners. Cattle driven on hoof to Juba, for slaughter for meat there, made healthy returns for the traders who had to hire men for the gruelling job for a pay that always didn't exceed two Sudanese pounds per a mission. Those who accepted the mission saw gain: such an amount was the price of a small heifer during times of hardship.

Imported food

When climatic conditions were favourable for cultivation, the population were able to produce grains to feed their families. But natural catastrophes such as floods, drought or visitation by swarms of locusts or grain eating sparrows created shortage of dura and the threat of starvation in the area. Under that situation, rich merchants would order huge amounts of grains from Renk, north of Malakal, or from Gedaref, in the eastern part of the country. According to the rules of supply and demand, it was the consumer who paid exorbitant prices, costs of transport included. Times of distress provided opportunities for struggling traders to get quick, easy and big gains in a matter of months. But things did not always happen that way; during rainy season, which at that time began in March and ended in late October each year, meant that movement of goods and people all over Upper Nile were very much restricted as roads became impassable. Shops in remote areas such as Kongor, had to stock their stores during the dry season. But some dealers came to grief when they bought large quantities of grains, to meet expected famine. When such predictions failed, the grains rotted in stores while the rural people were celebrating a bumper harvest.

Not every Northern Sudanese in Kongor was selling and buying; some of their cousins were successfully engaged in other occupations: tailors, bricklayers, masons and teachers especially after the government decided that an Arabic-language elementary school should be opened in a place that was basically a hardship territory for these civil servants from Northern Sudan.

Mahmoud Ibrahim was a tailor. Evidently a black man, he was of Shilluk extraction, but a Muslim who spoke Arabic as his first tongue. The Dinka tried "Mamuuth" at first before they settled for the descriptive appellation of Makër e Makän, derived from colour configuration of his ox name, *makëër*, and *makana*, Arabic for machine, in reference to his Singer sewing machine.

Then something of a phenomenon happened with the arrival, a couple of years later, of a young brown-looking youth in his mid-teens. Awadallah was his name; he happened to be Mahmoud's nephew or "the son of his sister", as Dinka are keen to define the gender of relationship. A hot-tempered young man, Awadallah during the early days – unlike his generally calm and friendly uncle – used to get cantankerous with almost everyone who crossed his path, either through business or simply by way of Dinka of the time's often unjustified and constant intrusion into individual privacy. Awadallah was a tailor's apprentice. Soon he took over from his Uncle Mahmoud who had succeeded in setting up his own shop, not far from where he used to work as a fitter of *lawa* or simple African attires especially made for women, which was wrapped over the whole body from shoulders down to knees.

Language proficiency

Over the years, Awadallah learned and mastered the Dinka language. With very few people in the picture, he called friends for a rehearsal of the song he had composed in Dinka. Privy to this was one young man called Diing-Magok, half-brother of the then-popular composer and singer Chan Awuol Chan. Diing was not only impressed but told the celebrity-in-the-making: "In the next round of dance, you and I will dance, sing and dance together".

Thus one of the extraordinary careers in Dinka art was launched. With Diing and Awadallah on stage there was a spectacular public expression of both curiosity and genuine admiration for a beautifully-executed piece of art. The lyrics were full of moving expressions and sung virtually without accent.

Awadallah who, with Mahmoud, were adopted members of Padool clan, remained a Dinka associate and married a girl from a clan living not far from the town. They had children. I have been informed that his son went to fight on behalf of the SPLA when Sudan's second civil war erupted in May 1983. His friend, Diing who grew up in the village and cattle camp decided to move to the town where he followed the example of his dance partner, becoming a tailor with his own sewing machine.

When the government decided – after independence – that the special education that was being offered to children in Southern Sudan should be replaced with what was called "national pattern", a system that removed the teaching of the indigenous languages and English in all "bush" and elementary schools from syllabus, a large number of people from Northern Sudan came into the area, as teachers for the new school. Kongor Village School –which this writer attended – became one of the victims of the "nationalisation" of education in Southern Sudan.

The new school was not to follow in the footsteps of the institution made of mud and thatch; it was going to demolish it – literally and metaphorically. Preparations began with the arrival of tradesmen in the area: bricklayers, carpenters, masons and people with allied skills. Almost all of these were from Northern Sudan. Unlike traders, these workers maintained limited contacts with the general population, except with labourers who were engaged in fetching water to be mixed with mud, felling of trees for burning bricks, and other back-breaking manual and odd tasks.

Integration and solidarity

The traders who had spent several years in the area were able to make friends among some of leading members of the host society, especially chiefs. It was common for the Northern Sudanese to be adopted as members of local Dinka clans. Such membership was more an honorary gesture and did not carry attendant rights and obligations. But there were times some of these Northern Sudanese volunteered some needed assistance to their indigenous friends. There was a report of a trader who offered an ox as his contribution towards efforts the people were making to build a dyke when flood waters were threatening to destroy crops in the area. The ox was meant to be slaughtered to feed the young people who were building the embankment.

Other acts of solidarity included an adopted trader attending and participating in dance during the weddings of offspring of their friends or from their adopted clan, or to support a team of wrestlers against an opposing team from another clan.

This identification of the merchants with local people went beyond the immediate neighbourhood; it involved crossing dialect divide. For example, a Northern trader from the Twï-speaking Kongor area travelled to Bor town, where he met his Northern counterpart who ran a shop in the southern part of the district where Gok is the main dialect. It is told the two men began with each boasting that he was more proficient in speaking Dinka than the other. In the course of their conversation, the trader from the south began to mock his interlocutor from the north of the district. "Listen to him. He talks through his nose. This is not Denka".[12]

"This is Twï Denka, the *rutana* [most Northern Sudanese regard any indigenous language as a dialect] of those people up there in the north. They speak like that", was the reply from a third person who had spent some years in the two parts of the district.

Strange telephone operator

A strong contingent of police force was stationed in the town immediately after the Torit mutiny of August 18, 1955. Its members consisted of men from Nuba Mountains and Darfur. As their job was maintenance of law and order they either confined themselves to their quarters or would be seen moving with their guns within or around the town. The police had a long-range communications radio. Its operator, who was said to have been from Shendi, was a weird man. He would obey nature's call anywhere in the open in full view of people, unlike the rest of the town-dwellers, who used pit latrines. As if that was not disgusting enough, Ibrahim, as he was called, would carry an *ibriq*, or tin water bottle in Arabic, full of water which he used for washing his backside, also in public. This puzzling behaviour was contrary to the customs of the hosts, who

---

12 Denka: Sudanese Arabic name for Dinka.

would perform such an act very far from human surroundings and behind the cover of a bush or at night. The exception to the rule of hygiene in the disposal of human waste were babies, a chore that fell to their mothers or older siblings. Toddlers and adults with disability were trained and encouraged, and also on their own will, would perform the act outside homestead and would ensure they were not to be visible to anyone while in the act.

Within two years the building of the school was completed. Made of red brick and corrugated iron, the school was a landmark complex. Consisting of classrooms, houses for teachers, dormitories, a kitchen and dining area, nothing of its kind had been seen before. (A modest veterinary office consisting of two rooms, made of red bricks and asbestos sheets was the second public building of permanent building at that time. The other one was 'Awad's shop). The school buildings stood for elegance and novelty. Soon teachers – almost all from the North – arrived before the pupils, who were selected from all the chieftaincies in Bor North (Bor Elementary which took pupils from all over the district was now to be for children from Bor south and Bor town and other parts of Southern Sudan). Kongor Elementary School had then introduced a cosmopolitan character and status to what was then a drab court centre. The teachers were, unlike the traders, informed and sophisticated. All of them spoke English. The new intake included girls. The school that I attended was an all-boys institution throughout its existence.

Pastime and entertainment

In the early days the world of commerce allowed almost no free time for its agents. Shops used to open as early as 6.30 in the morning, with short breaks for prayers and lunch. Even Friday – the Islamic day of rest – was also for trading. There was no mosque in the area. Most of the businessmen, whether from the North or South were fairly old men. That ruled out vigorous sports like football. In their free time some – especially the elderly – would play dice. Whenever they had time to spare they would go to watch weekly dance and, in later years, wrestling. Southern town-dwellers preferred playing cards or dominoes, which were very popular with some chiefs.

Years later, the new elementary school made football possible because of the number of students and their teachers, most of whom were young men. Throughout the rainy season Dinka frequently held dancing sessions especially when cattle camps had returned from *toch,* the swampy area east of the White Nile. Generally, dancing attracted spectators from all walks of life, from traders, teachers, nurses, chiefs, young and old, and visiting strangers. When wrestling matches were introduced into the area, the sport that also included a parading of "personality oxen" and dancing at the end of a session, was an exciting pastime.

Northern traders went bird-shooting for sport and food. Rainy season was the time when wild geese, ducks and other varieties of birds were abundant. This sport was the most ideal game for the Northern traders. I remember two Southerners had their shotguns, one of them a very senior chief while the other was a nurse. The chief who rarely had time for hunting or other diversions as he was always preoccupied with cases, never went bird shooting. Furthermore, he thought shooting birds for food would dent his image, as most Dinka of the day did not approve of birds – including chickens and eggs – as food for self-respecting people. The other gun owner, who was a crack shot, did not mind. He often shot birds for his pot.

I was one of the boys who used to accompany bird-hunting parties. The rifle owner would wade through water. We walked closely side by side with him. He would take aim. In fact, there was no reason to do that as the fowls were so many that a random shot would not miss its target.

Once birds had been sprayed with pellets, we would run through the flooded terrain where the water level would sometimes reach to the knee to capture the wounded fowls. This had to be done quickly. The bird had to be taken alive to the rifleman so that he could slit their throats in an Islamic way. A dead bird or animal was not fit, according to the Muslim religion, for consumption. At the end of hunting each of us would be paid, depending on the number of birds one captured alive, in piastres or tarifas. We would spend the hard-earned cash by buying dates or sweets, mostly from the very persons who had paid us previously.

The civil war of the 1960s

As the armed conflict between the guerrillas of Anya Nya and the government in Khartoum intensified and began to spread over much of the rural areas and remote towns of Southern Sudan in the 1960s, it became imperative that Northern Sudanese traders relocate their businesses and families, (most men kept their wives and children in their home areas in the North), to the relative safety of towns with bigger garrisons and a large army presence, commanded by Northerners.

Like their colleagues all over Bor district, Northern traders in Kongor moved to either Bor town, Malakal or to the North for good. Because delivery of commodities was interrupted by the war, Southern traders packed and relocated to Bor, or to their native villages.

From late 1964 to 1968, fighting between the insurgents and the government armed forces escalated nearly all over the South. The army adopted the tactics of targeting the educated within the population, and retaliatory killings of civilians in towns and villages. In 1966, 24 chiefs from Northern Bor were arrested and in early 1967 were assassinated by the government army. The paramount chief of all the Bor Dinka, Ajang Duot and Parmena Bul Koch, politician-cum-chief were among the dead. The army then set bases in several strategic points all over the area to monitor the movement of the rebels and their contact with the rural population. The soldiers were raping local girls and women, and intimidated men who dared to question the troops or protest their conduct. People were terrified and helpless. This rape and pillage of the area later resulted in births of some children with strong Arab physical attributes.

At this time, when the Ummah and National Unionist Party, NUP, coalition government, under Prime Minister Mohammed Ahmed Mahjoub declared the holding of country-wide elections to the Constituent Assembly, the main parties representing Southern Sudan expressed their fear that conducting polls under the prevailing insecurity in the region would not be fair and free. But the government had its way; after all it was the author of the reign of terror and knew exactly what to gain from state- induced rampant lawlessness. Few people were surprised that no candidates among the politicians born in the area were ready to enter into electoral fray. The result was that in Bor North constituency, Abdullah Elias Babiker, the candidate of the NUP, was "elected" to represent the area. Another trader, a certain Khojali was alleged to have been elected by the voters in Bor South as their MP. Only Bor Central was taken by a Southern Sudanese politician, Ezra Majok Chol Biar of Sanu. The area always didn't have the presence of Northern traders due to limited government activities and institutions such as health centre or a large school whose personnel would be the clientele of the merchants and their good and services.

Consistent with the prevailing ideologies of the day, Abdullah, a secondary school leaver who wrote and spoke good English, in his maiden speech, of course delivered in Arabic, accused "oppressive colonialism" for allegedly creating division between the North and the South. That was the pervasive view held by all Northern parties and even many among the masses. This position might have changed over the years, but it still persists, mainly in right-wing circles of Northern Sudan. Members of the Southern educated elite of all walks of life, however, used to – and still – accept that the British colonial administration had to some extent contributed to the problem, but argue that it serves no useful purpose to dwell on the past; the way forward is: let us get the right solution to the problem of disparity.

These developments confirmed the long-held allegations by the Southern Sudanese elite that Northern Sudanese merchants in the region meddled in political and administrative matters, and that they gave deliberately misleading advice to Northern administrators and security chiefs deployed in the region.

When relative peace returned to Southern Sudan, after the reconciliation between the central government and the Southern rebels in 1972, Northern traders were free to return to where they had operated businesses before the war. But times had changed; this time there were many local persons plying petty trade. That meant, in places like Kongor, the former monopoly of commerce had effectively ended as the field was open to cut-throat competition, with some Southern administrators favouring their own relatives in grant of business licences as a form of economic autonomy.

To be circumcised or not to be circumcised

As the traders and later teachers from the North were without exception Muslim, it also meant that they were circumcised according to the requirements of their faith. This custom in itself, as practised by new comers did not generate problems between the two communities except in rare cases of a local man engaged in heated argument with a circumcised one. Dinka boys and sometimes adults in that part of South Sudan used to – and continue to – throw verbal abuse at other persons during a bitter fallout involving a physical fight. One of the commonest and most provocative insults of the time would be for the opponent to shout aloud "*Yin ye aŋuala* (anguala) *de raan!*" On the face of it this is a statement of fact and should not cause offence – however the word was intended to be abusive and to hurt. What provokes the addressee in this instance arises from the connotation of the word "*anguala*" or the circumcised one and the scornful tone in which that statement is uttered in Dinka.

Eastern Dinka- those inhabiting east of the White Nile do not only reject the practice but also see the custom as abhorrent, detestable and something to be ashamed of. According to this thinking, calling a man anguala is to insult him, making him a laughing-stock among listeners sharing similar worldview as the accuser.

Some decades ago, attitudes towards circumcised men by communities that did not practise the tradition virtually verged on the irrational or obsessive with a tinge of revulsion. Any man from linguistic groups such as Bor as a whole, Ngok of Bailiet, Ager, Abiliang, Padaang, all east of the Nile, or Agar, Aliap, Ciec, Rel or Atuot as they like to be called, and Gok, Dinka inhabiting west of the White Nile, who underwent the operation either for medical or religious reasons, or from free choice, had to live in denial for the rest of his life. Peers and even young boys- females pretended the practice didn't exist or it didn't concern them- would snigger at him behind his back, calling him names, mostly in whispers. At times "*raan*", Dinka word for a person, would be applied as a code for a circumcised man.

The length to which such societies went to follow their customs is illustrated by an event that took place many years ago, in a village not far from my own. A woman had contracted a venereal disease as a result of liaison between her and a stranger she claimed had raped her. She then passed the disease to her husband. After the symptom appeared the two villagers who did not know the nature of their sickness did not report to a health centre for early diagnosis and treatment.

When the man's condition deteriorated, he was taken to a nearby health facility. The medical assistant recommended that the patient should undergo circumcision as well as to take a course of antibiotics. The man told the medico he preferred death to circumcision. And he was dead serious. Relatives were called to persuade him. Finally, he relented. More problems were brewing. As soon as he had recovered he and his brothers approached his in-laws with a complaint against their daughter for adultery and bringing difficulties to her husband. The in-laws agreed to give him a heifer as a form of compensation for the loss of his prepuce and for the slurs he was going to endure throughout the rest of his life. To conceal the identity imposed on him, he had to bathe when no other people were around or after nightfall.

These attitudes were also widespread among the Nuer and Shilluk of Upper Nile. Until recent times, members of these communities used to make fun of circumcised men. Like some of Dinka communities, Nuer and Shilluk, used to compose and sing songs ridiculing *thony*, the Nuer equivalent of anguala.

The reverse of circumcised is *ayuuk* in the dialects of Western Dinka, mainly from the communities inhabiting the former Gogrial, Tonj and Aweil districts. Ngok Dinka of Abyei and Pan Aru circumcise their men. The word is derogatory. Since these Dinka people carry out circumcision as a rite of passage, to them, an uncircumcised man is considered to be a boy. In these communities, there is a general belief that being uncircumcised would almost amount to poor bodily hygiene. The idea that the operation guarantees cleanness is common among the Semitic peoples and their neighbours such as the Ethiopians and Eritreans, Christian or Muslim.

In Africa the opposing concepts surrounding circumcision can become a political and leadership issue. I am thinking about Kenya. During the multi-party presidential and parliamentary elections of 1992, some members of the Kikuyu ethnic group whose community practises the custom, opposed the leadership of Oginga Odinga on the grounds that he was alleged to be uncircumcised – on the assumption that his Luo community does not perform the rite – and was, allegedly, not qualified on that account to be president. In a public reply, the old man said he underwent the surgery many years back.

During my intermittent sojourns in Kenya from 1992 to 2005 I often read of gangs in market places in Nairobi forcibly circumcising some Luo men, after the crowd learned there was a "boy" in their midst.

In Southern Sudan, time has softened attitudes. From the late 1970s through to the 1980s young Dinka Bor youth – mostly students – were flocking to hospital in large numbers to have the cut. It soon became so fashionable that it turned into a stampede. "The demand [for operation] was so high that we had to do it by appointment", a doctor who worked in the area at the time told me years later. When the war broke out soon after, those young people who had missed out at home had to have the operation performed on them in clinics in the military bases. These were men from those ethnic groups – some Dinka communities, Nuer, Shilluk, Murle – who had opposed the practice throughout their known history, making a reverse decision. Cuban doctors who came to Africa to provide health care to SPLA fighters at Bilpam, their most famous general headquarters, are known to have as well performed the operations on young men hailing from communities which had previously held the practice as a taboo.

Are people making a fuss over whether a man is circumcised or not circumcised? It seems so. However, if one's religion or community decrees that one has to undergo the operation, there is no reason why others would have cause to complain. Again, if a person gets a cut because of medical reasons or purely as a matter of personal choice, that also should be respected. On the other hand, if for cultural reasons other people do not perform the operation, that custom has to be respected. In a nutshell, cultural practices and belief systems don't always find universal approval or rejection. The best under the circumstances is for anyone to respect other people's value systems and their practices, as long as none of them has been proved to be harmful to those who practise them – such female genital mutilation, FGM, – or when they pose no dangers to others. Mutual tolerance should be the guiding principle.

This article was first published in Tore *journal of arts, South Sudan, 2006. The periodical appeared once.*

When Juba reeled under Ebola

In July 1976, *Nile Mirror* newspaper, which was published in Juba at that time, and on which I was its features editor, carried a story on the front page about a "mysterious killer disease". The disease first hit Maridi, a town in Western Equatoria. Little was known about how many people had contracted the illness or how many had died from it. Among its symptoms, were a very high temperature and massive bleeding through body orifices. The victim died within 72 hours from the time of attack. Doctors in both Maridi and Juba did not know the cause of the ailment, much less the cure. This kind of ignorance about the feared affliction gave rise to several names being assigned to the condition: it was first called Maridi disease, then haemorrhagic febrile disease, Green Monkey disease and finally Marburg, after a town in Germany where research was being conducted into it.

Since the unknown illness was highly contagious, travellers and patients from Maridi carried it to Juba. A doctor in Maridi hospital who was treating a patient of Marburg was infected through physical contact. Other unconfirmed reports claimed then that the doctor got infected either during burial or funeral service for a trader who had died of the disease. The doctor was rushed to Khartoum hospital where he died two days later. It was rumoured that his corpse was incinerated to avoid infection. A nurse in Juba hospital who had previously attended a patient of the Green Monkey disease came to the same tragic end. The medical institution was gripped by fear, to the extent some of its junior staff refused to look after the sick while others – especially the non-medical personnel – threatened to resign from work altogether.

Although there were more deaths from the disease in Maridi than in Juba, the capital city of Southern Sudan was in the throes of exceptional fear, gloom and a near mass panic, comparable to the mood of the Londoners during the Black Death in the seventeenth century. Children, women and men regardless of age or social status, lived in constant dread of contracting the disease whose victims died in a couple of days after horrific bleeding. There were reports of some government employees absenting themselves from work; parties and other minor social functions automatically came to a sudden halt; mutual visits by friends and relatives gradually decreased in frequency. Visitors from the afflicted Maridi were shunned like, shall I say… ugh, plague. Stories – mostly fabricated – circulated in Juba about the strange behaviour of some people as a reaction to the fear of this dreadful unknown disease.

Panic captured by cartoonist

One of those tales went as follows. A man alighted from a bus at the Yei station, in the Malakiya suburb of Juba. On saying that he had just arrived from Maridi, all hell broke loose as everyone, including those who did not know the cause of the stampede, fled in all directions. The stunned visitor, who was left virtually alone, was himself in a state of shock, wondering why people were fleeing the spot. His tribulations didn't end there. When he went to stay with a relative at the outskirts of the city, he was turned away, according to reports we in the media could not verify.

A couple of hours later a reporter who was on the beat came to narrate the story. I recall that all of us in the newsroom burst into spontaneous laughter. It sounded too fanciful to be a news story. But that did not deter Urbano Oyet, popularly known as Jobojobo, the quick witted cartoonist from making an example of the story, false or true. It was a suitable material for satire, for which Jobojobo had made a name for the weekly and for himself as well. A few days later thousands of the *Mirror's* readers had something to tickle them at that bleak time when merriment was becoming rare in the city. The cartoon depicted people running helter-skelter in all directions, fleeing the bus station, leaving only the empty bus and bewildered new arrival standing alone.

To report about the health situation citywide, I visited Juba hospital, where I found the mood of all except for the doctors and senior nurses, characterised by despondency, fright and uncertainty about the future. As a rule, public gathering was not evident; one could see at least a group of three, four, talking together in hushed voices. Leaving the hospital, the time was about four in the afternoon. Normally that route was a mass of humanity, moving in opposite directions. But throughout the time I was walking I encountered less than 10 people; everybody had gone home earlier than usual.

It had rained previously and the stench of human excreta on both side of the road having been invigorated by rain water, was terrible. The unbearable odour served as a reminder that this town was once inhabited by people, some so poor that they had no pit latrines and had to relieve themselves in the open when it was night.

Before reaching Khor Bou bridge – separating Malakiya from the main city – I passed by All Saints Cathedral. The edifice looked lonely, reminding me of a coconut tree in the uninhabited swamp land between my home area and Shambe in Yirol, on the western plank of the White Nile. There was no one to be seen within the compound, even the fowl kept by the workers had gone to their cages before dusk. Looking to the west, I could see the sun, looking dull orange, lonely and sad on its way, to its "hideaway". The external scene affected my mood: I had been smitten by the prevailing atmosphere and was now feeling very low and lonely.

A few days later the scene at the Cathedral had changed dramatically. The Archbishop of Canterbury, The Most Right Reverend Dr Donald Coggan, had come to Juba to enthrone Bishop Elanana Ngalamu as the Archbishop of the Episcopal Church, formerly the Anglican Church of Sudan. For the occasion, all the faithful, among them, government ministers, clergymen down to the street cleaners, turned in their hundreds for the rare event. The cathedral was full to capacity, so much so that the congregation outside the building was larger than that seated inside.

It was a solemn occasion, deserving of such a massive response and attendance. But some people had gone there, hoping that the English primate and the leader of the Anglican communion worldwide would pray to God to put an end to the scourge which had visited the territory. I was among the congregation in my capacity first as a journalist and second as an "Anglican". Earlier in my professional training I was taught not to be involved or identify with any participants whose occasion one was covering, otherwise impartiality would be seriously compromised. I therefore decided to keep my eyes wide open while all the participants were in deep prayer, humbly kneeling, eyes closed and chins on the top of the pews.

The Archbishop of Canterbury chose to dwell on the role and challenges of the new Sudanese prelate and the need and rights of the Sudanese

Christians to exercise their administrative right in religious matters. The visiting spiritual leader studiously avoided any mention of the disease. I suspect, many in the congregation must have been disappointed with the VIP for not saying anything about the illness threatening the lives of people he was visiting. Common sense has it that the clergyman had nothing to say about what was happening in the city; probably he might have prayed silently for divine mercy; nothing more than that.

When he was not preaching or praying, the top man of the cloth looked calm, composed and dignified. The same attitude was exhibited by his hostess, Dr Fatima Abdel Mahmoud who was minister of social welfare in the government in Khartoum and a trained physician. Abdel Mahmoud had accompanied the Christian leader from Khartoum to Juba for the occasion.

When the two were airborne, most of the people of Juba felt like a flock without a shepherd. Flight restrictions between Khartoum and Juba and the outside world were immediately clamped again. Juba was, once again, a huge quarantine outpost: no departures, no arrivals, by land or by air.

Despite the all-embracing fear which had seized Juba, there were people who saw the fright and the danger from the disease as over-exaggerated; others had a cavalier attitude which seemed to say "If I die, so what?"

Waiting, watching

One category consisted of what was known as Young Executives, or YE for short, a group of young men who were fresh university graduates, occupying middle ranking positions in the government of Southern Sudan. Strictly speaking, this was an unofficial social club of the intelligentsia who discussed issues of the day such the weaknesses and strengths of the regional government; ideas of thinkers such Herbert Marcus, Frantz Fanon; the death of Steve Biko, the South African anti-apartheid campaigner and his black consciousness philosophy; his place in history; the Soweto riots and the massacres that it provoked; the rapprochement or détente between West and East; the bicentenary commemoration of the United States of America as a nation; the role of black American leaders such as Rev Jesse Jackson or Andrew Young, then US ambassador to the UN. The group's unofficial venue was Senior Rest House, one of the two hotels in the city and both owned by the government. I was one of the regulars at that establishment. And an associate member of the YE.

When the Marburg disease became a talking point in town, some of the tales about the disease turned out to be a laughing matter. Filberto, as I will call him here, was a member of the YE. He was very talkative. He gave the impression that he was a very knowledgeable person. He loved to be considered an intellectual. Filberto, a graduate of economics in North America, asserted that Marburg was nothing but germs or viruses produced in laboratories of the developed world and to be tested in Africa as a lethal biological weapon. However, he was not well regarded despite the fact that he had studied abroad. Filberto was known as a loose talker. When he was asked to provide evidence for his assertion, he responded with "In the world of science nothing is impossible. Politicians also can abuse scientific discoveries, inventions and scientists themselves. You may be right or wrong. Anything goes." The conversation ended there and discussion moved to another, less stressful topic.

A remote brush with the killer disease

Personally, I had a brush – although not a close shave – with Marburg disease. Dr Abdin Abu Shanab, to whom I have previously referred, operated on me for an appendectomy in Juba, several months before his death. The operation was carried out at the time it was about to explode with predictable consequences: death. I was grateful to Dr Abu Shanab, but saving the life of one individual out of 17 million, then the estimated number of Sudanese, was of little consequence.

Dr Shanab, a fresh graduate from the University of Khartoum and a bachelor was known by the personnel in Juba hospital as the Mad Doctor. When I was his patient, I learned a lot about the man. He would move to the hospital wards at the first light. With the exception of brief breaks for meals, he would be in the hospital until about 10 pm. Abu Shanab saw to it that the patients were given full care, respect and devotion by all the medical personnel. On several occasions, the doctor had a physical fight with nurses who neglected their duties or showed laxity towards their charges. The death of Dr Abu Shanab was a loss to his family and to the country whose people he loved. He had devoted his entire working life to their welfare.

Another aspect concerned the death of a nurse. The nurse was a colleague of Joshua Koryom Nak, head nurse responsible for administration of the hospital. Koryom was my relative. I was staying in his house at the time in question. One afternoon while we were having lunch in the house, Koryom informed me about the death of one of his colleagues from Marburg disease. "When we wanted to take his body to the graveyard for burial, most people including some of his close relatives just disappeared. Dr Salama Hilmi, [senior medical officer in charge of the hospital] myself and two of the deceased relatives carried the bier. The four of us lowered the body into the grave," he said in a whisper, so as not to frighten the women and children who were within earshot. I was filled with fear.

"But, but... er..." I stuttered. He understood that I had meant to say that he had taken an enormous risk. "This is one of the professional hazards. We in the medical field are like soldiers. We sometimes die in the service of the people. I would rather die a dignified man than be branded a coward," he told me, before we began to eat.

This article was first published by the SPLM/A Update *newsletter, 1995 under the title of* "When even the Bravest Trembled with Fear" *and in early 2002 it appeared in the Kenyan* Daily Nation *as* "When Juba Reeled under Ebola". *This is an abridged version of the two.*

After all Radio is a Luxury

It is probable that many people have difficulty recalling the exact dates when they first listened to a radio broadcast for a length of time. A similar number, however, vividly recall the time they acquired or owned their first receivers. These two instances fit me.

People begin to listen to radio programmes because they want information, education and entertainment, the principal functions of any mass medium. Radio as one Arab poet has written, is like a "free" school at one's fingertips. It is a class at one's convenience any time and place of one's choosing. As a source of entertainment, mainly music and light talks or plays, a radio set is by far cheaper than cinema or theatre except that the listener misses pictures (with colours, gestures and so forth).

Though listening habits and interests in programmes vary from person to person, the overall pattern is virtually universal. For working people and the majority of students, the ideal periods for listening are early mornings and evenings, a fact which programme planners, audience researchers and advertisers know – and exploit – very well. As a rule, a serious listener tunes in to their regular favourite station programme(s) first thing in the morning, before teeth brushing and tea. In the evening he returns home from his place of work, with no barrier or excuse not to press and turn the knob and of dial of his set; he has to update himself with the latest developments in the country and in the world in general. Like a journalist, a regular radio listener is fixated to following up events: how has a crisis he heard being reported in the morning progressed or been resolved and in which manner and with what results? Or assuming that the enthusiast is a music or sport fan, he will want to know, literally almost on the hour, any new entry in the pop chart or which team has won and by how many points.

At this stage the listener is no longer a free spirit, but rather the captive of a habit which progressively becomes too expensive to maintain. If his set suffers from poor reception, the wave guide or advice from radio engineers will whet his appetite and spur him to buy a better set, likely to be costlier than the receiver being replaced. And as there is no end and shortage of what is better, the desire to acquire the latest and the most efficient-sometime the most elegant- is hindered only by the depth of one's pocket. Utility, hobby and even vanity, gets mixed up in such a way that the pursuit and acquisition of several and different sizes, shapes, colours and brands of radio sets have to be rationalised. The bulky gadget is for use indoors; the combination of alarm and radio set is ideal when one is in the kitchen; the other one with AM and FM is suitable for music while one is in the city; the portable is for safaris to areas where there is no electricity; the digital saves time in locating stations and is so powerful that it picks up communications between pilots in flight (or between them and control towers); the other saves money as it is economical with batteries and allows one to present particular stations and their programmes and so forth.

Radio enthusiasts are another class of users, with different interests. I knew of one radio buff who in the early 1990s used to claim that he could pick military pilots of the Sudan Air Force who bombed civilian installations, and he would know the aircraft were going to bomb their location only as they talked in Arabic and most of the time in code language.

There is yet another irrational side to this obsession. What on earth would an adult listener buy a toy-like FM/AM band set, whose size is that of a toilet soap tablet as already mentioned? There is a convincing reason for that, as the owner would like to justify. Examination time is approaching and he is not prepared to waste even a minute. Laundry, pressing clothes, cooking, scrubbing, shower, shaving and even listening to radio are time consuming chores. It is economical to shave and bathe while listening to news broadcasts, weather reports or music, behind the closed door of the bathroom. This way he is killing several birds with just one stone.

To wean someone who has been hooked to radio broadcasts in that manner for many years would be similar to removing a fish from water. They would miss what they are used to and could lead to self-imposed solitude even in the midst of people, however congenial they may be.

Several years ago I had to undertake a mission that might be described as "Destination Unknown" and "Duration Infinite", and to make ready for that trip in just 15 minutes. Details of the trip are "redacted" for now.

All the same I managed to obtain a three band (SW/MW/FM radio, a Japanese National Panasonic portable set with three dry cells after which I immediately set off for my Erewhon.

For the first night of the trek we bivouacked in a glade in a no man's land. It was that time which proved that although I was in the company of many, radio was the best friend under the circumstances.

The time was the middle of rainy season, characterised by incessant rains which poured with a vengeance, as if to compensate for the drought of the previous year. The land was full of water and the few remaining high grounds were soggy and slippery, rendering movement to mere wading and shuffling. As a wilderness, there was no shelter to speak of except for mosquito nets whose only good use was to protect the occupants against the bites of swarms of the demons of insects. Food, too, was insufficient and with the long march and a very long distance to be covered, the amount that one could carry (and to run out soon after), was miniscule. We were exhausted, cold, hungry and wet. Misery had engulfed us all; only a few were seen to have some morale, but it was a charade.

In the early morning, before we could continue with the virtually interminable journey into the interior of Erewhon – I request pardon for plagiarism as that is the title of Samuel Butler's novel – I tuned to my favourite radio station for a half-hour news programme. The bleak surroundings and the dark grey clouds which had covered the sky from the earth's four corners and threatening imminent downpour, dampened the mood and thoughts which turned sombre and blunt. The situation was reminiscent of the time when the Dinka men of older times would provoke the earth with "*Ye piny col amook!*",[1] an expletive without an equivalent in English, but is a traditional expression which the person uttering it intends as a means of releasing emotions against an invisible enemy or a very trying situation[1].

Suddenly a female voice came on the air at with the introduction "Hello, and welcome to the programme, wherever you are." In a split second, I found myself at the point of jumping up with "You have worded it right with 'wherever you are!' I am here in this damned, slushy hell of place, under a leaky sky!"

I had to restrain myself from doing so or the people around me would have concluded that I had lost my mind. Fortunately for me, the sudden change in my demeanour – from expressionless to jovial – was given a different but positive interpretation by fellow travellers, most of who were similarly exhausted. My comrades had assumed that I must have heard some "good news" from the broadcast I was listening to. They did not know the cause of my uplifted mood was that obscure "wherever you are" statement from a news reader in a far corner of the globe. I was happy, too, that none of my companions had taken the trouble to enquire what the good news was all about, if there even could have been such an item in the first place.

I did not personally know the presenter to stir the slightest of sentiments, but she was reading from inside one of the studios of a warm and cosy building of a broadcasting institution I sometimes frequented and where some of my friends I had known worked. In a sense, the chain reaction led to that place and the fond memories I had formed about it. I attributed this vicarious joy emanating from my receiver. I was grateful. I suddenly valued the radio a lot more. But that was not destined to last long. At last, we managed to trudge to our destination after several weeks of ordeal and deprivation.

There, I discovered that the people we were going to live with were very good at making do with practically everything. In fact, the only thing they considered basic was food. Water which should have come on top of the list of life basic requirements had earned itself the distinction of being a nuisance, a major source of their plight: the area was witnessing something like the enactment of a biblical flood.

Some of these wretched but fatalistic people in some of the villages and towns were forced to live in old and abandoned lorries, others perched on the flat rooftops of what used to be shops or government office buildings. Anyone looking for medicine, soap, salt or sugar was certainly asking for the impossible and therefore being unreasonable. In place of modern drugs, herbs were being introduced; bark of a certain tree became a substitute for soap; yet others concocted fresh grey ashes collected from the heath immediately after cooking to be added into food instead of salt. I never tried any of these chemical blends or other discoveries.

Dry cells for torches and other battery-driven appliances were among the rarest commodities in the area. Unconfirmed reports spoke of a man who exchanged a bull for six batteries, good enough to keep his radio working for about six months.

We divide the world into frugal and extravagant, but in reality, everybody becomes stingy to the point of meanness when managing severely limited resources. Accordingly, I had to cut down the time for the use of radio from two hours a day, divided into equal halves, morning and evening, then soon to half an hour. To deny others the use of my radio during my absence from the shared accommodation, I either locked the set in my attaché or removed and hid the batteries somewhere within the building.

Finally, the inevitable happened: the greatly exhausted power of the batteries, left the receiver inaudible and hissing, making it irritating. I had to remove and discard the used cells. It was a dark day as the radio had become just a toy. It was a truly an unpleasant end.

The people in the area, as was their custom, were in bed a couple of hours after darkness fell. By 9 pm at the latest, everyone was in deep sleep, with a few snoring. Although in my childhood, I lived under such conditions, this time was different; I could hardly come to terms with this somewhat traumatic experience. Without lighting of any kind and without books or newspapers, reading was out of the question. My lot was to cope with the long dark nights in silence, and unable to sleep early during the first two weeks without radio functioning.

Then one day an idea struck. We would arrange storytelling, mainly folktales. It was a fantastic and fruitful engagement. Joy replaced regret at missing the radio and consequently I began to regard radio as I did TV and electricity, as deadly enemies of folklore and storytelling, an old pastime in the traditional societies. To this day my view on this remains the same.

[1] In one of his writings, Dr Francis M. Deng quotes an elderly Dinka chief as evoking that utterance and which he translates to roughly mean "an earth with a black anus".

SPLM/A Update newsletter, 1995.

Sudanese Supermodel Alek Wek sparks African Beauty Debate

The rise of the "uncompromisingly black" (as one fashion magazine has described her), 22-year-old Alek Wek to stardom has sparked off a huge debate about beauty. The supermodel hails from Bahr el Ghazal in Southern Sudan.

Writing of Alek in the fashion magazine, *Elle*, Rebecca Lowthorpe describes the Sudanese model as "one of a kind". Magretta wa Gacheru, a Kenyan journalist, wrote: "Despite Wek's not conforming to conventional concepts of beauty (which traditionally have meant white features and pale skin to 'make it' in modelling), she has been reckoned one of the hottest and most photogenic models in the world to date."

The model's ethnic origin holds the key to her "difference". Lowthorpe writes "Hailing from Sudan's ancient Dinka tribe, she is far from the traditional ideals as the deserts is from the Paris catwalks- a six-foot statue carved from ebony and polished to perfection".

The fact that the jet-black Sudanese model was diametrically different from what the fashion business was used to was emphasised by a caption beneath a photograph accompanying the story: "Devilishly attractive: Alek Wek's once-seen-never-forgotten looks are a refreshing antidote to Barbie doll cutely-beauty".

For some (black) Africans, Alek owes her quick and stunning rise in the fashion industry, where competition is stiff, to the fact that she is original, in the sense of "noble savage". In a letter to the editor carried by the *Sunday Nation* of June 21, Abwao, a Kenyan reader wrote of Alek's controversy by stating that "authentic here means genuine. Just as in African art, the true beauty of this continent's women has sadly been misunderstood and misinterpreted by critics who do not have a true insight into aesthetic – natural or man-made – as seen through Africa's eyes." Because of this misunderstanding, the writer has argued that "for the height, the Sudanese super-model Alek Wek would not have made it even to the quarter finals of the M-Net competition had she entered," since the "M-Net contest, winners tended to be light-skinned."

Alek, who left her home because of war to land on a gold mine of fame and fortune, sees herself as an unofficial spokesperson for her long-suffering people. In the US and wherever else she meets the news media, Alek Wek says she wants to educate the world about the problems facing her people with a view to soliciting aid for the victims of war and famine. Recently, she flew to Bahr el Ghazal for that same objective.

The world of modelling, sports and music is a money-spinner, so Alek Wek's success means she has escaped the crippling poverty now pounding her people back home. However, there is a paradox here. Dinka cultural values denounce the use of skills, beauty, talents and other natural endowments for commercial purposes, even for a livelihood. Dinka openly scorn careers such as thatching huts, blacksmithing and traditional healing, since those who practise them demand pay. Singers, leading wrestlers and other public entertainers feel insulted at the hint of being honoured or given token gifts by their fans; believing that innate or acquired personal gifts should be offered to the public at no cost at all.

True to the spirit and social philosophies of her people, Alek Wek has said on several occasions that she will use her graceful features now as a means of awareness creation to help her war and famine ravaged people.

Beauty among the Dinka, seen from their own perspective and consisting of certain attributes, is universally admired and desired, but it has never been put to commercial ends. For example, since Dinka pay bridal wealth in cattle when marrying, this would therefore mean that the greater the girl's beauty, the more cattle will her family demand from a suitor. This is not wholly true. The determining factor in the number of cattle that accrue to a family in the form of bride wealth is the size of the girl's clan; the good looks of a girl play a minor role.

That the Western world, especially the fashion industry is eyeing black Africa to promote showbiz is hardly surprising. The process of discovery, whether of strange lands and peoples' practices and customs or ideas, of new mechanical devices or processes has always been at the heart of Western progress and civilisation. Intrepid navigators and explorers of the 15th century through the 17th century went to sea to "discover" new lands. In the Americas, such discoveries resulted in the establishment of colonies who began to grow cotton and sugar with the labour of black slaves brought from Africa. In the same capitalistic vein, the orient was "discovered" as a source of spices and so on.

The fashion industry by nature is always on the lookout for anything new as its operators are fully aware that people, in their search for what is novel and exciting, quickly tire of the familiar and the common. Alek Wek may be the blackest woman courted by fashion managers, but certainly, she will not be the last. Soon fashion houses in Milan, Paris and New York will send discoverers to virgin and relatively inaccessible outposts in the African jungles, in the Amazon rainforests, Papua New Guinea, Tahiti, Mongolia and others, looking for the next unspoilt "native" enchantress.

The EastAfrican, *Nairobi, Kenya, June 6-13, 1998. This weekly is widely read in Kenya, Uganda, Tanzania, Rwanda, Burundi and from 2011, in South Sudan.*

'Comrade' is neither a name nor an honorific

Sudan's civil war of 1983-2005 – like similar civil upheavals – brought people from the former Southern Sudan into contact with peoples from neighbouring countries such as Ethiopia, Kenya and Uganda. These Southern Sudanese were refugees, escaping the armed conflict. Interaction with the host communities resulted in some of the refugees learning languages commonly spoken where they lived. In the process the guests, especially children, adopted – to some extent – some of the hosts' cultural practices and social norms.

Kenya, in the later stage of the conflict, became one of the societies from which most Southern Sudanese refugees received a limited cultural influence. Unlike the case of Ethiopia, language was no longer a barrier to a sizeable number of Southern Sudanese and their Kenyan hosts as the two communities, especially members of the educated class, were able to communicate easily in English. Also, because many refugee children went to Kenyan schools, they were able to imbibe some elements from the local cultures and value-system.

In contrast, contacts and interactions with the Ethiopians were very limited. Nevertheless, there were few influences, direct or indirect, which Southern Sudanese in Ethiopia could not escape. One of these is the love of Ethiopian dishes among Southern Sudanese who spent much of the 1983-1991 period in different parts of Ethiopia.

Another "contribution" from Ethiopia was the adoption by Southern Sudanese of the word "comrade". The Ethiopians of the post-imperial era cannot be credited with having invented the word or its application; it was already in existence in other parts of the world, especially after the Russian Revolution of 1917. Use of "comrade" came to Ethiopia almost immediately after the radical left-wing regime came to power following the fall of the imperial system in 1974.

Doing away with titles and class

The revolution that overthrew the Ethiopian imperial system under Emperor Haile Selassie was avowedly Marxist-Leninist in its pronouncements and action. With a profound opposition to both monarchy and the class system associated with the ancien regime, the ruling Provisional Military Council or Derg, as they were known, branded titles such as "Ato" for men or "Woizero" for ladies as class markers. Regardless of their status, a person had to be "Comrade Tesfai" or *Guad* Tesfai"[13] in the Amharic equivalent.

When the SPLM/A was formed in 1983, the Ethiopian government of Mengistu Haile Mariam was the main backer and ally of the then Sudanese insurgents. The fact that Ethiopia was home to more than 400,000 Southern Sudanese refugees – mainly in Itang in the western region- made contact with the hosts and some of their influences possible. The first of these was the adoption of "comrade" by the top echelon of the Sudanese rebel leadership. They themselves were waging a war against the regime in Khartoum, described in their manifesto as a reactionary "clique" and a one-man "no-system" rule. As people who believed they were progressives, the rebels took to calling each other "comrade". "Mr" and "Mrs" and "Miss" or "Ms" were too imperialistic for the comfort of the Sudanese revolutionaries; at the time Western honorifics were seen as symbols for identifying counter-revolutionaries. There was no room for titles such as "His Excellency" or "Her Excellency" in a movement that was fighting a system run by a "bourgeoisified" elite in Khartoum. The other meaning of bourgeoisie was class of exploiters or "those who eat other people's things".

Also despised and discarded was the Arabic "Sayed". When this writer prepared a list of senior civilian members of the SPLM to take part in a roundtable discussion over Radio SPLA in late 1984, one of the discussants angrily rebuked him with "I do not own slaves", after reading "Sayed" written before his name as it was the case with the rest of his colleagues to participate in the radio talk. "Sayed" in Arabic means "master" and by extension this implies the existence of someone inferior to *as-sayed*, probably a slave. In a way, the protester had a point. The use of "Sayed" as an honorific for Southern Sudanese VIPs had ceased before the emergence of the SPLM/A. The editors of the government-owned weekly newspaper, *Nile Mirror*, insisted on using "Mr" instead of "Sayed", in defiance of the government's order.

---

13 Tesfai is a common male name in Ethiopia, mainly among the Amhara speaking people. *Guad* is an Amharic word for friend or comrade.

Nothing derogatory about 'comrade'

To poke fun at the SPLM/A leadership of the day for deciding to address each other as comrade, or to use the word when talking to their juniors, who would in turn address them as such without any loss of respect, would be unfair. It was a sign of humility consistent with the people and their organisation, the SPLM/A, whose objectives included promotion of egalitarianism in theory and practice. Today, some people use "comrade" as a title: "Your Comradeship", for example, when someone writes a letter to a very senior person in the ruling party, the SPLM, or in government. But this is clearly a misuse of the word. It was not meant to be a lofty title reserved for VIPs. To use it in this manner defeats the purpose it was intended to serve: to express modesty and narrowing of the wide class-gap between the most powerful people and the proletariats.

Being soldiers and patriots fighting a common enemy for shared objectives, the senior SPLA officers that included their commander in chief, were using the shortened form "comrade", meaning comrades in arms. And indeed they were. In practice, and regardless of rank, age group, ethnic, regional or any other parochial affiliations, *all* soldiers of all ranks, relied on the support of their fellow soldiers for safety, food, water, tobacco and company. Camaraderie was the glue that bound all the members belonging to an organisation, along with their shared ideology and goals. Whether one was a civilian or soldier, as long as you shared a common cause with your colleagues and were fighting a common enemy, you were a comrade.

It was the colleague next to you who would evacuate you to safety when wounded. His origin and mother-tongue were irrelevant. Sharing hardships, victories or food and water, cemented the relations of those soldiers. It was a common practice for any comrade to voluntarily declare to his fellow combatants anything of value – such as money – he had received from family or friends. By doing so, the object in question would be shared. In short, they were true comrades not only in arms but in matters of life and death. Those bonds in turn bred trust and mutual dependability. The need for kinship ties and support became superfluous when your comrade was your keeper and vice-versa. This spirit also prevailed within the movement's secret internal cells in cities and towns under government control, and who operated within the lion's den where trust was paramount.

Now with the war of liberation presumed to have ended on January 9, 2005, some former SPLA comrades in arms have changed so much that camaraderie – defined in the dictionary as friendship, amity, solidarity, companionship, among others - has become a dirty word in some circles. At the other end of the spectrum, some ignoramuses think it is a lofty title or a badge of honour and so they append "comrade" to their names each time they write, to advertise to the world that they once took part in the struggle. They love calling themselves comrades and desire others to call them so. They don't know what they do.

In the ensuing environment, a comrade is longer the trusted colleague of the past one would rely on during times of adversity; camaraderie has been replaced by base instincts and predatory practices: there is little sharing but plenty of greed; backstabbing has effectively replaced mutual support; humility is no longer the badge of the great; arrogance is blatantly on show, as modesty is seen by some people as characteristic of those lowly folk without an easily recognisable name or a past they can be proud of. Only the other day I overheard someone protesting to his counterpart, saying "Please don't call me comrade. I am not a communist. That was the way *the so-called liberators* used to address each other". The italics are mine.

For sure the bonds between former comrades in arms appear to be comatose at the intensive care unit.

'Romancing' Sudan

This title has been lifted from a travel book which was a bestseller in 1990s. I am referring to Justin Wittle's *Romancing Vietnam*.

Though tragic as it was the war in Vietnam had created stereotypes, perceptions and images, out of proportion with reality. The bloody conflict polarised the world into uncompromising camps: America, its allies, the government in Saigon, now Ho Chi Minh City, and their sympathisers in other parts of the world. The opposing side comprised Viet Cong fighters, the government of North Vietnam in Hanoi and their friends, especially in the communist world.

The war in this South East Asian country was virtually on the daily news menu. Since most powerful Western news media such as the Voice of America were covering the fighting, it was not surprising that the reportage was almost one-sided.

Whether the stories were balanced or not, the Vietnamese war produced some of the most memorable images of the last century. Two pictures stand out. One of these is what has come to be known as "The girl in the picture". This once-seen-will-never-be-forgotten photograph portrays a girl between three to four years, fleeing from napalm bombs dropped by the American B52 aircraft. The poor child, understandably in panic, is stark naked, just like when she came out of her mother's womb. In journalism classes, the picture is often used as a masterpiece of photography. The image has acquired a life of its own and its creator is said to have made a fortune out of it.

But what many people do not know about "the girl in the picture", is that the owner of the well-known image is a person of flesh and blood; she is not only alive, but also a respectable professional lady who resides in Canada where she runs an advocacy organisation for worthy causes. When I saw her three years ago giving a talk on TV I was amazed by how fiction and reality co-exist, sometimes in harmony.

Then, there is this picture of a captured Viet Cong fighter with an enemy officer pointing a pistol at the prisoner's head. The photographer was sensible enough not to capture the decisive moment (or if he did, withheld its publication) when the trigger was pulled, but all the same anyone seeing the partially closed eyes of a person on the razor-thin border between life and death, would not fail to be moved. Through photography the deaths we were used to hearing about the massacre in My Lai village where an American officer, Lt William Calley gave orders to his troops to shoot anything that moved...

Young students at the time, we knew of two Vietnams: the real and the other created by our imagination. Justin Wittle went to Vietnam after the war had ended. His first hand findings indicated that exaggeration was the word to describe much of had been written about Vietnam.

Vietnam and Sudan and their peoples do not have many attributes in common, but they share the burden, their identities and problems are defined and named by others. It is not true that all foreign writers and journalists show the Sudanese people and their cultures in poor light. But some, out of ignorance, arrogance, prejudice, or both, continue to poke cruel jokes at or invent absurd caricatures about the people.

Jokes may be innocent and light hearted or bitter and damaging, depending on the motives and occasion. For example, when the British journalist Anthony Mann made fun of the first MPs from the South when he reported that the legislators felt uncomfortable in their newly acquired Western style suits, that could not be taken as an offence although I am neither a fan of the author nor of his book, *Where God Laughed,* which he wrote in 1955 after several visits to Sudan. That were the days the country was preparing to become independent of Britain. Mann was a correspondent for *The Daily Telegraph*. On the other hand, an anthropologist referring to a people as savages should be declared an enemy. Most Western news media have a habit of setting agenda for African problems, especially when they are reporting civil wars. The conflict between the South and the North is about greater autonomy, some news agencies stress with devotion. Many ordinary readers and listeners are not sure whether greater autonomy is regional self-rule, federal or confederal system or outright separation. In their package of negative presentation is noun and adjective "animist" for describing the people. I have written many times that this is an insult as the people are not. But will they listen to facts and change? I doubt.

While the leadership from the South waging war against Khartoum say their practical movement is called SPLM, some media insist, it is not SPLM but SPLA, the military wing. When the SPLA decided in 1987 to create a new ranking system, the SPLM leader, who is an army officer was given the rank of the commander, Cdr, instead of his previous, colonel. Many news media swear the man is a colonel.

Some media have alleged that the man is surrounded by myths and when they are not there, new ones are created. One of the folktales about Garang is that little is known about him. False. As far as I know, he is always ready to meet journalists unless when he is busy or when one of his cronies lies he is busy. And he is not known to refuse to answer any question no matter how rude it may be. I remember him telling a journalist that his pastime was to do mathematical sums. On another occasion he asked: "What is Maradona?" to the question about the Argentine football wizard, Diego Maradona.

The fault is therefore with journalists who want to know about the man while at the same time not bothering to seek interviews. It seems such reporters prefer to read Garang's alleged dark side written by his enemies in books, articles and broadcasts.

If these misrepresentations come from foreign journalists, one could forgive them; African journalists are aping their Western counterparts. Recently a Kenyan paper listed John Garang and Riek Machar together with Somalia's General Morgan Hirsi as warlords. The journalist simply does not understand the definition of "warlord".

In 1994, the London *Sunday Telegraph* published profiles of African warlords. They included Farah Aideed and the rest of his Somali cousins, Jonas Savimbi of Angola, Charles Taylor of Liberia, Fodey Sankoh of Sierra Leone. Garang was not in the list. When in Nairobi I gave John Garang the copy of the paper, the then rebel leader laughed, very pleased.

Two main attributes of a warlord are that the cause of fighting is not national and second, the support base is narrowed to a clan or a district. But who cares when the Western journalists use the English language to project their worldview?

Away from war and politics, there is an aspect of Sudan which has been romanticised: modelling.

At about the close of the last century fashion houses and their publicists informed the world that they had found a gold mine in the person of a young Sudanese girl called Alek Wek. Women magazines including the famous *Elle*, were very generous with praises of the poor Sudanese refugee turned model who has escaped poverty and other forms of deprivation. There was frenzy about her.

In an article, I wrote in the *EastAfrican* weekly, I admitted that Alek was very beautiful by the standards of her Dinka people. However, I pointed out that the secret behind her selection and promotion by fashion industry was that she was different, defying the familiar and the conventional. I concluded that in this commercial environment model seekers would trot the globe to look for enchantresses in faraway places such as Tahiti.

To date Alek-mania and its attendant exaggeration, romanticism and the distortions that go with it, have not waned. In a recent article in a women magazine *True Love* Marriane Macdonald wrote this about Alek Wek "...is bouncing forwards with legs as thin as forearms to perch on the sofa like an animated paperclip".

When discussing with her interviewer about the idea of Dinka giving cattle in marriage, Alek is reported that "she seems totally at home with the idea of a dowry of cows". The girl now modelling in America was born and grew up in Wau, one of the three main towns in Southern Sudan yet it is written of her that "she grew up without electricity or water in the Sudan...".

A detailed description is given. "Her skin is an extraordinary gray-black colour, like charcoal, incredibly fine, her small eyes lively, and her face gorgeously shaped – not round, as people often say, but sculptured over her cheekbones. She has thin, bare, battered – looking hands..."

The people of Southern Sudan will continue to be shown as good, generous, proud and beautiful by outsiders. Others will find careers and means of livelihood to present them and their ways of life as stuff for entertainment. Foreign writers and media workers with an axe to grind with, will perfect the art of distortion. I am prepared to forgive a non-African making us a laughing stock, but not a fellow African. Never, ever.

Sudan Mirror, 2004

Is Complaining becoming our National Pastime?

Nations are sometimes portrayed as behaving like human beings. For example, some countries are described as sports loving, disciplined, xenophobic- hating foreigners- and so forth. South Sudanese pride themselves on being patriotic on the basis that they and their forebears have fought the central government in Khartoum for over half a century. That history of armed resistance is given as proof of South

Sudanese rejection of oppression and subjugation. In other words, they base their patriotism on their readiness to die for their country. The list of their virtues includes readiness to forgive one another even after bloody conflicts; generosity, pride in – and maintaining – their collective cultural or even individual identity.

But there is also a downside to these sources of national pride. Some of their compatriots – and some foreigners too – also come up with objectionable attributes such as the description of South Sudan as a nation whose citizens are lazybones; very rude; bursting with disrespect for time-keeping; disobeying rules of queuing to be served in crowded public places. These days, South Sudanese, especially members of the elite, are being seen as truculent, power-hungry and in the process have earned for themselves an unenviable description as warmongers.

What is not in doubt is that some of these negative characteristics, whether they are applied to South Sudanese or other nations, largely belong to stereotyping: the habit by which one draws a conclusion from a sample or percentage of a whole and used as a label for the rest. Certainly that brand of reasoning does the targeted group an injustice, as it usually distorts reality. Common sense has it that in every case there is an exception to the rule. What does one say about border cases of fringe groups or a minority opinion, or conduct in a society or nation whose beliefs and practices are lumped in a single adjective such as "peace-loving", "primitive" or "irrational", for instance? It is an indisputable fact that there is no group, be it a clique, clan, linguistic or religious, that can claim monopoly of virtue, evil, wisdom or idiocy. Practitioners who apply a monochrome blanket painting of a group of people do not realise that their act tends to alienate and even antagonise potential allies, especially when the image is negative.

The subject of national stereotyping is not peculiar to South Sudanese. For example, *Oxford Dictionary of Proverbs* attributes the following to the French leader, Napoleon Bonaparte: "…sneering spirit described English as a nation of shopkeepers (L'Angleterre est une nation de boutiquier". A visitor to England, in the past or today, would find millions of its citizens engaged in activities other than selling or buying goods or services; English shopkeepers are a tiny minority of the population as is the case with other nations of the world.

Nature and objective of complaints

It is a fact that many people become uncomfortable with someone known to be a habitual complainant. This does not mean there is no room for one to raise an issue that is bothering them or others, if by doing so the grousing person is hoping to get a desired response by way of explanation or practical solutions.

I am not sure that there is anyone who does not complain; even the most powerful and the richest people sometimes do. It is a way of life and a form of defensive mechanism when it is a response to an objective reality: babies cry when they are hungry and wish to draw their mothers' attention to feed or make them comfortable in a hostile environment; when we sit in a room that has become exceptionally warm we ask someone to turn on the air-conditioning system or a fan; we make a request to a hotel manager to reduce the volume of a machine playing loud music and so forth. These are some mild forms of complaining.

When complaints are justified

This category of complaints is justified and can be considered as legitimate. On the other hand, the negative and irritating brand, mostly personal, that goes under the name of grumbling, is undesirable, especially when the person doing it knows nothing can be done to solve the problem raised or when the audience is not to blame for the situation giving rise to the whingeing. For example, a line is crossed when an individual makes it a way of life when at every turn and in any company in a given environment, the person raises strictly personal grievances or criticisms to persons who have no power or means to address the matters raised.

The complainant simply becomes a bore, whose company persons who enjoy spending quality time are likely to avoid when possible. But this judgement is unfair. The case cited here involves a very tiny minority of people one would describe as uncouth and insensitive to the feelings of other people around them. However, there is no person in real life without a problem of their own, private or public. Existence of problems gives rise to complaint of one form or another. What matters is where the issue bothering someone would be taken for an appropriate remedy.

When complaints arise out of the public domain and on serious matters that affect lives of many people or conduct or omissions that tarnish the image of a nation, such expressions of concern are understandable. That concern is actually the job of agencies such as news media, legislative bodies, church, civil society organisations and even governments, to present the problem and propose possible ways out of the fix.

In this sphere I, as a practising journalist, have played – and continue to play – a part in articulating some of the issues that I think should be brought to public attention and addressed accordingly. I have complained and complained about the lax attitudes of our society to the protection of our environment and suggested planting trees as one of the remedies. My war against the destruction of our forests for making charcoal, for example, appears unwinnable. At the moment my efforts seem to be a lonely cause although I know there are thousands of my compatriots who share my views on the state of our ecology and how to keep it wholesome. But I digress. Back to the issue of grousing.

Four years ago, just to cite one example, I wrote an article in the *Citizen* daily in which I protested against the all-pervasive phenomenon of discourtesy in our society, especially from some officials in public places such as government offices. The article appeared under the title of "If rudeness were a commodity we would be the world's biggest exporter." I was not fantasising. People were complaining about this same problem but in private.

A year later, a minister who was one of the senior ministers from the South serving in Khartoum told a gathering of the newly-appointed ministers and deputy ministers during an induction course that one of the complaints foreign envoys in the country used to raise to him and other government functionaries was that "…your officials, especially receptionists and secretaries in government offices [in Juba] are very rude." The minister did not say what would be done to inculcate politeness in some of the people who have a problem with how to handle people, everyone, in a civilised manner. Ditto this writer. Despite the apparent despair, raising the issue is meant to alert the public so that right answers can be found; the intention is not to insult those who lack grace and social skills.

The mass media are among the leading forums through which journalists and other members of the public can channel their observations and suggestions about some of the complaints that require solutions from bodies and institutions such as legislature or government agencies at various levels.

News reports and analyses, comments, letters to the editor and talk-back with the FM radio stations can and do serve as platforms where public concerns can be expressed. But these forums should not be abused for personal objectives and incitement to hatred and violence. Topics range from high cost of living; rising crime rates; unemployment of youth; claims of the illegal influx of foreigners – especially drug traffickers and sex workers – into the country; cases of alleged mistreatment of foreigners living among us. The list is long.

The body that should join the grumbling train is our legislative body. Private members' bills and motions are some of the means available to our lawmakers. However, as I gather, most of their complaints are that most of the pieces of legislation they have passed are not being applied. So they are complaining like the rest of us. Their constituents, including this writer, are complaining against their MPs: for example, where are the laws criminalising hate speech without curtailing freedom of expression; acts of terrorism; drug and human trafficking; child abduction; marriage to underage girls; the care for mentally ill citizens who are now chained in prisons as if they were criminals? And so on and so forth.

We are a society where virtually everyone is complaining, and almost daily, about almost everything in our society. But we are justified: we have just begun as a nation and our expectations are too high. Can anyone blame us for complaining excessively? What is not acceptable is that our complaints should incite people to hate and violence or to resort to unconstitutional means.

Is setting too-high standards the cause of disillusionment?

On the eve of his 75th birthday in 2010, the veteran Nigerian journalist Peter Enahoro stated that he and many of his compatriots had learned one thing: "that you cannot build a nation in one generation." Aware of the fact that his statement would need further explanation, Enahoro added, "We – journalists and people who were critical of the way things were going on – set very, very high standards for ourselves. We had no experience [at independence in 1960] and we thought that almost overnight we could make changes if we wished to. But carrying these people along, changing people's way of thinking; those are the things that take time…let us accept that we don't build a nation in a generation". This statement may attract criticism in that its author appears to accept that progress is preordained and no matter how hard one tries, one would have to wait for 30 years – a generation – to see the fruits of one's labour.

When Enahoro made this statement about his country, Nigeria was half a century old as an independent country and for that he said he was "grossly disappointed that our politics is still without direction".

Well, one should expect Enahoro to have stated, for the sake of optimism, that a beginning – and a good and an encouraging one – has to be made. It would be interesting to know his reaction to the statesman-like decision of the former President Goodluck Jonathan when he gracefully accepted the people's verdict in favour of his competitor General Buhari; an act that probably saved Nigeria from potential civil upheavals arising out of disputed election results, as has been seen in several African countries in recent years. There was a latent fear as some stalwarts within the former president's camp were making noises telling the news media that Jonathan had won, contrary to the reality on the ground. That Mr Jonathan did not heed some of his myopic lieutenants who were prepared to rig the results was an act of wisdom and patriotism. I believe Peter Enahoro's opinion on that stand by the former Nigerian president would have been of compliment, not barbs.

SPLM Groping for Bureaucratic and Administrative Formula

When the SPLM and its military wing SPLA were formed in 1983, the movement's manifesto, now withdrawn, stated the objective was creation of a united socialist Sudan. The declaration generated mixed reactions throughout the country. In the North, there were sighs of relief that this new Southern insurgency was not bent on tearing the country apart. The Left was also divided over whether to cooperate or even join the Southern-based organisation. Although the Sudan Communist Party maintained sporadic contacts with the SPLM leadership, most of its members privately expressed their reservations about the ability of Southern Sudanese to lead a progressive armed liberation movement.

The sectarian groups and the Muslim Brotherhood saw the emergence of a non-Arab and non-Islamic force as a threat to their interests. Papers affiliated to the National Islamic Front, NIF, openly denounced the SPLM as an atheistic organisation.

After the fall of Nimeiri in early 1985, forces that had participated actively in the regime change began to call themselves new forces. Those were mostly intellectuals and fringe groups who had rejected both sectarian politics and ideologies of Islamic fundamentalism and Communism. The Nuba leadership, along with some educated members of Southern Blue Nile saw the SPLM as their natural party as it supported the unity of the country, predicated on righting the wrongs the system of rule had committed against marginalised areas, as they would be known.

These groupings together with the SPLM delegation met in Ethiopia. Although the Ummah Party and Union of Sudan African Parties, USAP, attended, the "progressives" called the shots. According to the Koka Dam Declaration, the war had little to do with the Southern Question, but was a Sudan problem that could be addressed in a national constitutional conference in which all Sudanese political forces would participate.

The profile of the SPLM and its leader, John Garang, had been promoted from regional to national stature. People who mattered in public life paid him homage at his headquarters.

The notion of unity was however very unpopular among Southern Sudanese, including those within the movement. But, since there was no appropriate forum to discuss the issue, opposition continued to be only private opinion, a fact that partly led to the implosion. The split in August 1991 caused great suffering for the people, especially in Upper Nile where the conflict took an ethnic dimension, and considerably reversed military and diplomatic gains the rebels had made since 1983.

Unity versus secession

The issue of whether Sudan should remain as it is today or split into two or more entities is so controversial and emotional that there is barely any room for a third opinion or party: it is either "you are with us or not with us"; with almost nothing in between. What is also absent in the two opposing camps is that proponents and discussants have never tried to assess and come up with positive contributions made by both sides of the divide.

It would appear, then, that both the separatists and the advocates of unity among Southern leaders have contributed actively to the acceptance of civil war as a national crisis that should be resolved through the participation of regional and international mediation and cooperation.

This exactly is where we are now.

Despite the disastrous consequences, including attendant ethnic carnage and the movement's loss of much of the territory previously controlled by SPLA, the Nasir coup directly and indirectly forced the SPLM to endorse, although reluctantly, the lukewarm reforms it undertook from 1991, and the call for self-determination.

Garang may feel vindicated that his erstwhile antagonists, in particular Dr Riak Machar and Dr Lam Akol, have returned to the organisation they left more than a decade ago.

But as Southern Sudanese appear to be uniting, his Northern allies both in the moment and in opposition as National Democratic Alliance, NDA, are crying foul that their ally has betrayed them after signing the Machakos Protocol – whose declaration of principles or DOP, has affirmed the right to self-determination, and the security arrangements.

The Northern opposition smells a rat in these developments and some of their members have openly expressed that they have been conned by their ally, the SPLM, to the extent that a Northern confidante of Garang is not only furious about the agreements but he is also calling Southern Sudanese abusive names. How the SPLM leader, the juggler and survivor, will handle this development remains to be seen. However, the next three to five weeks will witness North/South relations being redefined either for the good of the country or a return to the chronic mutual distrust between the two regions.

Administration

Southern Sudan may be one country geographically, but politically and administratively, it is a territory where various actors operate diametrically opposed systems with their matching nomenclatures. In fact, each system's purpose is to wipe out opponents rather than serving the people. The main rivals are the Government of Sudan, the Sudan People Liberation Movement, SPLM, and various armed groups. Since the administrative units and their names remained unchanged, Riek Machar's defunct organisations, South Sudan Independence Movement, SSIM, and South Sudan People Democratic Front, SSPDF, remain part of the subject in discussions regarding structures.

To understand the reasons beyond SPLM's emphasis and even the breakaway factions with military approach to politics, administration and so forth, one has to refer to history. The SPLA – the military wing – was formed as a reaction to Khartoum's refusal to enter into a sincere dialogue for a political solution to the grievances articulated by leaders from the South.

Before the emergence of the movement in 1983, many Southern politicians were arrested and detained after expressing views contrary to the government policies. Southern Sudanese who embraced the new movement were absolutely delighted to learn they now had an army which could give Nimeiri a bloody nose. This was popular with the civilians, some of who had just left prisons in Khartoum and Juba. Ironically, the Military High Command which had executive and judicial powers had no single civilian member.

Despite the fact that John Garang, the leader held a doctorate degree, anti-intellectual sentiments were widespread within the movement. Former bureaucrats in Juba and professionals were held in open contempt. Persons with experience in public life or had received higher education were classed as bourgeois, a class unfortunately held to be responsible for corruption and ruining the country. It was a false charge.

Some senior officers had been convinced that putting up structures such as the SPLM secretariat, political bureau or national executive council, would be to repeat Anya Nya mistakes which had "ministers" without actual ministries to run. This thinking was transferred down to recruits, most of them peasants and young students. In the training camps, soldiers in the making were told that formal education was not everything when it came to running a state. "An egalitarian society was one in which class differences should not bar a revolutionary from aspiring to senior office in the state", was a common utterance. This made sense, since the majority of recruits were either former high school students or peasants drawn from cattle camps, all who were unable to write or read. In the long run, this propaganda became an unwritten policy of the movement, which was stringently resistant to anything that resembled the discredited system of governance in Khartoum and Juba. The void had to be filled with a new apparatus. To this day, the system never emerged or, when what was conceived to be the desired substitute was put in place, never worked.

Until quite recently, some officers genuinely believed they would be ministers, permanent secretaries, and heads of parastatals. Such officers were disappointed and felt deceived by their leaders when, after the convention, the national executive council was composed mainly of civilians, mostly university graduates. And some of those personalities had just formally joined the movement on their return from Egypt, Khartoum or other government-controlled towns in the South. Because of these developments, there was – and still is – resistance to the implementation of resolutions of the 1993 Chukudum convention: the establishment of civil service, the police force and the empowerment of the SPLM and enabling it to supervise the management of the movement including the SPLA itself.

The holding of the first convention and its resolutions raised hope in many that the much-awaited reforms were on the way. The announcement of the formation of executive and legislative organisations, the National Executive Council body and National Liberation Council, was welcomed as they were perceived as opening the way for greater popular participation. This created the belief that the NLC would watch over the executive and pass laws for governing the people under the areas controlled by the movement. But the leadership had different ideas; the two bodies hardly ever held meetings. This meant that making and presenting progress reports, general supervision and the questioning of office-holders – along with any follow up – became impossible.

Instead of defining and strengthening the roles of these organs as the nucleus of institutional building, what has characterised the process is constant and sometime unjustified change of names and functions of organs of governance and those managing them. There is now the Leadership Council, which has effectively usurped the role and functions of the NLC; departments headed by secretaries have been renamed commissions and lumped- three to four- with a super commissioner at the top, along with virtually all members of the defunct "Politico" Military High Command as the supervisors of the commissions.

Sometimes, when one looks at the setup, one is tempted to think that the SPLM leadership is allergic to the conventional way governments or liberation movements are formed and how they function. Various roles within the movement are not delineated. For instance, several years ago the man in charge of police (a civil servant) was at the same time a secretary- minister and therefore political- in the office of the SPLM Chairman. There is also this appointment of a "Director General" of the National Liberation Council. The council was the rebels' legislature. The officer, whose title should have been that of a clerk- one in charge of administration of the law making body is the conventional title- had no single member of the staff besides him. By definition, a director general is the most senior director with more than two directors; a super director, so to speak. The policy makers responsible for these creations should use the military system as a guide: a commander in chief is the most senior commander who has many commanders under him or her.

In 1991 following the split within the movement, committees to organise civil service were set up. That included the police, administration, prison service, wildlife, information and others. the committees headed by senior civil servants did a job which, had their reports been endorsed and used as a blue print for running public administration, the bureaucracy would now be an effective, efficient and credible, civil service. (The writer was head of information committee). Apart from the proposals to be used for the creation of departments and units, every report emphasised identifying and recruitment of middle ranking personnel and training. Those reports have been conveniently shelved.

Sudan Mirror, November 2003.

The Civil Service Delivery Fiasco

During the days when the sun never set on the British Empire, the Sudan received the best colonial administrators. These were members of what was called Political Service. The system these men set up and ran in Sudan had no equal in the rest of the countries that Britain ruled in Africa or other parts of the world in the first six decades of the 20th century.

Of these officials who managed provinces and districts, many were army officers and graduates from Oxford and Cambridge universities. And whether the administrators were former soldiers or civilians they were men of robust physical strength and had the personality to cope with the harsh climate of Sudan: heat, humidity, mosquitoes, seasonal *haboob* or sandstorms and impassable roads during *kharif*, the rainy seasons.

The administrative structures were so clear-cut and the ladder so easy that a pupil in year two could understand the system. The country was divided into nine provinces, three of which were in the South. A province was made up of several districts and its top administrator was the governor. A district was sometimes divided into sub-districts. A District Commissioner who was assisted by someone (usually an Egyptian or Sudanese) who was in charge of the area, where he worked closely with traditional chiefs as a direct link with the rural populations. At the bottom of the hierarchy were court centres where the Sudanese exercised power in the so-called Native Administration. The most senior chief was the paramount chief or *nazir*, who wielded enormous power in their areas. One is writing this not out of nostalgia; but to suggest to those who want to invent the civil administration wheel that the structures are there only waiting for adjustment and modernisation to meet the needs of a changed world.

But while people have to embrace change for the better, the Sudanese politicians, especially the elite introduce change for change's sake and that sometimes destroys what time has proved to be working or durable. Let us look at the mess the Government of Sudan and Southern rebel groups have made of structures, units, territorial boundaries and how the units are run.

Version of the Government of Sudan

The government objectives can be understood within the context of el *Tawhaju el Hadhari*, which roughly translates into civilisational orientation, authored by the likes of Hassan el Turabi. Put in simple language the programme is about converting the whole world into Islam and its ways of life. And since charity begins at home, this orientation makes Sudan the launching pad. New structures were created as tools for the project and for accommodating loyalists and converts among Southern Sudanese. The former regions and provinces had to be fragmented and renamed *wilayat* or states in an attempt to give the ordinary people the impression that the system was truly federal. Now there are 26 states of which 10 are in the South. Then there is the "federal" government. The head of state government is a *wali*, a fitting Islamic title, not governor; the wali has a council of ministers, about five in number, who run mainly service oriented departments such as health, education, agriculture, finance and human resources.

Next in the hierarchy after the state is *mahaliya*, or province, whose administrator is known as el *ma'tamad* or superintendent. Beneath the province is *belidiya* or an equivalent of a district with a chairman at its head. This rung in the system is *el qura wa el mudun*, namely villages and towns. *El Lijaan esh'abiya*, or popular committees, mind the affairs of villages and towns. They are managed by chairmen.

Contrary to propaganda, it is a centralised system in which, for example, revenues collected by any of these units flow upwards and end in Khartoum (income from water and electricity is remitted to the "federal" treasury). The paradox in the splitting of the administrative structure means the system has created levels of government so physically small and with so little or no financial base, Khartoum has brought a genie out of the bottle: no one can amalgamate these bodies in the future without inviting the fury of the people who have enjoyed the fruits of "decentralisation".

The SPLM/A system

"Change" was the SPLM/A's catchword from its inception in 1983. Its main objectives were to change the "minority clique" and "one man, no system"- in the language of the manifesto- of rule in Khartoum and change the way the South had been administered, even by Southern Sudanese themselves.

Perhaps the most difficult task the SPLM/A leadership had set themselves was to change people's thinking. All these forms of political, social, ideological and psychological transformation were summed up in the vague slogan "Our objective is to create a New Sudan" whose posters used to greet anyone entering towns controlled by the movement in the second half of the 1980s and early 1990s. The SPLM/A leadership, most of whose members had belonged to Anya Nya, disagreed with the policies and approaches of the first Southern guerrillas of modern times. Former students and civil servants were all given military training and most of them deployed at the war fronts. For the first six years, formal education was completely non-existent and any talk about when schools would be reopened in the liberated areas or in refugee camps, was openly discouraged.

With a huge army at their command, the zonal commanders – who also were members of Military High Command – were able to make their presence felt in the rural South and later in the former government garrison towns. The territory was carved up into military zones, some following the old provincial/regional boundaries, as was the case in Bahr el Ghazal, while other zones could be part of a region in the case of Western Upper. In others, a zone could encompass two parts of two provinces: Central Southern Sudan comprised of northern Equatoria and the whole of Jonglei Province. District borders remained unchanged. Zonal commanders were in charge of the conduct of war as well as civil administration and administration of justice. They were assisted in the management of districts by what they called civil military administrators. These men, most of them young officers lacking skills and experience were, in all but name, military rulers who never hesitated to humiliate the local chiefs, whose power was greatly reduced. SPLA soldiers never appeared in customary courts even in civil suits such as torts or adultery. They considered customary court presiding over by a chief as beneath their status.

On the other hand, civilians, who were always referred as *muataniin* (ironically meaning citizens or nationals), were subjected to courts-martial as well as customary courts.

While discontent was present, few dared to complain, at least in public. Perhaps it was this militarisation of civil administration and other wrongdoings by the SPLA, which was exploited by the leaders of the 1991 split.

That split, although the forces of breakaway factions committed terrible atrocities and were no better in creating democratic, accountable, better working institutions, forced the SPLM/A to mend its ways to some extent.

Soldiers were gradually – albeit reluctantly – edged out of civil administration by these changes. The policy was later crowned when the First National Convention was held, paving the way for the current climate, which permits very limited criticisms – during meetings such as the officers' conference in 1994 – of the leadership and their performance.

Current structures

The highest policy making body is the Leadership Council, a recent creation. Even to non-constitution experts, many observers dismiss the Council as an illegal structure since there is no provision for it in the resolutions of the National Convention of 1993. Furthermore, the Leadership Council is not truly representative in that its membership is weighted heavily in favour of Upper Nile and Bahr el Ghazal regions at the expense of Funj, Nuba Mountains and Equatoria. The next most important executive branch are the commissions, which are the equivalent of ministries, but, unlike the conventional cabinet, chairmen supervise the commissioners. Many commissioners do not have permanent secretaries or directors, which means the commissioners run the day-to-day administration, including financial matters. The legislative body is the National Liberation Council. The legislative rarely meets to check or question the executive.

The areas under the SPLM administration consist of Bahr el Ghazal, Equatoria, Upper Nile, Nuba Mountains and Funj. The SPLM Secretary, formerly the governor whose cabinet is made up of only three officials, administers a region: Front Commander, Deputy for Political Affairs and Deputy for Administration. Except for the SPLM Secretary for Equatoria, those for Bahr el Ghazal, Nuba Mountains and Funj are perpetually absent from their regions since they are members of the SPLM delegation to the peace talks with the Khartoum Government. The SPLM Secretary for Upper Nile runs the region from Yei town in Equatoria, not far from the border with Uganda and Congo.

A region is divided into counties or districts or provinces, and the head of a county administration is a commissioner. Most of the counties suffer from lack of trained human resources. A county is divided into *Payams*, and a Payam is subdivided into Bomas. For those who are not familiar with

SPLM's newspeak, "payam" is a combination of "Pa" and "Yams". *"Pa"* is a common prefix in Acholi, Anyuak, Shilluk and Dinka languages. It means "the home of". Yams is said to have been the ancient name of Sudan. Perhaps.

Several new counties have come into being, some out of necessity and others by request of the inhabitants or both. Budi- an acronym from Buya and Didinga respectively- was carved out of Kapoeta county in order to accommodate the two communities who have been having troubled relations with their neighbours the Toposa, especially over cattle rustling. The creation of Turalei out of Gogrial, Northern Bor and the subsequent birth of Duk from greater Bor may be justified, but the leadership is unfair to those people who have not complained. The solution should be the formation of a committee with members from the five regions. Its terms of reference should include the following:

The size of the population of the original districts (counties).

Available human and natural resources and physical infrastructure.

Ethnic, if any, composition of the county.

Criteria for creation of new countries (that is, how many from the old?)

These points would enable the committee to create sound recommendations that, when implemented, would protect the leadership from blame, especially accusations of favouritism.

The civil administration and the administration of justice are being crippled by the lumping of departments into an entity called Law Enforcement Commission. The constituents are Administration, Legal Affairs, Judiciary, Police and Prison Service. While civil administration, police and prisons can operate under one umbrella, judiciary and legal affairs should exist separately (although not necessarily independently), especially at this time when there is a shortage of lawyers, particularly judges.

Sudan Mirror, April 2005.

All Patriots? Count Me Out

Since the subject, patriotism, is a heavily loaded word, I request readers to suspend passing judgement until they have reached the end of the article.

They say patriotism is the love of one's country or, more accurately, the unwavering love of fatherland or motherland, depending which word one prefers. A citizen in this kind of relationship is called a patriot. The patriot is prepared to do everything, including sacrificing their life in the interest of homeland and fellow citizens, also known as compatriots.

This is true of many ordinary people and a tiny number of politicians. However, most members of political elites, in government or opposition, white, black or brown, in developed or poor countries, tell lies when they claim they love their countries more than their lives or their wives. Pray, is a politician a patriot when he embezzles public property? Or when he incites racial or religious hatred? Or when he orders a war of genocide?

Such public figures display their version of patriotism with symbols, slogans and rhetoric, not always by positive action or sincere thoughts about the welfare of all the citizens.

I always have problems controlling laughter when I see people outdoing one another to prove that one is more committed to a national cause than others.

Today one of very lucrative businesses is the sale of SPLM badges (flag). One badge goes for 500 Kenyan shillings. I am yet to learn about the beneficiaries of the proceeds.

The badge gained currency and popularity during the Machakos round of peace talks.

The SPLM delegates and their advisers were given the badges to distinguish them from their adversaries, the delegates from the Government of Sudan. And ever since, they have been sported daily and are now inseparable articles of wear.

The rest of the members have joined the bandwagon; there was a scramble among nearly all the movement's members to get this item, which has almost become sacred; those who have not yet obtained, feel they are missing out. For its part, the government delegates did not want to be outdone by fellows who do not have a seat at the UN.

On formal occasions, government representatives dress in *jalabiya* with a matching turban. And whether you are a Christian, Muslim or atheist, as an ambassador you have to present your credentials while in that kind of national dress.

As for the flag, the Government of Sudan does not need to advertise it: it flies over one of the buildings in Nairobi.

Now a switch from jesting to more weighty matters.

Flags, anthems, religious symbols – the cross for Christians and the green crescent for Muslims, for example – mean far more than the words or items we see or hear. These objects and statements symbolise what is noble, spiritual and holy to their adherents. They represent unity, fraternity, and identity, solidarity (such as the hammer and sickle for Marxist-Leninists) pride, sovereignty and the common good based on political, ideological or creed values.

Over the years such symbols have been used to rally people to action especially in defence of what a symbol represented, or to wage war of aggression; to spread a faith or build or maintain an empire.

After the September 11, 2001 attack on America by members of Al Qaeda, the American administration appealed to the citizens to unite against the threats from Muslim terror groups. To President George W. Bush, the world is made up of evil people and freedom-loving people respectively. American values consist of freedom, democracy and respect for human rights, said the president.

And what symbolises these values? The stars and stripes. From that date, American officials, beginning with the chief executive and the members of his cabinet have been wearing the flag of the United States of America. Americans know very well how foreign groups opposed to American policies insult their country. It goes like this: a demonstration is organised amid cries of "Down with America", "Go home Yankees", or "Death to great Satan". A rowdy mob publicly burning the American flag usually marks the climax of an angry protest. We have seen this on TV many times.

To citizens who are not amused by such behaviours, the flags and anthems of both the Government of Sudan and those of the SPLM mean nothing to them. Let me explain:

Sudan may not be a failed state but since "independence", the country has been almost dysfunctional. Some reasons are that the system of rule has oscillated between Northern coalition governments and repressive military regimes, both exclusivists and that policy has been responsible for armed conflicts in the country over the years.

The governments in Khartoum, civilian or military, have used the civil war as an excuse for targeting and killing civilians. Apart from the military regimes, the government led by the Ummah Party have been very bloody. Examples to justify this point are given below.

In 1965, the government of Prime Minister Mohammed Mahjoub declared war on the South and its people. The result was the massacre of about a thousand innocent civilians in Juba town in a single night. The killers were government soldiers. Victims' crime? Being members of the Southern educated class. In the same year, over sixty wedding guests were killed in Wau. The perpetrators on this occasion were also security personnel. Again, in 1965, the government army wiped off the surface of the earth the village of Warajwok, a few kilometres south of Malakal. In early 1967, Prime Minister Sadiq al Mahdi ordered the execution of 24 elderly Dinka chiefs in Bor District. The list of crimes committed by Khartoum against Southern Sudanese is virtually inexhaustible.

Can one be proud of a state or leadership which kills its own citizens? Most Southern Sudanese have contributed to this mess; through docility or fighting among themselves, they encourage the Northern ruling class to continue to dominate the Sudanese state.

Many Southern Sudanese tend to blame the abrogation of the Addis Ababa Agreement on ex-dictator Nimeiri, and the Northern opposition. And yes, to some extent they had a hand in the end of the peace accord, but there are two indisputable facts which some Southern politicians try to suppress.

They cannot cheat recent history because many eyewitnesses such as this writer are still alive.

First, the politicians affiliated to the group that was known as the [Abel] Alier camp wanted to topple General Joseph Lagu, the head of the Southern government. When they failed in parliament to achieve that – which would have been legitimate and democratic – they flew to Khartoum and begged the President of the Republic to dismiss the regional chief executive, contrary to the provisions of the Addis Ababa Agreement. Naturally Khartoum was pleased and accordingly obliged. Those individuals had sold to Khartoum the rights of the South. The Addis Ababa Agreement vested that right – to remove the President of the High Executive Council – in the People's Regional Assembly, not in the President of the Republic.

Following the unconstitutional dismissal, a – rightly – furious Lagu went to Khartoum to retaliate. The project was code-named "further decentralisation". The agenda was being economical with the truth: put crudely, it was a move to kick the Dinka out of Juba in particular and Equatoria in general. In an interview with *The Middle East* magazine (April 1982 edition) Mr Lagu said the only common thing between the people of Equatoria and the Dinka was the dark skin.

What was essentially a power struggle assumed ethnic form, pregnant with violence and potential bloodshed. That power struggle has since reinforced – and contributed to – mutual hatred built on stereotypes, across ethnic divides.

Interestingly, many members of Alier and Lagu's respective groups are today masquerading as advocates of the unity of the Southern people. They are lying: they are hardened tribalists with a parochial agenda.

The formation of SPLM/A in 1983 to change the repressive system of rule and to correct the mistakes made by the Southern politicians, was a welcome development to me and that was the reason I joined the rebel movement. My assumption was – and still is – that any organisation dedicated to bringing about change for the better, must be exemplary; faithful in translating its objectives into concrete action. To me the SPLM/A has fallen short of my expectation. I will give a few examples.

It is a fact that the SPLM has been dormant. I want an SPLM model of the South African ANC, The African National Congress, which fought a spirited diplomatic and media war and won international recognition and moral support for their just cause.

I should not be understood to mean that the role of the SPLA is not important. In fact, given the nature of the Sudan's conflict, resort to armed struggle is crucial. It was the last and viable option. My point is that there is no contradiction in having a strong army and strong political machinery, as they complement and supplement one another. Because of the mere absence of a strong and active SPLM, some vices have crept in. This includes a wanton corruption among some senior office holders.

Third, I have found, to my utter dismay, that while many members of the movement joined to sacrifice, it is a fact that some people came to improve their lot, namely, power and wealth. I believe a revolutionary must fight for others, especially the disadvantaged.

Both the SPLM and the National Islamic Front regime, have debased the concept of public office. The two systems have a propensity for appointing to senior positions some persons who would not qualify even as headmen.

This celebration of incompetence and mediocrity is responsible for the poor performance we witness in public institutions. There is little respect now for some ministers and directors as they do not measure up to the role expected of them.

On the other hand, my disappointment with some of the policies and omissions of the SPLM does not mean I have reserved nice words for the government in Khartoum. What is there to admire in a regime that contradicts its slogans, *el ingaz* (salvation or rescue)?

Since it took power in 1989, the NIF-led regime has consistently denied people freedom of expression including the press (the *Al Ayyam* and *Khartoum Monitor* dailies were recently closed down by a government order).

Before the announcement of cessation of hostilities more than a year ago, Khartoum was in the habit of aerial-bombing civilians, schools, hospitals and relief centres, using high-flying Soviet-made Antonov aircraft. Many people have died as a result of those air raids, as well as leaving civilian populations in the territories under the SPLM/A administration perpetually scared for their lives.

Then there is that policy of conversion to Islam. Only imbeciles would be convinced that Southern Sudanese Christians woke up one morning after the NIF's coup to find Islam had become attractive more than before. In reality, many of these conversions are not genuine; they happen because of inducement: money and senior government positions, or both.

It is the right of anyone to change or not to change their faith. What is objectionable about these "conversions", however, is the method used. There have been cases involving disputes between the authorities and relatives of dead people. Since most of these changes in religion are secret, relatives of a dead person would claim the body for a Christian burial. On the other hand, the authorities acting on behalf of the Islamist regime, insisted to have the deceased was a Muslim and must be buried in an Islamic fashion. This is not only humiliating, it subjects the relatives of the dead to additional stress and embarrassment, as was the case with late Henry Jada, the former governor of the state of Bahr el Jebel in greater Equatoria who was believed to have secretly changed his faith to be Muslim.

Furthermore, induced conversions can break up families. For the head of a household who has changed his faith would like to have his children and wife become Muslims. It is probable that those who disagree will leave the family. This is not an assumption; cases of this nature have happened; one does not need to reveal names here.

With this dismal record by Sudanese politicians and their organisations, is there anything to make one proud of being a Sudanese? I know all the ordinary Sudanese are great: generous, hospitable, kind and quick to forgive, but it is an indisputable fact that most of their leaders are people to be ashamed of.

■

This piece was published in the *Sudan Mirror* weekly newspaper, a few weeks before the signing of the Comprehensive Peace Agreement, CPA, in Nairobi, 2005. After reading the piece, late Dr Samson L. Kwaje, a friend and then SPLM/A spokesman approached me with "What has provoked you to write this?" He didn't conceal his anger. I just smiled and gave him no answer. Kwaje was previously my boss from 1997-2000 when he was executive director of Horn of Africa Centre for Development and Democracy, Hacdad, an NGO affiliated to the SPLM/A. Hacdad published a monthly magazine, the *Horn of Africa* of which I was its editor.

Of corrupt governments and persons

It is easy for many people to recognise cases of corruption and persons behind malpractices, illegal acts and omissions. In some areas, corruption can be prevalent. Malpractice or abuse of office by public officials is easy to detect. For example, if a head of government department employs an unqualified relative instead of another competent citizen, and particularly when the vacancy was not advertised before the appointment was made, has committed a type of corruption called nepotism.

Since men and women run governments and states, these bodies sometimes engage in corrupt activities. There is no attempt here to provide an exhaustive definition of corruption. In a few cases what is considered as corruption in a given culture can be an acceptable behaviour in another. For example, in some African communities, it is perfectly proper and even expected, for people to present chiefs with material gifts such as money or goats in addition to feasting. In other parts of the world such presents can be categorised as a form of bribery and therefore corruption.

This piece will be looking at two forms of corruption carried out by governments and public servants. The case of thieving governments is the first part while the second and final section will deal with "the type of persons likely to be corrupt".

The line separating the behaviour and actions of a government or a state from its officers is thin. But if a cabinet, through the orders of a prime minister or executive president, enters into an irregular deal or unlawful payment of taxpayers' money, there is no doubt, the guilty party is the government in its collective responsibility.

First, there is the question: why do governments break the law in pursuit of corrupt acts?

Incidences of corruption among governments in the Western world are relatively low because the system of checks and balances makes it rather difficult for individuals to break the law and get away with it. On the other hand, weak institutions such as legislatures, permit office holders to abuse their positions. Pursuit and maintenance of power is another area in which corruption take place; again with weak and opaque systems of governance being more vulnerable to abuse than their stronger and more transparent counterparts.

While cases of corruption by the government of the day in Sudan will be cited in passing, it is better to begin abroad where cases of corruption have been substantially documented in newspapers, articles and books by investigative writers.

In 1982, the Nigerian government of Shehu Shagari decided to buy advanced and expensive military aircraft from Britain. Some senior ministers in the government of the conservative Prime Minister Margaret Thatcher argued that Nigeria did not need the warplanes, as the West African country faced no military threat from anywhere.

But what counted most was not morality or logic, but mutual interests. The Nigerian ruling party, which had mooted the idea in the first place, was going to compete in an election that year. The money they expected from commissions (which would amount to more than £30 million pounds was going to finance their election campaign, in addition to lining the pockets of senior government ministers in Nigeria. In this case the thief was the Nigerian government, plotting to steal people's money that they were supposed to protect.

A sensational revelation of a government being involved in vice came from a North American aircraft manufacturing company.

In the 1970s American aircraft manufacturer Lockheed Aircraft Corporation had set aside some money for bribing Japanese officials so that they could approve purchase of its passenger jets to All Nippon Airways. Investigation by the American lawmakers exposed the scandal which shook the government of Japan including the arrest and resignation of Japanese Prime Minister, Kakuei Tanaka and some of his senior ministers. In the US two of the senior managers at the aircraft manufacturing company committed suicide when they were being investigated for their role in the bribe scandal.

Sudan's various governments that have come and gone have been involved, in one way or another, in corrupt practices. Usually, cases of corruption became public because a successor regime wanted to expose its predecessor. This is exactly what happened in 1969. After the overthrow of the government of the civilian administration by the military in that year, the new regime headed by Jaafar Nimeiri arrested and tried former ministers of the ousted government.

During a televised trial, a former minister who was answering corruption charges admitted having paid out public money to a political organisation run by Southern Sudanese. The accused ex-minister justified his action by arguing that the money was used to soften the stand of what he called that body's hostility to what was Arab and Islamic. To him that was not corruption: he was serving the nation; he was being patriotic.

Ironically the May regime, which took power in the name of fighting corruption among other things, became very corrupt years later. Mansour Khaled's book, *The Revolution of Dis-May* records some cases under the rule of Jaafar Nimeiri.

Khaled, who was once minister in Nimeiri's government, reveals that a deal was struck by a minister whose docket was special affairs – a portfolio whose function was dubious as it raised numerous questions – with a foreign tobacco company. According to the terms of the agreement, the tobacco firm demanded a ban on rival companies to produce or import their products into Sudan. The president then endorsed the demand, granting monopoly to that multinational. However, during a cabinet meeting, so the story goes, Nimeiri, after seeing one of his ministers smoking one of the "prohibited" brands, flew into a rage and ordered the "offending" colleague to drop and crush the cigarette, which he sheepishly did. Both the president and the minister for special affairs had received bribes to enforce the deal.

Another story concerned purchase of heavy duty military trucks form Germany. The individual, who had the full backing of the head of state, went against tendering regulations and ordered hundreds of trucks, which had not been custom built for Sudan's environment. The departments of defence, finance and foreign trade were not represented. What mattered was not the suitability of the vehicles; the purchase had to be made so that the two would be able to reap hefty sums from commissions.

After the overthrow of Nimeiri a couple of years later, it was made public that a minister who specialised in bribes and commission taking had become so rich that he was said to have bought a new light aircraft as a graduation present for his daughter.

Although frequency and the amount of money involved in corruption cases by the regional government of Southern Sudan were not at the same scale of the abuses committed by the central government, the authorities in Juba were not clean nonetheless.

As the elections to the second People's Regional Assembly were approaching in 1977, the government in Juba decided to get some money for buying saloon cars for senior and middle-ranking civil servants. The arrangement, which was called hire purchase, turned out as either a gift or a bribe, depending on the way one viewed it. According to the regulations the recipients were going to pay a certain amount for many years, until the payment was completed. The owner was prohibited to sell the car before the debt was cleared. On top of that the officials who had received the cars were going to receive over 50 Sudanese pounds monthly mileage allowance, a huge amount at the time. The ministry of finance never deducted the instalments. Most of the beneficiaries, also in possession of government vehicles, began to sell their "private" cars during the second year of purchase. And the owners continued to receive their mileage allowance after the cars had exchanged hands. What appeared as the government's generosity was nothing but a cloaked bribe to the members of the ruling elite to influence them to vote for the incumbent administration.

The army who were not part of civil service stepped in with demands that senior officers should benefit from the free things. When their request was initially rejected, on the grounds that the army was not part of civil service, the army officers instructed the drivers of heavy trucks to make the city's roads unsafe for drivers of the hire-purchase cars. This intimidating tactic worked: those in charge of the programme in the ministry of finance pleaded with the authorities to allow the army get their "quota" of the hire-purchase cars.

Persons likely to be corrupt

There is no intention here to engage in gross and baseless generalisation when discussing traits, behaviour, conduct and other personal factors of individuals likely to be corrupt. To emphasise that the purpose of this article is *not* to insult innocent and honest people who form the majority in any society, I have included this story.

In a recent news story appearing in a Kenyan newspaper, a member of an airline cabin crew found a jacket forgotten by its owner. There was 5,000 US dollars in one of the pockets. The man, whose pay is modest, declared that big find, the owner was traced and the money returned – about 400, 000

Kenyan shillings – a big amount by many standards. The moral of this story is that because a person is poor, it does not necessarily follow that he or she will steal or be involved in other criminal activities to get a livelihood.

Having said that, there are documented examples to suggest that a handful of persons who happened to acquire absolute political power used their positions to steal with impunity from the public. Most writers on the Marcoses of the Philippines and the Ceausescus of Romania agree that the thieving first families grew up in poverty.

The behaviour of this small – but very dangerous – category is best understood through psychology: Despite being surrounded by wealth, they still feel insecure, and they want to prove to the rest of the world that they have made it in the face of all odds; want to see others suffer as a way of punishing society for being unjust – in their distorted worldview – to their parents who lived in poverty throughout their lives.

These kinds of people tend to be insensitive to the plight of others, cruel, envious and jealous; some of them are known to openly enjoy the suffering of others. Whether originally born into poverty or wealth, the kind of people who love to amass wealth for its own sake, not utility, are victims of what is called cupidity, the desire for acquiring wealth and more wealth as if it is a hobby. Available riches cannot quench their desire for greater wealth. And the means used are invariably not fair or honest.

In communities where cattle are an important form of wealth and in which polygamy is practised and seen as a form of investment – more children especially girls mean more cattle – some of the members who believe in these values would be prepared to resort to any means, including dishonest ones, to achieve their objectives. If a crooked person from such a background were to have access to public coffers, they would not hesitate to empty them of money for buying cattle, the main currency in bride price of an additional wife. Again, it is not true that all polygamists are prone to steal to buy cattle for marrying more wives.

The last example comes in the form of a hypothetical character described in these lines.

He loves to show off and to impress everyone around. As a dandy, he prefers to wear the latest and most expensive suits and shoes, especially the imported ones. While the use of wrist watches is in deep decline, our friend would go for a costly Rolex instead of chief Casio sold in the streets by hawkers; a mobile telephone handset costing about 30 US dollars would do, but his preference is for the one that cost multiple times those inexpensive gadgets and items. The rationale is not difficult to find: to be different from the "common spirits". He avoids and despises a car that many people would drive; his car of choice is the one he believes few can afford to buy although he knows its spare parts are not locally available.

Some of the people belonging to this class tend to be persons trying to cover up some shortcomings such as low self-esteem, academic achievements – or lack of them.

The people of Southern Sudan could be forgiven if they are found praying that the future government will not accommodate one or two elements exhibiting – or with a potential for – the foibles just described.

Sudan Mirror, April 2004

Criteria for Selection for Public Office Holders

Recently some of my Sudanese colleagues were racking their brains as they tried to write and produce a document of a semi-legal nature.

Present at the meeting was a Kenyan friend who reminded the professionals – most of them learned people enjoying vast experience and exposure to modern ideas – that what they were doing was essentially reinventing the wheel. Such a document, he said, could be obtained in Nairobi and all that would be required was to adapt, adjust and customise the information to suit the Sudanese situation.

Several senior SPLM officials, who are preparing to construct institutional structures, spell out job descriptions, academic qualifications and skills to meet certain assignments and appointments, are fumbling and groping in the dark; determinedly trying to reinvent the wheel, which is already in existence. The problem with such senior officers is that they are too shy to ask for help and advice from fellow Sudanese or non-Sudanese with experience in various fields, related to public appointment for – and management of – a modern bureaucracy.

When a government department or a firm invites – through advertisement – applications for filling a vacancy, potential applications are usually asked to send their CVs, or curriculum vitae, sometimes known as resumes, together with certified photocopies of certificates, diplomas or degrees. Nothing is wrong with that approach. The danger with paper proof, however, is that documents can be – and frequently are – forged. It is well known that fake degrees and the like are on sale in some countries. To prevent and safeguard against fraud, an employing agency must, when possible, countercheck with the authority purported to have issued documents given to them by candidates. An e-mail message, for example, will either confirm or dismiss the claim in a matter of hours, if not minutes.

During the period of regional self-rule from 1972-1983, some persons fraudulently obtained jobs. (There was this case of a fellow who almost ran away with a senior job after claiming that he had a master's degree from one of the developed countries. He did not have even an equivalent of the Sudan School Certificate). Today it is possible for an employing agency not only to prove that Juma has obtained a PhD from Harvard University, but also that a copy of his thesis can be downloaded upon request.

Forgery of academic documents is a way of life in several African countries. In Nairobi, on Kenyatta Avenue, one can buy a diploma, a certificate or a degree, complete with logos or stamps of some of the world's reputable institutions of learning. And they look very genuine. Employing authorities need to be on the lookout to verify what is authentic from a counterfeit.

Whether the person being considered for a top government or parastatal job has proper academic qualifications or not, the last word regarding acceptance or rejection – when the position to be filled is political – lies with the final authority, a minister or head of government- prime minister or president- as the case may be.

The SPLA used grades to determine military ranks when commissioning officers. For example, a secondary school leaver was awarded 12 grades, which translated into the rank of a lieutenant. A bachelor's degree equalled 16 units and in turn meant its holder was commissioned 1st lieutenant and so forth. Since there was no way for those in charge of commissioning to verify the validity of claims, statements made by the cadets were accepted in good faith; the conviction existed that someone volunteering and ready to die for a cause would not even think to engage in falsehood. The real world, however, was different. The result of this was that the system was often abused by unscrupulous individuals giving themselves more academic points than they really had.

As the post-war period will be – physically and metaphorically – a time of rehabilitation, selection of people for jobs needs to be based on transparent methods, not simply trust or goodwill. Crooks abound and taking things for granted can be costly. Academic achievements, work experience and aptitude form main criteria when people are being selected to perform technical or semi-technical tasks. With political positions such as ministerial or senior jobs in the civil service and the army, merit may count, but it is not everything. In the past, there were cases of DS (distinguished service) rank holders being catapulted four notches upwards, to Group One Super Scales, or an army major to major general, three ranks above. In those and similar cases, there was little or no room for complaint from the public since such accelerated promotions pointed at powerful interest groups desiring – and demanding – to be represented at the highest echelon of the state or government.

Affirmative action, the policy that favours elevation of members of minorities, disadvantaged classes or women, can be commendable as it aims at redressing historical injustice and operates as a means of putting inclusiveness into practice. Affirmative action, however, has negative sides to it.

First, special consideration, as it is known in the Sudan's political lexicography, is a temporary measure, which is not a cure but a palliative. In such a situation the beneficiaries may feel vulnerable, as they become what in Kenya has been dubbed political orphans.

Second, favours accruing from special consideration tend to make the recipients complacent and numb, instead of working hard to better themselves. In a recent interview with a radio station, in reference to the suggestion that in order to promote equality between boys and girls in schools, girls should be given more incentives than boys, my answer was both Yes and No. Yes, because any minority, as well as majority, deserves equal opportunities and rights, and no, because preference in the name of justice stifles competition, the mother of success and merit. To support that assertion, I cited the

American system. Before the mid-nineteen-sixties, and right through the eighties to the present, the establishment's remedy to black representation lay in affirmative action. It did not quite achieve its goal to the satisfaction of all. What has worked is individuals' efforts to prove themselves equal or even better in abilities and merit. Citing from the American scene, let's take the examples of: Andrew Young, the former US ambassador to the UN, Colin Powell, the current Secretary of State, Condoleezza Rice, the adviser to the president on national security; and a host of other blacks in senior positions in government or in the corporate world.

Virtually all those public figures owed their elevation first to their achievements in their areas of specialisation and only tangentially to the colour of their skin. The rational way to strike a balance between affirmative action and selection on merit is to apply the two concurrently. Appoint those who might not necessarily deserve slots of real power and empower the community or a class through special programmes, such as opening more schools and providing greater health and agricultural services, if the group occupies a geographic area. That approach has the potential of producing elements of the class concerned, equipped with the tools that will qualify their members as deserving, rather than unfairly favoured, a repugnant idea that insinuates patronage and condescension from the "giver". Appointments to public office are a right, not a favour from those who dispense them.

In a society plagued by ethnic, regional, linguistic or political diversity, justice can be achieved only when the authorities responsible for dividing the national cake and supervising the offices of real decision-making combine ability, merit, and authentic professional and academic credentials with ethnic, regional, intergenerational and gender factors and when appointments are being made.

Sudan, one may argue, is not the USA; competence of office holders sometimes comes third after the clan and region. And that means the list has to be in order as long as ability is not sacrificed to the god of particularism.

These elements, when adopted as criteria by those authorised to appoint people to public offices, can be described as minimal requirements for a just, fair and democratic governance. But human beings and their institutions are not always perfect, no matter how sensitive leaders may be to the rights of all their citizens. Some people will complain that they are not receiving their fair share of wealth and power (I know of a certain county where every clan wants to have a county of their own and to be administered by one of their number, an unreasonable and impractical demand).

Constitutions usually name collective or individual appointing bodies, who receive nominations or recommendations of persons to fill certain portfolios in several branches of state, such as in the cabinet, civil service, army or parastatals. The job of executive prime minister or executive president is to finalise the process, for instance rejecting or endorsing a nominee for public office. It is an unenviable responsibility, as whatever choice is made there will always be grumbling; it is rare for anyone, no matter how well-intentioned they may be, to satisfy everybody when dishing out public offices of power and prestige.

Whether the person being considered for a top government or parastatal job has proper academic qualifications or not, the final say lies with the head of the government; this is a political decision. In this case he or she has to consult with all relevant constituencies, special interest groups, peers or the community to which the person being considered for appointment belongs. In our situation this approach makes a lot of sense. The appointing authority should not be seen as imposing leaders on their constituencies; let the community choose who represents them or at least allow them to give the stamp of approval.

The heads of the defunct regional government of 1972-1983 were in the habit of telling a community or a district that they had been given a ministerial position and that it was up to the local members to select one of their own. The appointing authority, of course, had the veto and also the right to name a nominee of their own besides. To me, that made the people accountable rather than their representative: you don't choose for people because your choice, no matter how suitable the candidate, will be seen as a stooge.

Processing and promotions in the civil service are – although they have to be fair – different from political appointments. But the appointing department must not be left without guidelines. The appointing body must be gender, ethnic, regional and merit conscious in the interest of justice and fair play.

Sudan Mirror, vol. 1, issue 16.

Why Chiefs are still Relevant

The recent meeting between the leaders of SPLM and the chiefs from Southern Sudan was judged to have been very successful and satisfactory to both parties. The SPLM had called the chiefs to be briefed on the progress of the peace process, especially the protocols signed by the two Sudanese sides in the conflict.

The chiefs in turn would raise questions on issues they wanted to be clarified, their role before, during and after the interim period and in the implementation stage.

The grassroots leaders were particularly grateful in that, at long last, the movement had recognised them as important stakeholders and owners of the peace process. For their part, the SPLM leadership, who had woken up to the realities of a changed world of pluralism, had a reason to be comfortable, in having partners needed in mobilisation and who also carried a very powerful weapon – the vote.

Some people, however, think that the revival of the "Native Administration" – a scheme that was devised and put in place by the colonial authorities at the beginning of 20th century – is wrong. Their argument is that the system is a relic of colonial rule and has no place in modern African state, run by Africans. That is not wholly true. The involvement of chiefs in governance has always been dictated by practical reasons. The British clearly understood that their management of the colonies in Africa would be weak if the chiefs, as a vital link between the rulers and the subject people, were isolated.

The colonial authorities relied heavily on the chiefs for tax collection, keeping of law and order- through the courts which settled cases which might have led to fights and bloodshed- mobilisation of citizens for communal projects such as construction and repair of feeder roads, schools, health centres or courtrooms. In recognition of their effective role as agents of rule, the colonial authorities sometimes listened to – and acted on – advice given by senior chiefs. In fact, some of these community leaders such as Giir Thiik of Gogrial, Lado Lolik of Lirya in Equatoria, Deng Malual and Ajang Duot of Bor District, Reth Dak Padiet of the Shilluk and Deng Majok of Ngok Dinka – to name only a few – carried immense influence and weight, so much so that their roles emanated from their districts, through the province and eventually in Khartoum, the seat of government. After independence the system was not only left intact, but during the military rule of 1958 – 1964, the government allowed senior chiefs to attend annual provincial conferences to discuss issues that revolved around the effectiveness of local councils. Sometimes, the chiefs, accompanied by provincial governors, were invited to Khartoum to brief the minister of local government or even the president, about the problems facing the rural population. Following the coup that brought Jaafar Nimeiri to power in 1969, the then leftist regime abolished the "Native Administration" in Northern Sudan.

Chiefs in that region were loyal to the rival sects of Ansar (Ummah Party) in western Sudan and Khatimiyya (Democratic Unionist Party – DUP) in the east, respectively. In the South, the Local Government Act eroded the powers of the chiefs. In the past, chiefs were mainly hereditary; after 1971, elections were introduced; rigging and vote-buying crept into a culture that had before operated by consensus. The biggest blow to the role and prestige of the chiefly class came from the SPLM. The rebel administrative structure put civil administration in the hands of what were known as civil military administrators. Except in very few cases, these officials were overzealous and often insensitive, young men with a mission to change the society radically and overnight, while being hazy about a substitute system. The thinking of the time was that soldiers even privates, were senior – in any capacity in society – to all civilians including an undersecretary in the civil service, a university professor, an archbishop, a cabinet minister or even a head of state.

As expected, the chiefs were at the lowest rung of the civil administration. SPLA officers of varying ranks and assignments used to give orders to chiefs in the area where the SPLM/A was the de facto government. And, naturally, the chiefs suffered excruciating humiliation and indignities from these young rulers who were more often than not, arrogant and ignorant of customs and managing people. While serving in my home district between 1988 and 1989, I witnessed on three occasions chiefs being whipped in public. They swallowed their pride silently "because of the country", as a chief once told- while wiping tears from his eyes- an insensitive bully of an SPLA officer.

In Bahr el Ghazal, some parts of Upper Nile and Eastern Equatoria, some administrators were in the habit of dismissing chiefs either to give way to relatives or because of a quarrel over cattle. The chiefs had at that time lost their responsibilities including the job of settling cases according to customary law and their office was subsequently deprived of respect and dignity.

The Southern Sudanese political scene has seen changes that have reversed roles and actors. In the case of chiefs, the Kalashnikov in the 1980s had usurped the job of the traditional rulers. Now with the call for participatory democracy and the reign of the ballot box instead of the bullets growing louder, the chiefs have become the darlings of the competing political groupings and their divergent agendas. After unwittingly allowing themselves to be used by politicians and warlords to fight wars whose causes they did not understand and which caused tremendous suffering, the chiefs in Upper Nile decided to resort to the time-tested method: suing for peace, reconciliation, forgiveness and peaceful coexistence between clans and communities. Solving their differences through peaceful means, proves that the chiefs regard the welfare of their people as a priority

And they, unlike politicians, are sincere and do not often harbour sinister motives or ambition beyond their current position and duties. Examples show that local leaders scattered across all rural areas are laying a foundation for stability and harmony among the masses. And so far, the commitment of chiefs in reconciliation and normalisation of inter-ethnic relations has produced tangible results. For example, in the past two months Nuer chiefs from western Upper Nile have managed to collect and return to owners hundreds of Dinka cattle looted during the turbulent years following the 1991 split. In line with those positive steps, the Nuer chiefs and their Dinka counterparts in Bahr el Ghazal have agreed to compensate families of the victims of ethnic fighting.

For their part the Dinka community has vowed to return the stolen Nuer livestock. The Nuer community in western Upper Nile appears to be in the lead in translating peace agreements into reality. Almost at the same, the chiefs agreed to help the local authorities in collecting an estimated 50 unlicensed guns from civilians.

Although the move met some resistance as expected, the positive and welcome action was praised by the Dinka neighbours who have been reported as saying they would apply the same in their areas. In addition to peace-making and its consolidation, the communities in the coming months and years will be playing a leading part in different aspects of the ongoing peace process between the Government of Sudan and the SPLM.

When a peace agreement is to be signed, the communities and their leaders will play host to citizens returning from refuge in the neighbouring countries. The internally displaced persons, along with the expected exodus of thousands of Southern Sudanese coming from Northern Sudan, will put a heavy burden on the hosts, who are having their own problems in feeding themselves.

Whether voluntary or organised by international community, repatriation, rehabilitation and resettlement will present difficulties to those involved in the programme; the heaviest burden falling on the shoulders of those who will be receiving the returnees.

The immediate concern will be the receiving points. Since there is nothing known as no man's land in a society where the land belongs to a community, a clan or a family, there are bound to be problems arising out of claims and counter claims over ownership of pieces of land where new arrivals will be temporarily accommodated. As this is a sphere of law, chiefs will be the ones to arbitrate and adjudicate, using customary law to settle such disputes.

As most of those who will be returning home after the war will be persons with meagre or no means, the receiving communities will have to supplement what the UN agencies and other humanitarian bodies will provide particularly in form of shelter, food and possibly land for the arrivals to use for cultivation of food crops to be self-sufficient.

And since the hosts themselves do not have much even for themselves, this will be a great inconvenience.

But there is a precedent to follow. When the SPLA was formed in 1983, the then-guerrilla army depended on the rural population for almost everything. Chiefs – voluntarily – used to mobilise the people to contribute livestock, grains, dry fish and even native tobacco for the recruits on their way to training centres. On return from the camps, the soldiers would be received and offered whatever basic needs were available. Those SPLA members were not necessarily from the areas where they enjoyed public generosity and hospitality; the reason was solidarity fostered by patriotism. This time, humanitarian reasons will reinforce love of the country and the chiefs, like before, will be at the centre of rehabilitation and resettlement efforts.

Among the post-conflict activities will be demobilisation and disarmament. As it is difficult to draw a line between civilians and members of SPLA combatants and other armed groups, all efforts at disarmament and demobilisation will face problems without the participation of communities and their leaders. Deserters and those in "camouflage" will not be plucked out without the cooperation of chiefs in whose villages the former fighters are hiding with their guns.

For the common good of all, chiefs are expected to report armed relatives to military and political authorities for appropriate action, mainly disarmament or reintegration of those who will be fit for military service. The process of demobilisation will also be carried out by communities who will have to welcome former fighters to start a new life by living off the land or to go to school for those who may be still young.

The post-war reconstruction and physical rehabilitation will not be the sole responsibility of state organs and their foreign donors; part of the programme will have to be done by the people on the principle of self-help and self-reliance. Towards that objective, schools, health facilities and the like will have to be built with local materials such as elephant grass, wood and mud. This can be achieved through the mobilisation and supervision of chiefs. This experiment was tried before by the defunct regional government of Southern Sudan in the seventies for establishment of new provinces – Jonglei in Upper, Western Equatoria and Lakes in Bahr el Ghazal,

The project was an impressive success although some provincial authorities – especially in Jonglei – stole much of people's contributions in cash and kind. There is no reason why community contribution can't be repeated when the war ends. Formal education has been hurt deeply by war, to the extent that in some regions people are having to start virtually from scratch. Although the support by agencies such as Unicef to the SPLM's department of education has been and continues to be critical, the role of the ordinary people will be to supplement external assistance.

Like in the past, when many Southern Sudanese families, especially those from the cattle-owning peoples refused to take their children to school, authorities asked and at times forced chiefs to lead by example in enrolling their sons or nephews. In many parts of Southern Sudan, it is not automatic that a child will enrol even if a nearby school is empty. Local leaders will have to talk to their people to make education attractive for boys and girls. But since most of the chiefs have themselves not been to school, convincing them will have to be a combined task of local education, administrative authorities and the SPLM secretariat branches in the counties.

Chiefs in state structures, properly belong to civil service, not politics. But since they manage the affairs of citizens who, on the other hand, become voters (politics) they find themselves being wooed by competing political parties and other interest groups. Inevitably, political rivalries have in the past led to sharp differences among chiefs and their followers, sometimes to bloodshed. However, nobody – soldiers, chiefs and others included – can afford to stay aloof when the future of one's own society is being determined; one has to take sides. What I mean here is that the lead up to the exercise of self-determination will begin following the launch of a pre-interim period. Chiefs as leaders for over 90 percent of the population cannot be ignored, as they will take part in mobilising their people for the referendum exercise.

There will be intense lobbying by opponents and supporters of independence. The chiefs will be a major target as they command the support of their people. Certainly, even those who have been using these grassroots leaders as a means will have to treat them as an end, as they are king makers and true stakeholders of the peace process and its result at the end of the six-year period.

But as only a political novice can fail to realise the power the chiefs wield, courting them now has become the new ideology. However, if I were a chief, I would demand from these unpredictable members of the elite to make a public apology for dragging the chiefs into a war based on power struggles and personal antagonisms and rivalry. The power elite have also to say sorry for the indignities heaped on chiefs during the formative years of SPLM/A.

Will the office and role of chiefs remain unchanged forever? When one supports the chiefs and their role in society, it must be emphasised that in the current stage of socio-economic and political development, the chiefs play a critical role. Furthermore, they should continue to do so until strong and effective local government authorities emerge to perform what the chiefs do now. Chiefs are a stop-gap that has served the people well under the circumstances.

Sudan Mirror, vol. 2, issue 2004.

Democracy in an ethnically and culturally diverse society

Sudan is one of the countries that are characterised by geographic, cultural, racial and linguistic diversity. Each cultural community has its own customs, belief systems and practices. The impact of geography on the Sudanese is that some communities sharing a common language within the country or across the border of another sovereign state identify with each other as brothers as sisters. For example, most Darfuris in the west are at home with some citizens of Chad, as is the case with most Sudanese nationals sharing borders with some people in Eritrea. Sudanese speaking Acholi and Madi feel the same in their relationship with citizens of Uganda who speak the same mother tongues. Some Sudanese who claim Arab descent identify with the Arab world or with Muslim co-religionists globally. Internally, most Sudanese, like most of their counterparts in Africa and many parts of the developing world, feel secure and at ease with their kin and kith; sharing a common language or dialect, territory and ways of life. These factors create strong bonds of solidarity. There is nothing strange or wrong with such attitudes; after all countries that happen to be mono-cultural and mono-lingual are an exception rather than the norm. And let us not forget Somalia has gone to be a failed state despite the fact that its citizens speak one language and over 90 percent of them profess Islamic faith.

Spiritual matters also come into play, although in recent times, such as the case of Darfur and to some extent the Nuba Mountains, Southern Blue Nile and Eastern Sudan, confessional affiliation does not always necessarily translate into political cohesion. To conclude this introduction, it is relevant to cite how some politicians, both in the North and later during the Addis Ababa Agreement exploited ethnicity, faith and language to mobilise their adherents to support them against rivals seen and projected in the They-versus-Us dichotomy. In the North the sectarian parties used to mobilise their supporters on religious agenda. In the sixties over 70 percent members of the "national" army were drawn from Darfur and Nuba Mountains, except after the formation of the General Union of the Nuba, the two regions use to vote for Ummah was virtually 100 percent and fought Southern Sudanese on account of religion.

Undemocratic Northern system of rule

The rival Khatimiyya sect of the Mirghani family also used religion as their power base especially in Eastern Sudan and in the Butana plain, Khartoum and within mercantile and Muslim communities through the country. Democratic Unionist Party, DUP, an outcome of a merger of the former National Unionist Party and People Democratic Party, both which favoured unity of Egypt and Sudan had no programme for uplifting citizens who did not belong to the ruling circles.

Although the two sectarian parties, Ummah and DUP, disagreed on many issues they agreed and asserted privately and in public that Sudan was an Arab and Muslim country. This stance made nonsense of the claim by the ruling Northern elite that their governance, always a coalition, was democratic. It was a system that the late SPLM leader John Garang called "Double Apartheid", meaning discrimination on the basis of race and religion.

Southern Sudan's ethnically based politics

Southern Sudanese politicians of the time when these policies were in place and in practice had very little influence even among their own constituents. After the Addis Ababa Agreement of 1972, Southern political elite had the chance for the first time to exercise power in Juba and to some extent in Khartoum. But because of the weakness of the peace accord and the military-cum-one party state that obtained at the time, the South did not achieve its full democratic potential. The removal of Abel Alier as the chief executive of the South with active participation of many Dinka politicians and his replacement by the former Anya Nya leader General Joseph Lagu who hails from minority Madi people was seen by many observers as a proof that the people of Southern Sudan had risen above narrow ethnic politics. Critics, however, took the contrary view, arguing that the Dinka leaders who helped bring Lagu to power simply wanted to use him while pretending to be liberal; in other words, eating and having the cake at the same time.

Whatever view one endorses on these two opposing positions, political history of Southern Sudan is replete with records of the masses following leaders from their ethnic and linguistic communities. Even the war of liberation tended to chart that trend. For example, when the veteran leader of Anya Nya Joseph Oduho joined the SPLM a sizeable number of people, especially among the intelligentsia from his Torit home district, the Lotuho followed him in large numbers; the Dinka did the same and possibly for similar reasons because the top leadership consisted of members of the ethnic and linguistic group. After the split within the SPLA in 1991, opposing factions were largely ethnically led and based.

Hope for a democratic transformation

Is there any hope that the people of Southern Sudan will abandon ethnic agendas in favour of national and democratic direction? Although I am an optimist to the bone, I believe that unless the change comes from the intelligentsia, Southern Sudanese have a long way to evolve and practise the White Hall version of democracy. Ironically, it is the elite who can bring that transformation. John Garang's bold programme propounded in his call for restructuring the way Sudan was governed by an ideology that transcended ethnic, racial, religious and parochial considerations. Sudan today is completely different politically and psychologically from what it used to be before 1983, the time of the formation of the SPLM/A. It is because of that approach. There is no doubt that among the current crop of Southern Sudanese leaders there are some who genuinely believe in democratic culture and values. May be the climate for them is not right. Who knows that such an enabling environment will be ushered in by the birth a sovereign state in Southern Sudan?

This article was published as "Democracy and Cultural Pluralism".
Sudan Mirror, December 2003.

A Move Away from Cities

The delivery of development and social services to Southern Sudan is largely conditional on the end of the current war. But the future Government of Southern Sudan in cooperation with development and aid partners will first have to clearly spell out their priorities, and where the projects and activities will be located and carried out.

It is obvious, if not logical, that the much neglected rural areas will receive much emphasis and attention in development of physical infrastructure, agriculture, roads, health, education and the like.

Politicians often forget that the phrase "marginalised areas" and their grievances are a direct result of economic development and services having been concentrated in central Sudan and the former Khartoum Province, the country's capital.

If the share of services and wealth were equitable, the two civil wars in the South and now the insurgencies in the west and east of the country might have been averted.

The leaders of Southern Sudan should learn from – and avoid the mistakes of – their Northern counterparts, which have taken a heavy toll on the country, both in lives and wasted time and resources.

By definition, and by international standards, Southern Sudan has no single city. The estimated population of Juba, the biggest town in the South is below 300,000.

This is certainly good news for the future Government of Southern Sudan whose plans for urban development will be a clean slate compared with the experiences of Nigeria and Egypt – Lagos, the former capital, and Cairo each have more than 12 million inhabitants – which have been grappling with the problems of urban explosion. (South Africa is almost successful in the provision of housing, water and electricity supply, although crime rates stubbornly refuse to fall).

The problems of large cities, especially in Africa are a nightmare to governments. These include rising unemployment which leads to poverty, a reduced life expectancy, crime, and shortage of basic amenities.

There is no doubt that the first item on the rehabilitation and reconstruction agenda will be the physical infrastructure especially repairs of roads and bridges, and building of new ones.

The importance of good, functioning, and all-weather roads and bridges is too obvious to be stressed: they serve to link places and people and ease transportation of people and goods, particularly food from the regions of production to consumption destinations.

Good roads will be a prerequisite in expediting repatriation, resettlement, rehabilitation and reconstruction programmes.

As air transport is very expensive, repatriation of the refugees from the neighbouring countries, mainly Kenya, Uganda, Ethiopia and Eritrea will have to be conducted by road. That means that the Sudanese authorities and the international community should start levelling roads as soon as a comprehensive agreement is signed because there are refugees who hate life in the camps so much that they will want to return to their ancestral homes the same day the armed conflict ends.

Although the Government of Southern Sudan will be short of money and will depend on aid, that should not mean that the donor community or the Government of Sudan should be the ones to choose project sites.

That right will have to be based on two considerations: fairness for all areas and communities to benefit from the projects and services, and second, moving these away from towns to countryside.

Agriculture

The discovery and production of oil in the South has led many people including the Sudanese leaders to ignore the most vital assets in the region: arable land and abundance of rainwater. These resources are the backbone of agriculture, as is livestock. Except for a few districts the people and successive governments in Khartoum and even in Juba have never fully utilised agricultural potential of Southern Sudan; most communities even during peacetime have been reliant upon subsistence farming, whose harvests cannot feed families to the next harvest. Inevitably, famine has always been endemic in many parts of Southern Sudan because of this ineffective and outdated agricultural mode.

In addition to rehabilitation of some agriculture projects that stalled, even before the outbreak of the war, the government should plan for self-sufficiency in food. There should be a clear policy on land ownership and use in Renk District of northern Upper Nile, one of the grain-producing areas of Sudan. Renk alone can feed the whole of Southern Sudan if absentee Northern businessmen return the farms to their rightful owners who till the land for others.

The Aweil rice scheme, which began as an experiment in the early 1960s, was a success story. Like Renk, Aweil project can meet the needs of the entire South. These two are capital- and labour-intensive and will require greater involvement of the government and private investors.

However, it is unrealistic to expect that agricultural revolution, which turns Southern Sudanese from a hungry people to ones who are self-sufficient in food, will take place in a short time. Guided by that knowledge, the Government of Southern Sudan, NGOs and community-based organisations will have to encourage the majority of citizens who cannot afford tractors to train in and use ox-ploughs.

The idea of using cattle for farming was originally unacceptable to the Dinka and Nuer peoples who used to argue that the method demeaned their "noble cattle". But reports from Bahr el Ghazal indicate the device has not only been accepted but also that the people have seen yields have increased several times in comparison to the use of hoe. This success with ox-plough means also some conservative ideas about value and use of cattle will change: a cow has to be seen as a mere economic utility.

Fish is abundant in the White Nile, Sobat and the rest of the tributaries, streams and swamps of Southern Sudan. Fishing with modern equipment should be introduced to communities living along the rivers.

Equatoria is rich in cash crops, such as tea in Upper Talanga and coffee in Western Equatoria. Together with mangoes and bananas these could be produced for export, as well as for local consumption.

Large scale agricultural farming promises job opportunities for the large army of unemployed young people now residing in foreign cities, and also in refugee camps and centres for displaced persons. Those schemes could also absorb those who will be demobilised after the war.

Health

Health and education sectors have been severely affected by the war. UN agencies such as Unicef and other international NGOs have been prominent in providing these basic services.

When guns fall silent, it is expected that the Sudanese authorities with these organisations will concentrate and double their efforts to rehabilitate old health centres and build new facilities.

Probably lack of funds would be the impediment, rather than the absence of a blueprint. For decades, the World Health Organisation, WHO, and many developing countries have been operating primary health care, PHC, projects – small units built in the villages and suburbs of towns and cities. Usually, such centres – which treat minor ailments – do not necessarily require qualified physicians; paramedics such as nurses will do.

For Southern Sudan, health requirements will include building health centres and hospitals, the acquisition of medical equipment, training junior personnel and procurement of basic drugs. In the past, hospitals operated in provincial capitals (Juba, Malakal and Wau) and in district headquarters. There is now an existing need to take general hospitals nearer to the people in the rural South, while regional hospitals should be upgraded to referral centres.

Education

Unlike health, education has more peculiar problems, such as the apparent absence of a universal blueprint. The SPLM Commission of Education has a policy in place, but while it looks impressive on paper, its implementation will face hurdles. Children will return from different parts of Sudan and Africa, which run different educational systems. To unify these systems will not be easy; some pupils and students will inevitably lose out. However, whatever system emerges, the most important move the authorities should take is to concentrate on primary and secondary schools in the rural areas with post-secondary institutions based in the regional capitals and even in the district headquarters. The idea behind this trend is to relieve towns of congestion and make living in countryside more attractive since rural schools and hospitals will come with amenities such as potable drinking water, electricity and libraries. The schools will provide employment – manual in particular – to the locals.

One of the biggest difficulties to face the Government of Southern Sudan will be tertiary, or university education. The government in Khartoum has made a mockery of education in general and at tertiary level in particular.

The choice of Arabic over English at colleges is one example. This politically motivated decision has effectively barred the hiring of foreign lecturers who have always been an important element of university learning, not only in Sudan but worldwide. Consequently, the standards are appalling, shortage of qualified teaching staff, books and other learning aids, are the main features of this self-inflicted crisis.

There will be need for the two governments – the Government of Sudan and the Government of Southern Sudan – to evolve a brave new policy: one university, call it University of Southern Sudan with colleges in Juba, Wau and Malakal, modelled on that of the University of Wales (in United Kingdom) which has the main campus in Cardiff and colleges specialising in different fields spread across the region.

Whether these ideas are likely to be accepted or rejected is not the issue. The problem is the duration of the six-year interim period.

Politically, many Southerners are not comfortable with the timeframe believing it gives ample time for any of the parties to reverse or frame or even sabotage the process.

On the other hand, in the field of rehabilitation and construction, the period is too short for any tangible development to be realised.

Sudan Mirror Vol 1 issue 11 2005

This article was published a couple of days before John Garang, the SPLM/A leader, made his famous statement on "Taking towns to the people". Although Garang was a regular reader of the *Sudan Mirror*, which carried my article, there is no suggestion that the politician was influenced by this opinion. At the time I wrote the article I was no longer Garang's speechwriter. That there are similarities in the two was just a coincidence. But one thing is clear about the views expressed here and Garang's plans for rural development: they have remained just ideas as no action has been taken in that regard; instead, the reverse is the case as the influx of inhabitants from the countryside to towns has been taking place since the end of the conflict in 2005. Ironically, since that time the Juba-based government has been publicly reciting the slogan.

South Sudan: an unknown country without an identity

In anticipation of statehood the former region of Southern Sudan would obtain on July 9, 2011, the people and their leadership spent the months leading up to the great day organising symbols of sovereignty.

In late December 2010, for instance, a meeting directed by foreign experts on international law took place in Juba. Those legal heavyweights advised the Southern Sudanese political leaders in government, and legislators, to choose carefully a name for the they were going to have soon.

A name that would be contested, they said, would impede or even prevent the attainment of independence. The case of Macedonia, which Greece also claims, was cited as an example. So the choice of South Sudan made a lot of sense in comparison to names such as Kush or Nubia which some were advocating in the media to be adopted for the new nation: the two ancient kingdoms were located outside the present day South Sudan's territory.

On the eve of Independence Day, Juba was ready to meet the occasion with almost full instruments of a sovereign: a flag, an anthem, an emblem, a coat of arms, a currency – the South Sudanese pound – a transitional constitution. Unknown to the public, the Ministry of Culture, Heritage, Youth and Sports had also commissioned various medals of several classes.

The march to statehood was fast and smooth. Recognition of the new country came shortly after the declaration of independence, which the Speaker of the Legislator announced at John Garang's Mausoleum, with the Government of Sudan leading the world. A couple of days later, the United Nations welcomed the Republic of South Sudan as its 194th Member State.

Recognition hitting a glitch

The European Union, along with the five permanent members of the UN Security Council quickly and readily received the newly independent country. This recognition gave confidence to most South Sudanese that the new status of their country would confer on them the rights, responsibilities and privileges of citizens around the world. Unfortunately, some political and technical factors turned these hopes into disappointment and sometimes bewilderment.

One of the first hitches was the rejection of the code "SS". The two letters standing for South Sudan were rejected on political grounds: SS was abbreviation of *Schutzstaffel*, the dreaded Nazi special security police in Germany during World War Two blamed for committing genocide in concentration camps and other crimes against the German people. Objections raised by representatives of Holocaust survivors against the adoption of the code by South Sudan delayed issuance of passport and the country's admission to the International Telecommunications Union, ITU. The problem was finally solved in favour of South Sudan. So its email domain is now: abukalaam@edu.gov.ss, theoretically, at least.

Available information reads ". ss is the designated country code top top-level domain (ccTLD) for South Sudan in the Domain Name System of the Internet.... According to CIO East Africa, the TLD was allocated on 10 August 2011 following the country's declaration of independence from Sudan. The TLD was registered on 31 August 20111; as of 8 December 2015, it is not in the DNS root zone and thus not operational".[14]

No reasons are given to say why system is or was not operational at the time the report was made.

Another problem is the establishment of a physical postal address. In 2015 I went to a post office in an Australian city to send a package to Juba, the capital of South Sudan, only to be told: "Sorry, this address in not on the list I have checked on the computer. We have Sudan, not South Sudan", the clerk assured me.

To compound matters further, the country doesn't have street names or numbers for postal addresses. In that situation, your mail will only reach the addressee if you write the name of the government department or organisation where they work, or if they have friends who can receive and pass the items on to them. Homes and small private businesses have no street numbers.

Secession of South Sudan from Sudan has been described as an unfinished divorce. A particularly thorny issue is the demarcation of the common

---

14 Wikipedia.

border between the two sovereign states. As a result, Sudan continues to exercise its sovereignty over South Sudan's airspace. This situation has serious security and economic implications.

Personal experience

It is no secret; there are difficulties with the use of the South Sudanese passport in several countries, mainly outside the African continent.

In 2013, I was invited to attend an international media conference in Europe. When filling in the application form for the trip, I discovered that the name of South Sudan was missing in the form. The staff in the embassy in Juba of the country I was to travel to advised me to tick Sudan in the place where South Sudan was supposed to be. My colleague who was going to attend the same conference had to travel to Egypt to get his visa there. I was able to get my visa in the first European country where I made my connection to the venue. I was travelling on my Australian passport, so I had no problem entering Europe, or any other country.

Problems of national identity continued to dog my colleague and me while in Europe, one of these relating, crucially, to the currency. A central bank was contacted to give exchange rate: euro to South Sudanese pounds but the bank in the European country had no idea. The solution was for me to ring a friend from that European country who was in Juba. The friend gave me the exchange rate figures for that day, which we then used to complete our transaction.

On return to Africa via a neighbouring country, I wanted to open a new email account. The internet server gave me the list of all the world's countries. The only name missing was –predictably – South Sudan. And since people don't argue with online forms, I knew there was nothing I could possibly do to insert the name of my country in the list, so I had to give up, perplexed, upset, and left questioning. Who is to blame? Nobody but ourselves, as will be seen later.

That South Sudan remains unknown in many parts of the world is not surprising and remains a problem for our compatriots who travel outside our homeland. And for any citizen proud of their country, South Sudan has become disappointingly a joke, internationally. For example, in January 2014, airport authorities in an Asian country where I had disembarked to take an onward flight to Australia told me that their system did not recognise the South Sudanese passport. Fortunately, they were prepared to be flexible as their country was not my final destination.

Who is to introduce South Sudan to the world?

The role of diplomats accredited to foreign countries is to look after the interests of their country in the host country. These duties include promotion of good bilateral relations especially diplomatic, economic and cultural; presentation of a positive image of the country and its people and monitoring the welfare of compatriots there, among others.

For a young country like South Sudan, our diplomats should concentrate on making the country, its people and resources, known to the receiving nations. This assignment should not be a problem if the officials know their mission well. During the years of struggle for freedom and nationhood, Southern Sudanese had earned a reputation for being tireless and effective salespersons for their cause.

Former BBC presenter of "Focus on Africa" programme, Robin White, was an independent voice who recognised that characteristic when he answered a complaint from the Sudan embassy in London. A spokesman for the mission had accused the broadcaster of bias in favour of the then rebel SPLM, saying that the BBC ignored Government of Sudan's version of events. In defending the BBC, White denied that his employer was biased. The problem, he said, was that the representatives of the SPLM always went out to tell the news media their stories while the embassy simply waited to react with denials. That spirit of combative salesmanship seems to have died following the attainment of independence. The establishment should understand that no anyone or organisation other South Sudanese themselves who have the interest and are qualified to introduce their country to the rest of the world.

Are our embassies doing their job well? One single answer will not do; some are doing praiseworthy jobs while others are sleeping, turning their missions into dens of semiliterate idlers and recipients of sinecure. I back up this statement on personal experiences with two missions, one in Africa and another in Europe.

During a visit in 2012 to an African country – which shall remain unnamed – our embassy there arranged my meeting with a local media organisation.

Not only was my meeting with the CEO of a giant media house successful; my host told me that the embassy's constant contacts with journalists in their capital city had created a better understanding of the affairs of South Sudan. There had been some misunderstanding between the media in that country and Juba as copies of newspapers sent there were frequently impounded. Proprietors of the papers in that country saw the action of South Sudanese authorities as an attempt to censor them; it also resulted in financial loss.

The efforts exerted by the media staff at the South Sudan's embassy in that country succeeded to convince the management of those foreign publications that the mistake shouldn't spoil the budding good and mutually beneficial relations between the two neighbouring countries. By that time the media in that country had been convinced that the confiscation of papers was an act of rouge elements within the government, purportedly serving their narrow interests, not of the whole country.

In my view, those diplomats, especially the media representative, are doing a commendable job and deserve encouragement. Nevertheless, not all our diplomats abroad are carrying out their duties to meet expectations. In another visit to a European country where we have an embassy, my colleague and I discovered, to our dismay, a conspicuous absence of our diplomats at the venue.

The international gathering attracted over 2,500 high-profile participants including senior media executives, economists, politicians, environmentalists, scholars, and human rights and gender activists. That country's head of government was scheduled to address the meeting but had to send their foreign minister because an unforeseen development necessitated a change in their agenda. The venue of the conference was not far from the capital city where our ambassador is located. I knew the ambassador was there at the time but chose not to pay a visit to the conference on the opening day. That forum would have provided our embassy with an opportunity to introduce South Sudan to the world. None of the staff from the mission bothered to drive to the venue of the important international gathering, leaving the job to me and my colleague. Participants from Kenya, Uganda, South Africa and Ghana volunteered to go around with the message "Please meet our brothers from the Republic of South Sudan". They did that without prompting from us. One of them wondered whether my country had a mission in that country, a question to which I reluctantly replied with yes.

Words could not express my gratitude to our African colleagues for helping us to introduce our country to the rest of the world. However, for the ambassador and their staff who should have been the ones to sell South Sudan to the important participants from across the globe, it had to be barbs, if not outright curses. Well, since I know the ambassador's limited understanding of diplomacy as well as nearly everything else, it was unfair of me to expect much from that "diplomat".

A Long Journey to Authorship

"Success in literature depends on what you have to say as well as on how you say it"
George Bernard Shaw

This Shavian aphorism applies to almost all forms of communication, not only literature.

Looking back, I am amazed to realise that the road I have travelled to become a published writer has taken nearly my entire life. The story begins in a rural African village many years ago, when my first teacher, Thepano[15] Reng Arok, pressed my finger onto the sand – as he was bending over me while I was sitting – to copy the Dinka vowels, written on a blackboard in front of a class of three boys. We learned under a leafy tree which served as a class. When it rained lessons had to be abandoned as we and the teacher had to run to take shelter somewhere else. The medium of instruction was Dinka language which was also the subject besides scriptures and arithmetic.

The apex of learning the language – at that stage – consisted of understanding the rules of correct use of words and sentences. At the university, there was this professor of English telling the students – including me – that not all the words existing in English or any other language were ever to

---

15 Thepano: This is the Dinka version of Stephen.

be used. At the highest level of learning how to write, as a journalist, I was taught that the best writing is marked by clarity and simplicity of expression, and that for communication to be effective it should avoid labouring to impress, but to *inform,* educate and entertain. The following is the trail that has landed us together – you as the reader, myself as the writer – in this book.

My entry into the world of writing began at a newspaper. It was an unusual beginning, starting in a senior position with very little training and no experience at all. One day, in March 1975, I received a letter from the director of the Ministry of Culture and Information, Richard Mambia, appointing me as features editor of the *Nile Mirror,* a weekly publication owned by the Government of the Southern Region. Two weeks earlier I was one of the government employees, most of them clerks turned reporters, who had attended a five-day training in basics of journalism – defining, gathering and writing news; the "inverted pyramid" and so forth. The instructor was one George Bennet, a man of the cloak and journalist who was from Kitwe, a church-based training centre for African journalists, in Zambia. Mading de Garang, George Akumbek Kwanai (late 1950s) and Agatha David Lado, (late 1970s) were the Southern Sudanese journalists who trained there.

I had been a cub reporter for about a week. I protested that I was not up to the job but was told that being a degree holder in English language, which was considered a sufficient qualification, stood me in good stead. Thus began my four decades that included advanced courses in journalism in Khartoum and West Berlin to culminate in a master's degree in the history of broadcasting by radio in Sudan from the University of Wales, in 1984, in Cardiff, UK.

At the editorial helm was Benjamin Warille, who like me held a degree in English and Philosophy. Unlike me, he had trained in journalism at home and in Germany. His deputy was Kosti Manibe, an arts graduate from Makerere University, Uganda. Under those competent and diligent colleagues, I quickly learned on the job the basics of writing news, and features editing. Those were the times when journalism was learned in the newsroom, not at college. Two years later and after I had obtained a diploma in mass communications, I was appointed founding editor of a government monthly magazine, *Southern Sudan.* It was on the magazine where I practically learned the art of editing as the story below shows.

Natale Olwak Akolawin

The person I will always remember as my main mentor in teaching me journalism in general, and writing in particular, was Natale Olwak Akolawin, an unlikely person for the job.[16] Olwak was not a trained media person. An academic and a political figure, he was previously a lecturer in law at the University of Khartoum. At the time he decided to work with me, or rather, as I later realised to my pleasure, to help me, he was a government minister. That unsolicited help which I heartily welcomed was from July 1977 to February 1978, the time he and his team lost power to the opposition through an election. He was Minister for High Executive Council Affairs. This was another name for cabinet affairs portfolio. And he worked closely on a daily basis with the president.

Following my appointment as managing editor of the *Southern Sudan*, a monthly news and cultural magazine, the minister volunteered to help me with editing. Mading de Garang who was Minister for Information was therefore the magazine's ex-officio editor in chief.

Olwak chose to be an associate editor in chief, a position which appeared in the editorial listing. And unlike his colleague, Mading, he did the practical job, coaching me on editing the stories that our reporters, contributors or I had prepared or commissioned. I was not only grateful to Olwak for his professional editorial support he gave; I was surprised and impressed by his unaffected humility. The minister would walk to my modest office whose only furniture consisted of my desk and that of my secretary; no sofa set or coffee table or a bell for calling a messenger as was fashionable then.

When Minister Natale Olwak Akolawin was entering the magazine's office, a messenger was hurriedly sent to direct him to his colleague's office. When he was informed he had lost direction, he chuckled and casually told her he knew his geography of the building and that he knew where he was going and the official he was going to see.

I tried to give up my desk for him but he refused, saying he was going out and would come over the weekend. He had come to know where I operated.

16 More stories of my work with Natale Olwak on the *Southern Sudan* magazine will appear in forthcoming book, *Into the World of Journalism: From the Nile Mirror to Radio SPLA*.

"I am going to work with you here", he informed me as we stood in the middle of the office. He then left to see Mading. From there he was back at the Presidency, where he had his office.

When the information quickly spread within the ministry that Olwak was sitting comfortably in *my* office, there were murmurs and some consternation, especially within the ranks of senior staff. His visit to my office raised mixed reaction. This was not surprising. Ministers, seen by many as a special class were expected not to associate closely with ordinary people apart from their own office staff or family members. On the other hand, some colleagues read sinister designs in his interest to work with me: he was going to control all the contents and I was just going to be a figurehead, I was warned. Finally, others became jealous: why me? The group whose members didn't welcome what had happened to belong to "rankers", a derogatory name for senior officials who were not university graduates. Fearing for their positions, that clique, most of whom were heads of departments and units, tried all means within their power to block the progress of the young entrants. I was not an exception in that cutthroat rivalry, which had become a discernible phenomenon within the civil service.

Lacking extra furniture, and coupled with the protestation of the Professor, as the minister was known to his colleagues – that there was no need for a sofa set and an additional desk and chair to be acquired for him – I had to take over the secretary's place while we worked on stories.

As he was very busy with his work at the Council of Ministers during weekdays, the minister put aside weekends – mainly Saturday and Sunday afternoons, especially when an edition was being prepared for printing – for the magazine's job. To me these were useful days, as I was learning from him. The first lesson was that once Olwak had begun work, I had to brace myself for long and exhausting working hours. Since there were bound to be no breaks, a messenger from his office would bring from home a large flask full of coffee and milk. Whenever he wanted to take coffee Olwak rarely left his desk, as he continued to work; for him, every minute counted and should not be wasted only in an emergency.

"Hard work does not kill. You want a break? You are very much younger than I am and now you want to go out for a break!" Olwak mildly reprimanded me, when I was about to go out for a short break to smoke after working for more than five hours non-stop.

"They say a break at work is useful for one to get rid of lactic acid", I replied in defence.

"I have heard this thing being said before. That is an excuse many people resort to", Olwak replied, adding that it was a ruse lazy people used to dodge work. We laughed before he allowed me to go out to straighten my legs.

Natale Olwak was an unrepentant apologist for the use of formal and sometimes highbrow English. This was not surprising, given his background as a graduate of London School of Oriental and African Studies, where he gained a master's degree in customary law. He later on went to do a PhD at Oxford, where he left to become minister for the interior in Juba, a short time before completing it. He constantly reminded me to avoid slang, clichés, colloquial usages and jargons when engaged in formal writing "except when you are reproducing quotations made by someone else", he conceded.

As a lawyer, Olwak insisted that a serious writer should be specific. "Ambiguous expressions are usually misleading. Make sure you use a word or an expression that *hits the nail on the head*. Do not leave the reader to guess what you are trying tell him", he would frequently remind me. He was particularly irritated by the way many people used the word "southerner". "This is vague. southern United States? southern Italy? If you mean someone from Southern Sudan, please say Southern Sudanese, instead of 'Southerner'. People are being lazy to use this form. Go for the full word or phrase", he told me, before he resumed reading the feature article he was editing.

It was when we were working on a special issue report on the Ministry of Wildlife and Nature Conservation that I observed Olwak applying his meticulous editorial skills. The ministry had submitted to me over sixty single-spaced typed pages of their report the magazine was to carry.

"We have to go for *meaty* paragraphs", he remarked, adding, "much of what the pages contain has nothing to tell the reader. Much of the information in these pages is without the needed facts and figures. When you say for example, Khartoum is very far from Juba, you are not specific. State the distance in miles and the reader will know what you are saying. This is a sloppy way of writing a special report. The composers of this document do not know that the potential readers are likely to be intelligent people who will be asking questions. As a writer you provide those answers, unless you do not want what you have written to be read and unclear statements in it to be questioned".

Olwak, who was more knowledgeable about policies and what was going on in every government department than staff in charge in those departments, would often add the information he spotted to be missing and delete what was either irrelevant, incorrect or superfluous. He also hated flowery usages as he contended that they added no value to the information in hand. We ended up with just 10 typed pages – double-spaced – which together with photographs covered about six pages in the magazine.

When that issue went out, I received letters from excited readers from around the world. One of those who commented was Arthur Forbes, a British colonial army officer in Sudan and former director of wildlife service in the run up to independence. By then he was a retiree in his native England. In a letter to the editor, retired Captain Arthur Forbes expressed his joy that the new generation of Southern Sudanese was committed to the conservation of the environment and wildlife protection – he and his colleagues had carried out in the 1930s until the British departure from the country. Olwak was very pleased. We published the letter.

The majority of readers who were not aware of the real editor, Natale Olwak Akolawin, poured praises on me. The man who should get much of the credit did not use his name as a staff a writer. He didn't want to publicise his role; only a few of his colleagues, among them, the President and the Minister of Information, knew he was the man behind much of the publication's success. The self-effacing academic turned politician said he loved what he was doing: editing. The result: I became the envy of some of the journalists who were struggling and dying for recognition.

I must state here that Olwak's work on the magazine was absolutely voluntary, as he didn't receive a cent from the publication's items set aside for part-time staff writers. For me or Mading de Garang to have suggested paying Olwak would have amounted to not only an offence to the proud man; it would have meant terminating his free service as he would undoubtedly have quit in protest for being "insulted" or because "dignity *ca* touched", meaning dignity has been fringed upon, as a local Shilluk saying would have it.

Frank Burton and his 'biscuit factory worker'

Frank Burton was a British journalist who worked for the Kenyan press in the 1960s and was later director of the Zurich-based International Press Institute. Burton was well-known all over Africa for his book, *Inside African Newsroom,* then a highly recommended manual for the training of journalists. In 1978, Burton was one of a few veteran journalists with strong African backgrounds taking part in the training of Batch 35 – a team of journalists drawn from several sub-Saharan African countries. The International Centre for Journalism in West Berlin was the body organising the course. The centre also offered similar sessions to journalists from Asia and other parts of the world outside the countries of the Iron Curtain, Western Europe and North America. Countries from which practising journalists were selected were, as expected, ideologically pro-West.

As one of the journalists attending that three-month course, I remember in perpetuity Frank Burton the teacher, and his advice "Remember the biscuit factory worker". By that, the expert trainer meant that anyone writing news items or engaged in communication in general should not forget an ordinary reader or listener with modest formal education. To achieve that objective, the messenger should use simple words and shorter sentences. If communication is to be effective, Burton constantly emphasised, the sender should aim at making their message 100 percent accessible to the recipient; in that process there should be no room for one to show off knowledge or the vocabulary at the sender's disposal. His argument was that such a form of communication should be made accessible to all: primary school leavers as well as university professors and all people between those two groups. This is a universal truth that applies to virtually all forms of communication: journalism, creative writing, non-fiction, public speaking. Although I am not an ideal follower of this tested wisdom, I have always tried to be as simple as possible in choice of words, thanks to Frank Burton.

Another area in which Burton – like all good journalists – advocated clarity and simplicity of expression was the reduction of superfluous phrases. "Instead of 'He is a man of wild nature', write 'He is wild'", he told us. When applied to the South Sudanese scene, one could include inelegant expressions, such as "He is a Dinka by tribe" or, "Lako is from the Bari tribe". Following the above advice, these sentences would be pruned to "He is a Dinka" and "Lako is a Bari", respectively; nothing is gained by beating around the bush with vulgar or clumsy forms of expression. As learners it became clear to us that not all that we read or heard from others was there ready to be borrowed in whole.

Another area which came under Burton's scrutiny was the uncritical use of clichés. Some of the common expressions he warned his students to minimise their use or totally avoid included "at the end of the day"; "when all is said and done"; "in the final analysis". "Just say 'in the end' or 'finally', instead of wasting words and time", he told the attentive class, whose members were laughing at the expense of absent people they knew were fond of using such long-winded expressions.

Dr Douglas H. Johnson

Like Prof Taban lo Liyong, Dr Douglas H. Johnson's mentoring me didn't take place within the confines of lecture theatres. We met briefly in Khartoum in the early 1970s when he was doing his research into the prophesies among the Nuer in the early 19th and early 20th centuries, which later became the *Nuer Prophets*. However, it was in Juba during the second half of the decade that his job and mine brought us close. This was at the headquarters of the Regional Ministry of Culture and Information. He was the assistant director for archives, while I was editing the *Southern Sudan* magazine. Our respective offices were next door to one another. But there was more cooperation between us than one would expect the two fields would warrant.

The publication was an ambitious project, which styled itself as a serious cultural and news magazine. At the beginning the periodical didn't have professional and credible writers to contribute articles in several departments. When I approached Douglas to contribute short and general pieces on the history of Southern Sudan he readily accepted, an offer that gave the periodical high profile both with the Southern Sudanese as well as non-Sudanese readers – especially foreign embassies and NGOs based in Khartoum, whom subscribed to the monthly immediately following the appearance on the street of the maiden issue.

I remember an article Douglas wrote on Nuer prophets. A reader, Jeroboam Machuor Kulang, a Dinka from Duk-neighbouring Lou and Gawar Nuer, wrote in a letter to the editor, disagreeing that the Nuer prophets were men of peace. Machuor, a retired nurse, singled Ngundeng Bong, claiming that that prophet was a troublesome man. Douglas replied that he had no quarrel with anyone disagreeing with him on that. To the historian, different people could see the same object differently, depending on their respective vantage points. It was probably my second time – the first was when I was chair of a debating society at the University of Khartoum in 1973 – to referee a debate, as well as being an opportunity to appreciate the idea of the right of people to reply. The lesson – for a writer and debater – I was beginning to appreciate was that in the world of ideas, nearly everything was subject to debate and different interpretations. This is consistent with the exercise of freedom of expression; anything that tries to inhibit expression of opposing views belongs to the domain of totalitarianism.

Years later, when I was editing *The Pioneer* weekly newspaper, Douglas again accepted to contribute articles selected from the history of South Sudan. The readership was now wider than that of the *Southern Sudan* monthly. There were more foreign readers in Juba after the independence of the former region of Sudan, as the capital has now grown from the town it was in the 1970s and early 1980s into a thriving cosmopolitan city.

The articles which appeared under "Past Notes and Record" regular column have now been published as a book. *South Sudanese Notes and Records* covers famous historical personalities such as Ali Abdel Latif, and former slaves who later became outstanding figures in the Catholic Church. These include Daniel Surur and St Bakhita among many other prominent figures in history of Sudan/South Sudan.

I was not only handling his articles; like the general reader, I was also learning from those articles. The pieces contain information not easily available to a non-historian. Besides that, Douglas H. Johnson's presentation of narratives is characterised by his signature clarity and the overall sense of balance. Despite the scholarly perch he occupies, his writings are easily accessible to all: laypeople as well as his colleagues in the academia. It's not surprising that in reviewing Johnson's latest book, *South Sudan: A New History for a New Nation*, Justin Willis, a professor of history at Durham University, has described Douglas H. Johnson's knowledge of South Sudan's history as "unrivalled" and that his approach is "both sympathetic and critical". Deborah Scroggins, author of *Emma's War*, acknowledges Johnson as the "most prominent living historian of South Sudan".[17] Douglas H. Johnson's *The Root Causes of Sudan's Civil Wars: Peace or Truce* has become a standard reference for researchers and general readers interested to understand recent history, especially conflicts involving what are now the two Sudans.

Reference to the scholar as "sympathetic" requires clarification and context. "Sympathy" or "sympathetic" would generally imply bias in favour of someone or something. But for a person such as a scholar or a journalist, with a professional and personal integrity to maintain and protect, being sympathetic takes the form objective presentation of the subject in question. There is no better tool to use to achieve that than semantics. For years I have been fighting what appeared to have been a lonely campaign against the use of "animist"/"animism" by most Western journalists and pseudo-academic writers when talking about South Sudanese. Unlike me, Dr Johnson bases his rejection of the term on available body of knowledge accumulated by linguists and social anthropologists as well as his own, having studied aspects of belief system and spirituality as practised by some South Sudanese peoples. In his opinion, for one to describe South Sudanese people as animists, whatever their social and educational attainment may be, is incorrect. For me Johnson's rejection of "animism"/ "animist" has become an all-clear signal: the terminology has no place in any discourse on spiritual matters relating to the peoples of South Sudan.

For years I have been convinced that "tribe" is an outdated word when used in the context of South Sudan and because of that I "banned" it in my writing. Now I have retrieved the word from the reject list and now use it cautiously in limited cases. This happened after my reading of Johnson's recent critical analysis of the term: when and where the use of "tribe" would be appropriate.[18]

I look towards Dr Douglas H. Johnson as an old friend and a teacher, whose lessons- through his writings- keep me updated in the fast changing world of ideas and epistemology.

---

17 Johnson, D. H. *South Sudan: A New History for a New Nation*, Ohio University Press, 2016.
18 Crystal, David, *How Language Works*, p.289, Penguin Group Australia, 2008.

Professor Taban lo Liyong

While an undergraduate at the University of Khartoum in the early 1970s, I stumbled on a publication called *Eating Chiefs*. Going over the small book, my eye caught "Makal" and "Malakal". The introductory lines were "Luo culture from Lolwe to Malkal, selected, interpreted & transmuted by Taban lo Liyong". These words were enough to pin me down. "Ah! This should be about me", I told myself and decided to sit to read the contents and part of the book. For a start I went straight for the blurb to get information on the author whom I thought might be Shilluk. As someone from a province whose capital was Malakal and Makal in Shilluk, my interest was less than a passing curiosity. The writer was a complete stranger to me – I had never heard or read about him before. At that time African literature in English was not part of our syllabus. I decided to read the book that introduced itself as "transmuted folktales", from Luo-speaking peoples. *Eating Chiefs* belonged to the African Writers Series which included works of Chinua Achebe- who was also the series' editor- published by Heinemann.

During my youth, meeting a famous public figure, especially a writer whose book one had read, was a big deal. At that time, Professor Abdalla el Tayeb, then an authority in Arabic literature and culture, was probably the only writer I met in person. He was the Dean of the Faculty of Arts at the University of Khartoum. The Nigerian writer, Cyprian Ekwensi, was another writer whom I met in West Berlin, Germany in 1978. He was there for a couple of days lecturing to us- journalists from Africa- on the responsibility of writers and journalists as educators whose role in their societies was to tell the truth regardless of cost to the messenger.

In 1976, Dr Oliver Duku, a specialist pathologist and a fellow member of the All Saints Cathedral – Episcopal Church of Sudan at the time – met me at Juba Hotel one evening and gave me some interesting news.

"I have an important visitor in my house now. Do you know Taban lo Liyong?" he asked me.

"Really? Yes. But not in person. I want to meet him" I said with an excitement I couldn't conceal.

"This is why I have come to tell you. Nobody else [among the journalists] knows his presence here" he emphasised before we sat down for tea.

The good doctor didn't need to worry. In the Juba of the 1970s there were very few serious fellow hacks to fear losing to a rival. The presence in Juba of Taban lo Liyong was news that could be a scoop.

With a young cameraman I had hired from the office of information in Equatoria Province, I met Taban lo Liyong at the former Juba Senior Guesthouse. The newsmaker was sitting under a tree where he was sipping a soft drink. He got up to greet me. He was friendly and warm as he told me to take a seat. After brief self-introductions, I was amazed by the simplicity he showed. By that time, I was learning about life in general and of great people in particular. I was beginning to note that one could be a celebrity yet be modest. Taban was probably the first VIP I found to be down to earth. This was in sharp contrast to some bullies of ministers who openly treated reporters haughtily. While on the staff of the *Nile Mirror* my colleagues and I imposed a boycott on reporting about a ministry because its snobbish minister had rejected to talk to a young female reporter the editor had sent for news coverage; he wanted to be *interviewed*, and only by the editor.

The interview Taban gave me was one of the longest I have ever done in my whole career. He talked about his books and other writers and their works; that Alexander Pushkin, the famous Russian poet had African blood in him; had heard from him the saying "If someone has built a pyramid for you, don't ask him whether he washes his hand before eating".

After writing up the interview, I sent the typed version to *Sudanow*, published in Khartoum and whose chief editor was Bona Malwal, then Minister for Culture and Information in the central government. Within a short time, the publication turned out to be the best monthly magazine in the whole of Africa of the day. After the publication of the interview – which was given prominence by the periodical – I was pleasantly surprised when I received a cheque whose value was just three (Sudanese) pounds short of my monthly salary.

It was my first lesson that journalism was a job that was well rewarded. But the most important benefit I earned from the interview was not only monetary; the final product was a very useful lesson about how a good copy editor would turn a raw material made dreary by the question-answer format into an interesting read. Without addition or subtraction, the staff writer at *Sudanow* breathed life and character into the ensuing feature which was very entertaining and informative, even to me. I soon adopted their style, unfortunately without acknowledging my indebtedness to the editors.

We had become friends with Taban, who encouraged me to write fiction. While an undergraduate, our literature lecturer, had introduced us to fiction writing. *Khartoumers*, a collections of short stories by her class, was in imitation of James Joyce's *Dubliners*. *Khartoumers* carried my "Two Lives", which incidentally was along the line of transmuted folktales. I hadn't yet seen *Eating Chiefs* at that time. Through Taban's encouragement I sent the story to *Sudanow*. The magazine immediately accepted, published it and asked me for more. "Murder", a short story followed. It is a story about someone who because he has become Christian, goes to his native home and kills a snake which is a family totem. The family is in panic as they fear some divine retribution for the killing the reptile that the clan worships. While writing short stories as well as working in the local press, I was voraciously reading the world's best short stories by authors such as Kurt Vonnegut, Hemingway, William Somerset Maugham, along with a host of French, Arab and Russian writers.

Taban lo Liyong, who would become Professor of Literature at the new University of Juba, was promoting creative writing among young writers, some of them journalists. My literary cooperation with Taban solidified with him supplying his creative writings to the *Southern Sudan* magazine – launched in July 1977, and of which I was founding editor. And goodness me, Taban lo Liyong could be savage in his satirical pieces. Each time I published any of those searing poems or tales, I waited anxiously for a summons or explanation from my employer, the Regional Ministry of Culture and Information. The man is full of humour. On paper his words can be devastating especially when those targets are the powers that be.

Our shared interests in writing, however, didn't extend to politics. In the 1977/8 elections to the People's Regional Assembly, Taban lo Liyong offered to contest one of the seats allotted to university graduates. He approached me to be his campaign manager. Although I have always spurned politics (and continue to shun it) I agreed to work for him, only to be told as a civil servant I shouldn't get involved in matters political.

In 1981 I moved to Britain to continue my studies in media. During the second civil war, Prof Taban lo Liyong went to teach literature in Japan and later at the University of Venda in South Africa. An author of over 20 books on poetry, fiction, literary criticism, among others, Prof Taban lo Liyong has taught at universities in Kenya, Papua New Guinea, and is now at the University of Juba, South Sudan.

It was in the late 1990s, while I was in Nairobi, that a Kenyan academic surprised me with a parcel which she handed to me. It contained a book of collected stories about women from Southern Sudan. The editor of the anthology was Prof Taban lo Liyong. My story, "Two Lives" was there again. He sent me a certain amount in dollars as my honorarium. Of considerable interest was that I had to sign a document confirming the receipt of the sum. The paper had to be returned to him. In turn Taban was going to send the form I had signed to an organisation which had provided the funds to support creative writings by Southern Sudanese. This was typical of Taban, a man who hates corruption so much that his criticisms are directed – more often than not – against the corrupt and always against African ruling elites who abuse public office.

On many occasions Taban has urged me to write and publish. Each time I asked him, "Write what? Write on what?" his answer would be "Write. Just write". He didn't need to elaborate. And he means it. Seriously.

In 2013 when Dr Peter Adwok Nyaba, Prof Taban lo Loying fellow academic and an author in his own right, launched *South Sudan: The State We Aspire To* at New Sudan Hotel, Juba, Taban approached me with "The next launch will be of your book". A few minutes later, Taban's daughter, Census, as if acting on a cue from her dad, caught up with me as I was leaving the venue to tell me that the public was waiting for my book.

■

Francis Mading Deng

Apart from British anthropologist Dr Godfrey Lienhardt, author of *Divinity and Experience: The Religion of the Dinka*, there is hardly any other person who has done more in writing on Dinka people and their culture more widely and in depth than Dr Francis Mading Deng. A lawyer and international diplomat, Mading is also highly prolific, his writing traversing areas ranging from fiction to ethnography. These include (but are not limited to): songs, folktales, philosophy, biography, history, politics, current affairs, humanitarian work and novels, among other genres. Whether the reader of his works is a Dinka with a background in culture or an outsider, Mading brings freshness to whatever subject he tackles as he combines an unrivalled knowledge of his people, their history and ways of life.

My introduction and subsequent interest in the writings of Francis Mading Deng began with The *Dynamics of Identification*, followed by *Tradition Modernization: Challenge for Law Among the Dinka of the Sudan*. From there, I became an avid reader of whatever he wrote and on any subject. One of his books – which I consider to be his best – is *The Man Called Deng Majok*, a biography of his father, the late chief of the Ngok Dinka. The account is a record of the chief's life as an influential and powerful public servant, who was adroit in building relations with his neighbours, the Baggara Arabs of Kordofan. Chief Deng Kuol Arop, his son, tells us he was not a saint: the chief is presented roundly, with his virtues and faults such as corruption. Despite this, as an author, Francis Mading Deng hasn't lacked unforgiving critics over the years.

Earlier on, one of his fiercest detractors attacked me when he saw me reading one of Mading's new releases, *The Dinka Cosmology*, a bold attempt at philosophy. When I wanted to know what irritated him about the Mading's works, he laconically responded with "I do not like the man and his books". Ugh, the man! I was temporarily speechless. Since there was bitterness in my interlocutor's voice it was clearly a waste of time for me to continue arguing with this highly-prejudiced man who regarded himself as an intellectual. Sadly, I later found out the man, a graduate of social sciences from the University of Khartoum, Mading alma mater, had not read a single work by the writer he disliked with a fashion.

That encounter opened my eyes and mind to the world out there where mere preconception prevents some people from first reading a piece of writing and then critically judging the contents on their merits and demerits. The lesson I drew from that discovery was that anyone writing and hoping for a universal approval of their writings was in for a rude shock.

Francis Deng, the author, has often been criticised for allegedly using his Dinka Ngok tribe and society as a mirror of the entire Dinka people. Despite the fact that Mading is of very high calibre as an intellectual who is also a polyglot – very fluent in Dinka, Arabic and English – his "microcosm" approach to ethnography is right and logical. An American academic whose mother tongue was English told me in the early 1970s that Francis Mading Deng wrote English better than he.

It makes a lot of sense for one to talk or write on what one is familiar with, rather than engage in a vast area beyond one's grip. Interestingly, this was the problem I later faced in the early 1990s over my "Far Away from War" series of press articles in which my village of yesteryear was the scene of my recollections on Dinka culture. I was warned that I had "demoted" myself from a "national" writer to a "tribal chronicler". I managed to water down that baseless charge because I had expected it, thanks to the experience of Francis Mading Deng.

I have borrowed a lot from Dr Francis Mading Deng the writer. I am happy to emulate him in several aspects of writing especially when it comes to someone documenting the cultural aspects of a traditional society. While a good number among South Sudan's ruling elite give lip service to their pride in their cultural identity, few care to do anything creative to preserve, promote our national heritage and diversity. There is an urgent need for those with an interest in writing to capture and record cultural aspects, especially, the traditional ways and values of the Dinka people – indeed all our collective national heritage- currently facing extinction due to modernisation onslaught. It is no secret that I have two manuscripts in Dinka language of my recollections of Dinka society of childhood and youth. There are ideas and concepts in Dinka English or any other language cannot successfully convey to a reader without any solid background in Dinka language and culture especially of the past centuries and decades.

I was inspired by the writings of Francis Mading Deng. He remains a driving force in that regard.

Antipas Arok Biowei: learning English in the street

Antipas Arok Biowei was one of my first teachers in what was known as bush school. The day-school was exactly a mile away from my childhood village. Antipas Arok really revolutionised teaching methods. Here is just one example. While I was in second year at Kongor Bush School, Arok took the whole class outside to roam the town, collecting items in the street and from some households. He gave the English names of all the objects thus collected or seen. Those consisted of a water well, drums, hides and skin, ropes, sticks, cooking utensils, grass for thatching huts, poles, branches of trees, stones, spears, cow horn, names of some birds, feathers and shells. In one of the shops we visited, the class was given names of some items such as beads, ankle bells, needles, razor blades, pieces of cloth, salt, onion and sugar.

By the time we were back in class we had many items of different kinds and with their names written down in English. We had learned their names; this was our biggest vocabulary in a day and from one source. With an adequate vocabulary, the possibility that one could talk and write and be understood was enhanced. Grammar then was the required glue for correctly stringing together those words to make communication possible. And this brings us to another builder of a kind.

Samuel Lual Dhoka: 'Column method'

Grammar in virtually all languages gives learners, especially those using non-mother tongues, a serious problem. When I went for elementary education at Malek, the school headmaster, Samuel Lual Dhoka, was teaching English. Lual, a graduate of Rumbek Secondary – then the only school of that status in Southern Sudan – equipped its students with what was the best educational available in the land. In his teaching of grammar, Samuel Lual had devised his famous "column system" – divided into main three categories: yesterday, every day, tomorrow. (As I can recall, there was no column for the past participle). "Yesterday he came, every day he comes, tomorrow he will come", he would say as he pointed to real columns and their contents he had drawn on the blackboard. In fact, we made a song of out of the column model.

For the pronouns, Lual demonstrated how to use them in this manner: "I, we and they never take an /s/; she, he and it takes an /s/", he would intone. Verbs came, in different shapes and forms: regular and irregular. Verbs such as "cost" or "cast", including "cost" and "broadcast", he taught, never change whether under yesterday, every day or tomorrow, columns. The method in a way involved some elements of rote learning.

The approach to what was a very complicated subject was simplified to make learning fun and easier, to the point that even the least intelligent student would have no problem understanding such rules, which govern unpredictable tenses that behave like a moody person. By the time I was in year four, most of us could write and sometimes use grammatically correct tenses. It's a truism that without grammar, the amount of vocabulary a person amasses in any language would be like having a team of football players without regulations.

Well, ungrammatical English continued to flourish within the student community of Malek. I can still recall a fourth year student whose skill in the language was challenged by a colleague. In response, "I have a danger grammar", he boasted. One is left guessing what the student meant to say.

Many years later a 12-year-old South Sudanese child who was brought up in Kenya where he was receiving his education would ask me, "Uncle, to which school did that man go?" He was referring to a sleekly-dressed public figure who was speaking for a VIP. The official was giving a statement to a public news channel we were watching in a family living room, when the man was heard saying "… as broadcasted yesterday". I had no answer to the child, although I have heard from several South Sudanese that the man was in England for several years during the 1983-2005 war. But even if that information were to be correct, people don't imbibe knowledge of a language by merely living where it is widely spoken; it is not in the air people breathe.

Samuel Lual Dhoka's teaching of grammar laid a firm foundation for his students, most of whom later had to earn their living using English as a tool for their work whether as clerks, journalists or full-time writers, including this author.

Pasquale Rumunu

My time at Atar Intermediate School was one phase in my education where I learned more subjects in some depth. These were geography, life science, mathematics, Arabic and English. While most of my teachers were very good at teaching their subjects, one teacher was exceptional. His name was Pasquale Rumunu Karlino Modi. The master – as a teacher was known at the time – was a darling to nearly all the students. Although Pasquale Rumunu taught other subjects besides English, his essay lessons were so popular that even some of the students who were listed sick with minor ailments would attend and then return to the dormitories to recuperate or rest.

Pasquale Rumunu would give a topic for the class to write on. After marking the essays, he would come around with the exercise books. He would comment on mistakes in grammar, peculiar expressions and areas that he wanted the rest of the students to avoid. Usually, Rumunu would pick the exercise book where there was a particular mistake that drew his attention most, read aloud, sometimes followed by students laughing at the unnamed colleague. Rumunu sometimes would slightly make a passing simile, with a reminder, "We learn through mistakes, our own or those made by others. Please stop laughing".

Some of the errors he would point out, consisted of words which were incorrectly applied. For instance, there was this student who had used the word "fellow" when he was referring to his father.

"Do not call your father 'fellow'. This is not polite", he warned not only that particular student, but the whole class.

"Came" versus "come" came under spotlight.

"Are you not going to return to your village when the school closes this year? Do not say 'In my village where I came from'. You have not stopped coming from or going to your village. Say 'the village I come from'". The topic was "Life in my village during the rainy season". Another student had written "returned back". The teacher said that form was wrong. "You are repeating yourself. 'Return' and 'back' mean the same. You should say either 'turned back' or 'returned'". It was the kind of mistake that the students including those who had not committed it had to avoid for the rest of their lives.

Prepositions and their use was another area where the teacher paid particular attention. Arbitrary as they appear, some prepositions, like idioms have to be taken as they are whether they appear incongruous where they are assigned. One of those was "sitting under the veranda" instead of "sitting in the veranda", as the speakers of Arabic are prone to fall into that trap.

Expressions which commonly gave students trouble included "malaria caught me", instead of the person catching an illness; the same problem of "thought transfer" applied to vehicular movements. In conventional English usage, for instance, a person catches a train or a bus. On the other hand, in some African expressions people don't catch those machines that move; cars, trains or wagons take and carry passengers. "The car took me from the town and carried me to my village" is a typical way of expressing that.

Pasquale Rumunu kept reminding us to avoid the practice of "thinking in one's mother tongue" and then literally translate an idea or an idiom into English. He warned that such a method did not always work well and should be avoided as far as possible. We began instead to "think in English" when writing or speaking in that difficult tongue we were determined to master.

Those instructions were not all about criticism for its own sake and how to avoid mistakes in grammar or misuse of words; the adored teacher often commended a student who had creatively used a sentence, phrase or word in his composition. "Make your story interesting by being imaginative", he would advise. He praised one of the students whose essay contained "We bent double as we followed the antelope through the tall elephant grass. The hunter who was ahead of us turned to us. He put his hand to his mouth. He wanted us not to make any noise because he feared that would scare the animal and run away ...". His voice still echoes in my ears as if it was yesterday Rumunu read to us the sentence he had selected from an essay written by one of our fellow students. He commended the writer of that composition whose name he withheld. On three different occasions, Pasquale Rumunu did the same for my essays, whose writer he also accorded anonymity which as a shy boy, I liked very much.

Mrs Margaret Kheiry

Mrs Margaret Kheiry was British by birth. She was married to a Sudanese. A trained teacher, Mrs Kheiry was one of the students' favourite teachers at Rumbek Secondary School. She joined the staff when I was in second year. For three years in that school she taught me novels of Dickens' *David Copperfield*, Robert Louis Stevenson's *Treasure Island*, George Bernard Shaw's *Arms and the Man* and Shakespeare's *The Merchant of Venice*. Her style of teaching made literature interesting and reinforced my ambition to become a writer in future. (Earlier, my ambition was to study agriculture at university but after realising that competence in natural sciences and maths – the last being my weak spot – I abandoned the dream).

Thomas Madit Aleth

Thomas Madit Aleth, who is a medical doctor by training, and currently a senior staff member of the University of Bahr el Ghazal is one of my former schoolmates who has helped greatly in shaping my ambition to be a writer. I first met him at Kongor Bush School. He had joined the school after his father, Timothy Aleth Gueny, who was a medical orderly, had been transferred to work in the dispensary in the area.

Madit's literary influence on me began when we were attending Rumbek Secondary. He was an exceptionally voracious reader. Simplified novels in the school were not enough for him. At Omdurman our school was located at the premises of the former Afhad Intermediate School for girls, not far from the Mahdi's tomb. A British Council library was next door to the school. The library was well stocked with books, mostly by English writers. Its membership was open to all, so we applied. Like me, Madit used to borrow books every week. I didn't know that there were books by African writers until one day Madit showed the books he had borrowed the day before. Those included ones by Nigerian writers led by Chinua Achebe, Cyprian Ekwensi and Elechi Amadi. I recall hearing from him the name *Things Fall Apart*. Unfortunately, it was not until several years later that I would read Achebe's first novel and his other works of fiction and non-fiction.

During our free time Madit would narrate to me the stories from the novels he had read. I began to ask myself: if those Africans were able to write books in English, why couldn't I do the same? To Madit, there was no special requirement for one to write novels. He told me that Cyprian Ekwensi was not an artistic person but a pharmacist. He also cited another person who had a strong taste in the arts while his background was in medicine. That was Dr Tigani el-Mahi, a polymath Sudanese known to the public for his expertise in psychiatry. The renowned psychiatrist later bequeathed his collections to the University of Khartoum Library- books in English, Spanish, French, German, English and Arabic. Dr Tigani el-Mahi is said to have known Latin, Persian, Hausa (widely spoken in Nigeria and other West African countries), besides English and Arabic.

Madit read Bond stories by Ian Fleming, the English novelist and creator of James Bond character. A habitual moviegoer, Madit loved the arts. He watched American movies and Indian films of which *Janwar* was his favourite.

Later, when I entered the University of Khartoum my ambition was no longer a passing whim: I had decided to be a future novelist. Thomas Madit, the man who loved literature, ended becoming a medical doctor, most probably trying to become one of the people his father had worked under for years.

I thought we had parted ways as far as things related to books, the arts and love of reading were concerned. I was wrong. After a separation lasting more than three decades – we met in Juba in 2013. One midday, Chaat Paul Nuul, a mutual friend, rang to inform me that Dr Thomas Madit was in town and that we should meet for lunch in one of the hotels in Thongpiny area. Excited to meet a long lost friend we hugged and sat down to a meal punctuated by an exchange of stories of what each of us had been doing all those long years.

"I never stopped reading your writings even during the war", said Madit who added "Those days when you were in Juba we used to get copies of the *Nile Mirror* in Malakal. I bought my copies to read your writings. Again when you were in Ethiopia and later in Nairobi, I was reading your articles and keenly following how you people were faring. Our thoughts were with you always", Madit fondly recalled. During the war, however, some of my writings were considered subversive by the Government of Sudan. People who received those "contraband" publications sometimes had to read them underground.

I was deeply moved.

Prof McMillan

Prof McMillan was a career British educationalist. When he taught English to preliminary students of the Faculty of Arts of the University of Khartoum in 1970, the elderly teacher was going to retire at the end of that year. A small man with a deep and commanding voice, McMillan taught literature and elements of phonetics as a guide to correct pronunciation. During one of his classes which he delivered to more than 200 students, the professor asked for one of them to volunteer to pronounce the adjective "doctrinal". Either out of shyness or ignorance of the right answer, none came forward to try.

He explained that the /i/ in the adjectival form had to be pronounced as /ai/ in "fine", for example, while in the noun, "doctrine", the /i/ was to sound like that in "fish". That was not the end of the explanation. The professor told the attentive class that he doubted any of those students sitting in the hall one day in their lives would use "doctrinal".

The message was that not all the words in any language that a person knows will ever be used. I was among those students. In all the years I have been speaking and writing English – amounting to hundreds of thousands of words, probably millions, and writing on as diverse topics as religion or ideology – there has never been a time I have ever used "doctrinal" or had the need to use it. It's simply because there has never been an appropriate context in which the word would be required. What McMillan meant was that words, particularly the difficult and rare ones, are vehicles for clear communication and not really a means for one to show off. A sound piece of advice I have adhered to well, although I occasionally err one way or another.

Mrs I. G. Abaza and Dr Rashid Abu Bakr

These were my lecturers in linguistics. This subject is defined – by one source – as "the scientific study of language and its structure, including the study of grammar, syntax and phonetics". In addition to improving correct use of language, the subject taught by these lecturers helped in demystifying popular concepts with political overtones. It was common – and little has changed over the years – that many Northern Sudanese, including members of the intelligentsia used to refer to languages spoken in the then Southern Region as *lahjat, rutana* (dialects) and the like. The languages spoken all over the South were derided. It was Arabic that enjoyed the hallowed status of *al-lugha* or *the* language. Such attitudes ignore important facts about language, any language.

Writing in his book *How Language Works*, David Crystal[19], a distinguished British linguist and author, says "People often hold negative views about dialects, because of traditional social association of the term. Languages in isolated parts of the world, which may not have been written down, are sometimes referred to pejoratively as 'dialects', as when someone talks of a tribe speaking 'a primitive kind of dialect'". Prof Crystal goes on "But this fails to recognize the complexity of the world's languages". Indeed. "There is no such thing as 'primitive language",[2] concludes one of the world's leading linguists.

At the personal level, I am one of the losers as far as the survival and future of mother tongue is concerned. Long ago, Twï, my mother tongue and that of the people inhabiting the territory that has undergone several administrative nomenclatures, known previously as Sub-district (under Duk District), Northern Bor, Kongor People's Rural Council, then again Bor North, and until a year ago, Twï (East) County, was spoken by nearly 100 percent of the population as a first language. (I have no inclination or stomach to know the number and names of clan enclaves that have been created out of Twï County after the Batustanisation of South Sudan in 2015).

Now, the number of speakers is dwindling by the year. There is fear that within the next 30-50 years Twï dialect and it variants will join Latin as a dead language – without anyone speaking it as a mother tongue. The reason for the decline has nothing to do with natural factors; it is a man-made situation. The idea of people abandoning their mother tongue in favour of what some of them consider to be a more fashionable language/dialect and that "outsiders" aspire to acquire and speak so as to keep up with the Joneses is not new nor it is peculiar to any particular language/dialect group. The reasons accounting for members of a community dropping their mother tongue for another may be due to social factors but since that is not my concern here, it is necessary to report the justification children normally give: "others make fun of us" when they speak their native tongue. This is not theory. Twï dialect has its peculiarities that easily alert listeners speaking other Dinka dialects because of a distinctive phonological feature that even speakers of other foreign languages can detect in the way their own words are pronounced. The dialect has this rare feature /l/ and /n/ deceptively alternating but at a closer look are not interchangeable. By way of example, take "Malakal", the name of a major town in South Sudan. Invariably it would be – to a typical Twï speaker, "Manakal", "Malakan", or even "Malakal". Nothing seems to be a constant in this regard. And when listeners or let call them "outsiders" come to notice this, they wonder; others laugh at the speaker. Extended to other languages, one gets in this hypothetical speaker carrying the phenomenon a foreign language. Let us take this English sentence "He runs slowly" becomes- in an idealised case- "He ruls snowny".

Anyone who doubts the veracity of my statement should look for the speeches of the late John Garang, the leader of the SPLM/A who spoke his native Twï (and some Rek dialect- which did nothing to affect his Twï[20] "accent"- he picked up when he was a student in Tonj and Bussere in Bahr el Ghazal). Whether he is talking in Dinka, Arabic or English, the /l/-/n/ phenomenon is there for anyone with a sharp ear to note.

During the 1970s, the name of the Cambodian soldier, General Lon Nol was a perfect case for teasing Twï speakers. "My friend, what is the name of the army officer who has overthrown government in Cambodia" was the joke poked at students who spoke Twï dialect.

The problem is not confined to the puzzling and unpredictable case of /l/ and /n/, and their seeming "interchangeability"; certain words fit into what others may consider as "primitive". In those days Twï speakers had "*mom*" for *nom* or *nhom*, head in the rest of Dinka dialects. With the exception of the very old people over 80 years and above living today in Twïland, South Sudan's urban centres or in the diaspora, the word has died out, and so has the exclamation "*Mawoou!*" or "*Eŋoŋ*" (engong) for "really". I have randomly selected these three examples out of many words now on their way to disappear from daily usage; some are actually long dead. And the queue of words which are terminally ill is quite long. They include the phrase "*Ca nin?*", a phrase for "Good morning", now overtaken by "*Cï yï bäk?*" and strangely by "*Kudual*" which is a general form of greeting similar to "Hello".

■

Prof A. N. Tucker

Tucker was project adviser to the British administration in Sudan on language teaching policy which culminated in the holding of the Rejaf

---

20 Twï or Twi shouldn't be confused with Twi which is spoken by between 6-9 people in Ghana, a member of Akan family of related languages.

language conference of 1928, where several Southern languages were selected to be used for educational purposes. An authority on the study of African languages in those days, Prof Tucker was a visiting fellow at the Institute of Afro-Asian Studies, at University of Khartoum from late 1974-75. I became one of his students at the centre. The elderly scholar spent several weeks investigating Dinka vowel system. I was with him most of the time. Nearly all the sessions were devoted to the investigation into some aspects of Dinka phonemes. He would ask me to supply examples to support a theory or what was already known. His attention was on the nature of the vowels, particularly the difference between the so called breathy and non-breathy vowels. As a native Dinka speaker, I could pronounce any of those vowels as requested although I was not then aware of the importance of the study and – more importantly, the role that knowledge was going to play in the development and writing (improved) the language in the future.

Without going into details, the two types of vowels are explained below:
Non-breathy vowels– known in Dinka as *akëër cie yäu* are /a/, /e/, /ɛ/, /i/, /o/, /ɔ/

Breathy vowels- known as *akëër yäu* are /ä/, /ë/, /ɛ̈/, /ï/, /ɛ̈/, /ï/, /ö/, /ɔ̈/

Although /u/ is a vowel it doesn't fall into any of the two categories. The "breathy" vowels are differentiated from the "non-breathy" ones by the presence of diacritic or umlaut on top character. Before the Summer Institute of Linguistics, SIL, introduced these symbols to the writing of Dinka, the reader had to guess the difference in the word- its pronunciation and meaning- with a vowel by context. Vowel quantity and quality act as major determinants of pronunciation and meaning of a given word. For example, in those days one would not know what to make of these sets of words: *"gak"* and *"lony"*. *"Gak"* (without umlaut), means crow, while *"gäk"* is a word for "plentiful". *"Lony"* on the other hand is a Dinka word for civet cat while *"löny"* means noun "fall". Before the introduction of diacritics to differentiate the breathy from the non-breathy vowels, it was not easy for a ready to know whether *"riŋ"* (ring) meant "meat" or "run". Now thanks the symbol *"riŋ"* is the Dinka for meat *"riŋ"* is "run".

Linguistics involves knowledge that is mostly technical. As an undergraduate, I was fascinated by the study of phonology and morphology.

Lectures on these greatly helped me in understanding the complexities that are the vowel system in Dinka. Years later, I found a convenient application of that introduction to the subject when I took up the job of Dinka-English translation while in Australia. Many friends and colleagues don't know that my main source of livelihood for more than 10 years has been – and continues to be – English- Dinka translation. Also unknown to them is that the role of translator I have been involved with over that period to the present, is largely a secure and more rewarding employment in terms of recompense, than teaching, for instance. And it has other advantages over other jobs, too. It's a job one does at home; anywhere in the world as long as one is computer literate and uses online communication. And the most important aspect of the employment is that one doesn't have a boss to breathe heavily over their shoulders or an employer who out of whims or spite would fire you without warning. What the client wants is a quality job and to be delivered on deadline; no loyalty is required from the translator.

I sometimes wonder whether I would have acquired fluency in written Dinka without what I learned under Prof A. N. Tucker. The study of linguistics has been one of the few labours that have been truly and practically rewarding to me. With that background I have now completed three typescripts in Dinka – recording recollections of rural South Sudan of my childhood and translation of some of Aesop fables. I am grateful to late Prof A. N. Tucker and to my friend and former colleague, Prof Job Dharuai Malou, the linguist whose book, *Dinka Vowel System,* remains an important guide in the subject.

War
& Peace

The Origins of 'Far Away from War'

On the second Sunday after my return from Australia to Juba I arrived a little late for a church service. As usual the congregation had filled the church to overflowing, so I took my seat at the wing that appears to be an addition to the original structure. The congregation that numbered over 1000 souls consisted of children, youth, middle aged men and women. There were senior members in the Government of Southern Sudan, GoSS, several generals in the SPLA and senior officers in other regular forces.

Just when the service was about to end it was announced that if I were present I should report to the podium to greet the congregation. I slowly picked my way towards the pulpit, or was it an altar? After receiving the microphone, I was not sure whether I was going to say "I bring to you the greetings of our people in Australia. They send their greetings to you in the name of the Father, the Son and the Holy Spirit" and then walk back to my bench.

I thought that doing that was not enough. I had an important message to deliver. Since I went to Australia immediately after the signing of the CPA, many people, distant friends and others, frequently kept asking several questions such as: Why had I to leave at that particular time? Did I not like the agreement? Some people drew some conclusions concerning my motives, suggestions so absurd that I had better not repeat them here. I found the invitation to speak publicly an opportunity to end some of the wild rumours that had filled the air since my departure for Australia in 2005.

Because of the war conditions I had never had enough time with my family to the extent that my children did not know me very well, I revealed, adding that I had and still have nothing against the CPA or any individual or groups of people in or outside government. I further disclosed that I had told the late leader John Garang at Naivasha that I sincerely supported the protocols that constitute the CPA; but despite that stance I would not be part of the administration to be set up after the signature of the agreement. To drive the point home that I was not making it up in the absence of the late Garang, who would not be able to deny or contradict my claims, I had to mention, for verification, three senior SPLM/A members who were present during my talk with Garang. One of the witnesses I had named, an SPLA general, was by chance in the congregation. Since I had to be brief and that the subsequent utterances were of little import I have, at this juncture, to bring to an end the substance of my "lecture".

Why being addressed as 'Far Away from War' offends me

In about 1999, when I was in Nairobi, one of my young nephews wrote a letter to me. The missive began "Dear Uncle Far Away from War..." I instantly lost my cool and threw away the offending paper. The people in the room were stunned at my reaction. Was the missive carrying some bad news? they asked. The boy might have thought the title of the paper's column had become my nickname. He was wrong; only peers create and exchange nicknames. Usually, nicknames have their roots in circumstances best known and kept as secret among friends. Some of these could be light-hearted or based on a special circumstance which when taken out of context would be extremely insulting. There was nothing in "Far Away from War" remotely similar to the situations just cited to make that title in a newsletter my sobriquet.

"How can this boy be so rude as to write this?" was my reply. Even after I had repeated what the letter contained the people in the room did not see any reason behind my rage. After I had cooled down I realised that the boy had made a mistake out of innocence.

"This boy thinks that this is my nickname. It is not. And even though it were one, he is not my age-mate", I told them.

"*M'aleish*[21]. He did not intend to insult you", they assured me.

The origins of the column and its name

On my return from West Africa where I had gone to work as an editorial consultant at the African Development Bank and after my reunion with my family who had been "stranded" at Nasir which was the headquarters of breakaway rebel faction for over two and half years, I chose to settle in Lodwar, Kenya. The town unlike the nearby Kakuma refugee camp had better schools and amenities such as a public library and electricity. I enrolled my children in a primary school there. I also took up a teaching job in Lodwar High School. North-western Kenya is usually dry, hot and humid

---

21 [1] *M'aleish* is Sudanese colloquial Arabic for "take it easy".

for many months of the year; afternoons were particularly unbearable. I had to spend much of that time under a tree near the rented family house. The tree's shade provided some mild relief from the searing heat. Nearly every day, while sitting under there I would either read a book or write an essay, a short story or a press article. I even ventured into poetry, some of the poems were published in the *SPLM/A Update* newsletter.

The subjects of these pieces ranged from culture, mostly childhood recollections of village life; to customs or emergence of slangs that contain words such as *"thiai-dit"*, Dinka and Nuer corruption of "CID", or Criminal Investigation Department, to refer to a Southern Sudanese informant working for Khartoum security apparatus. In the cultural domain, for example, I wrote a piece that explained the possible reasons behind the taboo that prohibit initiated men especially among the Nuer and Dinka people from cooking or milking cows.

Nowhere in the column did ever I write an article denouncing the war of liberation that was being waged by the SPLA against the army of the Government of Sudan or SAF. I also did not express in writing or verbally that the forces of SPLA should stop fighting when the causes that led to the armed conflict had not been adequately addressed and given appropriate solutions. I am neither a militarist nor a pacifist but I am firmly convinced that the armed struggle conducted by the SPLA was justified as a last resort by a people denied their birth rights as citizens equal with others before the law.

What I meant by 'Far Away from War'

When I sent the first articles, the editor of then SPLM/A mouthpiece, the *SPLM/A Update* weekly newsletter my colleague George Garang Deng Chol was happy and encouraged me to feed the publication every week. Within a short time, the column had attracted a large readership, especially among non-Sudanese expatriate community in the Kenyan capital, Nairobi. Letters of praise for the contents of the column came from Sudanese sympathisers of the SPLM resident in the Gulf and from areas controlled by the government in Khartoum who read the paper under cover. The central message from "Far Away from War" was that despite the prevailing war conditions, Southern Sudanese people in refugee camps, in rural areas under the SPLM/A administration and in the diaspora and even at the war fronts, continued to live their normal lives. Children were being born, marriages and wedding were being celebrated, cultural values were either being observed while others were being questioned or discarded. To me this there was nothing unusual in that phenomenon; peace or war, life must go on. Wars, it has to be allowed, disrupt lives, cause deaths, maim people and separate families but the human resilience makes it possible for war-affected people to live their lives as normal or a semblance of that. Indirectly, even without the writer being aware of that, the column was a voice of optimism. I was saying the obvious.

Others, for different reasons and motives, viewed the contents differently, some with jaundiced and venomous bias against the author; some approached the essays with closed minds to the extent that I was informed that some persons who had not read a single article were known to seethe with anger whenever they saw a copy of the newsletter containing a piece by me.

Because of that campaign of denigration and distortion from my detractors, word went out to some members of the SPLA that I was "contributing to lowering the morale of the fighting forces", an allegation that could equate the accused with treason and of course with serious consequences, given the military mind-set of those days. Anyone known to have done anything to dent the morale of the SPLA was seen as someone working against the people and their just cause. That was the job of the enemy, not of a member who happened to be a commissioned officer in the rebel army.

Self-inflicted hate
Some of the movement's members who believed I was wrong did everything they could to tarnish my personality; some of those who were maddened by my writings were reportedly said to have gone to the leader of the SPLM/A, John Garang, asking him to order the editor to stop publishing my column. He is reported to have said nothing in response, an indication that he disagreed with my critics. And the column continued until the publication died a natural death several years later.

To be fair I must admit that I frequently stepped on some sensitive toes. For example, in one article I ridiculed people, without reference to soldiers, for buying and carrying several expensive pens at the same time to advertise that they were educated and therefore "intellectual". In another opinion piece I challenged the then pervasive belief among some Sudanese officer classes for priding themselves on belonging to a career that they thought was superior to all other professions. I conceded that being a soldier, anywhere and throughout history, has always played a noble role in defending fellow citizens and their values and sacrificing one's life in the process. I mentioned some well-known generals in world history who defended their countries from foreign aggressions and that some military leaders were on record as liberators of their people from foreign invasion or oppressive internal rule.

On the downside of the scale I reminded the braggarts that soldiering had the distinct disadvantage that it was an occupation that could not be exported as is the case with medicine or teaching. If and when a former soldier wanted a job outside his home country, the only vacancies on offer were membership of a mercenary army or guarding of public buildings and establishments, I wrote. For months I was a pariah within the SPLA officer corps for my audacity to state indisputable facts.

I believe that no harm came to me for my "sins" of "Far Away from War" because the SPLA top political and military leadership enjoyed reading "Far Away from War". They loved the pieces and they told me to my face. Years later some friends within the diplomatic and NGO community based in Nairobi informed me that they subscribed to the *SPLM/A Update* because of my column which they said relieved them of the dreary propaganda material that filled the rest of the 11 pages. Having myself been a propagandist – a job and name I am loath to adopt – during my tenure as director of Radio SPLA from 1984 to 1991 I have come to realise that propaganda is the most boring form of communication human beings have ever devised. "Far Away from War" provided the non-partisans as well as core SPLM readers with a break from a litany of invectives hurled against the movement's enemies and from grim statistics of the dead enemy soldiers. I have no regrets and this is why I have included those pieces in this collection.

When Gaddafi and SPLM/A Played a Game of Wits

Our story takes us back to the year 1969. On May 25, 1969, a group of Sudanese Army officers staged a successful coup, replacing civilian rule. The coup leader, a colonel named Jaafar Mohammed Nimeiri, who had promoted himself overnight to the rank of major general, told the world that among other things his "revolution" was not going to do business with Zionism, imperialism, nor another evil, called neo-colonialism.

On September 1, 1969, a Libyan Army captain with a difficult name to transliterate, overthrew the monarch, King Idris es Sanousi. The officer, Mu'amar el Gadhafi, a name written by the media with different spellings and corresponding pronunciation – now standardised as Muammar Gaddafi – who was just 27 years old, vault-jumped his rank, becoming a colonel on assuming power. He told everyone that his military rank was all that he cared for, and that no one should address him in any form other than *Al-Aqiid* or Colonel. To him and likeminded revolutionaries, the honorific title of "president" smacked of cultural imperialism. His admirers, though, defied the taboo with two endearing modifications for him, that is *Al Akh*, meaning Brother and *El Qaid* meaning, the Leader.

The two radical soldiers in Libya and Sudan admired their neighbour, the former Colonel Gamal Abdel Nasser of Egypt, who had discarded military uniform many years before and was happy in Western style suits and the title of President, rather than that of a military rank. Nasser had mellowed with age, and tasted humiliating defeat at the hands of the Israelis during the Six Day War of 1967. Those experiences had made him more guarded about the revolutionary rhetoric from Khartoum and Tripoli, but the changes were music to the ears of Nasser whose lifelong dream was complete unification of *Al Ummah al Arabiya* or the Arab Nation, and the liberation of Palestine from what they termed "Zionist entity", a euphemism for the State of Israel. Nevertheless, the former soldier was happy with the advent of the untested young revolutionaries on the Arab political stage.

But Gaddafi was the most impatient and restive of the trio: he wanted immediate unity of the Arab peoples and countries stretching "*Min el Khaleej lil Muheeth"*, meaning, from the Gulf to the [Atlantic] Ocean. An understanding, dubbed The Tripartite Agreement, was hastily set up as a nucleus for future Arab unity. But matters did not favour Gaddafi; Nasser died in 1970. More frustrations were in store for the young Libyan proponent of unity.

The Libyan had no patience with Arab kings or presidents who kowtowed to the West. However, his nemesis was one of the kings he despised - King Hussein of Jordan. During a meeting at a summit of Arab heads of state, taking place in Cairo in the early 1970s, Gaddafi and the Jordanian King Hussein had to be separated when the two were about exchange blows across the conference table, after Gaddafi had thrown insults at the Jordanian. This brawl gave the Libyan leader the moniker of *El Majnoon el Libi*, or the Mad Libyan.

Nimeiri as a black chief of the Arab world

With Nimeiri left as Gaddafi's partner in his grand design for the unity of the Arab world, things went from bad to worse. The Sudanese leader was dragging his feet; Arab unity was desirable but its pursuit could wait for more opportune times; first, he believed, he had to put his own house in order. The African Sudanese in the south of the country were up in arms against the system of rule in Khartoum and were bent on separating their region from the rest of the country. Nimeiri's solution was to prevent the fragmentation of his country while, at the same time, allaying the Southern Sudanese nightmare that they were not going to be frog marched into the fold of Arab unity.

Nimeiri knew that the civil war in his backyard was not child's play. The President had seen action in the war zone of Southern Sudan. He still remembered his days in the region; a handful of the now nearly extinct veterans class of Anya Nya guerrillas still recall to this day the time they repulsed the forces under the command of the then Major Nimeiri at Boma plateau on the Ethiopian – Sudanese border in the 1960s.

Gaddafi's solution was different from Nimeiri's – let the South go if it stood in the way of the unity of the Arab nations. Nimeiri and his colleagues saw that proposal as a chalice full of treason that no sensible Northern Sudanese leader could countenance, without inviting ignomiy and even ostracism by the people of his region.

Abortive communist Coup of 1971 – the last straw

They say one offence can easily be forgiven but a repeated one requires a saint to overlook. Not so with Gaddafi. In 1971, Nimeiri's former colleagues in the ruling Revolutionary Command Council, whom he had dismissed the previous year, carried out a coup in broad daylight. The daring military takeover was executed by Major Hashim Mohammed al Atta at 3 pm. Atta, later described by Nimeiri as an active member of the Sudan Communist Party, broadcast a statement that Nimeiri had to go to give way to what he called *"Al Thawra el Tasihiya"* or revolution for reform. Lieutenant Colonel Babiker el Nur, was going to be the head of the new dispensation. He and Major Farouq Osman Hamdallah, also a member of the new Revolutionary Command Council, were in the British capital, London. The two held a press conference, detailing their itinerary and the airline that was going to take them to Khartoum to form a government.

No soldier worth his salt could possibly commit such a blunder. That piece of information was ammunition for Col Gaddafi who, although he claimed left-wing credentials, was an ideologically morbid anti-communist. While a BOAC, or British Overseas Airways Corporation – forerunner of British Airways, Khartoum-bound aircraft was flying over Benghazi in eastern Libya, Gaddafi's men ordered the plane to land or face being shot down. The pilot complied. Col Nur and Major Hamdallah were taken out of the aircraft and handcuffed by Libyan authorities, who then drove the Sudanese soldiers-cum-politicians to a location within Libya.

Arrest of coup leaders triggers pro-Nimeiri counter-attack

The news of the arrest of the coup leaders emboldened Nimeiri's loyalists back home to go out and demonstrate against the regime in the making, and in support of Nimeiri, who had been under arrest in the palace during the 72 hours of tenuous control under Major Atta. The tables were turned on the communists as their grip on power quickly collapsed like a house of cards. It was all over in a matter of hours. A vengeful Nimeiri emerged from his confinement to take charge of the country once more. The Chairman designate Col Nur, and Major Hamdallah were flown to Khartoum to join Comrade Atta and other colleagues who had been overthrown, rounded up and arrested. A hastily convened court-martial sentenced the ring leaders to death by firing squad. All of them were shot while their civilian accomplices, who included the secretary general of the Sudan Communist Party, Abdel Khaliq Mahjoub, Joseph Garang, the former Minister of State for Southern Affairs, and a senior party member, were hanged for their involvement in the putsch.

'No thank you' to Gaddafi

Gaddafi naturally expected Nimeiri to be grateful to him for helping him crush the communist inspired takeover. He saw his part in sabotaging Sudan's short-lived communist bid for power as so crucial that the Libyan leader expected Nimeiri and his government to repay the debt so, the Sudanese leadership would be at his beck and call all the time and under all circumstances. That was not to be: but Gaddafi was not giving up his dream of reviving the Arab glory and power it once wielded in ancient times. Gaddafi again brought up the issue of Arab unity, but Nimeiri had other domestic matters to attend to that he considered more urgent than the Arab unity project.

Now a close friend of the West – after the failed coup, that he blamed on the Soviet Union as the mastermind – President Nimeiri was listening attentively to advisers who wanted him to implement his government's June 9, 1969 Declaration, that had promised a regional self-rule for Southern Sudan. Gaddafi was not amused by the turn of events in Khartoum. The Libyan strongman summed up his disappointment in a telegram he sent to Nimeiri. The brief and paradoxical message read in Arabic *"Samahaak Allah"* – May Allah forgive you. While offering divine forgiveness to his foe, Gaddafi did not, as events later showed, pardon the Sudanese ruler.

From that day – until the day Nimeiri was overthrown in a popular uprising in early 1986 – the two men were sworn enemies. In 1976, Gaddafi unleashed armed Sudanese opposition – allied to outlawed political parties – to topple Nimeiri's regime. The rebels, who were trained and armed by Libya, and officially branded mercenaries by Khartoum, managed to capture the state-owned radio station and broadcast their message to the Sudanese people and the world, but failed – by a whisker – to take full and sustained control of Khartoum.

This is the genesis of the Libyan support for the SPLM/A. The Southern-based rebellion began in May 1983, waging a bush war against the regime of Jaafar Nimeiri.

Gaddafi's support for SPLM/A

The SPLM/A public declaration stated that it was fighting to change the system of rule in a united Sudan. The new insurgency made reference to the establishment of a socialist Sudan. Being perceived as a progressive liberation movement, the rebel organisation was treated in some African and Arab quarters as a friend, and as an ideological ally that would join their ranks in opposing Western and American economic, political and military dominance in the developing world.

The question of whether the leadership of the SPLM/A were simply a bunch of opportunists, or men who were very shrewd in understanding and exploiting the advantages of their organisation and its objectives, the contradictions prevailing at that time in Sudan, and in the world at large, is irrelevant here. Whatever future historians will say about the period in question, the SPLM/A leadership was able to convince Gaddafi to arm and clothe a very large number of their fighters. Gaddafi was not a charity-giver; he had his conditions, but neither side were prepared to be used and gain nothing, so the relationship between the two had to be established as mutually beneficial. Time later proved that Gaddafi and the SPLM/A cooperated while, at the same time, harbouring suspicions of the other's sincerity and their respective long-term objectives.

One of the strings attached to his generous support was his insistence on the teaching of his much talked-about book – which academics regard as superficial – the Third Universal Theory, at the SPLM/A training centres. The theory claims that both capitalism and communism as systems of running societies are bankrupt. The alternative, the argument goes on, is the Third Universal middle way approach. This philosophy had the *Green Book* as it platform.

Although the Popular Bureau – as Libyan foreign missions had been renamed – in Addis Ababa supplied many copies of the *Green Book* to the SPLM/A, nobody bothered to read the book, let alone teach its contents to the Southern Sudanese insurgents, who had little time for theories with tangential application to their cause.

After providing armaments to the military wing, the SPLA, Tripoli authorised its embassy in Addis Ababa, the Ethiopian capital, to meet – from time to time – some of the needs of the Sudanese rebel movement. One of the projects to benefit from Gaddafi's generosity was Radio SPLA. Accordingly, Tripoli provided the propaganda radio station with two vehicles, (four-wheel station wagons) for the use of its staff.

SPLM rejects Libya's offer of allowances

The assistance did not stop there. The Bureau offered to pay hefty allowances – about US dollar $500 a month – for the staff of the radio. It appears the Libyans were extremely reckless with how they spent money on their foreign friends and allies. The Bureau had decided that the staff, numbering about 12 men, would be receiving regular stipends throughout the duration of the war. This arrangement was agreed, in September 1984, between a junior SPLA officer – who was not known for being scrupulous, especially with money – and one of the senior diplomats at the Bureau. That murky understanding was reached behind the SPLM/A leadership's back.

When the leader of the SPLM/A, John Garang got wind of that arrangement he reacted angrily and gave orders that the scheme should be immediately scrapped. His argument was based on the premise that the entire SPLM/A membership – especially the fighting force – was a voluntary organisation. He further contended that for anyone to single out a few individuals to benefit financially, while the majority of rank and file struggled to survive, was conduct that could give room for accusations of unfairness and favouritism – if not actual resentment – within the movement. The third reason was that, being unpredictable as the Libyan regime and its leaders were, entering into such a financial deal in the long run would be a recipe for disappointment for some of the recipients when the "grants" would likely be terminated without warning.

A final reason, which Garang did not express, but which was the strongest one behind the rejection of the "free money", was the belief that the offer did not only carry strings; it was really dirty money. Gaddafi's henchmen appeared naïve, but they knew exactly what they wanted and how to extract maximum benefit from the recipients of their largesse. Gaddafi's agents were very good at planting divisions within the people and organisations they sponsored.

In the case of the SPLM/A, two Sudanese, one from the greater Northern Sudan, and the second a Southern Sudanese, who reported to join the rebels but later had to leave after failing to implement the Libyan agenda. At that time Tripoli and its embassies employed either its nationals or members within organisations they supported to spy or foment discord from within, a method the Libyans developed to perfection in the interest of control of the beneficiaries. With the benefit of the hindsight this was a smart way Gaddafi made sure his treasury did not waste funds without some forms of check and balance, and clients who had to be pliant, beholden to his representatives, rather than independent spirits, benefiting from his bounty but acting and behaving according the dictates of their own free will. The SPLM/A was fully aware of the strings that were closely linked to the Libyan generosity.

Despite that ruling, Libyan money continued, secretly, to reach two or three low-key members of the SPLM/A, in one way or another. I still think that the Libyans who doled out money in what appeared a haphazard manner might have made an illegal fortune from the kitty for helping foreign "revolutionaries", who were to be found in every corner of the globe, pursuing all types of conceivable causes that shared nothing in common. These included armed groups, such as the Muslim Moro Liberation Front in the Philippines and the Catholic IRA in Northern Ireland.

Tripoli pays hotel accommodation for SPLM/A personnel

At the time of the cooperation between the SPLM/A and Libya, the latter was happy with the results of its assistance to the Sudanese rebels, who were scoring military victories against the government of Nimeiri. When Khartoum began to jam the broadcasts of Radio SPLA in early 1985, Gaddafi offered a frequency and access to the broadcasting facilities of the Libyan state to the rebels for rebroadcasting their programmes, beamed to Sudan from Tripoli. An office was opened in the capital for the use of the SPLM/A. Libya met the costs for maintenance of the delegates, who led lives similar to that normally accorded to bona fide diplomats in a host country.

But the costliest Libyan offer – after the arms – was the provision of full-board accommodation for SPLM/A members in transit to or from foreign countries, the sick, and officers on missions. A complete floor in a four-star hotel in Addis Ababa was hired for the rebels. When the hotel opened its doors to the Sudanese guests, their stay looked permanent. Even some moved in with their families. Time proved that the accommodation was contingent on political developments back home in Sudan. The SPLM/A leadership kept on reminding their members staying in the hotel to be ready for eviction at any moment without any prior warning. That advice did not need to come from a prophet.

In early 1986, Sudanese began to openly oppose the rule of Nimeiri, on the grounds that the president had increasingly become more autocratic and erratic. Having antagonised the South shortly before and after the revolt in Bor on May 16, 1983, through abrogation of the Addis Ababa Agreement of 1972 and the imposition of Sharia or Islamic laws in September that year, it was the North's turn to become active in planning to overthrow the May dictatorship by all available means. The sentencing to death and hanging of the ageing Islamic reformer, Mahmud Mohammed Taha for alleged apostasy in early 1986 provided the Northern opposition with additional reason in their campaign to remove Nimeiri from power.

Libyan objectives achieved

As an interested party in the events unfolding in Sudan, Gaddafi was keenly following every move being taken by the Sudanese. When it was clear that Nimeiri – who was outside the country after returning to Egypt following his visit to the United States – had been overthrown, Gaddafi was very pleased that his archenemy had finally left Sudan's political scene. Hours after it was clear that the Sudanese dictator had gone for good, Col Gaddafi rang the SPLM/A leader John Garang, who at the time was in the Ethiopian capital, Addis Ababa, where he was monitoring the developments in Khartoum. An elated Gaddafi congratulated Garang for the role the SPLM/A, especially the armed component, the SPLA, had played in the downfall of their common adversary.

Garang thanked Gaddafi for the Libyan material support to the SPLM/A. Gaddafi had a piece advice to give to Garang. It was time for Garang, and the movement he led, to pack and report to Khartoum, Gaddafi opined. For his turn, the rebel chief said he did not think that the type of change he and his colleagues were fighting to achieve was still to be seen. Speaking in a friendly and diplomatic tone, Garang was able to cling to the objectives of his organisation while at the same time giving no hint that future cooperation between Tripoli and the SPLM/A was a possibility. Though disappointed, Gaddafi had no reason to be bitter with the SPLM/A: after all, the military defeat the rebels inflicted on the Sudanese Army in Southern Sudan had made the regime in Khartoum very vulnerable and unpopular in the North, hence accelerating Nimeiri's exit from power.

The popular uprising in the streets of Khartoum gave the Army officers the pretext to topple their commander-in-chief – in their words, on behalf of the masses. A transitional administration to organise free and democratic elections was put in place. The military kept their word by holding elections, and a civilian government was put in place in 1986. The leader of the Ummah Party, Sadiq el-Mahdi, became prime minister. The SPLM/A, on the other hand, judged that the elections – which did not take place in much of the rural Southern Sudan because of the prevailing civil war at the time – were not truly democratic.

The rebels also contended that an all-party constitutional conference, on the problem of war and peace and system of rule, should have preceded the holding of elections country-wide. Since these conditions had not been met, the SPLM/A refused to recognise the legitimacy of the Mahdi government. Later in the year, the rebels toned down their anti-government stance and expressed their readiness to talk with representatives of political forces, and even the government of the day. In fact, months after Mahdi had assumed office as prime minister, the two parties met in Ethiopia. But the talks achieved nothing, not even a photo opportunity, as Mahdi refused to be photographed with Garang and his team.

It is to be recalled that Gaddafi gave sanctuary in the early 1970s, to the Ummah leader in Libya, where he was plotting the overthrow of Nimeiri. It came as a surprise to few that Prime Minister Mahdi and Col Gaddafi soon developed close ties. Despite his public utterances that his government was ready to end the armed conflict through peaceful means, Mahdi was more militaristic than the men in uniform he had succeeded, namely, Field Marshal Nimeiri and the Transitional Military Council headed by General Abdurrahman Siwar Dahab. Soon after taking office, the prime minister embarked on intensification of military operations against the SPLA. Although it was known that the relations between Khartoum and Tripoli had become warm and that Mahdi was receiving military and financial assistance from the Gaddafi regime, few knew the extent of the Libyan military involvement on Khartoum's behalf, and its campaign against the SPLA.

End of Libyan support

The game was up for the SPLM/A-Libyan cooperation. It began with the closure of the rebels' office in Tripoli, and the termination of broadcasts of the SPLM's propaganda using the Libyan radio station. Though the embassy in Addis Ababa remained outwardly friendly, all types of assistance ceased immediately.

A couple of days after that, the management of the Ethiopian hotel that had accommodated SPLM/A members at the Libyans' expense, informed the SPLM officer in charge of foreign relations that if the Sudanese rebels continued to be his guests, they must prepare to pay the bills from the date of Nimeiri's departure from power. This information was passed on to the residents, some of whom had to leave the hotel immediately, while others did so at midnight to avoid the embarrassment of being forced to evacuate, or face paying a lot of money none of them had. There were jokes about the new developments, however. "They [the Libyans] can stop their support, but can they return the weapons they gave us?" asked a former hotel guest, in jest. Of course, there were cheaper hotels in the city; but those who really had no business there had to report either to the war zone or to their families, in the refugee camp in south-western Ethiopia.

Paradoxically, the loss of the Libyan support did not weaken the SPLM/A. By 1986, the rebels were firmly entrenched within much of the rural areas of Southern Sudan, while arms deliveries were increasingly getting to thousands of newly-trained recruits, who included citizens hailing from Northern Sudan, particularly the Nuba Mountains. Politically, the SPLM was gaining acceptance within many liberal circles in Sudan – and in most countries of sub-Saharan Africa – as a force that could no longer be ignored when deciding the political future and direction of Africa's largest country of the day. Surprisingly, it was Mahdi, the politician who used to project himself as a democrat, who managed to rekindle doubts in the Arab world – after the rebels who were often associated with black Africa and the Christian faith had succeeded to either win to their side or neutralise many Arab and Muslim nations – that the movement was not anti-Arab or an anti-Muslim organisation.

The result of Sadiq el-Mahdi's diplomatic thrust against the SPLM/A in the Arab region was that Libya, Oman and Jordan backed his government against the rebels; Egypt, under President Mubarak was publicly seen as wavering, although Mubarak allowed a discreet presence of the movement's representative in Cairo.

Libya caught red-handed in the South
There is always a tendency, at times of grave social upheaval in societies where religion plays an important role in the lives of people, for them to regard themselves as victims and their enemies as the aggressors. In the same vein, this thinking leads to the conclusion that God has deserted them when things go badly. Conversely, an expected turn of good fortune for their cause is seen as a proof that God is with them or has heard their supplication for salvation. During the last Sudan civil war, such sentiments were often heard being expressed by some Southern Sudanese, even among members of their political elite. This episode fits into the thinking revolving around divine intervention.

In late 1988, Khartoum constantly sent MiG-23 planes to gather intelligence and bomb SPLA positions in various warzones in the South. Flights of such aircraft created panic among the civilian population. Alarms were often sounded so that people would take cover, usually in shelters. The planes were so fast and some flew so high that the SPLA was often unable to bring them down with heat seeking missiles or other conventional anti-aircraft guns.

But on midday of a clear, December day in 1988, the inhabitants of Lilir village, about 30 kilometres north-west of Bor, the capital of Jonglei, watched an event that they later described as divine intervention on their behalf. Two aircraft were flying overhead, from south to north. That meant the planes had at first gone southwards when they came from Khartoum and were then on the return flight northwards. As was their custom when sighting such frightening planes, people took cover in shelters. But there was something unusual with the weapons of death; instead of unloading their lethal cargo and speeding off as fast as they had come, they were losing speed and altitude. One flew northeast while the other hurriedly hobbled towards the ground to land on the narrow strip that was the road, the only dry piece of land for many kilometres, as the area had been under flood during the year. The military aircraft missed the gravel road, to land a few metres away in a long and narrow drain full of water. The soft soil acted as a brake and the craft came to a bumpy and thunderous sudden halt. The second aircraft landed or was believed to have dropped like a stone, in a no-man's-land area, about 60 kilometres northeast of Bor town.

There was an SPLA camp, two kilometres from the location where the first aircraft had crash-landed. The soldiers, who were a platoon strong, moved to the crash site where civilians had already surrounded the plane and its pilot. About an hour later, senior officers arrived from nearby Baidit, then the headquarters of Central Southern Command for the rebels. The news was too good to be true. The aircraft was a Soviet made MiG-23 belonging to the Libyan Air Force, and the pilot was a Libyan flight lieutenant, who gave his name as Shiteiti. The Libyan refused to give proper and reliable identification besides his name and Libyan nationality.

Before the arrival of SPLA forces to the scene, people from nearby villages – men, women and even children – thronged to the site of the strange event. The excited villagers were singing war songs, brandishing their spears in a mock fight to frighten the Libyan. According an eyewitness, the young pilot remained composed and showed no sign of fear at all of the martial show, enacted by scantily dressed African villagers.

Throughout investigation on the spot and, later, at different SPLA units, the pilot said nothing about their inexplicable crashes, except that he and his colleague, who was flying a second plane, were staying at the Hilton Hotel in Khartoum. Virtually nothing was known about the other pilot who died, or what happened to his aircraft, which crash-landed several kilometres northeast of that site. A couple of weeks later, a woman who had gone out in search of wild fruits found the wreckage of the plane. I accompanied the overall zonal commander, Cdr Kuol Manyang, to the scene of the doomed plane. There was no trace of the remains of the pilot. The prevailing opinion was that wild animals, most likely, hyenas which had developed a taste for human flesh as a result of the availability of corpses of soldiers from both parties in the civil war, must have carried away the cadaver of the second Libyan pilot.

At first Shiteiti claimed they had run of out fuel. That was unlikely because for each flight a pilot had to make sure that there was sufficient fuel for the duration of the mission, emergencies included. At the time of incident, no unit or a gunner with the SPLA ever claimed to have fired at the aircraft, nor do any former SPLA fighters recall having brought down the planes with their pilots. It is a mystery that has not yet been solved as the pilot refused to explain what exactly happened to him and his plane while his other comrade was dead and his body never found.

While what had happened to the Libyan pilots and their aircraft remains a mystery, the SPLM/A had what they believed was God-given evidence to prove to the world the role of foreign countries in the Sudan's civil war. It is ironic that when Khartoum used Libyan military warplanes against the SPLA who had received similar material help against the government in Khartoum several years earlier- the rebels complained vociferously against what they described as foreign interference in the Sudanese armed conflict on the side of their enemy.

The rebel movement accused the government of Prime Minister Sadiq el-Mahdi of using foreigners to fight on his behalf. They also appealed to the UN and regional organisations such as the then-Organisation of African Unity, OAU, the precursor to the African Union, and the League of Arab States, to stop Khartoum and Tripoli fighting the Sudanese insurgents. The SPLM/A, their message stressed, were fighting for a just cause.

The pilot was marched overland – walking over 300 kilometres – to one of the SPLA training camps, where he was paraded before scores of rebel cadets awaiting commissioning and deployment to the war fronts. That was late 1988.

As expected, the reaction by the international community was at best muted. That silence was understandable: there was a defence pact between Khartoum and Tripoli. Being sovereign states, Libya and Sudan had more rights than a non-state actor, the SPLM/A. Moreover, the world still remembered at the time, the military and propaganda assistance the SPLM/A received from Libya during the rule of the ousted Nimeiri. What the event scored for the rebels was a feeling of embarrassment that silently engulfed Tripoli and Khartoum, for what amounted to a passing cloud of bad luck. Time, the great healer of such mishaps, was on the side of the governments of Gaddafi and Sadiq el Mahdi. The world of the time was going through more dramatic events that overshadowed an apparently isolated development in Africa. Other more serious and epoch-making events were occurring in other parts of the world, such as the rumblings in Eastern Europe – which later gave rise to the fall of Berlin Wall – and subsequent disintegration of the former Soviet Union.

Shiteiti a pawn in the regional interests
From 1988 to 1991, Shiteiti remained in custody as SPLA's valuable POW. In addition to being living evidence of foreign involvement with Khartoum in its war against the rebels – most of them from the African South – some members of the movement thought Libya might one day request the release of its national, perhaps in exchange for arms. There is no doubt that the SPLM/A was keeping the Libyan pilot as evidence but also a tool to be used for extracting from Libya some material gain – more likely to be released in exchange for weapons. The Libyan leader- it would seem- was not very keen to have his compatriot freed, even gratis.

However, in late 1989 or early 1991, Libya contacted an African country to approach the SPLM/A leadership, for the release of Shiteiti. The SPLM/A said they had no objection, but there was need for the two parties to talk prior to the pilot's release. The release procedures would involve a fourth country, the Libyans, the SPLM/A and the Ethiopian government under Mengistu Haile Mariam, whose country would be a transit point for the Libyan POW. The release looked all but agreed. However, it was suspected that the fourth party – a country I have chosen not to name here – and the Ethiopian authorities had certain conditions, likely to be branded as national interests, which stalled the process.

Shiteiti's release was conditional and each of the parties staked some claims to benefit from the deal. But the talks dragged on. Meanwhile, Ethiopia, where Shiteiti was being held, was going through turmoil of its own. As the rebels of EPDRF were closing on Addis Ababa, the capital, negotiations about the pilot took a back seat. Shiteiti, who had been transferred from an SPLA base on the border between Sudan and Ethiopia to Addis Ababa during those tumultuous days, in anticipation of his release to a mediator (from one of Sudan's neighbours), who would then hand him over to Libya after a deal was reached, was actually in an Ethiopian jail. An SPLA junior officer was attached to Shiteiti, ostensibly as a companion but, in reality, a guard.

In May 1991, the Ethiopia rebels took power after defeating the government headed by Mengistu Haile Mariam, then a friend of the SPLM/A. There was a delay in the proposed transfer of Shiteiti to that country and then to Ethiopia, where he would be handed over to the Libyan Popular Bureau in Addis Ababa. There have been suggestions that some individuals within Ethiopian security organ – who were sympathetic to the Ethiopian rebels – sabotaged the process. This writer has no convincing evidence to support the suspicion. Whether the speculation was baseless or not, the ensuing interregnum chaos effectively put an end to the process leading to the release by the SPLM/A of the Libyan pilot.

Meanwhile, the civil war in Ethiopia was intensifying daily. It was clear it was a matter of when – not if – the days of the Mengistu's regime were numbered. In May 1991, Mengistu [2] was chased out of power by an alliance of rebel groups. The victorious insurgents entered Addis Ababa, after brief fighting around and in the capital. Although the rebel forces adhered to a strict code of discipline, there was something of a breakdown of law and order; during the interlude some institutions ceased to function, since officials loyal to the defeated regime had either fled or gone into hiding, or did not report to their stations for fear of arrest by the new order. One of the affected institutions was the prison service. We later learnt that Shiteiti, like most Ethiopian inmates, found himself walking – a free man – in the streets of Addis Ababa, but one who did not know where to go, as he had no idea of the location of the Libyan mission.

Some of us could not understand why a POW should have been kept among convicted criminals. I have no idea why a man – who was supposed to be handed over to his country –happened to be wandering alone in a strange place. Luckily for Shiteiti, help was not far away. He was with an SPLA officer, his minder in one of the SPLA bases before their relocation to Addis Ababa and, as they walked aimlessly in the streets of the city, they were told that all the Sudanese affiliated to the SPLM/A had gone to Khartoum and some to the US. Soon after that, they met an Ethiopian of Sudanese descent, an ethnic Anyuak, who came to their rescue.

Shiteiti and his former guard were taken to the Libyan embassy, where they were welcomed by the officials there. Shiteiti was now at home, while his former guard was given money in local currency. The Libyan embassy gave money and wished Chau Manguak, the SPLA officer, luck wherever he would go. Indeed, luck was indeed on Chaw's side. A couple of hours later, he learned in the marketplace that some of his comrades had taken refuge in an embassy of one of the African countries bordering Southern Sudan. That day those Sudanese, mostly the former staff of the SPLM office in Addis Ababa and the team of the clandestine Radio SPLA, were preparing to fly out of the capital, the first flight to leave Ethiopia after the fall of the city to the rebels. By another stroke of luck, some members of the SPLM people were shopping, before departure for Nairobi in Kenya in a matter of hours. The shopping SPLM personnel stumbled on Chaw. As they approached him with excitement, Chaw who looked bewildered, was not ready for their embrace: he had been abandoned and he was rightly bitter with the comrades who did not care about his safety. It took him and the other members some time to agree to come to the embassy where we were sheltering.

We left Addis Ababa by plane the next day, having spent more than a fortnight under the new administration of Meles Zenawi. Our flight was the first to leave or land in the city since the regime change. We flew to Kenya on our way to Southern Sudan in June, 1991.

[1] The full story of the fall of Addis Ababa to the EPRDF while my colleagues and I were in the city is told in a volume of my memoirs that will be released after the publication of this book.

[2] Mengistu: The Ethiopians do not follow the Western naming system of given and surnames. For instance, the former Ethiopian leader Mengistu Haile Mariam, could be referred to as Col Mengistu, or in full as Mengistu Haile Mariam, not Col Mariam (Haile Mariam shouldn't be seen as two separate names; the combination means Spirit of Mariam or Mary).

The speech that John Garang rejected

Although my main assignment was to initiate, direct and supervise the programmes of Radio SPLA since the launch of the clandestine broadcaster on October 12, 1984, I sometimes performed other activities for the then-rebel movement. These included attending meetings with visiting delegations – Sudanese or foreign – active participation in peace talks- in Ethiopia, Kenya and Nigeria- and the preparation and writing of speeches for the late SPLM/A leader, John Garang.

Speech writing and its presentation were not a frequent affair; important events and political developments at home always made it imperative that the position of the movement was made clear on particular issues. When such a situation arose, senior members of the SPLM would hold a semi-formal meeting during which the subject would be open to discussion. By consensus, points would be jotted to be expanded and made into an official statement for public dissemination, more often than not, over Radio SPLA, always by Garang himself.

From 1984 to 1988 and then briefly in the first half of 1991, I served as secretary of such tasks, taking notes that I would later write in full after the exchange and sharing of ideas and opinions had ended in an agreement. In turn Garang would go over the text, indicating points he preferred to be added, expanded or deleted. Persons who have had experience with speech writing especially on difficult areas such as crisis management, can testify that the job can be nerve-wracking. It mostly involves changes after changes for clarity and, above all, taking into account the kind of multiple audiences and their varying – and sometimes conflicting –expectations or capacity to understand and absorb the subject matter, and the language of the statement or speech. Official statements, especially those to be made public by a high-flying dignitary, are expected to be formal and stately in content and delivery. Unless for special effect, such speeches have to avoid slang, jargon or colloquial usages; above all, they should never engage in abusive language.

In early 1985 I made a brief personal visit to a centre run by the movement at the Ethiopian-Sudanese border. This coincided with the beginning of political upheavals in Khartoum, where popular uprising against the regime of Jaafar Nimeiri were boiling over. The leadership of the SPLM/A, who quickly made it public that the rebel movement stood in solidarity with the people of Sudan, decided to closely follow the developments in Khartoum. That evolving situation stipulated that the rebel movement had to – confidentially and publicly – take a stand so that its leadership should not be caught unawares by the unfolding events and their uncertain outcome, especially in regards to relations between the insurgents and the internal opposition, whose leadership was a loose alliance of all shades of political leanings – from extreme ideological right wing, centre, radical left and some grey areas.

One morning I received a verbal communication that I would have to attend a meeting that afternoon, at a social centre in one of the movement's bases on the border with Ethiopia, where I was briefly staying. I was given the names of the comrades – this was the common form of address at the time, and no sarcasm was meant as is the case these days – who would go to the meeting. The person who was going to chair the meeting was an SPLA officer, known for his communist credentials which he openly advertised. I will not reveal his name. He bore intense aversion towards me because he believed, falsely of course, anyone who did not belong to his group was a reactionary, for whom he held immense amount of loathing. He was convinced I was not a progressive.

As expected, I had been named secretary of the meeting, charged with the drafting the skeleton of a speech that Garang would deliver to the Sudanese people in about a week's time. Generally, I enjoy working as a team member and rarely feel intimidated even by the presence of the high and mighty at the helm, chairing discussion. But in this particular environment, I was seized by an undefined sense of helplessness. To put it bluntly, I entered the *tukul* or thatched hut where the meeting was going to take place. I was feeling anxious and tense. I was aware that there would confrontation between me and the officer who was going to chair the meeting.

Present in the room were three other members and the chairperson of the committee. Two of these were graduates of economics, one of them with a master's in the subject from the US in the late 1960s, while the second graduated from the University of Khartoum three years after I had left. The third member was a veteran member of the Sudan Communist Party and a sober man in his handling people and contentious issues. The team leader, whom I faintly knew from my Juba days, had his professional background in an area that was related to animal production. People who didn't like him- and they were not few- used to speak of him as a person who knew only "how to look after chickens", by which they meant animal production in general and poultry in particular. That statement was an exaggeration intended to put down the man they loathed.

The chair introduced the topic. He looked confident and enjoyed the authority the assignment had given him in addition to his official task. There was no doubt that he was now in full control and that it was his views and will that must prevail. But I suspect he accepted the assignment as a burden for he was one of the civilians trained and commissioned as officers who equated any form of dialogue or negotiation with political forces in Khartoum, opposition or government of the day, as a form of betrayal.

In the early days in the life of the SPLM/A, there were some members who believed that the SPLA would defeat SAF, the government armed forces and march victorious to capture political power, to the total exclusion of non-members. The fellow who was going to chair the meeting was one of these; he never tried to hide his disdain for dialogue and give and take formula – which he equated with surrender. This was not, of course, the official position of the SPLM/A and its top leadership.

Our task was to discuss and agree on policies that revolved around several areas such as war and peace, the forging of an alliance between the forces of uprising and the SPLM/A, the national economy and foreign policy. I vividly remember that it was the last item where I received a dressing-down from the team leader. What led to my humiliation and being categorised as a "reactionary" began with my suggestion that the SPLM/A's foreign policy should unequivocally be non-aligned.

"A what?" asked the angry chairperson.

"Non-aligned", I repeated after I had gathered some courage, mixed with suppressed indignation and scorn. To my surprise the rest of the team agreed with me.

"How can revolutionaries be non-aligned?", he wanted to know, adding that "it is a fact" that we were intricately linked to the progressive world and that anyone talking of "nonsense" such as non-alignment in the international relations was ignorant of the ideological divide that obtained during our time. Honestly, he saw me as the embodiment of a negation of a revolutionary.

"But Cuba and Yugoslavia are progressive countries, yet they are members of Non-Aligned Movement", I added, knowing that I was pouring salt into the wound. He deliberately refused to engage with me, thinking that he would be stooping too low to do that.

Doing that, in his view, would give me a modicum of respect, which he believed I did not deserve. He considered the "debate" closed on that item: our foreign policy should be geared to side with the progressive forces world-wide led by the Soviet Union.

Minute-takers are expected to honestly record the gist of talk and to avoid negatively influencing the contents of their notes. That was exactly what I did in my final draft, which he read. He was happy that the contents were a true reflection of his views and that our contributions were marginal points, mere footnotes. Mission accomplished, I travelled to Addis Ababa to present the draft to John Garang for approval before a final version would be prepared for him to broadcast over Radio SPLA.

In Addis Ababa I went straight to Garang's residence, where I gave him the draft. He put it aside and we began to chat. It was evening. There was nothing much we discussed. After taking leave of him at about 10 pm he told me he would go over the draft and that the following morning I would get the document with his comments.

At 9 am the following day we met in the living room. Garang who rarely showed emotions, looked unhappy. I knew the reason: the contents of the draft speech. Since I was going to work he told me to see him that evening. When I came at the appointed time, I found Yousif Kuwa Mekki deep in review of the developments in Khartoum. The two welcomed me into their company. Yousif had already been informed that he would be chairing the meeting to draft the speech since the first one had been literally shredded. Yousif, I and three other members of the SPLM, all civilians, were given the assignment to rewrite the document. As usual I was to be the secretary. We were given three days to finish the job, a sufficient time for that kind of an undertaking that did not require research. We operated in the SPLM office not far from Hilton Hotel, Addis Ababa.

Although Yousif was barely a year in the movement and had been a stranger to me until he joined the SPLM, I found him a pleasant and friendly person to work with. He was polite and as a former schoolteacher and legislator in Khartoum, he treated people courteously. He was a good, soft-spoken team leader and a good listener. As far as knowledge of the affairs of Sudan – especially the politics of Khartoum – went, Yousif was a moving encyclopaedia. He was not only fluent in "standard" Arabic but wrote poetry in that language, and English, too. Being a Muslim, his understanding of sharia law and its politics was of immense value to the SPLM. The contribution of the other three team members was very relevant and addressed the problems of the day from the Southern viewpoint although they and I made sure to steer clear of ideas that would project the movement as a tool for solving only the Southern Problem; the agenda then was the Problem of Sudan, not the traditional Southern Question.

In two days' time, we finished the speech, after implementing minor alterations. Garang was very happy with our job and thanked – I think three times – Yousif for a job well done. My next task was to prepare for the recording of the speech that John Garang was going to read. Two days later, the speech was broadcast by Radio SPLA. The copy of that speech is in some of Garang's collected speeches,[22] edited by Mansour Khaled under the title of *John Garang Speaks*, published in London, 1986 by Keagan Paul.

---

22 It is interesting to note in that speech, Garang mentions me by name as "the commander of the unconventional battalion", a reference to what he considered as a commendable role Radio SPLA of which I was its director. That statement and the praise he heaps on other forces, units and their commanders, were not in the original text of the speech I had typed. He later inserted them a little while before he went to read the speech in the studio. I first heard my name mentioned at the studio. Modesty made me shrink at discovering that the speech contained my name and that recognition of my work with that of my team. What worried me was that the memory of my disagreement with the chairman of the first committee over what could be included or excluded was still fresh in my mind. But under the circumstances in the studio there was nothing possibly I could do to ask Garang to read the rest of the names of the field commanders but skip over my name.

Weeks later, I learned from friends in the refugee camps that the part of the speech devoted to thanking commanders, me included, was universally condemned as very boring, although allowance was: its purpose was mainly to raise the morale of the fighting forces at the various warfronts. I and my team didn't need that.

Yousif Kuwa: back to his roots

The people of the Nuba Mountains in western central Sudan share three commonalities with their compatriots inhabiting the southern third of Sudan. First, the British colonial administration placed the two regions under cultural, social and political entity called the "Closed Districts". The ordinance governing the entities that included Southern Blue Nile, which some political commentators describe as social quarantine, was enacted to purportedly protect the "indigenes" from Islamic and Arab influence. Second, the peoples of Southern Sudan and the Nuba Mountains are characterised by great linguistic and cultural diversity. Third, the two regions were – until recent times – the South, since the Addis Ababa Agreement of 1972 ran its internal affairs such as administration, local security; health and education – among the most neglected by various central governments in Khartoum, in the provision of basic social services and economic development. The similarities end there.

Emergence of radical politics in the Nuba Mountains

The struggle of the Nuba people for survival and recognition as equal with other Sudanese in their own country is a long history. However, without belittling the role of Nuba leaders throughout modern history, one would say the period after independence in 1956, especially after the October 1964 popular uprising that overthrew the military dictatorship of General Ibrahim Abboud, and the emergence of the General Union of the Nuba, or Gun, under the leadership of a priest turned politician, Rev Philip Abbas Gaboush[23], became a turning point for the Nuba people, whose existence as a political force the Sudan's ruling elite could no longer ignore.

The formation of the General Union of the Nuba or Gun, in early 1965, under the leadership of Philip Abbas Gaboush, gave the Nuba people in general and their youth in particular, a fearless leader who was known for blunt talk about the condition of his people in the capital city, and in their

---

23 Although Philip Abbas Gaboush was an "Anglican" clergyman, Arabic language media and many Northern Sudanese used to refer to him as Ab or Father Gaboush, a title normally used for Catholic priests.

ancestral home in the Nuba Mountains, in the Kordofan Province.

For the first time since independence, the Nuba people were able to have their articulate representatives in the Constituent Assembly. Their undisputed spokesperson was Gaboush. Under his leadership most educated young Nuba were able to take pride in themselves. He also played a role as one of the architects of the rural alliance, which brought together some leaders from the South, East, and Darfur in the far west; a development some political analysts believe was a precursor to the New Sudan ideology.

It would be a mistake for one to write here that the Nuba were all under the umbrella of the priest-turned-politician; there were other leaders jostling for the leadership of the Nuba people, who are a multilingual society also divided by religion: Islam, Christianity and traditional African beliefs and practices. It was in that atmosphere where one Nubawi[24], Mahmud Haseeb, a retired army officer came out as a pan-Arabist. Lt Col Haseeb was later appointed minister for transport and telecommunications in the first government of Nimeiri. He was chosen on the pan-Arabism ticket.

Yousif Kuwa once believed he was an Arab

Much has been written about the early life of Yousif Kuwa Mekki and his political ideas. Some of the writings about that time and views of late Yousif are contained in the works of writers on the Nuba people, among them fellow Nubawi, Dr Omer Shurkian, and the British journalist, Julie Flint. Much of the episodes I record here are based on my first-hand experience I gained while working with Yousif or in several conversations or interviews between the two of us.

I was privileged to have been one of the few SPLM members to meet and talk with the late Yousif Kuwa Mekki, and Daniel Kodi Angelo, among others. Abdel Aziz Adam el Hilu later followed. When Yousif and his comrades from the Nuba Mountains arrived in Addis Ababa, Ethiopia, in 1986, I led the SPLM team, in my capacity as the head of the movement's department of information. Before that they had met several times with the SPLM/A leader, John

---

24 A male from Nuba Mountains is called *Nubawi* and a female is *Nubawiya*. This is to contrast with *Nubi* or Nubian, for a male Nubian- someone from Nubia region in the extreme north, south of Egypt. Female from Nubia is *Nubiya*.

Garang, and senior colleagues in the political wing of the movement, who had exchanged views on the issues of the day as well as the objective of their trip.

In a modest and simple ceremony that was announced as a news item over Radio SPLA, there was jubilation within the rank and file of the movement, at the war front, at home and outside Sudan by members and sympathisers. The reason was simple: we – by then – could justifiably claim and even boast of the SPLM/A as a national political force, not an insignificant and isolated Southern outfit made up of some disgruntled people who had left home, protesting the division of the South into three and impotent self-governing regions. During the early days, the armed struggle being waged by the SPLA was seen and projected that way by its opponents.

Borrowing a leaf from Southern Sudanese

Following the ceremony, my chat with Yousif gave me the impression of a serious man who was widely read, logical in his reasoning and, above all, a man with vast experience in public life as a leader, student, teacher, politician and poet. The longer I came to exchange ideas with him the more I discovered the depth of his thoughts, and his unshakeable commitment to serve, and even to sacrifice his own life for the rights of his downtrodden people. The Nuba politician, while he was an accomplished orator, almost a demagogue, he was also a soft-spoken person, an attribute rarely found in rabble rousers of the late Abbas Gaboush's calibre.

While addressing recruits from the South, who were being prepared for military training, the visitor's presence raised a lot of curiosity. Incidentally, I overheard someone whispering to a friend, "See this man [John Garang]; he is even bringing the Nuba who killed us during the Anya Nya war".

But when he opened his mouth, he held the audience spellbound; he moved the crowd of over 10,000 Southern Sudanese almost to tears.

"You had your government and you had ministers from the South in Khartoum. You even had one of your own as vice president of the whole Sudan. You got those rights because you fought. We [the Nuba] shall fight also, along with you, to get our rights", he declared.

On our return to Addis Ababa, Yousif Kuwa and his few fellow Nuba companions became a huge asset to the SPLM/A, mostly on the basis of their mastery of Arabic and knowledge concerning the affairs of Northern

Sudan. By the time he had been commissioned major and junior member of Political Military High Command, Yousif Kuwa had become an indispensable adviser to the late John Garang on national politics, especially the role of the sectarian parties in the North. During the much-publicised meeting between the former Prime Minister Sadiq el-Mahdi and the SPLM leaders in Addis Ababa in 1986, Yousif Kuwa Mekki and Major Arok Thon Arok were said by some of the members in the meeting to have been some kind of irritant to Sadiq el-Mahdi, because of their in-depth knowledge of Khartoum's political culture and its power brokers. The nine-hour[25] long meeting was a none-issue event.

Mr Mahdi went to meet the rebel leadership to show to the world that he was not a warmonger while at the same time he was uncompromising on the contentious sharia laws which the SPLM wanted to be scrapped. The prime minister of Sudan, too, did not know that some of the people he was going to discuss the matters with were not the Southern politicians he had often known for their limited grasp of the national issues. With Yousif and Arok, the head of the Sudanese government was in for a rude shock.

When the two leaders were approaching each other, I tried to take the photograph of Garang and Mahdi about to greet with a hug. However, Mahdi waved me away and Garang asked me to leave the room, as Sadiq el-Mahdi did not want any picture of him with a rebel and his colleagues. I complied and left to wait outside the building in the company of the prime minister's driver and his security personnel, provided by the Sudan embassy in Addis Ababa.

On several occasions, during conversation between Yousif, myself and others, the Nuba leader used to poke fun at himself. He said, in all seriousness

---

25 The statement the movement made to the media after the unsuccessful meeting between Prime Minister Sadiq el-Mahdi and the SPLM/A, that the meeting lasted nine hours, is not true. I was covering the event. The time was not even six hours. What is true about the failed meeting was that each party was not ready to make the first move to say the talks had failed, and therefore all of them should leave the venue, a nondescript house at the outskirts of the Ethiopian capital, Addis Ababa. There was a fear that the party going out first would be accused by the other party of having "walked out" of the talk and therefore would bear blame for the "collapse".

that he used to believe he was truly an Arab. Someone has written that the late Yousif Kuwa "saw the light" when one of his teachers of Arab origin asked the Nuba student why he was wasting his time in school, while like the rest of the Nuba people, his place was to be a house-boy.

Another factor he said contributed to his rethinking his belief in racial affiliation, was his reading of the writings by the Tanzanian leader and thinker, President Julius Nyerere. Kuwa was fond of repeating Nyerere's expression of "We have been oppressed a great deal". The second idea that made him question his belief in being an Arab was the frequent claim by the Northern ruling elite, that any attempted coup by men from the Nuba Mountains or in combination with others was a racist plot. Unlawful regime changes by military officers of Arab stock were always dubbed "a revolution".

Baptism of fire for Kuwa

Commander Yousif Kuwa, who had received military training in Sudan – but left before completing the training and therefore could not get commissioned and later went to university– was fully convinced that a combination of armed and political struggle, to change the way the country was being governed, was the best option left to the politically and economically marginalised regions of the country. He rejected the separation of any region from the rest of the country. That unwavering position often generated heated and sometimes angry exchanges between him and some young officers from the South who either innocently or deliberately said they wanted a separate South; even the movement's official stand was opposed to secession as a matter of principle.

Controversial clandestine mission to the SPLM

It is clear that the Nuba leaders who joined the SPLM/A, were working closely with secret internal cells within the Nuba community in Khartoum and at home in Kordofan. The late Gaboush constantly sent messages of support to SPLM/A leader, John Garang, whom he often addressed as "my son John". The cells' nameless and faceless operatives and their networks accelerated the spread of support and the recruitment drive within their own communities at home and in Khartoum, the capital. Messages, mostly by word of mouth, were able to flow clandestinely to the Nuba Mountains that young men should prepare to travel to Southern Sudan where they would receive military training before returning to wage guerrilla warfare in their homeland. Nuba Mountains is suitable for guerrilla activity.

Not all the members in the underground organisations saw things that way. Sometimes in the late 1980s, a handful of politically ambitious elements within the Nuba community, who had joined the movement and who harboured secret rivalry against Yousif's leadership, began claiming that he and company had been sent to discuss – with the SPLM/A leadership – the type of cooperation that would exist between Southern Sudanese fighters and their Nuba political activists. They claimed their mission was initially exploratory, and Yousif and his colleagues had hijacked the Nuba leadership by joining the SPLM/A instead of reporting back to Khartoum for briefing.

I am not prepared to argue here for or against these allegations, but I believe that whatever the case was, any return to Khartoum by the Nuba politicians – who had hobnobbed in public with the Southern rebels – should they be foolish enough to do so, would be suicide.

Again, time later proved that Yousif Kuwa Mekki showed by example that he was a capable leader in his own right.

Long trek to the Mountains

At the time Yousif had been made member of the SPLM/A Politico-Military High Command, the SPLA was one Africa's largest armies. Because of that the SPLA command dispatched a force to get recruits from the Nuba Mountains. As a commander, Yousif Kuwa led an army that was entirely Southern in composition. On arrival in the Nuba Mountains, a huge mass of recruits – numbering more than 15,000 – was waiting; ready to walk to north-eastern Southern Sudan for military training. Surprisingly, there was a sizeable number of girls who had decided to train for combat. Among the female recruits was Hanan, a Christian who was among the recruits. She became Yousif's second wife, and has remained Christian to this day.

While commanding the forces to the Nuba Mountains, I met Cdr Yousif Kuwa Mekki in 1987, at Pibor garrison town, which had just been taken by the SPLA. In a private conversation he told me how sad he was. One of his colleagues from the Nuba Mountains was not going with him, as he was sick. I suspect Yousif believed the officer was malingering. Said Yousif of the officer: "What he is doing is wrong. We are making history. It is true that there are dangers in this mission but it is our duty to shoulder it". He was both angry and sad, almost shedding tears.

After graduation as soldiers, and highly motivated and battle-ready, the SPLA fighters from the Nuba Mountains had to fight on their way home. Some of the government garrisons the Nuba fighters cleared were in Western Equatoria. Crudely put, the SPLA fighters from the Nuba Mountains, famed for their gallantry, were paying the debt to the South for escorting them to the training centres, where they were moulded into fully-qualified and armed guerrilla forces and under the command of their own officers. The officers who commanded the forces included Commanders Aziz Adam el Hilu, Yousif Kara, Ismail Jalab and Telefun Kuku.

Leadership test

After the split of 1991, the SPLA forces in the Nuba Mountains were cut off. The new government, under the ideological guidance of Hassan Abdalla el Turabi, had declared jihad on the Nuba people. Getting logistics by the SPLA GHQs to the area became impossible. The choices available to guerrilla forces in the Nuba Mountains, under the overall command of Yousif Kuwa, were unfortunately limited and both unpalatable: surrender to Khartoum, or fight to the last soldier.

But Cdr Yousif Kuwa, and fellow commanders, called a meeting of the local leaders and the SPLA senior officers in the area, to decide the course of action to be taken in the face of what was an imminent defeat by SAF. The overwhelming view was that surrender was not on the cards; they must fight on. Even civilians were prepared to take part if necessary. Luckily enough, for the forces and the people of the Nuba Mountains, some amounts of ammunition had reached the area through northern Bahr el Ghazal. And as they say, the rest is history.

My last days with Cdr Yousif Kuwa Mekki

In 1998, I was appointed head of information at a think tank that was closely associated with the SPLM. That non-government organisation was the Horn of Africa Centre for Democracy and Development, Hacdad, for short. I also became editor of the centre's monthly magazine, the *Horn of Africa Vision*. At that time, the Nuba Mountains community had a humanitarian organisation. Like Hacdad, the organisation for the Nuba operated in Nairobi. Cdr Yousif

Kuwa had just been diagnosed with prostate cancer at an advanced state. But he fought the condition bravely, almost unperturbed by his impending death. One day, I went to see him in his office. He looked relatively well, and cheerful as usual. When I enquired about his condition, the answer in Arabic was *"Ma bathal"* or not bad. To my surprise he asked me whether I had time to spare to discuss a matter and do him a "favour".

The favour he wanted me to offer had something to do with a job he wanted me to perform, for the people of the Nuba Mountains. He told me that his office had received some amount of money from well-wishers. He had decided that a certain percentage of that donation should be used for training journalists from the Nuba Mountains and that I should be both the main trainer and course director. Much of the money would go to rent the centre and maintenance of the students and stationery. I obliged. Together with three fellow Southern Sudanese (Henry Lasu was helping with English, while I taught most of the subjects half the time in Arabic. Obede Kunde gave instruction in photography). The three months' course ended in success. One of my former students on that training course was Sufian Mohammed, now a prominent media practitioner in the Nuba Mountains.

Approaching the end

One day I paid a visit to the SPLM Nuba Mountains office in Nairobi's Riara suburb, which was not far from Hacdad premises. His office manager was Captain Waleed Hamid, a friend of mine and an SPLA officer from Central Sudan. Waleed, whose wife is from the Nuba Mountains, was at the time assigned to the office of Cdr Yousif Kuwa in Nairobi. When I asked him about the health of his boss, Waleed's reply was a gloomy *"sarthan, sarthan"*, which is Arabic for cancer is cancer, meaning the prognosis was not good. The message was clear: it was terminal. What has amazed me to this day was by the time this brave man was nearing his end on this earth, he was busy, working for the movement and the cause of his people, while his family was leading a life that could be described as mere survival. In fact, the family did not have money. His two wives had to migrate to North America and Australia, respectively, for the education of their children. Some leaders in Yousif's situation would have found the temptation irresistible to convert the organisation's funds to his own to care for the families he was about to leave in poverty. But his selfless character had put honesty, principles and the future of the millions of his compatriots above his family's welfare.

By the time he passed away, I had gone to join my family in Australia. I was very sad at his passing. However, I welcomed the news that Cdr Yousif Kuwa Mekki received a hero's send-off as his body was taken to several towns in Southern Sudan – then under the control of the SPLA – before his coffin was flown to Kauda, in the Nuba Mountains, for final repose in his ancestral home, although he hailed from the Miri ethnic group, some distance from where he lies buried.

On my visit to the Nuba Mountains, in transit to Kurmuk in Southern Blue Nile in 2003, time did not allow me to visit the grave of one of the great and selfless Sudanese freedom fighters of our time. But at Kauda, I witnessed a situation worth recording. After our plane made a stopover to pick up Kuwa's successor, Cdr Abdel Aziz Adam el Hilu and comrades from the Mountains who were going to attend – as observers – SPLM's regional congress in Kurmuk, Abdel Aziz received us. We sat under a young and leafy mango tree. Nearby, there was a small thatched hut. This was Governor's Hilu's "palace", where his wife and children lived. The young ones were attending a school there. At the time children of some of the governor's SPLM/A colleagues were receiving their formal education either in Uganda or Kenya or far afield in England or the US. And, for probably for the first time in the history of the region, the medium of instruction at school was English. There is nothing special about English language in itself, but as an international language, and while Sudan's neighbours to the south and east use that medium in education, that choice made a lot of sense.

Yousif Kuwa Mekki died a brave and tolerant man. Although a Muslim, he never tried to convert his wife and her children. Hadi Diba, an SPLM member from the North, and a Muslim, recalls that the late Yousif allowed his children and wives to follow the faiths of their choice. He added that Fatima's children have converted to Christianity of their own accord, while a daughter by Christian Hanan has embraced Islam. Following Yousif's death in a London hospital, Hadi said, the body was taken to a chapel and later to a mosque for prayers. To this day, Yousif Kuwa Mekki's grave is draped with a crescent and a cross, two symbols of Islam and Christianity, respectively. That spirit of tolerance would have saved this country many lives, and prevented chronic civil wars, which have held back development and prosperity for all citizens.

Kuwa's successor

Some people love criticising the SPLM for almost everything that goes wrong in government, in party, and its performance in society in general. But except for people who deny hard historical facts, the SPLM has surprised both friends and critics in the manner its leaders conduct smooth transition when there is a leadership vacuum. Abdel Aziz Adam el Hilu succeeded the fallen Kuwa with little or no opposition. Abdel Aziz's leadership credentials are impeccable: a man of humility, with rare records for gallantry in military action in the Nuba Mountains, Southern Sudan where he once helped privates in carrying food items over a distance of more than a kilometre, in Eastern Sudan and Darfur – where Cdr Dawood Bolad was captured by the SAF and later executed in the early 1990s.

Although a quiet man, Abdel Aziz Adam el Hilu can argue his case patiently, persuasively, and devoid of emotions. Abdel Aziz and I have known each other for years, so I am making these statements from personal experience.

This piece was published the same day in three Khartoum by Arabic dailies: Al Ayyam, Es Sahafa *and* Rai al 'Aam *in 2010.*

Kerubino Kuanyin Bol as I knew him

The episodes I narrate here about Kerubino Kuanyin Bol, his relations with his boss, John Garang or with the author are not arranged in a chorological order.

It was in August 1984 when I met Kerubino Kuanyin Bol for the first time. From the time of the Bor mutiny in May 1983, Kerubino Kuanyin was a man many people, particularly Sudanese, were talking about. Although he was a newsmaker to some extent, his image- in the early days- was not available in newspapers or on television at home or in foreign news media. This was also the case with his boss, John Garang. I had no idea what Kerubino looked like, nor did anyone give me a description of his figure or appearance. I did know he was the deputy leader of the movement, and that he had gone into history as the soldier widely believed to have masterminded the fighting in Bor garrison on May 16, 1983, and that in the ensuing fighting between the mutinous forces and those loyal to the Government of Sudan he was wounded and later evacuated to rural Bor. That much I knew about Kerubino Kuanyin Bol, the man who now has a place in the history of South Sudan regardless of the divided opinion that surrounds his actions and personality.

Meeting the famous man

I met Kerubino Kuanyin Bol in an office in Addis Ababa, Ethiopia. He had just come from the war front in Southern Sudan, en route to West Berlin, for medical treatment. During the fighting in Bor that signalled the beginning of the second civil war, Major Kerubino Kuanyin as he was then, was wounded; a broken shoulder bone. The future SPLM/A leader John Garang, was also there with him in Bor.

Now we were in Addis Ababa. It had rained during the day and the weather was a little chilly with a cloudy sky, concealing the setting sun.

My recollections of one of the most talked about members of the new insurgency were products of imagination that bore little relationship to reality. The man the British *Independent* newspaper of September 24, 1999 described in an obituary as, "[a] flamboyant, trigger-happy southern Sudanese soldier, best remembered for supposedly firing the first rebellious shot when the imposition of Sharia law in September 1983 triggered a second round of civil warfare in the undeveloped, largely animist and Christian southern regions of the republic of Sudan", was a completely different human being. My concern with the quotation I have reproduced here is not to waste time with the erroneous facts, date and cause, included, and biased Western view of Africa in general and South Sudanese in particular, then and now. What interests me is the difference between the flesh-and-blood man, as opposed to the portrayal of the person either through imagination, or media distortion, or word-of-mouth.

Kerubino's mien and manner of speaking shattered the mental image I had formed of the man. He appeared calm, taller than I had imagined and showed a friendly and youngish face. He also appeared deep in thought. He talked quietly and in a measured tone. His hue, relatively speaking, was not very dark. He was pleasantly nice-looking.

I vividly remember Kerubino Kuanyin Bol expressing- that afternoon in Addis Ababa- to his colleague, Garang, a complaint without any hint of bitterness. The point he was making was that there were some people in Khartoum, especially among Southern Sudanese, whom he said talked negatively about the movement, with its leaders – Garang and Kerubino Kuanyin – in the top list of the figures commonly being vilified. Garang who also appeared calm replied that the expression of such dismissive views about the rebellion and its leaders were to be expected. The diatribes should not detract them from doing what they were doing, Garang said. I was listening to them quietly. Since I was going to stay with them for a long time to come, so I was not in a hurry to push some of my questions to understand certain aspects of the rebellion they were spearheading.

Our drive – in the only Toyota station wagon at the disposal of the SPLM and later to acquire notoriety (details in another account) – from Addis Ababa to Nazareth, a hundred kilometres southeast from the capital, was mostly quiet and uneventful.

The weeks we spent in Ethiopia with Kerubino, mostly in the company of his bodyguards, were without any incident I could recall, with the exception of a minor disagreement between Kerubino and one of Garang's aides, over matters concerning the plan for his pending trip to Germany. Again, during his brief stay in Berlin, there was some misunderstanding that led to his abrupt return to Africa, but on the whole I paid little attention to those episodes, dramatic and controversial as they were.

Work supervision and friendship

Despite the fact that Kerubino, who was known as an impetuous person, felt at easy in my company almost from the first meeting, became a talking point. Many people within the SPLM/A then- and even now- could not understand why the two of us got on so well; some of my associates even called our rapport a friendship. But I know why I was one of the persons the second-most powerful leader in the SPLM seemed to have singled me out for liking: I gave him the respect he deserved as the leader he was, and, above all, as a human being who was older than I was. In African tradition seniority in age demands the young should respect the older person who must, in turn, reciprocate. Besides that, I never contradicted him – even when there was a point of disagreement during a conversation, especially when making a statement that might not be true in my opinion. I was not being submissive or a power worshiper; as always, rocking the boat is not my way, except when under extreme provocation, or subjected to anything I suspect to be humiliation or when there is no principle or anything of value was at stake.

Although much of our time then was spent in some apparent indolence because there was really little to do, there were times Garang gave his deputy assignments, some of which Kerubino would then pass to me to do when it was paperwork. One of these assignments was to gather and prepare information that the SPLM was to present to visiting foreign guests, during the founding congress of the Ethiopian Workers Party, taking place in September that year.

Our team consisted of two former ministers and MPs in Juba Joseph Oduho, as chairman, and Martin Majier. Oduho, the veteran leader of Anya Nya, was head of the SPLM's department of political and foreign affairs, while Majier, a former minister – like Oduho, in the defunct Regional Government of Southern Sudan in Juba, was in charge of legal affairs and civil administration. The other members of the committee were Mayom Kuoch Malek, formerly in the department of planning in Juba and Philip Ajak Bol, an ex-official with the City Bank, Khartoum. There were others, but with little to offer in form of the type of information that would be contained in the proposed SPLM document.

The paper, which was to present in detail the socio-economic neglect of Southern Sudan by successive governments that had ruled the country since independence in 1956, was to be used as a reference outlining reasons behind the grievances of the people of the South and other marginalised areas. The data in the proposed was to be presented to justify the case for resorting to armed struggle. After three days of meeting to piece together figures on budgetary allocations for services and development in the South; kilometres of railway lines all over the country; tarmacked roads and so forth, I took the notes for rewriting and editing.

Kerubino had booked me into Hotel d'Afrique, in downtown Addis Ababa. He also hired a typist to do the job. Although I had been a fast touch typist, and loved the job since becoming a journalist, Kerubino insisted I be given a VIP treatment, and therefore should not be involved with what he considered to be a menial job such as typing, which he thought was beneath my status. I accepted the offer, but I had to sit near the Ethiopian woman, who had problems with Sudanese place and personal names. Her English was also rather inadequate. The deputy SPLM/A chief gave me cash, despite the fact that my accommodation was full-board.

When the 16-page document- which was more of a student essay than a product of serious research work- was ready, I passed it to Kerubino Kuanyin.

"What do you think of this?" Kerubino asked me. My answer was a cautious hint to the inadequacy of the document as it lacked credible figures, quotations from reputable sources, books and other relevant publications on Sudan. This was the pre-internet world of the 1980s. He then suggested that we should discuss the contents with Garang. A fast reader, Garang went over the documents in less than 15 minutes. After reading the report, Garang shook his head twice, disapproving, saying such a piece of work would raise a lot of questions about the competence of the entire leadership of the SPLM. The document was scrapped. I later learned that Garang went to prepare an alternative paper that I have never had the chance to read and which he presented to the delegates attending the Ethiopians' launch of their political party. I also do not know the sources he used to support whatever statements he made in his presentation. As the rebel masterminds were understandably not to be seen in public places- for their own security- such as university or libraries in Ethiopia, I still do not know where Garang would have obtained his information. Perhaps the Khartoum's SPLM secret cell, which had a number of academics, might have come to Garang's assistance with the accurate and up-to-date-information that was required for the presentation.

Launch of Radio SPLA

For reasons that I will not discuss here, it took Garang and both of his colleagues, Oduho and Majier, and myself, months to have a radio station go on air. It was a very frustrating time for most of us; on several occasions we promised the SPLA commanders in the field that we would be on-air soon. We would give the frequency, the time and the date for the first test broadcasts to begin, but nothing happened. The launch was also timed to coincide with a suspended graduation of about 12,000 fighters- of Koryom Division- ready for military operations, but such schedules passed without the clandestine station opening.

Garang and I were grappling with problems I do not need to reveal here, and which I believe he did not disclose to his field commanders, for fear of his messages on the subject being intercepted by the government in Khartoum, as long radio communication was not always 100 percent secure.

However, at midday of October 12, 1984, I rang Garang's residence at Nazareth. I was calling from a small hotel at the periphery of Addis Ababa. The receiver was one of the commander in chief's bodyguards. I asked him to connect me with the Big Man. Garang came on line, rather reluctantly as I was later told.

"We are on air today at three sharp, Sudan local time," I told a virtually incredulous Garang, my voice hoarse from extreme exhaustion. I had been working days and nights, sleeping for an average of four hours daily for a whole week, preparing five days' contents, putting together messages, slogans, war songs, statements and extracts from the movement's manifesto. I also worked with the help of a foreign friend on the design of the famous signal opening tune "SPLA Oyeei! SPLA Oyeei! Koryom Oyeei! Agreb[26] Oyeei! Hujuum! Hujuum"[27], accompanied by the sound of machine-gun shots. Garang received the news with some scepticism, for he had lost trust in the promises that were made by others in charge of the station. Previously I bore the brunt for being the proverbial messenger blamed or shot for carrying bad news. Happily, I didn't meet the second eventuality otherwise you wouldn't be reading these lines.

Spontaneous celebrations at Nazareth

About five minutes past three in the afternoon, a waiter from the hotel where I was staying knocked at my door; someone was on the line, waiting to talk with me. I went to the reception. It was Garang on the line. "*Mabruk*

---

26 'Agreb was a battalion of Koryom Division. 'Agreb in Arabic means scorpion.
27 Oyeei and Hujuum: Oyeei is a battle cry whose origin is subject of debate; some people in the SPLA think it is from Amharic language, while "*hujuum*" is Arabic for assault in the sense of someone giving orders for an attack.

[Arabic for congratulations] for a job well done", Garang who was very pleased and sounded excited, told me. I can't recall the other words which he said but he and his companions were all glowing with compliments. The next was Kerubino who, in addition to singing praises of me and what I and my team had done, promised to see me the following morning; in turn it was Oduho, Majier, and Lt Col Francis Ngor Maciec, followed by other lesser spirits in the hierarchy of the SPLM/A.

Like the rest of the new audience, I was listening to the broadcast. Although I had been listening before to the programme- now on air- many times over during preparation and recording, the fact that it was coming from a radio set had given my handiwork something akin to magical, sounding alien and powerful; it had acquired a personality of its own. I was also aware that thousands of people out there were listening to the product, much of it, I was one of its creators. I was happy and enjoyed a sense of achievement; the days and nights of toil were now paying off; I was as proud as a peacock, except that there were no people to affirm one of my few rare moments of glory and self-satisfaction. Since I was pleased with the clarity of the signal reception, as confirmed instantly by reports from all over Southern Sudan, and as I was dozing off, I went to sleep for more than three hours. While I was rewarding myself with a well-earned rest, the group at Nazareth, a small town 100 kilometres southeast of the Ethiopian capital Addis Ababa, which served as a hideout for the SPLM/A members during the early days, organised an impromptu party; a ram was hurriedly bought for slaughter and a feast that went on to almost 10 pm began, to mark the birth of what John Garang later dubbed as the "Unconventional Battalion".

Reconciliation

Being a politician in the making, Garang did not lose the happy occasion to reap some benefits from the cordial environment prevailing among those gathered and celebrating at his residence. Lt Col Francis Ngor on the one hand and Lt Col Kerubino Kuanyin and Lt Col William Nyuon on the other, were not on good terms before that date. Garang had taken Lt Col Francis Ngor and Col Solomon Majur Nhial Makol away from the frontline to minimise the friction between the three senior officers.

Garang is reported to have led his deputy to one of the adjacent rooms in the house where according to that source, the two men spent less than five minutes. Garang and Kerubino emerged from the room, smiling after the brief meeting. To the applause of everyone, Garang told the celebrants that Lt Col Francis Ngor had been appointed to command the Hadid Battalion,[28] then waiting deployment at a training centre on the Sudanese- Ethiopian border. The news was received with clapping, hugging and ululations from the few women who were present. For reasons that have remained unclear, Col Solomon Majur Nhial, who was in a similar situation as his colleague, Lt Col Francis Ngor and who was at Nazareth where the celebration was taking place, didn't benefit from the day of joy, by way of an assignment.

My finest moment

I enjoyed my deserved sleep that might have lasted more than eight hours. At about nine in the morning, Garang and Kerubino were driven to my hotel, a third-class facility at the periphery of Ethiopian capital. I was fresh and in my best spirits when I met the two soldiers, who themselves were all smiles, pleased with what was to going be one of the most effective weapons in their arsenal. Kerubino pulled me aside to have a word with me. He congratulated me again and handed me an envelope containing 600 Ethiopian birr, about 300 US dollars at the time. That amount was the same monthly salary for an Ethiopian officer with the rank of a brigadier. When I told him that I did not need that sum of money since I was on full-board accommodation, he argued that since I was a *bäny* – the Dinka word for a chief – I had to, and must have money and other resources to give to my junior staff when needed or necessary. As a team leader who gave no gifts to his subjects, meaning subordinates, I would not be respected or obeyed, he said.

As he was about to join Garang and leave together, a member within my staff I had just engaged, approached Kerubino with a request for money for himself. Having known the man for some years for dishonesty and self-centredness, I was not surprised but greatly embarrassed. Kerubino on the other

---

28 Hadid Battalion: the SPLA battalions and divisions were given names of some fierce wild animals such as Lion or Tiger and Timsah, *timsah* being Arabic for crocodile. *Hadid* is Arabic word for iron.

hand, responded in a rather loud voice intended to be heard by those present, taunted the man whom he told to get lost.

Soon Garang and Kerubino were gone to another part of the city for official contacts a couple of foreign embassies there.

The origins of SPLM/A policy of sparing lives of captured government soldiers

Before Radio SPLA had gone on air, Kerubino wanted to know from me what the station would be broadcasting. I explained to him that we, the staff, would be telling the Sudanese people – and the world – the reasons why the SPLA was fighting the army of the Government of Sudan; we would be telling true stories to debunk Khartoum's habitual and pathological lying; that we would be boosting and maintaining- with their own war songs- the morale of the fighting forces, and so forth. He was listening keenly before he asked for more, with, "And then?"

"Broadcast statements of captured government soldiers", I said, before he put in another "Why?"

"So that the relatives of the soldiers, the Sudanese people and the world will know that we are humane and civilised people", was my answer, before adding, "and to embarrass the government [in Khartoum]."

"You will get that", he promised, shook my hand and walked away to the orange car, parked outside the hotel where I was staying.

In January 1985, I went to the Jekou area in Nasir District, to cover the fighting going on between the SPLA and government armed forces, who were being supported by elements of Anya Nya II. The fighting was fierce and cost many lives on both sides. By then I had not yet received military training and commission. My base was Marial, which was a tactical headquarters for the SPLA forces of Koryom Division. Two members of the Military High Command were in charge of the operations. These were Lt Col Kerubino Kuanyin and Major Salva Kiir. Major Kuol Manyang Juuk – formerly a civil servant fresh from military training and by the time he had not yet been appointed to the leadership position – was one of the operational commanders during those battles.

Intelligence reports reached the SPLA, that the government was reinforcing the beleaguered Jekou garrison on the border between Sudan and Ethiopia. The SPLA had taken the necessary preparations, that included laying ambushes along the road. As the battalion plus force, commanded by Col Balaa', was approaching their destination, the SPLA struck, almost annihilating the enemy force. The commander, Col Balaa' was killed in action. The SPLA celebrated their victory; I had an additional reason to join in the victory party. The SPLA forces had captured a member of the government forces, who was a non-commissioned officer, NCO. The overall commander, Lt Col Kerubino Kuanyin, had given strict orders that the captive should be taken alive to the headquarters of Major Salva Kiir and promised dire consequences to any SPLA soldier who dared harm the NCO, SPLA's ever first prisoner of war. After the debriefing was over, the soldier was sent to me. I was assisted by Malaak Ayuen, a former Radio Juba broadcaster who like me at the time, had not yet trained as a soldier. We recorded the captive's statements that included his full name, military rank and number, village of his birth, names of his parents and so forth. This was what is called a scoop in journalism, only that we didn't have any rival for the news. I immediately left the war-front to broadcast the first of what later turned out to be a political and moral asset for the SPLM/A: sparing the lives of government soldiers captured in battle.

In our next meeting, Kerubino wanted to know whether I was pleased with the catch. "Yes, Comrade. But it would have been very good if the soldier was a senior officer", I said.

"Next time I will bring you [captured] an enemy officer of my rank [lieutenant colonel]", he said, in the manner of someone promising to buy a gift item from a supermarket. But it did not take long for him to make good his promise.

Several months after this exchange, Lt Col Kerubino Kuanyin led SPLA troops into Southern Blue Nile territory where they came under attack by the government forces. Their commander was Lt Col Abu Illa Adam Juma. In the engagement that followed, the SPLA routed the government forces, with heavy casualties and their commander taken captive. 1st Lt Mohammed Mirghani was also taken prisoner. At the time the government forces were defeated, I was at the officers' training centre. Lt Col Kerubino Kuanyin gave orders that the prisoners of war be transported to what was known as Institute of Revolutionary War Studies. I was called to interview the two officers for Radio SPLA. Assisting with recording of the interview was 1st Lt Kuol Atem, one of the officers initially trained for the station and was later attached to the GHQs. Having fulfilled his previous promise, Kerubino later told me I had no more demand on him. But what he did not know was that capturing and keeping government soldiers had become, by default, an official policy of the SPLM/A. To prove to the public that the rebels were not telling lies, their leadership invited the International Committee of the Red Cross, ICRC, to visit the POWs and exchange letters between them and their families. A couple of years later, an official of the ICRC told me that, legally, the ICRC did not consider civil war as applying to their rules and regulations regarding POWs, which she said were designed for conflicts involving nation states, not those in which non-state actors such as insurgents were party to. Hundreds of prisoners were in different SPLA centres. Some who chose to return were allowed to re-join their families, while those who wanted to be members of the SPLA went into combat to face their former comrades in arms, members of SAF.

Changing times and changed fortunes

In 1987, Kerubino Kuanyin Bol was arrested and detained for allegedly [since he was not tried to prove his innocence or guilt, this is an appropriate way of putting it] plotting to overthrow the leadership of the SPLM/A. In early 1991, Kerubino and his fellow inmates broke out of detention and fled to Uganda, then to Kenya. Being bitter mostly for his incarceration, Kerubino turned hostile against his former boss and anyone who was still loyal to him. He finally went to Khartoum where he formed an opposition armed body, SPLA Bahr el Ghazal, and worked hand-in-hand with the Government of Sudan in fighting the movement he helped in setting up. He carried his war to his home district of Gogrial, where he conducted attacks against the locals, reportedly to punish them for their loyalty to the SPLM/A under Garang's leadership. But in 1998, Kerubino turned against the government- for a second time- and re-defected to the movement of which he was a co-founder. But the organisation was already completely different in terms of hierarchy and leadership structure. His number two slot had long been filled, and so were the other positions made vacant by either deaths or defections to the enemy. Where Kerubino fitted within the movement's chain of command was not an easy walk. Since his absence was not a sabbatical approved by the organisation, for Kerubino to reclaim his previous position of deputy leader raised a lot of practical but difficult questions. But again, that is another story for another day in another medium.

On his return, I was surprised to know that his attitude towards me had remained the same: friendly, although he knew I was a member of what was known as SPLM/A mainstream, which meant being on the side of his opponents following the bitter and sometimes deadly, rift.

Still friends

While in the SPLM office, in the Kenyan capital, Nairobi, Kerubino rang me when I was at another outfit affiliated to the SPLM, located in another part of the city. In the conversation that followed, he complained that some people within the system were not taking good care of him. He was partially joking. In reply I said in Dinka *"Bäny, acïe piath bï bäny cam apiath ku cɔk anäk kɔc"*, which when literally translated is: Chief, it is not good that a chief eats well when famine is killing [other] people. I was referring to the grinding famine that had hit Bahr el Ghazal that year. He laughed. He told me he was happy that I did not fear to tell him the truth. The following day I went to meet him at the SPLM office. After the exchange of niceties and my expression of joy that he had come back, I told him in English that he looked in good shape and that he did not need to eat more than he was taking. His face beamed; he liked what I had told him. However, one of his lieutenants who had always held a baseless grudge against me, was not amused as he looked sullen, fidgeting in his nearby seat as Kerubino and I chatted heartily.

Some memorable episodes: John Garang and Kerubino Kuanyin

Since I have written- in some of my unpublished documents- about issues such as the reasons for the arrest and detention of Kerubino Kuanyin Bol in later years, I have confined myself here to only a few anecdotes, some seemingly insignificant; others dramatic incidents or those in between, involving the two men which I witnessed at a very close range. In general, the relations between the leader of the SPLM/A and his deputy oscillated between being fiercely protective; warm and friendly to detached and sometimes prickly; depending on the situation obtaining at the time. The following narratives- although by no means exhaustive- serve to illustrate the assertion I have made.

Standoff at a military base

An incident which demonstrated Kerubino's loyalty and regard for the dignity and welfare of his boss happened in August 1984 at Addis Ababa military airbase. I was accompanying the two leaders and their bodyguards. As we were preparing to board a military helicopter the Ethiopian government had placed at their disposal, an Ethiopian army major ordered all of us to open our hand-held bags for inspection and that he was going to take the weight of each of us, one by one, on a nearby weighing machine. On hearing this, Kerubino accepted but told the Ethiopian that Garang should be exempted from the procedures.

"Why?" asked the Ethiopian.

"He is my boss. He is a big man. You do not know that?" interjected Kerubino.

The request and explanation fell on deaf ears. Looking serious, the officer insisted that we obey his orders. His insistence that we should comply with his measures led Kerubino to wonder: in whose interest the major was taking those steps?

"Do you think we are going to hijack the helicopter? Where to? Khartoum?" Kerubino who was understandably puzzled questioned the Ethiopian officer. We couldn't suppress laughter. Although these were logical questions and not intended for jest, the major wouldn't budge: we must do what he was telling us to open our bags for inspection and get everyone weighed before boarding the aircraft. We must do what he was telling us to do or the helicopter wouldn't leave, he repeated. The situation was getting tense each passing second. On our side, there were moments Kerubino, who was very agitated, appeared as if he was going to strike the Ethiopian with a fist. He was also armed with a Makarov pistol in a holster, which was dangling under the belt on his right side. It was scary, as I can now recall that scene of the incident of more than 30 years ago.

What at first was a minor disagreement was developing into a problem likely to come to the attention of higher echelon within the Ethiopian bureaucracy. It was clear that if the row continued, a very senior army officer, for example, would suddenly turn up at the scene to sort out what was delaying the flight. In that case, the major was likely to face punitive measures for his disrespectful treatment of important state guests. Garang was aware of that prospect and wanted us to avoid a potential fallout among the Ethiopians on our account even though he didn't like the apparently irrational behaviour of the major. For that reason, Garang told Kerubino we had to save time by accepting (and swallowing our pride) to go through the inconvenience which he, Garang, knew was humiliating to him and his deputy. And he ended the standoff by opening his attaché after which he walked to the weighing machine. The rest of us followed suit.

There was something strange in what appeared to be security procedures: neither Kerubino nor the bodyguards, who were all carrying pistols, were told to surrender their weapons to the plane's crew as one would expect in such a situation.

By early afternoon we had landed at Gambella where we were going to spend the night in transit to another border area.

Seen from a detached vantage point, each of the three men involved in the wrangle had what could be considered as a convincing reason for what they did or said. For his part, the Ethiopian officer was probably acting on orders "from above"; Kerubino saw the decision as insulting to his leader; and finally Garang wanted to avoid a quarrel that was likely to create problems among the hosts and which he didn't want. The episode also had a message, at least as far as Kerubino was concerned. His reaction said a lot about his relations with Garang as his colleague and leader. In the real world, a test of genuine love and loyalty comes from action not by words only. And this was what Kerubino Kuanyin Bol had proved that he was ready to stand by his comrade and boss.

Fathoming the officer's behaviour

Several months later, a senior Ethiopian official casually confirmed the obvious, that not all his compatriots supported the Sudanese rebels and their cause; the behaviour of the major at the airport should therefore be understood in that context, he rationalised. But was the major not taking a risk as his government wouldn't approve of his action? Anyway, in similar situations, which weren't uncommon albeit subtle, Garang used to take an open mind and flexible position. When any of his colleagues or personnel in his office complained of their relations with uncooperative or covertly obstructive agents representing a friendly state or an organisation, Garang would remind fellow Sudanese that the Ethiopians, for example, were sovereign in their land and that their assistance to the Sudanese in general and the SPLM/A in particular was not a right to be demanded forcefully. The hosts, he added, could withhold their generosity if they chose to and the would-be-recipients had no justification to complain, disappointed as they might be.

"It is their country. It is their money. We do not owe them a debt", Garang once joked after a visit to another African country. The remark came when his aides complained that the amount of financial assistance the president had offered to the SPLM/A's delegation during their joint meeting and which they had just received, was far less than the declared figure. The implication was that the officials in the host country had short-changed the rebels. Interestingly, when I retold the anecdote to a friend who was also a fellow member of the SPLM/A, he smiled. After a pause he retorted:

"Do you believe the veracity of the story? Would you discount the possibility that two or three of our own comrades might have been the ones responsible for the shortfall and since they were confident that nobody would return to check the exact figure, they could go about falsely casting doubt on the honesty of the generous hosts?" We both laughed. He could be right. But considering that the whispered accusation of impropriety against some officers in charge of the movement's scarce resources were not a secret, I had no reason to trouble my lungs, arguing in defence of "our comrades". There was no reason we could be an exception although the core policy of the SPLM/A was to fight injustice of which corruption is an integral part. In bureaucracies of some African countries and organisations, such abuses are not in the realm of imagination; they sometimes do happen. One has just to read Che Guevara's experience in the Congo when the Argentinian revolutionary was training the anti-government rebels in the 1960s.[29]

Such an allegation would have sounded blasphemous in those days. At the time, anyone publicly and openly criticising SPLM/A's policies or perfor-

---

29 One of the books is *Che in Africa: Che Guevara's Congo Diary*, published by Ocean Press (Australia), 1999.

mance of the leaders or making hints of office abuse, ran the risk of being branded a quisling. Nevertheless, in fairness, the SPLM/A leadership had put in place some guidelines to curb possible misconduct by members. One of those was the regulation that stipulated that when a foreign country or organisation was giving cash donations "for air tickets" as they were politely dubbed by the benefactors, a team of not less than five members had to be formed to receive, *count* and *certify* the amount in question. The committee's role, however, ended at that stage as its members would not follow up how such sums would be spent or who would be the "end user" or the beneficiaries.

Mysterious disappearance of a lamb

After landing at Gambella airport we were driven straight to an SPLA base, not far from Gambella town. Zinc, the base, lies on a swift running stream. It was both Garang's hideout as well as a centre for training mostly young men in specialisation in various fields such as intelligence, signal, political- being a euphemism for ideological orientation, mostly Marxism-Leninism- among others. There were four thatched huts, the larger one being used as a sitting room. The structures were built purposely for the use of the Chairman and Commander in Chief. Since the SPLM/A leader used to settle- just for a night- at the base while in transit either to Addis Ababa or to many camps at the border area, there was no permanent staff deployed there to provide services.

On our arrival at Zinc I decided- in deference to the two leaders and Costello Garang being a guest – to run errands for ourselves. I approached John Garang for some money for the evening meal which he gave plus some for drinks. The Ethiopian driver went to town where he bought drinks, beer for John Garang, soft drink for Costello who is a confirmed teetotaller, and dry gin for Kerubino and me. Aware that the diet for the young trainees who were living next to us didn't include meat, I approached one of them to volunteer to buy a ram before dark. Abu Kalaam or Abu for short, as he will be known in this story, took the money and rushed to the neighbourhood. His mission included fetching the animal whose small portions he and his colleagues should prepare for our supper while the rest should be for their consumption. I returned to the tukul to join the three. We then began to sip the drinks the driver had brought.

A typical Sudanese meal involving slaughter of a domestic animal begins with *afash* (consisting of roast ribs or boiled liver, for instance, being served as entrée) to be followed by mounds of meat and stew, going together with kisra or asida. Since there were no women in the area to prepare either kisra or asida, bread was going to be a substitute.

At about seven, I began to wonder why the starter had delayed in coming. I went out not to check the progress but to order the young men to serve the long awaited meal. I was in for a rude shock; it was not that the meal was not yet ready: the lamb had broken the rope with which it was tied to a tree within the compound. The lamb had disappeared without a trace. I returned to the room with the fiction-like report. The Chairman who since our arrival, was hard at work, writing with a pen and loose pads, raised his head and uttered "*Billahi!*"[30] and immediately went back to his writing without saying another word. Kerubino on the other hand, made no comment or any form of surprise. Costello being a guest, conveniently said nothing. I was the only person in the hut who was deeply concerned, if that was the right way of putting it, with what I had been told.

About 15 minutes later, Abu who was breathing heavily came and called me outside. When he and his colleagues had realised that the animal was missing they went out, combing the neighbourhood for it, but all in vain, Abu told me as his voice sounded broken with sadness; probably feigned. They had crossed the nearby brook several times, looking for the lamb but to no avail; showing his pants which were wet up to the thighs for a proof. And Oh, yes, he had a suspect: this was not a human being having stolen the animal; this was another ram. Ayele's ram. Sounded familiar. Captain Ayele was one of the Ethiopian technicians in charge of the training courses being conducted at Zinc. He had a lovely ram which he kept as a pet. This ram weighed more than 40 kilograms and was always with people during waking hours, never seen going past the fence. Now according to the story I was hearing from Abu, the lamb they had bought had broken free, joined Ayele's ram which in turn walked out of the compound with the lamb; the ram returned alone without the lamb. Apologies after apologies. I said nothing. I should have answered him with "Really!" but chose not. End of the story.

---

30 Although *Billahi!* – often accompanied by an exclamation mark- invokes the name of Allah or God, the expression is normally used as a form of surprise.

Knowing that there were not going to be roast chops or boiled amounts to be washed down with gin, Kerubino and I stopped taking the stuff; we would be drinking on an empty stomach.

Garang's first press conference
A day after the airport saga, the same helicopter flew the following morning to pick Garang and Kerubino from Gambella. We were flying to Tedo, a sparsely populated Anyuak village at the Ethiopian Sudanese border. Garang, Kerubino, Costello and I had spent the previous night at Zinc.

An SPLA unit which had just returned from Aweil in Bahr el Ghazal where they had gone for recruitment had camped at Tedo. In Aweil area, a unit of Jamus Battalion- whose commander was Lt Col Kerubino Kuanyin Bol – captured two German nationals who at first were described as hostages but later were said to have been taken away from area for their own safety. The government of the Federal Republic of Germany wanted their nationals to be released unconditionally. The rebels agreed. Costello Garang Riiny, a long term resident of what was at the time known as West Germany, and the man who was instrumental in persuading the SPLM/A leadership to set free the Germans- a retired police officer and a young man in his early twenties- was with us for the event.

Having walked almost a thousand kilometres and unused to the types of food the guerrillas lived on, the Germans were exhausted although the ex-cop appeared hale and cheerful. There were several Sudanese who were being held on suspicion they were government agents when they were arrested in the area. Two of these were Mario Muor Muor, a law student and well-known activist at the University of Khartoum. For lack of evidence, Muor Muor was later released, sent for officers' course and was commissioned as an SPLA officer. Muor Muor rose to become one of Garang's senior aides. The second man was Arop Achir. Arop later escaped and went to Khartoum where he became a thorn in the movement's side, with his vitriolic attacks on his former captors; converted to Islam and became one of the Islamist regime's powerful leaders from Southern Sudan, in the process earned for himself the revered title of "Sheikh" before he died of natural causes.

Major Salva Kiir who had come from Pochalla where the forces of Tiger and Timsah under his command had withdrawn was in attendance, as was Captain Chagai Atem Biar, then commander of Bilpam headquarters. What was expected to be a minor function turned out to be an important platform for John Garang who since the outbreak of the rebellion in May 1983, had remained an unknown and shadowy character to both the local, regional and international news media. In that news "blackout" the world's perception of the rebel chieftain was that of a bogeyman, as he was being portrayed by the Government of Sudan under President Jaafar Nimeiri. For the release of the Germans and possibly to give Garang the chance to reach out to the outside world, the Ethiopian government had sent a contingent of reporters. Posing as an independent foreign journalist, I joined the Ethiopian newsmen who were of lower category working for the state controlled news agency, radio station and a daily in Amharic language. The story was relevant to the Ethiopians as their country had offered passage for the Germans.

I was armed with a still camera and a bulky radio-tape recording machine which someone had to hold for me as I was taking photos. The Ethiopian journalists didn't do a good job. As civil servants serving under a military dictatorship, attending press conferences or asking a VIP any question, let alone a probing and hard one, was out of the question for them. I wasn't therefore surprised by their dismal performance. Little was known about the objectives or the ideology of the new Sudanese rebel movement, yet the reporters never asked Garang about any of those issues. I should mention here that the press conference was the first for both the newsmaker and the Ethiopian reporters. This was Garang's ever first face to face with news media since the rebellion broke out at Bor's army garrison in May 1983, and his subsequent assumption of the insurgency's leadership soon afterwards. And his performance was just that of a novice; he stumbled over words; spent an awful lot of time on minor matters instead of big the picture, and so forth. I recall him using Americanism when he referred to Nimeiri as having "*gotten* himself into...the problems he is in now". (Late Garang spoke and wrote British English despite the fact that he studied for his degrees- bachelor, master's and doctorate – in the US).

When it was clear the Ethiopian reporters had failed to raise pertinent questions such who was supplying the insurgents with arms, I took advantage my phoney identity, shot up to confront Garang with "What are you fighting for?"

Garang lurched into a lengthy answer which should have been a summary of what he would describe in years to come- the time he had become adept at handling the press- as "things that make people angry". His answer was the story of grievances by the people of Sudan against the system of rule by Nimeiri's dictatorial regime…I don't remember the exact time John Garang talked; but his explanation lasted more than 20 minutes just to answer a single question. Captain Deng Alor, one of the officers from the Jamus Battalion returning from Bahr el Ghazal and who had been wounded in the leg during a recent skirmish in Pibor area between the SPLA and the Murle militia-men of Chief Ismail Konyi, was interpreting – from English to Arabic- for the soldiers who like everyone else including Garang were standing in the open air "press gallery".

With the mission accomplished, Costello Garang, the two Germans, the Ethiopian journalists and I boarded the Ethiopian military helicopter that was flying us back to Addis Ababa. Garang and Kerubino remained at Tedo with the other colleagues.

A couple of weeks later someone who was in the company of the three members of the leadership[31] and other senior SPLA officers told me that during the conversation after supper, Kerubino came up with what had been bothering during the day: the question I had put to Garang at the press conference. According to that report, Kerubino was wondering why someone who was a member and had been with them for several months, didn't know the objectives of the movement.

---

31 The Military High Command, later renamed Politico-Military Command consisted of Col Dr John Garang de Mabior, Chairman of the SPLM and Commander in Chief of the SPLA; Lt Col Kerubino Kuanyin Bol, Deputy Chairman of the SPLM and Deputy Commander in Chief of the SPLA; Lt Col William Nyuon Bany; Major Salva Kiir Mayardit and Major Arok Thon Arok. William Nyuon and Arok Thon were at the front and didn't go to Tedo.

"If he does not know what we are fighting for, then why is he still with us?" he was reported as asking. Garang, who was sitting next to him was said to have replied that I had to ask that obvious question because none of the other journalists had raised it. That I had asked the question was to give him, Garang, the chance to explain to the rest of the world the main objectives of the war, Garang explained as Kerubino was listening.

"Then he must be a *Mangok!*"[32]

This was a compliment. This word was a slang commonly used by the SPLA fighters to refer to someone smart enough to get out of a tight corner without a scathe.

The Ayele affair

Quarrels between John Garang and his number two in the rebel leadership were not infrequent as the following anecdotes will show. One morning, my team and I drove- as was the case every weekday- to Garang's residence not far from down town Addis Ababa. We were going to pick the news items from the various war zones, which were being received via long range radio being operated there. Each time we were in the house, we would be waiting at the lounge for the operator and the bundles of papers containing handwritten reports. Sometimes there were delays in the release of news reports which as a rule had to be approved only by Garang. Despite the fact that I was chief editor of news (as well as director) of Radio SPLA, I never saw the original reports from the warfront before any details of top secret had been removed. More often than not, casualty figures were subjected to alteration, with enemy losses increased and the SPLA's kia (killed in action) or wounded either missing or greatly reduced.

It was about nine in the morning. There was a delay in the release of news reports to us that morning. Kerubino and Cdr Martin Manyiel Ayuel, the director of the Addis Ababa office and a junior member of the leadership,

---

32 Mangok this is derived ŋɔɔk (ngook), a Dinka word for a type of fish that pricks its victim with a dorsal fin. *Maŋɔɔk* (mangook) then means a person not to be messed with; a tough guy. This was Kerubino's favourite nickname.

were together in Garang's bedroom which doubled as office. The bedroom was some distance from the lounge. We could hear some angry words being exchanged between Kerubino and Martin Manyiel. Kerubino and Garang were locked in a quarrel and Manyiel had intervened, openly chiding Kerubino for something wrong he might have done. Soon Kerubino rushed out of the room, obviously angry. As he was walking very fast by us he began to yell at us to "Get out from here", meaning from the sitting room. Manyiel could no longer control himself as we heard him utter "This conduct is not acceptable", he said in Dinka as he also walked past us, returning to the office in the market area about fifteen-minute drive. We were stunned, confused and became sad, although not surprised. Quietly my team and I left the building, going to work. Garang remained inside the bedroom; we never saw or heard him. No member of his immediate family was available as they were out of the country at the time. As we were driving to the station, we hardly talked to each other about what we had witnessed or on any other topic. Later we learned the quarrel had nothing to do with how the movement was being run by Garang, for example, but that the issue was related to unmet and "excessive and endless" financial demands. Kerubino had just returned from Britain where he had gone for the operation on his shoulder. The previous three days he and his bodyguards were shopping- most likely for gifts to friends and family members- in the city in preparation for their trip to Itang refugee camp.

On return from work- recording the news and programmes for the 3 pm broadcast- and as usual I went to the office at the market place. Garang, Cdr Martin Manyiel and his deputy, Cdr Deng Alor were all within the building. We had offices on the first floor of an apartment building within a crowded market area not far from Addis Ababa Hilton Hotel. (One still wonders why that location- of all the office spaces in the capital- was selected as a centre for a guerrilla organisation and its activities).

In that building the SPLM/A maintained three offices, one for the top leaders which was also director's office. The deputy's office occupied by Deng served as a secretariat. The third room was allotted to me as the head of Radio SPLA and editor of the SPLM/A newsletter. There was huge lounge which was sparingly furnished. At the entry there were always two Ethiopians for security, a man stationed outside and a woman inside, next to the door to the apartment.

It wasn't long before we started hearing boisterous noise emanating from below. When we enquired, the woman replied in Amharic *"Tinish shigir ale"*, or there is a small problem. It was an understatement; there was a serious argument going on at the car park below. These were bodyguards attached to Kerubino's headquarters quarrelling with some Ethiopians and among themselves; between those pressing for restraint and the authors of the commotion. Nobody upstairs had any idea of the person causing the noisy exchange or why. Soon an Ethiopian security officer came up to tell us that the soldiers didn't want the driver sent to take Kerubino to Gambella that day. When Garang learned that Kerubino was there while the altercation was going on, he ordered that his deputy should be told to report to him without delay. And Cdr Martin Manyiel, a graduate of Sudan military academy went down to execute the order. Late Martin Manyiel, like late Kerubino Kuanyin, hailed from Gogrial area.

As they passed us on their way to the office where Garang was waiting, Kerubino cast an angry look at the two colleagues sitting near me. We decided to quickly get into my office; the elephants were fighting and we might end up being their grass. After realising that it necessary for me to have someone in the lounge to tell any visitor to go away so as not to know what was going on inside the senior office, I returned to take my seat on a sofa set in the middle of the room. The office of the director remained closed and no sound or human voice from it was audible. Whatever was taking place behind the closed door lasted close to an hour. Then the door swung open and out came Kerubino, looking a bit subdued and followed by Deng Alor. Out of respect, I arose. He acknowledged that with a wink. He went down to where his bodyguards were waiting and wondering about what was happening upstairs.

"Let's go", he told his bodyguards as he was entering the front seat of the station wagon. When one of the soldiers asked about Ayelo or Ayele, the order was again "Let's go", this time anger and impatience in his voice was evident.

Ayele was elderly Ethiopian driver the Ethiopian authorities had assigned to drive SPLM/A leaders. There were unconfirmed stories that the *derebe*, as the Ethiopians call a driver, once served the deposed Emperor Haile Selassie. Ayele, a patient, friendly and dignified man, was loved by all the SPLM/A people he worked with. We later learned that the cause of all the noise was about Ayele. According to the same source, one senior bodyguard had convinced Kerubino that they shouldn't accept any other driver; it had to be Ayele. This was the root cause of the crisis.

With the turn of events, Kerubino and his team were going to be driven to Gambella by another driver, not by the universally venerated granddad of a driver, Ayele.

Cdr Deng Alor, bound by office code of confidentiality, refused to tell me and my team what had transpired between Garang and Kerubino in the office as he and his boss, Cdr Martin Manyiel Ayuel were there. It would not be too fetched to guess that the Commander in Chief was subjecting his second in command to a military disciplinary action and a lengthy lecture on how to behave; no doubt about that.

False accusation
Year: 1984; Stage: Itang refugee camp, western Ethiopia.
It happened that one of the SPLA junior officers approached me with a request that I should include the name of his wife in the list of the persons I was looking to recruit for voluntary work at Radio SPLA whose launched I was organising. The wife had no background in journalism, print or electronic. Before she married the officer, she was working as a junior clerk in the department of information in one of the provinces in the late 1970s. Moreover, for those personnel to work at the underground radio station, the job involved a lot of sacrifice, for which mothers taking care of young children would not be suitable. Unconvinced, and unhappy with me, the officer went straight to Kerubino, claiming that I was recruiting only people hailing from my Bor home district. The reverse of the allegation was the case. For a better understanding of the saga, a digression here is necessary.

Within the SPLM/A there were highly qualified broadcasters who like me were born in Bor area. These were George Garang Deng Chol (known to friends as Michael George), a graduate of English and Political Science from the University of Khartoum. He was a former editor of the *Nile Mirror*; trained for a year at the German international broadcasting system, Deutsche Welle; a holder of an advanced diploma in journalism from West Berlin; former director of Radio Juba. The other was Chol Kuany Deng and Chau Mayol Juuk, former news readers on Radio Juba and had trained at Khartoum Institute of Mass Communication (Chol) and Cairo (Chau), respectively. There were other journalists from Bor area who had similar backgrounds in media but for this purpose, citing the three will suffice. Although not all those broadcasters were in Itang at the time the charge was made, they were in different locations administered by the movement where they could be ordered to report to the station at a short notice if and when needed.

Despite the impressive backgrounds and experiences the three journalists had in broadcasting, John Garang who was born in Bor area flatly *refused* to engage any of them on what was actually a voluntary assignment. Although he didn't give a reason for his refusal to have the broadcasters taken by Radio SPLA, it was common knowledge that the guerrilla leader judged that deploying the three experienced radio journalists to Radio SPLA would amount to turning the mouthpiece of a national organisation, the SPLM/A, into a "monopoly" of "his clansmen", an eventuality which would negate the slogans of the movement that was fighting against all forms of injustice, particularly discrimination on racial, ethnic, regional, gender and religious grounds.

Ironically, the SPLM/A leader was later forced to accept the deployment of Chau Mayol Juuk to the station to back up Jok Yousif Ngor, from Renk District, northern Upper Nile, then head of station's Arabic department. Despite his intimate knowledge of Arabic language as well as his beautiful voice he effectively applied as a newsreader, Jok Yousif had serious difficulty with formal and professional writing and editing of news in that language.

For similar reasons, Garang was often reluctant to appoint persons related to him by blood or regional affiliations, to positions seen to offer power and perks. However, though commendable as his understanding of fairness and social justice went, he obviously ignored, knowingly or otherwise, giving a job to someone who happened to be sharing ties such as friendship, consanguinity or geography with him, and who had the required qualifications, and that the selection was not at the expense of someone else deserving the position, doesn't necessarily violate the norms of fair play or good governance.

Interestingly, using the same standards, Garang tried to block my appointment as project manager future Radio SPLA when in early 1984 the SPLM/A had mooted the acquisition of a broadcasting station. The plan also necessitated the search for someone suitably qualified to organise and manage the project. Joseph Oduho and Martin Majier, former ministers in Juba and by then senior office holders in the SPLM/A, proposed me for the position of director of Radio SPLA. Garang vetoed the nomination; I was his relative –a distant one, of course- he told the politicians who knew me in Juba of the 1970s and early 1980s where I worked as a senior journalist. The two politicians prevailed over Garang, who reluctantly endorsed the appointment. Up to this day, I don't know the person John Garang had in mind for the position of Radio SPLA director.

Case dismissed

The officer who had accused me to Kerubino knew the *facts* about the former broadcasters of Radio Juba because he once worked for a short time as an unclassified junior staff at Radio Juba. He was a secondary school leaver who later left work at Radio Juba to study abroad where, I was told, he gained a degree in unspecified discipline, but certainly not media studies. When he was telling Kerubino the story he had made up there were several other people in the guestroom listening to the charge being made against me.

When Kerubino learned of my alleged misconduct- alleged promotion of nepotism within the movement – he sent three armed soldiers to bring me to him at the guesthouse. The soldiers who were Kerubino's personal bodyguards and who knew me very well, found me in a friend's house where I was reading a novel. The guards gently knocked at the door. Unlike what was a common practice at the time – suspects were often roughed up by soldiers acting as law enforcers – they politely told me their boss wanted to see me and that I should accompany them to the guesthouse.

The young soldiers were very polite and tried to give me the impression they were merely acting. I complied and walked side by side with them instead of walking ahead of them, which would have sent the message of an offender being driven, perhaps to jail. On nearing the guesthouse, the guards started to pretend to be rough and rude to me. I was ushered in. My "enemy" was sitting quietly in a corner of the room, looking unconcerned and as innocent as a baby. I knew that despite his feigned indifference, he was secretly enjoying the spectacle and humiliation I was being subjected to. I was not allowed to sit but ordered to start up at attention although I was not yet a soldier. I obeyed the orders, remained composed as explained- point by point- everything that Kerubino had demanded that I should explain.

After listening attentively to me and while I was mid-way through my defence, convinced of my innocence, Kerubino stopped me and stunned some of the listeners when he declared he had been misled. He didn't name the culprit. The tables had turned against my adversary who also belonged to the opportunistic and self-proclaimed progressives. Kerubino then allowed me to go. One of the officers who present when the allegation against me was being made, later disclosed to me the officer's name: he was the husband of the lady whose "application" for a place on the staff of Radio SPLA I had refused. Her husband wanted her to be assigned specifically the position of a newsreader in Arabic.

Manner of man: personal experience

Although I do not claim to have known the man very well, one of the traits in Kerubino Kuanyin Bol which sometimes made him vulnerable to being taken advantage of was his trusting nature. In the vernacular languages of the two Sudans a "person with a white heart", is an idiom used to describe an exceptionally kind person who can get involved in a quarrel, even a bitter and serious one, but with a passage of time, as short as a day, the feeling of ill-will or annoyance, has completely evaporated; and the bygones become bygones. Such attributes neatly fitted Kerubino Kuanyin Bol. The reverse side of the coin of that commendable trait is called in Dinka "*Acol puɔ̃u/ piɔ̃u*" (puou/piou), literally meaning, "with a black heart"; a projection of someone who never forgives; has a propensity to brood over past slights, real or drummed up, and always looks- waylays adversaries as it were- for the slightest excuse to strike sweet vengeance.

From my personal experience, Kerubino Kuanyin Bol, it wouldn't be an exaggeration to state that his heart was as white as snow, metaphorically speaking. Whether one loved or detested him, Kerubino had a soft side to him.

The man was also generous to a fault; he loved to share the company of other people, food or drinks with others including people who were not his peers.

Two days exactly after the incident I have retold above, Kerubino sent one of his bodyguards, this time not for questioning but to be taken to his house for a meal. When I arrived, Kerubino who was dressed in his official camouflage uniform, rose and hugged me as if he had forgotten the drama of the past days. Having before witnessed similar incidents involving him and others and how quickly he would put aside previous quarrels, I wasn't surprised.

A man of the people

There were several officers of different ranks and ethnic communities of Southern Sudan. When I arrived they were chatting inside the thatched tukul. I hadn't met some of them before, but had heard about their various stories- of valiant fighters in combat or former student activists and their role in mobilising local students to support and join the movement in the early days, and so forth. Nearly all of them were happy to meet and chat with me, too. The lunch that was later served consisted mainly of huge chunks of roast meat, stew and kisra. The conversation that followed became the beginning of the acquaintanceship that later developed between me and some of the officers. Several of those men have remained friends with me to this day. One of them was 1st lieutenant Garang Mabil, who had the reputation of being a caring officer and brave fighter. He is now a general in the South Sudan's national army, the SPLA. Captain Johnson Gony Biliu whom I first met in Addis Ababa 1984 when he was head of Lt Col Kerubino Kuanyin Bol's guards, was present on the occasion and in the same capacity. He is also a general and still a friend of mine. Gony prefers to address me with my occupational label, "Journalist" which he thinks confers honour to me. I don't mind having a "title" in the honorific-thirsty society of South Sudan where it is not unusual to hear someone telling friends or family members "I Doctor James" or "I am Brigadier-General Santos".

Abuse of trust

On several occasions when I socialised with the late Kerubino, I found him as a person who was ready to trust associates, me included, to the point he would confide intimate and strictly personal information to that person.

Although that attribute should not in itself be a personality defect, some unscrupulous individuals – and there was no shortage of such characters in his entourage – exploited that innocence, sometimes to the detriment of Kerubino himself in the long run. My observation was that the behaviour of the folks around Kerubino Kuanyin Bol tended to influence him; he would be a congenial and considerate person – consistent with his baptismal name, "Little Angel" or Kerubino in Italian – while in the company of good people. Conversely when surrounded by a gang of self-seeking and malicious hangers-on, the consequences – ill-advised and intemperate behaviour, for instance – which naturally were not good for others, and Kerubino himself, would follow. I think it was that tendency to change full circle which led some of his critics, including one of my former colleagues- whom I will not name here- to draw conclusions such as *"ee amuɔ̈l"* (amuol) or "he is a crank". I disagree and consider such an interpretation as unfair. The depiction conveniently ignores some of the man's brighter side to his life, public or private, as seen above and also in the following paragraphs.

No tribalist

"A person who shows or feels discrimination or prejudice against people of other **tribes**, or who believes that a particular **tribe** is superior to another" is how the online Oxford Dictionary of English defines a racist. The words in **bold** are my substitutes for **people** and **races,** respectively. This is the definition whose African verbal cousins are **tribalist** and **tribes,** respectively.

I can also attest that Kerubino Kuanyin Bol didn't always behave or act as a tribalist as explained above, unless when he was misled by minions serving and advising him to act in a manner that would later be judged to be parochial. And because he was not a *practising* tribalist, he was always very comfortable in the company of persons speaking languages other than Dinka. For Kerubino, differences in age, rank, religion, region of origin or gender couldn't justify discrimination against other people. A sizeable number of his aides and guards were from other tribes of South Sudan; in the early days, those soldiers were mostly drawn from the Nuer and Murle communities as well as Dinka. Consistent with that attitude, it was not an accident or strange that two of his wives were from Murle and Anyuak heritage, respectively. And everyone who intimately knew Kerubino and his families bore witness that his wives, whether they were Dinka, Murle or Anyuak, were responsible and respected mothers, wives and citizens. They remain so to this day. Nyandeeng[33] and Kaka, two of Kerubino's widows, are public figures in their own right – known for their advocacy of social and national cohesion among all South Sudanese at home and in the diaspora. They and their children have friends from across the entire linguistic diversity of South Sudan.

Brave or reckless?

Kerubino Kuanyin Bol, the soldier was known to many people as a brave fighter. He commanded several battles, some in which the forces under his command scored stunning victories; while in others, his forces suffered heavy losses. In the first battles and skirmishes against government forces around and in Jekou garrison in 1984, the losses in lives were so great that some of his critics branded him as a soldier who didn't differentiate between valour from recklessness bordering on suicide, and that he believed in the superiority of numbers and attack in waves over the application of tactics taught at military colleges or familiar to guerrillas, and so on. However, the second battle for Jekou a year later, turned the tide against his detractors; he had the become a hero after the forces under his command almost annihilated the government forces that were moving to reinforced the besieged garrison at the same Jekou. He was accorded similar accolades were conferred on him when his forces routed the SAF battalion and captured its commander, Lt Col Abu Illa Adam Juma in the Blue Nile region.

I leave what would be an objective judgement of Kerubino Kuanyin Bol as a soldier to experts in military strategy and history of modern guerrilla warfare.

Little did I then know that the man's name, Kerubino, means "Little Cherub" or "Angelo" in Italian, or that there would be children in a country to be

---

33 Nyandeeng, is a feminine of Deng. The widow of John Garang, Rebecca, has that name but is usually written as Nyandeng. She however, appears to prefer to be addressed as Rebecca de Mabior.

called South Sudan who would carry this name. I have no figures but there are many young men of South Sudanese origins- probably in their hundreds- who bear the name Kerubino. Just as an example, about two years ago, a young Dinka man, approached me at the end of an occasion held in Sydney, Australia, to mark the anniversary of the 1983 mutiny- and on which I was one of the speakers. He wanted to be in contact with me because he said he was interested in the history of the struggle for independence, mainly the early days of the SPLM/A and that from time to time he be would directing his questions to me. Although I told him I didn't know everything about that period or the history of the struggle, I agreed. As a result, he gave me his business card which showed his first name as "Kerubino". It is a common practice in some African societies for a family to name their child in honour a VIP even if that personage is not related to them. Such an honour is normally not extended to contemporary evil figures or ones in history.

Problems of interpretation

Kerubino's undisputed physical courage has spawned several conspiracy theories among different South Sudanese analysts. One group posits that the events that led to Kerubino's arrest and detention in 1987 were engineered by an alliance of the self-styled progressives' faction within the SPLA and elements with an ethnic and regional agenda. Though diametrically opposed ideologically- the "progressives" dismissing Garang as not fit to lead a Marxist-Leninist revolution, while the ethnic chauvinists believed they were trying to redeem the hijacked leadership they believed was hijacked by Garang, to its rightful leader (Kerubino)- saw Kerubino Kuanyin Bol as the soldier with the guts to remove Garang by any means, including the use of military force.

Not everyone agrees with this interpretation. What is certain, however, is that the disagreement that resulted in the arrest and long detention of Kerubino and several officers, had elements of power struggle, personal animosities, absence of open debate within the SPLM which would have amicably addressed the policy direction or grievances which were boiling but without an outlet for airing them. What may not be known to the public is that the differences between Garang and Kerubino and their respective camps, had reached an explosive stage to the point that had restraint on both sides not prevailed, a scenario similar to the aftermath of Nasir declaration of August 1991 would have been happened.

And this leads us to the most important question: application of double standards in apportioning blame on defectors. After escaping from detention in early 1990s Kerubino and fellow detainees, bitter with what they saw as unjust treatment, became an effective opposition that went to the government side and in the process turned their guns against their erstwhile comrades. There is no doubt that the alliance between the former SPLM/A senior leaders and the Government of Sudan, gave Khartoum an advantage over the rebels (so called mainstream) and their cause as well as causing a lot of deaths among the civilian population. What is commonly referred to as stabbing the SPLM/A at the back is blamed on all who left and fought alongside the government forces. Kerubino and his SPLA Bahr el Ghazal were equally and roundly condemned for their role in that alliance.

After the return of the factions of the former defectors and the reunification of the SPLM/A, beginning at the end of the last century and the beginning of 21 centuries, some of the former defectors began to brag, projecting themselves as the champions of the right of self-determination who made, in their view, the independence of South Sudan possible. Kerubino was not among those peddling the transparent lie that joining the enemy- on the enemy's terms- won the South its statehood.

Such boasts are completely silent about the destruction those former defectors inflicted on the armed struggle and on the rural communities in the loss of thousands upon thousands of innocent lives and the stealing of their livelihoods which resulted in the mass starvation of the early 1990s in which almost a million perished in what was called "Hunger Triangle" (in Jonglei- Pan-gak, Wat, Akobo and Bor areas).

In the interest of reconciliation and unity, such arrogance has been overlooked and forgiven. Kerubino, likewise deserves to be forgiven for his role in aiding the enemy, but more so, in not insulting the intelligence of rational persons by turning an abominable mistake into a credit.

Sad end

When Kerubino Kuanyin developed misunderstandings with his boss, John Garang, for a second time, he left for western Upper region where he died under controversial circumstances. Although I didn't always agree with some of his actions and ideas, his death was a loss not only to his family but to all who recognise appreciate positive contributions others make to the public. I mourned his death when I learned of his passing away. He was a friend and, despite his obvious shortcomings, Kerubino Kuanyin Bol had made contributions to the liberation struggle which outweigh his failings; after who among *all* of our freedom fighters was/is blameless? He belongs to the heroes who made the achievement of our nationhood possible, his shortcomings notwithstanding.

Martyrs: We Shall Not Forget Them

South Sudan has put aside July 30 every year as Martyrs' Day. This was the day when John Garang, the founding leader of the SPLM/A died in a helicopter crash in 2005.

Although the current economic difficulties the country is going through – due to an austerity programme resulting from the shutdown of the pipeline early in the year – significantly reduced attendance at the function at Garang's Mausoleum, the occasion received the solemnity it deserves. (Garang's widow, who was on the VIP speakers' list was absent, to the consternation of many observers).

The Martyrs' Day is important to nearly every South Sudanese for two main reasons. One, the sacrifices made by all the citizens, dead or alive, young or old, soldiers or civilians, male or female or from all tongues, different creeds or ethnicity, in every walk of life and through numerous decades, have made the attainment of independence possible. Second, as President Kiir who himself participated in the two armed rebellions, Anya Nya and SPLM/A, stated in his keynote address this week that virtually every family in the land has lost a dear one during the long struggle. In some cases, there are families that have been known to have lost almost all their young men during the last war.

Who exactly is a martyr?

Any thought that remotely insinuates impropriety – in words, actions or omissions – to the memory of a martyr is tantamount to sacrilege that no rational person can contemplate, let alone utter in public. This perspective is understandable. However, there are legitimate issues that resolve around the words "martyr" and "hero" ("heroine" is plainly sexist and its use should be avoided since "hero" has been neutered to make it unisex just like "chairperson").

According to *Oxford English Dictionary* "martyr" has its origin in religion. Says the good word guide, "a person killed because of their religious or other belief". In the early days of Christianity, "witness" from Greek "martur" simply meant a someone laying down their life on religious grounds.

Although tens of people – mostly members of the clergy – of what is now South Sudan met their fates in the hands of the security organs, acting on orders from Khartoum on the basis of their faith, the majority of martyrs fall in the category of "other beliefs". Citizens of this country who died because of their religious affiliation, mostly Christianity, were killed by soldiers of SAF. One such victim was Rev Pastor Gideon Adwok Deng who was murdered in his Melut parish church, northern Upper Nile in 1964.

Political conviction tops the list of these beliefs. The people from what is today South Sudan who lost their lives for political reasons are so many that any attempt to put a figure, such as 2.5 million persons, would do injustice to the victims of foreign aggressors and invaders for centuries, or all the victims of Khartoum based government policies from 1955 to 2005.

Our martyrs can be divided into several categories, namely: direct combat with the enemy, assassination of nationalists suspected of being members or sympathisers of a rebel movement, victims of Khartoum targeting innocent civilians through events such as aerial bombardments or war-related factors such as starvation, when humanitarian relief food was prevented by Khartoum from reaching the vulnerable people. These are tackled case by case with examples. The last part of the article will examine proposals for memorial symbols for the martyrs countrywide.

Leaders who either took up arms against foreign invaders in the wars of resistance belong to the class of combatants. Our forebears who engaged in these wars used primitive weapons such as bows and arrows, spears, shields and clubs which were no match for gun powder used by the invaders. That disparity in military might meant that large numbers of our ancestors were mowed down like insects.

In our time freedom fighters were able to use the guns they laid their hands on but they too were no match for the arsenals in the possession of the rulers of Sudan after the departure of the British colonial rule in 1956. That too, meant very high losses were incurred by the insurgents of Anya Nya and later Anya Nya II. These victims are, by all accounts, martyrs.

Freedom fighters, who fell in battlefields all over Southern Sudan from August 18, the day of Torit Mutiny of 1955, to 1972, then from the beginning of Anya Nya II in the mid-1970s, through to the birth of SPLA in May 1983, run into their thousands. Prominent – but not excluding many officers, NCOs and men – are figures such as Bernardino Mou Mou whose daring attempt to capture Wau the capital of then Bahr el Ghazal in 1962. More than two decades later, Major Ngachigak Nyachilluk, member of the SPLM/A Politico-Military Command met martyrdom while fighting SAF around Kapoeta town in 1987. His headquarters was virtually wiped out as his bodyguards valiantly fought off the enemy attacks.

Assassinations of leaders and mass murders

Nineteen-sixty-five will stand out in the annals of war of liberation for South Sudan as one of the bloodiest episodes in the North-South conflict. After the failure of the Round Table Conference early that year to find a peaceful solution to what was known as the Southern Question, and after the election of Mohammed Ahmed Mahjoub of the Ummah Party as prime minister – the coalition government gave an ultimatum to the insurgents of Anya Nya to lay down their arms or face dire military consequences – Khartoum declared war on the people of Southern Sudan. That year was also the tenth anniversary of the 1955 Torit Mutiny. It was obvious that Prime

Minister Mahjoub and his minster of the interior, Ahmed el-Mahdi, Sadiq's uncle, used the occasion to avenge Northern Sudanese who died during and after the rebellion, that was later described by the departing British colonial authorities as, "Disturbances".

Following the inclusive closure of the Round Table Conference, authorities in the South, backed by the government in Khartoum, embarked on targeting for physical liquidation members of the intelligentsia from the South, the prime suspected them as fuelling and replenishing the rebellion with fighters, ideas and money. Among government officials to meet their deaths at the hands of the security organs were: Police Inspector Joel Akech, who was killed by his colleagues in Bentiu, and, months later, Prisons Inspector, Paul Nuul Bior was gunned down by members of the government armed forces. Such killings took place all over Southern Sudan. Most of the victims were school teachers, students, administrators or local community leaders. In 1967, for example, many chiefs in what was Bor District were killed in cold blood by government soldiers. These included Paramount Chief Ajang Duot Bior, Chief Parmena Bul Koch, Ayom Dor and Jogak Deng. That was in 1967, at the time Sadiq el-Mahdi was prime minister and who is known to have personally influenced the decision to have the chiefs eliminated.

Most memorable of the tragedies that the Mahjoub's government unleashed all over Southern Sudan occurred in August 1965. July 8, 1965 was a night of bloodletting by soldiers of the Sudan Armed Forces that went berserk, shooting on sight any Southern Sudanese that came their way. Death estimates at the time of the pogrom was put at more than a thousand innocent civilians. Many residents of Juba at time believe the figure was an underestimate. Barely a week had passed when mass murder was perpetrated by SAF in Wau, the capital of Bahr el Ghazal who shot to death over 50 wedding guests. Most of the victims were among the cream in the whole province: doctors, senior civil servants and other notables.

Upper Nile Province had its share of what could qualify for genocide on July 15, 1965 when 126 males belonging to the Shilluk nationality were shot dead in Warajwok village, several miles southeast of Malakal town.

All of these victims of government extra-judicial killings are, by all means, martyrs. The other groups that could justifiably be considered martyrs were those who died as a result of government scorched earth policy, aerial bombardment, and starvation because Khartoum denied the hungry civilians relief food and medicine. Also included are civilians and rebels who met their deaths in the hands of government-sponsored militias.

Prominent politicians who were assassinated were in some cases, martyrs. Fr Saturnino Lohure, Anya Nya patron and the former legislator who once told his Northern colleagues that if they failed to solve the problem of inequality in the country no force on earth could stop Southern Sudan to become independent it so wished. Fr Lohure was killed in Uganda in 1967 by the agents of the Government of Sudan. In 1968, William Deng Nhial, the president of Sudan African National Union, Sanu, was assassinated by SAF while he was campaigning in elections in Bahr el Ghazal.

Fitting memorials for martyrs

In the Western world, soldiers who die for their countries are honoured in many ways: streets and airports are named after intrepid generals; other memorials are erected in various parts of a country where names of war victims are inscribed on marble slabs, with the names of the battles, places and dates concerned written large. South Sudanese need to honour their war heroes in a similar fashion. But there is likely to be a problem of the "borderline heroes". By this I mean persons who are considered heroes by some and traitors to others. I have written about this controversial topic before and I do not need to go into a detailed account again. However, to clarify what I mean, I have to repeat what I wrote several years ago. The question is: was John Kulang Puot a hero or a villain? Before I explain the point, I must say I do not intend to insult the memory of the former SPLA commander.

It happened that, after differences between Anya Nya II and the inchoate SPLA resulted in armed confrontation in early 1984, remnants of Anya Nya II under the leadership of William Abdalla Chuol Deng sought military assistance from the Government of Sudan. The SPLM/A declared their rivals as enemies. On one encounter between the two opposing armed groups, the SPLA forces, under the command of Major Kulang Puot, fought Anya Nya II, who lost the battle in which their leader, William Abdalla Chuol was killed. Major Kulang became a hero to the SPLA, who elevated him into junior membership of the Military High Command. Several years later,

Cdr John Kulang differed with the leadership of the SPLM/A who had him arrested and detained for several years. After breaking out of detention and absconding, he defected to the Government of Sudan. John Kulang was appointed Khartoum's administrator of his home area of Pan-gak (no such thing as Fangak). The SPLA forces in the area intercepted the Khartoum administrator designate, on the way to his headquarters at Zeraf Mouth. Kulang was killed by his former comrades in arm. The SPLA headquarters received the news of his death with joy. I refrain to give my opinion whether late John Kulang is a martyr or not. The reader, especially anyone who is familiar with the country's recent history, is the best judge, not the writer.

[1] Although this piece cites- more examples and in some details- the atrocities the Government of Sudan committed against innocent Southern Sudanese in 1965 through to 1967, those cases are also mentioned in my opinion piece "All Patriots? Count me out", which is also included in this collection. I should have deleted those examples from either of the two article to avoid repetition, but to do that would affect the flow of argument and weaken the point I was trying to make in each of the articles. For that reason, I left the two intact. My apologies.

Do our heroes have to die to be recognised?

The death in Nairobi this week of Dr Kameri Jango Gribani is a heavy blow not only to members of his family, friends and colleagues, but also to the entire nation of South Sudan. Kameri died from complications arising out of diabetes which he had battled for years. A graduate of medicine from the University of Khartoum in the late 1970s the young GP began his work in Juba and later went to qualify as a surgeon in Kenya.

At the university Kameri was one of bright and prominent students from Southern Sudan. He was particularly popular with his peers and lecturers because he was an affable human being. Although known as one of the academically bright students who always scored high marks, he was nevertheless and epitome of modesty, always found smiling and in company of many of his friends from different political, ethnic and regional backgrounds.

After becoming a surgeon, Kameri landed a job with Norwegian People's Aid, NPA. NPA was the major humanitarian organisation to move in mid-1980s to assist the civilian population in the SPLM/A administered areas of Eastern Equatoria, mainly Kapoeta District. The 1990s was a trying time for both the movement and the people of Southern Sudan following the split of August 1991. But the services rendered by NPA and the late Dr Gribani will be remembered for a very long time to come. Those services to the civilians in the war zone, mostly the many among the war wounded and patients suffering other diseases he treated, cannot be sufficiently quantified: they fit into the local African saying that the person who visits you while you are sick is a true friend or relative indeed.

When the international community deserted the people of South Sudan

Following the defection in September 1992 of William Nyuon Bany from Pageri in Eastern Equatoria, then the movement's second in command, and the killing of several relief personnel and a visiting Norwegian journalist in the ensuing fighting, all the humanitarian organisations operating under the UN umbrella body, Operation Lifeline Sudan, or OLS, withdrew their personnel and services from the area. That decision left the population, numbering over 100,000 internally displaced persons, mostly women, children and elderly, who had fled their homes as a result of the factional fighting of the previous year, at the mercy of starvation and disease. The NPA which had deliberately not registered with the OLS, stepped in with the much needed food and health care for the IDPs at what was dubbed "Triple A"- Aswa, Atepi and Ame.

While the war wounded from the opposing factions were flown by the International Committee of the Red Cross, ICRC, to their base at Lopiding in Lokichoggio, north western Kenya, the NPA decided to establish their own health centres inside Southern Sudan at Chukudum, Yei and Nimule. The facility at Chukudum was upgraded to handle major operations. Dr Gribani, a hardworking man, was in charge of all operations assisted by his Ethiopian and Norwegian colleagues. It was a success story as many lives were saved. Most of the victims had wounds which required amputations especially of limbs hit by anti-personnel mines, bullet shrapnel or wounds inflicted by fragments of crude bombs that aircraft belonging to Sudan Airforce frequently dropped on civilian settlements in SPLM/A controlled localities such as schools, health, feeding centres, places of worship or food distribution gatherings.

The fame blended with admiration of Dr Kameri Gribani spread far and wide and he was generally seen as an embodiment of patriotism at work, comparable to that of his colleague Prof John Adwok Adieng of the Nairobi School of Medicine whose clinic used to provide treatment at a discount or sometimes free of charge to his compatriots, most of whom were members of the movement who had little or no means to pay for their treatment.

Always it is a posthumous recognition

After the end of the civil war in 2005, Dr Kameri Gribani surprised many people when he continued to work the NPA when high profile jobs were opening up for South Sudanese elites because of the peace agreement of that year. There were ministerial positions in Khartoum as well as in Juba. Besides those vacancies in the civil service that included heads of departments (undersecretaries), commissions or embassies (ambassadors), for example.

As someone known on personal basis (and respected for his personality and his positive contribution the war) by some senior decision makers in the new SPLM/A led Government of Southern Sudan, Dr Gribani had all the chances of being appointed to any of those posts. But his humility and being someone who lived by giving to the public rather than taking from them, stood between him and prestigious public office. He was just content to do what he loved to do best: healing people. With that decision Gribani the surgeon, continued to work where he was virtually invisible an anonymous until he left us a few days ago. A mutual friend has informed me that he was happy where he worked.

Kameri's conduct is in sharp contrast with that of a few among his colleagues whose contribution to the people of South Sudan and their struggle, remains doubtful but who at the same time have exploited their proximity to leaders to climb to positions of prestige and privilege even when they lacked the required credentials and qualifications. This statement needs to be made clear. Many South Sudanese doctors, whether they were trained SPLA officers or just civilians, did commendable work during and after the war. For examples, several South Sudanese doctors, not to be named as they were many, looked after the health of the recruits at the various training centres, at the refugee camps and at the warfront especially during the early days of the struggle. Some of those who had stayed in rural areas looked after the population that was left without medical service after the outbreak of the war, while those in government towns cared for their people when it was within their capacity. However, there were very few bad eggs within the medical fraternity of South Sudan as indicated by the episodes I will retell here.

I remember, as if it was yesterday, what I saw during a two week long visit to Bilpam the SPLA general headquarters and Bongo training centre in the second half of 1984. By that time the Koryom division (12,000 volunteers undergoing military training) was about to finish a three-month course at Bongo. Death from malaria, dysentery and other gastric diseases was very high among the recruits, sometimes as many as 10 to 15 a day. Fortunately, when a doctor, whose name is withheld here, who had just arrived from Europe to join the movement began looking after the sick, the situation changed dramatically almost to zero death a day.

At that time while I was one of the members who had just reported to the headquarters and being taken around in the company of the former leader of the SPLM/A John Garang, our next place to visit was Zinc, not far from Gambella. There, soldiers who had been wounded during the battle to capture Pochalla, had been taken to that base was a training centre for radio signalists. We were surprised to know that the two foreign nurses sent to look after the wounded did not know how to dress wounds. We did not have our own people there at the time. An angry Garang sat down and drafted a message which he gave to a signalist: a doctor who had promised to report to the headquarters was ordered to fly to report to the headquarters within two weeks. There was no ultimatum for failure to turn in. And what happened years after that? The officers he should have treated when they needed his services most and who until now have no idea about this story salute him: he is one of the VIPs of the sovereign state of South Sudan.

It does not make sense for those who dedicated their lives to serve their nation and its people to be recognised only after they are dead. Many people like Dr Kameri Gribani do not sacrifice their time, resources and even their lives in order to be paid by the public; they are not the type of people who feel they have served the country with tears and blood, and well; therefore, they are more entitled to public resources and positions than others. No; for them patriotism simply means selflessness and they are happy and content that the goal they worked for has been achieved; they do not suffer from "where is my share?" syndrome.

It is certain that sure such people would not reject token recognition in form of medals or other non-monetary forms of honour. So are we stingy in giving out honours that do not affect the treasury? Are we jealous of them for outshining us, we the mediocre, the praise-singers and the leeches who reap where they have not sown?

What we need is for the legislature to enact a National Heroes and Monuments Bill for all our heroes, living or dead, soldiers or civilians. It is as simple as that.

Conversation with Mansour Khaled

It began with a telephone conversation. As it was raining heavily the talk was rather inaudible on both sides. Mansour Khaled, a veteran diplomat and politician, was in the capital of Southern Sudan, Juba on an official mission from Khartoum. "I am here, bringing a message from the President to the President", he told the composer of these lines. That was Khaled's typical style of communication. Some persons in his shoes would have said "...message from the President of the Republic HE Field Marshal Omar Hassan Bashir to the First Vice President of the Republic and the President of the Government of Southern Sudan, HE Lieutenant General Salva Kiir Mayardit." Nothing is wrong with this last piece of information, or with the particulars of the mission or titles of the office holders involved. However, to Mansour Khaled the writer, communication must not be a bland and a boring chore; it has to be fun and, at times, make recipients think for a while. Despite this attitude, the man can be very serious when a situation demands that. Over the years, as a politician, and as an individual, or a team leader or member, Mansour Khaled has grappled with grave matters, some of them bordering on life and death for his fellow citizens.

Dr Mansour Khaled is a man with many hats. He trained and briefly practised as a lawyer before he became a diplomat, and, in later years, a politician. Khaled is an accomplished and prolific writer in Arabic and English. He speaks and writes fluent French, the medium he used in writing his doctoral thesis at the University of Paris. He was quick to dismiss the widely-held belief that he studied at the famous Sorbonne by saying that the institution is part of the university that is for the study of the arts.

The prominent Sudanese public servant is well remembered as a long-serving and popular foreign minister in the 1970s, and for his role as member of the Government of Sudan delegation to the talks with the representatives of the former Southern rebel movement, Southern Sudan Liberation Movement, SSLM, and its military component, the Anya Nya. The negotiations that took place in the Ethiopian capital Addis Ababa in the last part of 1971 ended in the peace accord of March 1972 that bears the name of the venue, the Addis Ababa Agreement, or simply, Triple A.

The man from Omdurman

"I was born in Omdurman..." he said with a pause before he chuckled to warn, "but don't ask 'when?'", a request that I politely accepted. No matter what age he is, Dr Mansour Khaled has been around in public view and life for over five decades [this was 2010]. Young Mansour received his basic education in Omdurman, from where he moved to the neighbouring Wadi Seidna Secondary School, not far from his birthplace. This educational institution was one of the first and best in the country. It has produced a host of Sudanese young men, some of them who later rose to positions of leadership. Two of these were Jaafar Mohammed Ali Bakheit, Mansour's senior schoolmate and Abel Alier who had to redo his fourth year there. Mansour proceeded to study law at the University of Khartoum, the only tertiary centre of learning in the country then. After graduation he briefly served in legal practice.

Since post-graduate studies were not locally available the ambitious lawyer was the first Sudanese to be granted a Fulbright Scholarship, that took him to do an MA in law in Philadelphia, Pennsylvania, USA.

UN system employee

The attainment of independence by many African countries in the 1960s opened more opportunities for educated Africans. Mansour, who had been employed by the United Nations as legal officer, was posted to serve as legal assistant to the Resident UNDP officer in the newly independent Algerian nation. Knowledge of Arabic and French secured him the job easily.

After a stint in Algiers, Mansour Khaled moved to the office of United Nations Educational and Scientific Organisation or Unesco, based in the French capital, Paris. His choice to work with the UN system in Paris, he says, was motivated by his desire to do a doctorate in law. At the law school, one of his contemporaries was Hassan Abdalla Turabi, the future leader of Sudan's Muslim Brotherhood movement. For the rest of their lives in the public domain, the two men have not always seen eye to eye, ideologically speaking. Their chemistry does not mix to this day.

Member of Nimeiri's government

Although Nimeiri's regime was "a hotchpotch of leftists and pan-Arabists", Mansour Khaled, who was minister of youth and sports stressed that there were members of the government who were nationalists, of whom he was one. Members of this group were – according to him – interested in changing the political situation in the country for the better. One of their objectives, he reveals, was to end the war in the South. Those who shared that approach included Nimeiri himself, Dr Jaafar Ali Bakheit and Ibrahim Moneim Mansour. After years of ideological wrangling, Mansour says they succeeded in reaching an agreement with the SSLM, with the grant of regional autonomy to Southern Sudan, embodied in the Triple A.

Before he became minister for foreign affairs after 1971 the diplomat-cum-politician worked to turn the ministry of youth into an instrument for change since there was, in his opinion, an ideological gap between the elders and the youth. But things did not go his way, forcing him to take up the job of Sudan permanent representative to the UN.

Foreign Ministry with a difference

On becoming minister for foreign affairs, Mansour Khaled worked to make the department a vehicle for the promotion of national unity. He conceived diplomacy as an agent for development because – in his reasoning – no meaningful development could take place in the absence of an active diplomacy.

Asked whether the pan-Arabists in the May government were opposed to the Triple A, the former foreign minister replied "No. They were not against the end of the war as such", adding that, "their opposition was against the means used to achieve the peace agreement". He reveals that the opposition was based on the involvement of the Ethiopian monarch, Emperor Haile Selassie, the All Africa Conference of Churches and the World Council of Churches. "They [the pan-Arabists] saw it as a Western plot. But Nimeiri prevailed because he wanted the war to be ended", attributing Nimeiri's intention to the fact that the president was a soldier and knew firsthand the problems inherent in war. He also thinks that Nimeiri believed making peace would bring stability to his rule.

Contrary to the widely-held view of many Southern Sudanese that Babiker Awadalla, Nimeiri's first prime minister, and who later went to live in voluntary exile in Egypt after the accord did not want the agreement, Mansour Khaled denies that allegation.

Enter Turabi, el-Sadiq Mahdi

Mansour Khaled blames the change of attitude by Nimeiri upon the pressure exerted on him by both Hassan Turabi and Sadiq el-Mahdi of the Ummah Party. The two men, according to him, were against the Triple A and wanted it to be abrogated. Nimeiri, he reasons, made a miscalculation. Thinking that he had already secured the support of the South, he went on to make himself an imam to please the Islamists in the North. By making such a move, Mansour Khaled says Nimeiri was implying that he personally introduced what the Islamists wanted, but that would take him a long process to achieve. In both cases, concludes the former cabinet minister, Nimeiri was wrong.

With that turn of events, the diplomat quit the May regime. But he did not leave quietly. While based abroad, the former senior minister published *The Revolution of Dis-May*, a scathing attack on – and shaming of – a regime that had become synonymous with the whims of a leader whose behaviour was unpredictable, excessively corrupt and vindictive. "Dis-May" itself says it all: destruction of what the government that came into power through a military coup in May 1969 stood for. The play on the word also explains the resulting shock with which those who had placed their hope in the change of system of governance, judged the performance and the attitude of the leader.

Contribution to the South

Although there was no hint of boasting in his voice, Mansour Khaled counted some of his contributions to allow Southern Sudanese have a fair amount of representation in the national government. "By the time I took over Foreign Affairs, there was only one diplomat from the South. That was Yithaya Achol de Dut," he recalls, adding that by the time he left the ministry there were many young diplomats from the South. Most of these, whom he rates highly, like him were lawyers. He remembers with special respect the late Isaac La and late Achol Deng, among several others. "They were very bright, hardworking and efficient people", he says.

Although his decision to take more Southern Sudanese into the foreign affairs ministry was a matter of doing justice for the South, which he believed was being neglected, he concedes that the young diplomats from the South were qualified for the jobs in their own right. He denies having given preferential treatment, or playing a patronising role in the selection.

While minister for education for a while, Dr Mansour Khaled has revealed that he worked hard to reactivate the recommendations of the 1965 Round Table Conference on the South in respect to higher education. Towards that end, the establishment of the University of Juba – and the University of Gezira in the North – was part of his efforts which later bore fruit long after he had left government.

Was he the victim of an envious president?

At the time he served as minister for foreign Affairs Mansour Khaled was a very popular figure both at home and within the African region. On the social plane, the man was a trend-setter for the youth especially in fashion. Young people from the South admired his style of dress to the point that the broad tie that was in vogue in the 1970s was dubbed "Mansour", after him. Did the president become uneasy with his rising fame and celebrity status? "In such a type of government jealousies are rampant". He would not further elaborate on the claim.

Personal friends

A congenial personality, Mansour Khaled always enjoys the company of like-minded people, whether inside or outside the establishment. He says some of his personal friends while in government included Dr Jaafar Bakheit, Dr Francis Mading Deng, Ibrahim Moneim Mansour, Dr Bashir Abadi, and the two soldiers who each held the post of first vice president of the country at different times, Major Abul Gasim Mohammed Ibrahim and General Baghir Ahmed. The late Hilary Logali, who served in the South as the minister for finance and economic planning under Abel Alier, was also Khaled's good friend.

Regrets

It is on record that Foreign Minister Khaled and Vice President of the Republic Abel Alier, who led the Sudan government delegation to the talks with the SSLM leaders, openly rejected the rebels' demand that regional self-rule be extended to other areas of Sudan (West, East and far north). The Government of Sudan's representatives told the SSLM delegation that they should confine themselves to issues pertaining to their own region, since they did not have the mandate to speak for others other than the South. Khartoum carried the day. "I regret that. If we had done that [accepted the SSLM's proposal that regional rule should be extended to other parts of the country in the North] we would have solved the problems of the peripheries", says the remorseful veteran politician.

With the benefit of hindsight, he thinks the creation of four autonomous regions in Sudan would have reduced the powers of the centre in the interest of the regions, in relation to share of power and resources. He also believes that, with all the areas of the country running their local affairs, Nimeiri would have feared antagonising the Sudanese by tampering with the regional set-up, as all would be fighting to preserve the self-rule arrangement.

These views are contained in two of his important books, *The Government They Deserve, The Tales of Two Countries* and in the forthcoming book on the CPA, whose final title is yet to be decided. This publication is a lucid factual account, full of supporting references, of the difficult and meandering peace process. The author thinks the achievement of peace was made possible due partly to the patience on the part of the negotiators, mediators from the Igad Secretariat and the international partners, and the consistency of the SPLM under the late John Garang at Naivasha, and Salva Kiir at the early stages at Machakos. The book is due out before the close of this year.

Memories of pre-independence period

At the time Sudan was preparing for independence, Mansour Khaled was in his final year as a law student. He admits, as he had no political role at the time, he was just an observer. He notes: "It was a hectic time, full of excitement and expectations. Khartoum was a hub and beehive of activities and jubilation over the evacuation [of foreign troops from the country] and celebration for approaching independence. But few people were thinking about issues concerning the creation of sustainable unity and stability ahead".

He fondly recalls knowing politicians from the South he thinks were men of unquestioned integrity, whom he admired. One of these was Stanislaw Paysama Abdalla who hailed from Western Bahr el Ghazal. In fact, Paysama was an ethnic Darfuri and a freed slave who lived with – and was educated by – Catholic missionaries in Wau.

Mansour Khaled tells a story to support his belief that those personalities were honest public servants. He remembers Benjamin Lwoki from Equatoria, a government minister, going to Prime Minister Abdalla Bey Khalil to return a briefcase. The stunned head of government asked the outgoing minister why he was taking the attaché to him. Lwoki replied, "Sir, this belongs to the government".

Were all the leaders from the South decent and public-spirited persons?

"No. Not all of them, of course. There were some hooligans on both sides [from the South and North]", was his retort, amidst sniggering.

The problem with Sudan

Most Sudanese prefer to conform by jumping in with the crowd when there are issues that divide people. What does Mansour Khaled, who often and openly castigates some among his fellow Northern leaders in power, think of this allegation?

"I think this is a sheep mentality. The role of a leader is to lead, not to be led, acting as a bandwagon driver at the steering wheel, leading an unquestioning crowd. This is shameful", he deplores. He cites the late SPLM Chairman John Garang as an example of a leader who sets an agenda.

"What was great about John Garang was that he always led from the front and that was the reason why people respected him", explains the man who served as adviser to the former rebel chief and was a personal friend. But did that style of leadership not earn him enemies as well?

"Yes, it did," he admits.

Mansour Khaled knows the price people pay when they speak their minds on subjects considered by many as taboo, or when one supports a cause that might be unpopular at a certain time. One example stands out. During the Koka Dam Conference, held in Ethiopia in 1986, to allow nearly all Sudanese political forces to discuss what was called the "Problem of Sudan" (previously known as the Southern Question), Mansour Khaled, who had just joined the SPLM, was a participant.

In the first session, a delegate representing Ba'ath Party [Country Sudan] rose to demand the expulsion of Mansour Khaled from the gathering. Reason? His membership of the overthrown regime of Jaafar Nimeiri. Stoic as usual, the publicly-maligned man continued to occupy his seat, unperturbed, his face almost expressionless. Major Arok Thon Arok, member of the SPLM/A Politico-Military High Command and its spokesman during the conference rose to rebuke the protesters.

"No-one has a right to choose who should be member or not member [of the rebel movement]". Arok went on to defend Dr Mansour Khaled. The former minister did not only leave the May system when Nimeiri deviated from its objectives; he also wrote an indictment of the system in his book, *The Revolution of Dis-May*, Arok argued.

The attack on Mansour Khaled was not apparently for his past association with the May regime; it was a pretext. His presence was tacitly resented by some Northern Sudanese participants because of his robust intellectual weight and, as a Northerner, he had given the movement whose top leadership at the time was wholly from Southern Sudan, the epithet that it desperately craved: national player, not a regional and military force, as the Northern establishment would like to project it.

On the Comprehensive Peace Agreement, CPA

"It gives the people of Southern Sudan two options: unity or secession". Commenting on the notion of unity, the veteran politician says, "It was unity based on full implementation of the CPA; the creation of institutions and enactment of laws and edicts in the constitution. The decision by the end of the day is in the hands of the people of Southern Sudan. The role of the SPLM is to enable the people make their free choice. It is not for the SPLM leadership to second-guess the decision the people of Southern Sudan will make. But it is for them to make people make a correct decision", he explains.

On writers and writing

"It is sad". This is his reaction to the kind of writing being carried out these days by some public figures. "If you are a writer who wants to be taken seriously, you have to take your reader seriously. Respect the mind and intelligence of your reader. You are mistaken if you think that they [the readers] can't distinguish between truths and lies. If you respect yourself and your reader, you must respect facts. Facts are facts, not embellishment," is his advice to any aspiring Sudanese writer.

"There is a lot of laxity in the way people treat events now; lack of seriousness in analysis, perhaps this is because of the desire [by some writers] to be good to all. You cannot be good to all", he warns, adding that "The books I have been writing are comments on how the North has denied the legitimate rights of the people of the South. Being nice [in not telling the truth] will never bring respect to you but narrating the facts in the service of the truth will help in correcting things", Mansour Khaled, the writer, asserts.

Disciplinarian at work

It is rare to have a full-time politician who is a regular writer of books or columns in the press. Mansour Khaled is one of few exceptions to the rule. (He once maintained a column in *Es Sahafa* Arabic daily, of which he was chair of board of directors. He later compiled those pieces to produce *El Hiwar ma' es Safuwa*, or Discourse with the Elite.)

The veteran politician, writer and diplomat is a member of the SPLM Political Bureau. He frequently visits Juba, the capital of Southern Sudan for scheduled or emergency meetings of the party leadership. He is unofficially an adviser to the leader of the SPLM and head of the Government of Southern Sudan, Salva Kiir. The two men are known to enjoy a friendly relationship. On the social level, Mansour Khaled gets time to relax and have meals with friends in the evenings when there are no meetings.

At the time of the interview for this profile, that took place in his Juba hotel room at 9p.m., he had books and typed papers on his desk. He was working on another book project. An hour after the conversation he would be off for dinner in another hotel with a former SPLA commander, now minister in the GoSS.

How does a man past the age of 70 manage to have time for public engagements, social interaction and serious writing at the same time? One word: discipline. People who work closely with Mansour Khaled know the man's strict observation and proper management of time. It is an open secret that he does not hide his open disapproval of people who are lax with appointments and punctuality. Once a research assistant for a book he was writing (*The Government They Deserve*) arrived five minutes late for an appointment with him. When he learned that the fellow did not have a watch, Mansour Khaled bought him one on return from an overseas trip. The gift was followed by what sounded like a warning. "What excuse will you tell me next time you delay?" he asked, rhetorically surely.

Mansour Khaled is reportedly in the habit of subtracting a couple of hours from his sleep-time when he happens to spend time on an unplanned function.

This article was published in *The Pioneer* weekly newspaper in June 2010 under the title of "Mansour Khaled Remembers Good and Bad Times".

The origins of Garang-Mirghani summit of 1988

It is surprising how small events can sometimes lead to major developments of historical proportions. The meeting between the former leader of the SPLM/A, John Garang, and his counterpart, the patron of the Democratic Unionist Party, DUP, Mohammed Osman el-Mirghani, in December 1988, had modest beginnings in which I was the first point of contact. The summit, which took place in the Ethiopian capital of Addis Ababa made headlines both in Sudan and in the international news media.

Some commentators thought the meeting was a breakthrough in the search for a peaceful resolution to the Sudan armed conflict at the time. Others believed that Mirghani, whose party did not take part in the Koka Dam conference in 1986, had pulled the peace carpet from under Prime Minster Sadiq el-Mahdi, of the rival Ansar sect and its political wing, the Ummah Party which attended the conference. The all-party forum brought several Sudanese political parties, trade unions and independent intellectuals as well as the SPLM. The participants were able to define the nature of the problem and find a lasting solution by peaceful means.

The national gathering, the first of its kind since the outbreak of the second civil in 1983, was convened in the Ethiopian tourist resort that bears the name of the conference resolution, Koka Dam Declaration. Critics of the Ummah Party and its leader accused them of dragging their feet to commit themselves and their coalition partner in government – the DUP – to implement the letter and spirit of the declaration of principles.

In the first half of 1988, I took charge of the SPLM coordination office in Addis Ababa after its head, had gone on a foreign mission. At that time, I received a call from a stranger who wanted to meet me. The man, who spoke English with an Arabic accent, talked to me with some familiarity; calling my full name almost flawlessly. He must have practised how to pronounce it correctly, probably with the guidance of someone who spoke my language as a mother tongue. I responded cautiously; as was characteristic of guerrillas and members of underground organisations, who usually are guarded in what they reveal to or share with non-members. I was not an exception.

"Where and when can we meet?" asked the stranger. After hesitating for some moments, I responded with a sort of stammer "Er ... er, who are you, please?"

Aware that there could a third party listening to our conversation, the caller proposed he would like to meet me in the SPLM's office. This was an impossible request. The office, in the area between the Hilton Hotel and the headquarters of the UN Economic Commission for Africa, then a marketplace, was out of bounds, even to supporters and sympathisers of the movement, except when accompanied by a member of the accredited team.

As a rule, we had to meet people on business in hotels in the city, or rarely, in the residences where some of us lived.

I told that unseen interlocutor that his suggestion was not possible. A very determined character for whom "No" meant almost nothing; if he could not come to my office could I propose where we could meet?

Aware that there was no risk meeting the stranger anywhere in the city, I told him we would meet outside Ghion Hotel, not far from where the SPLM office was located. But one problem remained to be fixed: the issue of identification. He was the first to propose that I should give him a description of my general appearance and what I would be wearing at the appointment time.

I told him that I was slightly tall, rather slim with a dark skin. To complete the picture, I told him that I would be wearing a crisp white short-sleeved shirt over a black pair of trousers. For his part he told me he was going to be sitting at a corner outside the hotel. He added that he would be wearing a white shirt and blue jeans and dark sunglasses, and that he would be sitting alone around a table, facing westwards from the hotel. He said his colour was that of an Egyptian. Well, not dark or brown as a few Egyptians are, I thought he should have known that fact.

It was around four in the afternoon when I arrived at the hotel. We sighted one another, almost at the same time. He raised his right hand, to beckon me to join him at the table he had already booked for us. When I approached him he got up to greet me. Of medium height and build, probably in his early forties and appearing friendly, he greeted me in Arabic. I replied in the same language. He gave me his name, which I doubt must have been a borrowed one. After I had taken my seat, the Egyptian asked me to order whatever beverage I liked. I declined to take any despite his protestation. Seeing that I would not change my mind he ordered coffee for himself. We went straight to the business at hand.

While he was waiting for his coffee, he removed his dark glasses. His face revealed appearances and mannerisms of someone used to giving or receiving orders from very high-up in the pecking order, either in the political or military system. He did not attempt to hide his huge ego.

"I am here without the knowledge of anyone in our embassy; even the ambassador does not know my presence here in Addis Ababa. I come directly from the office of Bresident [President] Hosni Mubarak with a message for you beoble [people]".

Although I was surprised at hearing that piece of information I did not show my misgivings, which I tried very hard to conceal. I could not understand why an ambassador should be kept in the dark on matters relating to that country's contacts with anti-government insurgents. It was common knowledge that relations between any government of the day in both Khartoum and Cairo had always agreed on their policies towards the armed conflict in Southern Sudan: condemnation of the rebels and their demands, and resorting to military as well as political solutions. Egypt sometimes gave Sudanese authorities ruling Khartoum military assistance to fight the rebels in Southern Sudan. This was an open knowledge during the first civil war in which Egyptian warplanes were known to have either gathered intelligence on rebels' positions or bombed them.

Despite that knowledge I was confident that I had no reason to refuse listening to what he would say. The problem, however, was that this was one of very few occasions that I or any other member of the SPLM/A had to meet and discuss weighty matters alone with a stranger whose motives were not known to the movement and its top leaders.

The president's envoy, as he wanted me to know him, came to the heart of the matter. He wanted to know whether the SPLM/A leader, John Garang, would be willing and ready to meet Mohammed Osman el-Mirghani, the head of the Khatimiyya sect who was also the political spiritual leader of the DUP. I told him that the rebel movement had made it public that it welcomed meeting and conducting dialogue with all members of Sudanese political forces without exception. I further told him that, on that understanding, Garang would be ready to meet Mirghani as a matter of principle. The Egyptian envoy appeared to have been taken off guard by my statement: the reply to him sounded too good to be true.

"Do you mean what you have just said?" he asked, expressing a genuine disbelief.

He might not have been sure that the main role of the office I was representing at the time served as a link between the leadership – especially while inside Southern Sudan, and Khartoum, the Horn and Eastern Africa – and the rest of the world.

"Yes. I mean it. And for you to believe what I have told you is true, just wait for 72 hours for a reply from the field. Garang is in the field now". I assured him, although he did not show any hint that Garang was actually where I said he was. There was always a belief in many circles, Sudanese included, that the rebel chief and his colleagues in the leadership were always inside Ethiopia, especially within the capital, Addis Ababa. Many people outside the movement – this envoy included – did not believe that the SPLM/A was available and running much of Southern Sudan, particularly its entire rural areas.

After a few minutes of dry conversation on issues of no importance and not related to politics or the war in Sudan, we decided to leave for our respective destinations. He said he would call me after 48 hours to check whether I had sent his message or, when possible, for an earlier response from Garang.

As we were preparing to leave, he offered me a lift in the car he was using, since I had just walked to the hotel. I accepted his generosity. Should he drive me to where I live or to the office? He wanted to know. Neither, I told him. I took a ride with him in the rather rickety Peugeot car that he drove – that did not bear a diplomatic plate number – and ask him to leave me at a place I would show him later. He agreed and off we went in the direction of Harambe Hotel, a few minutes' drive from Ghion.

As he drove, he kept glancing at the side mirror from time to time. At one time, he would detour to another road for no apparent reason. When we arrived, he pulled up to let me alight. I walked into the hotel lobby, where I took a seat to have tea. No sooner had I made myself comfortable than someone patted me on the back. I turned to see the person – it was someone I knew very well; he sometimes worked with us, especially as an adviser in matters related to security. He was the one trailing the car I was in with the Egyptian.

After a brief exchange of information, he confirmed to me that my companion was actually an Egyptian. He was not sure whether he was a special envoy for President Mubarak but he guessed the Egyptian might have exaggerated his role and importance.

That evening I sent a radio message to Garang, who was inside Southern Sudan. The following morning, I received his reply. The message stated that the movement was ready to meet the DUP leader and that the details and date would be agreed at a later date.

Just 24 hours later the Egyptian rang me to check the progress in my communication with the front. He was ecstatic to receive the piece of news he was waiting for; he wanted to meet me immediately at the same venue. I agreed. When I saw him approaching he was smiling. He seemed lost for the right words to express his joy at what he interpreted as his successful mission.

"I will give you gift you will not forget for the rest of your life for what you have done. When that meeting takes place, I promise you will meet and shake hands with President Mubarak".

I almost asked him what I would gain by meeting his leader; after all I had before dined, in the company of other VIPs, with several heads of state and government and other foreign dignitaries, but none of these encounters had increased my standing by a nano-inch, so what was the big deal with a photo op with the Egyptian head of state? I asked myself. I am also yet to read any data by a self-respecting person listing in their CV shaking hands or sharing a state banquet with monarchs or presidents as part of their experience. Except in memoirs or for a family album, maybe.

We parted as the best of friends. The Egyptian was certain he was on top of the world as he prepared to return home after accomplishing his errands; for me it was just a routine, doing my job. I do not recall any importance I attached to the event until about six months later that year. A couple of days, afterwards the head of the coordination returned to resume his position. Even before I had handed over the office to him, he gave me to read a two-week old message ordering me to report to the war front. In less than half an hour I was on my way to Southern Sudan, where I had been deployed in accordance with the aforesaid radio message from the Dr John Garang, in his capacity as the commander in chief of the SPLA. Unceremonious as my deployment sounds, it does not belong here, as it is an episode for another day and another medium – a memoir.

'Historic' Garang-Mirghani summit

In December, 1988, the two Sudanese political leaders held, in Addis Ababa, what was described by local and international news media as an historic event. To some extent the summit bore most of the hallmarks of an important development in the Sudan's political landscape. As seen earlier in this piece, the DUP was one of the two parties who refused to attend the March 1986

Koka Dam conference. The party's hostile attitude towards the SPLM and what organisation stood for was public knowledge.

The other absentee at Koka Dam was the National Islamic Front – now the National Congress Party, NCP, – led at the time by Hassan el Turabi. This party, along with the DUP, publicly called all parties from Northern Sudan not to have any dealings with the rebels, whom they branded a public enemy, guilty of treason against the Sudanese state. After this necessary digression, it is imperative that the reader wonders why DUP and its leadership took that decision to meet and hold talks with an organisation and its leader held in utter contempt? The answer is simple: DUP was a coalition partner with the Ummah Party of Prime Minister Sadiq el-Mahdi. DUP and NIF believed that the prime minister was not strong – or militaristic – enough to crush the SPLA in the battlefield. To appear as a peace-maker, Mirghani and his party's move was to outmanoeuvre Prime Minister Sadiq el-Mahdi. The Addis Ababa summit was the right tool in that strategy.

On his return to Khartoum Mirghani received a hero's welcome; some called him a man of peace. Hundreds of thousands of DUP members and supporters flocked to Khartoum Airport to reinforce what was, to them, a triumphal return. Ironically, the praises showered on the DUP leader were directly extended to the rebel chief, John Garang, praise by default. As was expected, the loser in that game was Prime Minister Sadiq el-Mahdi and the Ummah Party. Critics accused the prime minister of procrastination in the move towards a peaceful negotiated settlement of the war.

It was all a charade

The Mirghani's peace initiative- in which I was involved at its early phase- was nothing but a political gimmick, whose sole purpose by the DUP's leader was to undercut his rival, Sadiq el-Mahdi. With the benefit of hindsight, the DUP's public pronouncements on their agenda were completely at variance with their confidential policy framework of the time. I have a DUP secret policy towards Southern Sudan in general, and the SPLM and its Chairman John Garang in particular. Two quotations from that document will suffice to support the assertion that Mirghani and his party were deeply involved in doublespeak. Regarding the South, the paper in part states:

... we wish to correct the erroneous assumption that the division of the South in 1983 was the work of the deposed President Gaafar Nimeiri. The truth of the matter is that despite differences between our party and the butcher Nimeiri over his many tragic policies, the party leadership had endorsed Nimeiri's fragmentation of the Southern Region for the sake of Islam through his policy of divide and rule... and a good step towards the creation of an Arab and Islamic state.

The DUP document, prepared by the party's secretariat, had this to say about the SPLM/A leader:

With little respect for the sentiments of Arabs and Moslims [sic] in this country, [Rev Philip Abbas] Ghaboush has repeatedly declared his open support for the defector Col. John Garang, agent of international communism and the Church, and the secret advocate of separatism.

While these events were taking place in Ethiopia and Khartoum, I was nowhere near the scene as I was following the developments via radio. At the time I was fully occupied as a captain at the headquarters of what was called Central Southern Sudan Zone, under the command of Cdr Kuol Manyang Juuk. Up to the time these lines were being written, I had no idea whether my friend, the Egyptian came to the Addis Ababa summit between Garang and Mirghani or not, to witness what we had begun. Still, I am not sure whether the visit to Egypt he promised me would have taken place, had I been present during and after the summit. Nobody cared to inform me of how the Garang-Mirghani summit was organised or whether the Egyptians had any presence, visible or discreet.

Garang and Mirghani did in the end meet. Despite the media publicity the news generated, the event was simply hot air; it did not bring the attainment of peace any nearer. Instead, the development gave the Islamists an excuse to mount their attack on the rebels and – to some extent – contributed to their preparation for the military coup of June 1989, that was carried out by officers affiliated to the National Islamic Front, NIF.

Why some people dread peace

Whether it is declared by a country or an armed group to achieve specific objectives, by another country, or whether imposed on a people, war is an evil activity. Whether brief or protracted, armed conflicts kill and maim people, separate families and force others to flee their homes to seek security and survival as refugees in foreign lands or internally, in displaced persons' camps. This situation limits people who otherwise would be self-sufficient, to depend on others. War also destroys a country's infrastructure and the environment.

Peace, however, is not mere absence of war, as the hackneyed saying goes, but a just and durable harmonious environment in which people can enjoy –unrestricted – their rights such as the pursuit of happiness, freedom of movement, association and expression and self-actualisation. It is the foundation of human progress and civilisation.

The people of Sudan are desperately yearning for a genuine and just peace. The recent agreement between the Government of Sudan and the SPLM on security arrangements during the interim period makes the chance of the 20 year-long war being ended more likely than at any other time before. But it should not be forgotten that not all the people of Sudan, and non-Sudanese – and even some countries –will embrace that peace when it is signed. There will be individuals, political organisations and countries who will oppose, some mildly and others vehemently, the peace accord.

Opposition to the peace agreement will come from individuals, groups of people and political parties or armed factions whose reasons would be mainly political, ideological, constitutional and then ultimately self-serving. This was the case with the Addis Ababa Agreement of 1972, which a few Southern Sudanese and many Northern Sudanese rejected for various reasons.

The Northern opposition will be based on the fears that the peace agreement will offer too many concessions that would eventually lead the South to separate, as the exercise of the right to self-determination is easily equated with the partition of the country. In several circles within the North, there runs a deep distrust of international monitors who are seen to be biased in favour of the South and against the North, on a religious basis.

Egyptian and Libyan leaderships share this fear, as can be gleaned from the text of Joint Egyptian-Libyan Initiative, ELI, which makes no mention of self-determination. "Egypt possesses cards it has not used in preventing the separation of Southern Sudan,"[34] said Egypt's ambassador to Sudan in 2000. On the other hand, the Southern Sudanese who will reject the agreement will use the argument that the deal will favour Khartoum, and therefore influence the cause of unity. Indeed, there will be no guarantee that the international monitors will not be biased against the South. They also fear that the government in Khartoum will use unfair means such as giving of bribes to some among Southern politicians and military leaders during the interim period, in order to influence them to convince their supporters to vote for unity.

War has always been – and can still be – a very profitable business, especially in the developed world where the sale of weapons brings enormous profits. Arms dealers will lose substantially with the end of Sudan's war. Apart from China, one of the suppliers of the tools of destruction was Russian weapon trafficker, Victor Bout who sold weapons to Sudan, one of his 16 African clients. According to the *New York Times Syndicate*, "without [Victor] Bout, there would be peace in Africa". Bout and his comrades in the lethal business do not care that their wares kill and disable people; their interest is more in making money than caring for peace in far-flung corners of the world.

The Sudan's war has sucked in more foreign elements than is known by the public. When the Sudanese decide to reconcile and forgive one another, one of the biggest losers will be the Ugandan terrorist group, the Lord Resistant Army, LRA, who are certain to be sent packing to the great relief of their arch-enemy, the government of President Yoweri Museveni.

But in Sudan not all will be well. The breakdown of law and order at an outbreak of a rebellion and the response to quash it always encourages illegal behaviour and activities among the combatants on both sides. It is public knowledge that both the Government of Sudan and the SPLM authorities do not care enough about the discipline of their soldiers. Each camp thinks the superiors would be asking too much from soldiers – and creating a potential problem – to impose strict punishment on commanders and their insubordi-

---

34 ¹ Johnson, D. H. *The Root Causes of Sudan Civil Wars*, p.176, 2003.

nates who have sacrificed everything, including their lives. This understanding has been abused by both Sudan Armed Forces, SAF, and the SPLA.

It is an open secret that some senior Government of Sudan Army officers have been using military planes and trucks to transport resources from the South to the North, and from North to the South they ferry items for sale or for personal use. Similarly, some SPLA officials have been stealing booty in the form of vehicles and cash after capturing government garrisons. Although few, these officers will not take kindly to the peace that will deny them the sources of their illegal wealth.

Other groups whose role is likely to be affected by the end of the conflict are the peace activists and advocates. There is no intention here to tarnish the name and good job done by many organisations and individuals, who have been active in funding and holding peace conferences. But there have been very few individuals, especially among the Sudanese crooks masquerading as peacemakers, when their business has always been globetrotting, staying in expensive hotels and pocketing part of the money intended for the peace process. Such elements will bitterly lament the advent of real peace, which will put them out of their unethical business. They will hate the peace for which they had paid lip-service while deceiving the world that they cared for it.

Neither the Government of Sudan nor the SPLM can boast of wholesome democratic credentials. This has produced two vices: a personality cult and the culture of preference for mediocrity over persons with proven qualifications, competence in performance and personal integrity when selecting people for public office. The minions whose qualification only is loyalty to and blind obedience to leaders are aware that the next stage to be implemented by both the Government of Sudan and the SPLM will require the application of universal criteria such as academic achievements, work experience and some outstanding leadership qualities, including a genuine commitment the subject shows to serve the people, not for money or to please the whims of leaders. The groups of bootlickers used to acquiring power fraudulently and wealth without working for them can become dangerous when they lose these privileges. Experience shows that such persons are capable of turning anywhere else in order to reverse the situation.

And what about what has been dubbed as "the options" – a euphemism for defection? After the end of the war, the phenomenon of people leaving an opposing group for another will become a thing of the past. Since the Government of the Sudan and the Government of Southern Sudan are going to be the two entities of one state and are expected to coordinate and cooperate, there will be no room for defection, a weapon some Sudanese from several camps have in the past used as blackmail: "give me this or do this for me or else", was always the implied threat. Habitual turncoats and deserters will find little or no room to squeeze favours out of their superiors and will have to turn to conventional methods of negotiation and persuasion. For them, peace will have exposed their vulnerability. In future, one will have to be content with what they have and their abilities or lack of them. This would mean a return of sanity and transparency.

The return of peace to Sudan will be fraught with many challenges, among them several, sometimes unrealistic expectations from the masses. The leadership both from the Government of Sudan and the SPLM will have to be prepared to meet all manner of problems with patience, cool and sober judgement, and to avoid taking anyone or anything for granted. Failing to do that, they will be shocked to learn that although peace is desirable and beautiful, it does not always solve all problems such as some of the bad habits known to be common among many Sudanese, one of which is disrespect for punctuality and misuse of time in their workplaces while discussing politics which consumes zillions of work hours every year.

■

This opinion piece was published by *Sudan Mirror* -vol 1 issue 2 a couple of weeks before the Comprehensive Peace Agreement was signed in Nairobi between the Government of Sudan and the SPLM on January 9, 2005. Some of the fears I had expressed in this comment did not happen, fortunately. Anyone having some fears about the current Agreement for Resolution of Conflict in South Sudan, ARCISS, between the Government of South Sudan and the armed opposition of the SPLM-IO should keep what people – friends or foes – are writing now about the agreement. It will be interesting in future to see how time or unforeseen events could change attitudes and perceptions. Unless one is an incorrigible cynic, it can be a pleasant surprise when events turn out differently; proving one to be wrong after having predicted serious problems or even prophesied doom. To preserve the message – including nomenclature – of the time, the entire comment has been left unaltered in form and contents.

Of Unity and Independence

This article was provoked by a public discussion in which some individuals who had fallen out with Garang, the SPLM/A leader, including the speaker who had become very critical of Garang was known as an avowed Marxist-Leninist and an ally of the rebel chief before his arrest and detention for alleged conspiracy to overthrow the leadership.

In his talk, this man appeared as if he didn't know the ideology of the movement, for which he was seen as one of its chief apologists. I did not agree with him and was wondering whether he had changed his view or if he didn't know what he was advocating in the heyday of the insurgency. His virulent attack on the SPLM/A agenda for a united Sudan, openly contradicted what the speaker had stood for all those years before he parted ideological ways with Garang. My goal then was to put records right, regardless of whether I personally endorsed those facts or not.

For a start, it can be emphatically stated that, without the foreign political, military, financial and diplomatic support, there would be no SPLM or SPLA the way it is today. The anti-unionist bag of contradiction knows this very well; if he has forgotten I have to remind him about the dividends he and his former bosom friend, John Garang, and the SPLM/A reaped from the unity slogan.

First, the SPLM/A was not the only armed anti-government organisation; there was Anya Nya Two in Upper Nile and Bahr el Ghazal. Although Anya Nya Two can be credited with keeping the flame of Southern rebellion alive, its main problem was that it called for an independent state in Southern Sudan. Almost all countries bordering Southern Sudan –although some of them were, and still are, sympathetic with the cause of their fellow black

African and Christian cohorts in Southern Sudan – none of them ready to publicly or materially back an insurgency against an OAU member state. The defunct OAU's charter prohibited member state's interference in the affairs of another state.

Many African countries have ethnic groups that harbour secessionist tendencies and any state encouraging such was by definition making a contradiction. Kenya, which has been lucky not to have experienced a civil war or military rule, would be the last to provide military bases and arms to a rebel movement; Uganda, which, under Obote, cooperated with Khartoum to crush Anya Nya, was having its own internal problems: coups and guerrilla warfare; the then Zaire was bled to death by a corrupt and despotic Mobutu, who could not afford to pay his army or rent of embassies and their staff, let alone financing an insurgency in a neighbouring country.

Naturally, Ethiopia was an exception. Before and after the overthrow of Emperor Haile Selassie in 1974, Ethiopia was fighting the Eritrean secessionists. With the Marxist-Leninist oriented government of the Derg, Jaafar Nimeiri, who had initially toyed with socialism and had since become a friend of the West after a short-lived communist coup, began to lend a helping hand to the Ethiopian dissidents.

Ethiopia's embrace of the SPLM/A was not altruistic; it was tit for tat. Although not told, the newly-formed armed Southern opposition made sure it sang the tune of the benefactor. And the refrain was: fighting for a united and *socialist* Sudan (italics are mine).

This state of affairs raises two moral questions. Was the SPLM/A – read Garang – being opportunistic? Did the movement's programme about unity and socialism have the backing of the majority of the people of Southern Sudan? Answers to these two questions are simple and they could be both yes and no. As shown earlier, the choice of Ethiopia as a friend and base for SPLM/A was the best under the circumstances. It was imperative that the guest, the SPLM, should not undermine or question the way in which the host, Ethiopia, managed its own house. Add to that the concept of opportunism, which refers mainly to individual political or business behaviour; states and political parties are naturally opportunistic. Insurgents are not an exception. Winston Churchill, the British statesman, famously summed up this position when he stated "There are no eternal friends or eternal enemies, only eternal interests". He is referring here to national interests. The same applies to all the nations and any other organisation, political or otherwise. Southern Sudan is not an exception.

This leads us to the unavoidable conclusion that if the SPLM/A – or John Garang, as some people would like to put it – sang "unity and socialism" like parrots, and if that brought them guns to fight a system they loved to hate, then what was the problem?

Do not ask whether I am a unionist or a secessionist, but I have outlined what the SPLM/A, or John Garang, has achieved by ostensibly stating it was for a united Sudan on new terms. When the SPLM/A announced its manifesto – that it was not fighting for an independent Southern Sudan, the reaction in the North in general was a bit of indifference; since separation, it has always been and still is an emotive matter. The government of Nimeiri picked and dwelled on the movement's "Communist ideology", a bestseller to the West under the conservative American administration of Ronald Reagan. Attempts by Khartoum to label the SPLM/A as a puppet of the state of Israel flopped: the majority of people in the Arab and Islamic world don't believe the Jewish nation does political business with the Reds.

Not only was the government of the day disarmed by the movement's unity agenda, but also some liberals and progressives among the Northern elite flocked to the rank and file of the Southern-based rebellion. The Nuba, a warrior nation, identified with the programme of the SPLM/A. In the famous words of the late Yousif Kuwa Mekki, the South received recognition and some of their rights from Khartoum because they had taken up arms from 1955-1972. If that was the language Khartoum understood, reasoned the Nuba leader, then his people had to resort to armed struggle. They did. For the sake of record, it is relevant to remind people here that Khartoum used the gallant Nuba soldiers to fight Anya Nya guerrillas on the basis that Southern rebels were enemies of Islam and Arabism because most Nuba army members were Muslim and some were convinced they were Arabs, contrary to the colour of their skin.

Regionally and internationally, the SPLM/A's policy on a united Sudan- on its own terms- won friends. Libyan maverick leader, Col Gaddafi, was the first to recognise and extend support to the SPLM/A. Libya armed and dressed up a complete division of SPLA. Its embassy in Addis Ababa took care of the wounded and officers on duty. Although Gaddafi's interest in supporting the SPLM/A was ideological and selfish – the then anti-West Libyan leader was against Nimeiri, whom he saw as an American stooge – there was no way he could have supported a separatist organisation as he was a fierce pan-Arabist. South Yemen – then a radical socialist state – warmed up to the SPLM/A. Contacts between the SPLM/A and Yemeni authorities were established in 1985. Although a poor country, Yemen was able to contribute some weapons, including two sniper rifles for the protection of the leadership. Some Palestinian factional leaders met SPLM representatives, whom they assured that their causes were in many ways similar and that their organisations would morally support the Sudanese rebels. It is self-evident that what neutralised or attracted Arab or Islamic states, organisations and individuals, was the movement's agenda: socialism in a united Sudan. Progressives, it is presumed, are not prone to racism and religious intolerance. But not all Muslim and Arab governments stood with the SPLM. For example, the tiny state of Oman, Iraq, Jordan, Egypt which claimed it took no side until its ambassador to Ethiopia boasted his country had provided 53 million US dollars to the government of Nimeiri to support his army.

One does not need to narrate at length how the SPLM, or John Garang, succeeded to either neutralise or win over the traditional and perceived enemies of the South – Arabs and Muslims in Sudan, the Arab and Islamic world, but by all accounts, the SPLM's political programme in this area was able to achieve its objectives.

Although the SPLM leader is on record as saying they had to shed separatist blood, it is not easy for one to conclude that the man is genuinely for unity or that he has been using the slogan to neutralise, and win friends and members from the North.

Having worked with Garang from 1984-1988 almost on a daily basis, I have no idea whether he is a unionist or a separatist. When I interviewed him several years ago about the subject, he used a guarded language. My question to him was "Why do you insist on unity when it is unpopular in your constituency, Southern Sudan?" His answer was that calling for separation does not bring independence. The Anya Nya programme was separatist, yet its leader Joseph Lagu ended by signing an agreement based on unity, he argued, adding that Dr Riek Machar called his organisation South Sudan Independence Movement. Riek Machar's Khartoum peace agreement affirmed unity, not separation, Garang concluded.

I think three factors may work in favour of the South voting for unity. One of these is what a man from Western Equatoria described to me: "the Dinka are worse than the Arabs". This man was a signatory to a document written last year by members of the Zande community, who echoed the same sentiment. That thinking, in my opinion, appears to be widespread. If the Dinka, who are perceived to be dominating the SPLM/A, are going to rule an independent Southern Sudan, then it is logical that such people would vote for what they consider to be a lesser evil; in this case the Northern monopoly of power and economy.

Second, given the fact that there is discord, suspicion and rivalry among the communities in the South, Khartoum will work hard to magnify the existing differences and create potent new ones. This will inevitably make the people regard the most important issue – voting for self-determination – really marginal. Finally, the Government of Sudan accepted the right of self-determination because it was confident it would scuttle it like the Khartoum Agreement of 1997. The Government of Khartoum will do everything in its power, including rigging, in the interest of unity. These are genuine fears.

For this, the Southern Sudanese who cherish the birth of a new nation in the South after the referendum have to educate the population on how not to vote for unity. Accusations and counter-accusations among the politicians will help foster antagonism and division, all of which are not in the interest of the quest for independence.

Sudan Mirror, vol. 1 issue 13, January 2005.

Garang and Taha deserve sympathy

On arrival at Simba Lodge complex on January 7, to witness the signing of wealth sharing agreement between the SPLM and the Government of Sudan, a person I have known for years came straight to me. "The oil has been given away. This is a sell-out…" I was stunned and silent throughout the monologue.

The speaker was not a youth or a woman activist; nor was the speaker an ordinary person. However, I must not reveal the identity of that Southern Sudanese.

What is relevant in the saga is that the main Sudanese negotiators, Dr John Garang and First Vice President Ali Osman Taha, are taking a huge amount of blame, even from within their own constituencies, for what they do or do not do. I feel sorry for these two politicians, whose roles only a fool can envy.

First, step by step: John Garang – who is reported to have said that insulting him was a way some people were making their livelihood- used to be accused by his enemies as a warmonger who did not care about the suffering of the people and that he would fight for the rest of his life. Another charge is that he was not negotiating in good faith.

And now since the SPLM leader is negotiating – I believe that he has always been- in good faith to end the war, he has come under attack, mostly from the same critics who are now accusing him of giving away the rights of the South to Khartoum.

Vice President Ali Taha is not free from criticism from his own colleagues. What was reported in the media as the resignation from government of the former presidential adviser on peace, Dr Salahudin Atabani, was nothing other than President Bashir ridding his system of elements opposed to peace. Atabani and company are known to be hostile to the right of exercise of self-determination for Southern Sudan, security arrangements and possibly the wealth-sharing agreements.

Taha, to Northern hardliners and ideologues, whether in government or opposition, is seen to be giving in too much to the South. In fact, some of his enemies could go as far as labelling him a traitor. To the rest of the people, Sudanese and non-Sudanese, who support what the two men are doing to end the war, there is some comfort.

John Garang, whatever his shortcomings, is an extremely hard-working and patient man who gets by, despite the behaviour and curses hurled at him by his opponents. I know nothing about the personality and temperament of Taha, but watching him twice during the press conferences with his calm-looking face and gentle- albeit constrained- smile, would suggest self-confidence and the ability to cope with stress, although appearances could sometimes be misleading.

For one to have some understanding of this phase of Sudan's peace process there is an important question to be answered: what is new in a situation that has enticed the SPLM and the Government of Sudan to the edge of a peace agreement, which has eluded the country since the present regime came to power in June 1989?

Besides its Islamist agenda, the National Islamic Front toppled the civilian government of Sadiq el-Mahdi – in my opinion, he is more militarist than the men in uniform; he is the father of aerial bombardment of civilian targets – in order to crush the SPLA militarily.

The regime took advantage of the internal problems within the movement. After the split of 1991, and following the cooperation between the breakaway factions with the government, Khartoum retook virtually all the garrison towns previously controlled by the SPLA. There was a time the SPLA was pushed to Nimule like a cornered rat. Khartoum was convinced that the "rebellion" was all but finished. But then in 1993 the SPLA took the initiative and recaptured several strategic garrisons in Equatoria and, four years later, in Bahr el Ghazal.

By the time cessation of hostilities came into force, now more than a year ago, the balance of power was a semi-stalemate, one would say *hors de combat*. This seesaw game, convinced both the government and the SPLM that an outright military victory, although none would admit that in public, was almost impossible.

But the biggest factor behind the parties-negotiated solution to a military one, in my opinion, has been the changed global political climate, beginning with the fall of the Berlin Wall and ending with the bombing of the World Trade Center and the Pentagon on September 11, 2001, by members of the al-Qaeda group. The last event has more impact on American foreign policy than the collapse of the former Soviet Union.

We live in a world of one superpower instead of two. In the past, a country or liberation movement had a choice between the US and the USSR -Union of Soviet Socialist Republics- for ideological, political, economic or military support. This is no longer the case.

Although the phrase "international community" is understood to refer to the UN, these days it could mean either the same or the US and its allies.

The Sudan peace process is officially being mediated by the regional body, Igad, but facilitated financially and in other ways by several European countries. The US administration has thrown its weight behind the Sudan peace talks and has made no secret that it wants the parties in the conflict to end the war, and immediately.

American interests in the Sudan peace process was demonstrated by the visit late last year of the Secretary of State, Colin Powell, to Naivasha, the venue of talks where he met the principal negotiators, Garang and Taha. The office of the US Secretary of State is not that of your local minister for foreign affairs.

The fact that President Bush sent Powell to talk with delegates from a country the president may have problem finding on a world map, says a lot about the interests of the American administration and its world agenda. After his brief stay at Naivasha, Colin Powell declared that the Sudanese protagonists would reach an agreement by December 31, 2003.

When realities did not allow that, American officials began to talk to President Bashir and Chairman Garang, urging them to speed up the talks to reach a final agreement. Now, Powell is not a personal friend of the two men in the sense that the American calls to enquire into the health of the Sudanese leaders and that of their families; there is something more than that: pressure.

How much pressure and what the consequences are, I do not know, but both Garang and Taha and their respective delegations are not fool enough to fail to understand the position of the American government. The persons who do not appreciate this situation are the critics of the SPLM and the Government of Sudan. And that brings us to the element of realities in the situation.

While inside the hall where the agreement on wealth-sharing was to be signed, a friend and I heard someone grumbling in a whisper that the agreement was bad. My friend[1], who in the past, used to condemn the movement and most of its policies, replied, "if you don't like the wealth-sharing ratios, you go and stop production so that there is nothing to share". I agree with this reasoning. The Government of Sudan and the SPLM are sharing because SAF are controlling the oilfields. Were the SPLA there, the matter would be a non-issue.

The fact that the SPLA was unable to defeat the SAF in the battlefield is partially the result of the actions and omissions of some Southern Sudanese organisations and leaders. I am not about to open old wounds here, but there are facts that should not be put aside when reviewing the current problems.

The breakaway factions did a lot to weaken the fighting capacity of the SPLA from 1991-1993. When the excuse for schism was the bad leadership style of John Garang, one would have some sympathy with the mutineers, but that could not be a justification for the destruction of "seventeen taskforces[2] of John Garang" as one Riek Machar, the leader of the breakaway faction, later boasted in a BBC interview.

These forces were part of the army to fight and win political rights for Southern Sudan, not of that much demonised man, John Garang.

Most of the critics of the SPLM leader have contributed to the phenomenon of desertion by SPLA fighters. In 1998, a fellow Southern Sudanese met me in a Nairobi restaurant. He was smiling and in a very expansive mood. "Have you heard the latest news?" he asked. "No," was my answer. "My friend, the forces Garang was to command to capture Lirya [not far from Juba] and Torit have deserted, leaving him alone"[3].

I later learned the fellow was involved in inciting the forces to desert to their home region. The argument was that any success of SPLA under the command of Garang was going to make the job of overthrowing him very difficult.

The point being made here is that when a guerrilla movement defeats a sitting government as was the case of Eritrea, Uganda under Museveni or in Rwanda, talk about power, wealth-sharing and the like becomes redundant.

This piece would be incomplete without a brief look at who has gained what or who has lost what.

The first and most important score for the SPLM, no doubt, is self-determination, which gives the people the choice between union and independence.

Depending on how the interim period is managed, the outcome of the referendum will be solely the responsibility of the people and the SPLM leadership will have the right to say "it was the people's decision, it wasn't us," especially when the result would not be to the expectations of the majority.

Although some Southern Sudanese had wished complete separation of forces, the fact that there will be separate SPLA forces alongside SAF is in itself a kind of guarantee, which was not the case with both the Addis Ababa Agreement of 1972 and the Khartoum Agreement of 1997.

The involvement of the international community in the implementation of the future agreement, which again was not the case with the two accords mentioned earlier, will be another formal, although not absolute, guarantee.

Khartoum is not a loser either. Perhaps the most critical gain by Khartoum is the duration of the interim period. The six-year transitional span will give an opportunity to Khartoum to "make unity attractive" or make mischief, in the words of some critics.

Having the presence of some SAF units in the South will assure many Northern Sudanese that the SPLA would not declare a unilateral declaration of independence, or UDI.

The agreement on wealth-sharing favours Khartoum in that the Government shares half the oil from the South, while oil from the North will not be shared. In all fairness, I do not believe the points of agreement are ideal to all. But in the circumstances of win-lose, the parties have done very well.

However, it is obvious the Government of Sudan and the SPLM have been very unreasonable on two issues. It boggles the mind why the Government takes 50 percent of the oil from the South, while denying the latter to share oil from the North. It is simply mean. At least a token 10 percent would be good "window dressing".

For its part, the SPLM's demand for a sharia-free Khartoum is unreasonable. As long as the South remains exempt from Islamic laws, the North should be treated the same way; let it have sharia, since the majority of the population are Muslim.

Garang's Unenviable Task

Sudan's armed conflict officially ended on January 9, 2005 with the signing in Nairobi, Kenya, of the CPA. Six months to the day, the practical side of the agreement came into being after President Omar Hassan el Bashir signed the draft interim constitution into law and the subsequent appointment of Dr John Garang as the country's first vice president. These developments were given further importance and regional and international recognition by the presence of the UN Secretary General, Kofi Annan, South African President Thabo Mbeki, the Ugandan Head of State, Yoweri Museveni, President Mwai Kibaki of Kenya whose country hosted the peace talks for years and Kibaki's predecessor Daniel arap Moi. A huge crowd of Sudanese citizens turned up in their hundreds of thousands, in what a senior SPLM official who attended the occasion has said was an unofficial form of referendum for peace. He might as well agree with the claim that the massive popular reception was a kind of support for the former rebel movement and its leadership.

Even with the goodwill of many Sudanese, Muslim, Christian, women, young or old, from the west, south, north, east, the new First Vice President of the Republic of Sudan and the future head of the Government of Southern Sudan, the former rebel chieftain, Cdr Dr John Garang de Mabior as he is known to his friends and supporters, is going to face serious problems arising from his responsibilities in those roles. One of the main problems is the complexity that is Sudan, culturally, ideologically and ethnically. I believe even a saint will find running Sudan a nightmare in that he or she will not please everyone. But try, mortals have to, do the right things or make mistakes. That is life.

As number two man in the whole country, what will a man who for more than 20 years has been behaving and being treated in some countries, minus red carpet reception at airports, as a head of state and administering a territory the size of Kenya, Uganda and Rwanda, put together, feel? That really, is not the issue. Most of problems he will face will relate to his role as national office holder and the chief administrator of Southern Sudan.

On arrival in Khartoum Garang has been welcomed by thousands upon thousands of Sudanese, mostly from the South and from what are called marginalised regions of the West and East. There is more to numbers than politics. "Triumphal" may not be the exact adjective to describe the event, but his return to Khartoum bore the hallmarks of an achievement which is truly historic.

First, the man who by all accounts is a headline news personality is virtually an outsider, both in the North and his native Southern Sudan. Governing or ruling people you do not know or understand well is or can be a serious disadvantage. Ironically, there are very few Southern Sudanese leaders who have seen many corners of Southern Sudan, travelled and lived in many glades, villages, towns or crossed valleys and climbed hills and mountains or crossed rivers and streams, more than John Garang.

The man of the hour has been in Khartoum for several years in various capacities while an officer in the army in which at a certain stage he was an instructor at the country's prestigious military academy and later as an adviser to military economic corporation. Nonetheless, Garang remained an outsider in every aspect of the Northern Sudanese society. Educated in Tonj, Bussere and Rumbek, all in the former Bahr el Ghazal Province, he left the country before completing his secondary education. Before joining the guerrillas of Anya Nya, he attended school in the then Tanganyika. Even after his return home at the end of the first civil war in 1972, the soldier and academic later to direct the second armed struggle, was known to few people; the majority of the Southern elite most of whom are going to be members of his team were educated at the University of Khartoum or some of the politicians and civil servants who managed the affairs of the South in Juba. Most members of Sudanese educated class tend to be cliquey and usually prefer to work with, and trust colleagues, past or present.

True, while in the North Garang interacted with the people there and made friends with some of them. Although he can be considered literate in Arabic up to a certain point, he expresses himself at best in colloquial version.

As far as I know, it is not a necessary condition for a senior constitutional office holder to be able to write and read or speak formal Arabic. Former vice presidents from the South and most of their Southern compatriots who were ministers in Khartoum knew little or no knowledge of "standard" Arabic. The point being made here is that in Khartoum, a vice president or a minister from the South will have to have a cleaner, receptionist, a driver and so forth from the North. More often than not these individuals, mostly less educated are more likely to look down on their "illiterate" bosses from the South.

Garang will have a platoon of his own staff drawn from SPLM/A Arabic speaking aides from the South, Nuba Mountains and even from the North. These fellows will help in translating official daily correspondence or periodic briefings and reports, but given the sensitivity of his duties, a second rendering would not be sufficient.

Although the agreement is supposed to put an end to the conflict which pitted the South against the North, only a few would believe that the whole population of Northern Sudan has welcomed the deal. Even within his office, Dr Garang will operate with a handful of elements that may harbour antipathy towards the agreement and the role of Southern Sudanese in the Sudanese state. These same persons may not show their true colours but they may try to sabotage the peace agreement and the plans of the first vice president. Civil servants are not supposed to engage openly in politics, but some of their colleagues may be supporters of opposition parties. How does a civil servant sympathetic with Sadiq el-Mahdi who is against certain clauses of the CPA, for example, carry orders from the former rebel leader? The likelihood is that such an officer may not express open defiance but may resort to others obstructive means such as procrastination.

Garang's dual role as first vice president of Sudan and the head of the Government of Southern Sudan has its own difficulties. He will not be in Khartoum and in the South at the same time. As one to represent the interests of the South in the central government, First Vice President Garang is expected to be in Khartoum most of the time. In that case the South which is his turf and where a lot of activities such as reconstruction and rehabilitation will be taking place will miss him or put another way; he will miss his daily stamp of authority there. Certainly, his deputy will be acting but major decisions such as appointments, promotions, retirement, transfers or dismissal of senior army officers and civil servants are not always the prerogative of a deputy performing in acting capacity.

Although Garang is expected to have been making consultations and continues to do so with different Southern interest groups, appointments of teams to various levels of government are not likely to please everyone. First, most of persons who are looking towards being made minister or other senior members of government may not take kindly to being left out. Experience of Southern Sudan is that principles and programmes count for less when politicians miss public office. In some cases, exclusion sometimes leads to opposition, open or underground, mild or violent.

Another thorny issue is the ethnic diversity of Southern Sudan. Even with the best of intentions no leader can accommodate the more than 100 communities, especially in Khartoum and in Juba. Practically, that is impossible. But as he often talks of an inclusive government, Garang could reduce ethnic marginalisation by allowing representatives of the three regions and their 10 states to sort out the issues of power sharing and percentages, in that his role would be to either endorse their choices, or convince them about some of his objections.

Not all who will be appointed to government posts will jump with joy; some will feel demoted since not all cabinet posts carry equal weight. There are personalities who would desire to operate in the South to prepare for future elections or to influence the outcome of the referendum. Such figures are likely to be disappointed if they are told to be ministers in Khartoum which may sound like being exiled. Others love to be governors to run their small fiefdoms where they will enjoy local authority and its many perks.

But the biggest challenge of all will be performance of Garang's appointees. Most of those who happen to be close, ideologically or socially to the leader, are not known for probity, competence or hard work; some have no idea about how to run a public office. The failure of such elements, unless they change their wayward conduct and begin to learn, will be a heavy blow to the SPLM and its administration. The electorate will be watching keenly. Good governance and satisfactory delivery of services and development endear the people to parties in power. Conversely, very few governments which fail to deliver are returned to power especially in democracies and Sudan is to embark on a democratic path whether the parties to the agreement like it or not.

It is not bleak, however. Although Garang's bitterest critics dismiss the man as devoid of leadership qualities, Garang does have virtues which he could deploy to enhance the image of his administration. One of these attributes is patience. People who have worked with the man at close quarters know that he is prepared to put up with the most frustrating situations and very irritating people including a few among his colleagues. The Arabs say *Es subur jameel*, meaning patience is beautiful [is a virtue]. In the captious society of Southern Sudan this trait can be an asset of immense proportions.

Coupled with that is his gift of hard work. But that is not enough if directed at less productive activity, for example when the boss has to type a lengthy document, a task that should be left to trusted personal aides. Even Garang's opponents and enemies find it hard to deny his intelligence. But again, that gift *per se* may not be enough; what matters is how it is utilised and directed. History records that some of the most dangerous leaders were not morons.

Sudan Mirror, 2005

South Sudan tragedy
choice of words for waging peace, reconciliation

*"I am a chief, but my power to make war
is gone, and the only weapon left to me
is speech. It is only with the tongue and speech
that I can fight my people's war."*

This stanza is from a book-length poem, *My Heart Soars* by Chief Dan George, a leader of the indigenous American Indians. He laments the fact that he doesn't have weapons any more, and presumably, an army to fight for the rights of his people. He now takes consolation in the use of words instead. The chief needs feel no regret as the alternative, words – spoken or written – have been known for being more powerful than the sword or any other tool of death nations use for settling disputes through the ages.

It is this awareness that makes some people reject the use of force in preference to words on the basis that arguing cases or negotiating claims is a better option, morally. In a conflict that is resolved through dialogue there are no losers, only winners: each party, through compromises reached, wins some points while peace emerges as the biggest victor.

In conflict situations, people desiring peace are always overwhelmingly in the majority but their voices are often stifled and drowned by a barrage of propaganda from warring parties, which usually manipulate news media, whether it is their own or external.

A peace advocate by choice doesn't need tools of war, unless they were a Christopher Okigbo, a promising young Nigerian poet who took up arms to join the combatants and was killed in battle during his country's civil war, more than four decades ago.

A fight for a good cause does not need to be violent to require soldiers; peace can be achieved by words: a rational and civilised mode of talking – dialogue or negotiation. Alternatively, it could be done in writing, not an exchange of expletives and hate speeches, that incite people to violence and more hatred. For example, much of the struggle to end apartheid in South Africa was conducted in words, namely diplomacy at various forums such as the UN, an approach which, in turn, mobilised international public opinion against the system, through media, pamphleteering and literature. Some anti-apartheid activists employed poetry and fiction as their medium of choice, to put their message across intellectually.

During this difficult time in the history of South Sudan, people committed to achieving peace and reconciliation must take words, spoken or written, as a leading tool. And words – like fire, a good servant and a bad master, as they say – must be handled with great care. Words have the ability to inflame passions, or a frenzy of hatred, violence, killing and destruction. On the other hand, they are capable of building bridges across different divides; words can promote healing, love and forgiveness, and reconciliation.

Well-grounded fears of the worst to come

The armed conflict that broke out mid-December in 2013 is not the usual political and social development in which South Sudanese pro-peace activists and media practitioners can afford to be indifferent, and report it from a detached position. It is not the stuff of ordinary news reporting, analysis and commentary. It is a shooting war which has already caused cataclysmic mayhem, resulting in thousands of victims – mostly women, children and elderly persons – being killed; a million – again from the same category – have been displaced from their homes; and the frightening spectre of imminent famine to hit headlines soon, unless a sustainable solution to the war is hammered out to arrest the human-made catastrophe.

In addition to the humanitarian crisis already grinding, the conflict threatens to tear the nation's social fabric to shreds as cycles of attacks and counter-attacks, culminating in vengeance, escalate.

In this environment, ethnic hatred and hardened feelings are fast replacing mutual trust and national cohesion in diversity. In the process the small, albeit ambiguous, feeble and half-hearted attempts by the ruling elite at laying foundations for nation-and institution-building, have already been wiped out in less than five months.

There is also a growing fear that the conflict is drawing in actors within the region. That three governments in the region [Khartoum, Juba and Kampala] and non-state actors [South Sudan's armed opposition, Sudan's pro-government Misseiriya and Janjaweed militias, Sudan's rebels of the Sudan Revolutionary Front, SRF and Jem] are trading accusations against each other gives credence to this anxiety that the conflict that began as an internal dispute has mutated into a wider and more complicated boiling cauldron with wider regional implications.

It would be an understatement to describe the current situation in South Sudan as unsettling. It is not only the lives of the people that are at stake; the very existence of South Sudan as a sovereign state and its territorial integrity are in the balance; the next target – and casualty – goodness forbid, is likely to be the soul of the nation.

With the targeting of people, especially civilians, on the basis of ethnicity, nationality and real or perceived political affiliation or sympathies as a weapon of war, the international community has constantly expressed grave concerns that the country's next destination is genocide. One does not need to research for proof; the images TV stations have transmitted globally to living rooms shocking the sensibilities of viewers tell the grim story, making brutality our – we South Sudanese – a badge of shame. This media coverage, coupled with the reports taken from the accounts of witnesses and survivors and independent investigators, are sufficient testimony of the viciousness of the conflict.

Khartoum must be gloating, to be sure
These observations are not an expression of paranoia. The regime of the National Congress Party, NCP, which had vigorously resisted the secession of Southern Sudan, is keenly watching the developments, and its leaders are gloating over the tribulations the country, now South Sudan, is going through.

As we fight each other to the death, Khartoum plays the role of Iago, the scheming character in Shakespeare's tragedy, *Othello*. Iago, the play tells us, welcomes the death of whoever gets killed in the fights that involve several sets of protagonists who are antagonistic to each other. In our context, Khartoum rejoices not so much in the defeats or victories of the Government of South Sudan or those of the South Sudanese rebels; to the NCP what *does* matter is that any side gets hurt and ideally – in the NCP's fiendish wish – if and when the two destroy each other. Sweet revenge achieved via enemy's suicide.

The analogy in short translates into: in South Sudan's conflict, it is in Khartoum's skewed interest if any of the parties – or both – get reduced in numbers, weakened or annihilated, leaving the entire country bleeding to the point of disintegration and where the surviving populations will live in reciprocal hatred afterwards.

Already Khartoum is revelling over a bonanza: because of the war in South Sudan, post-independence issues, such as the stalled Abyei referendum and border demarcation among others, have been pushed to the bottom of the national agenda, since ending the armed conflict now occupies the attention of the regional and international community, as well as that of the South Sudanese leadership.

Before Southern Sudan became independent, some of the NCP-led regime's hardliners, together with some of their allies from the South, publicly campaigned hard and long against secession, arguing that South Sudanese were not a nation, but a collection of "tribes" without any common denominator, and that they would be fighting each other once Khartoum's "protection" was no longer there.

Unfortunately, some elements within the power-elite in South Sudan recklessly – intentionally or otherwise – allowed the wishes of the old oppressor to come true. Those who opposed the independence of South

Sudan must be gleefully declaring what may later turn out to be a short-lived exoneration: "Did we not say so?"

Recent allegations have been made by the NCP leader, Omar Bashir, that leaders of some countries he did not name – clearly Western powers – had apologised to him for "allowing" the secession to take place and that they had asked him to reunify the two Sudans. These pieces of fiction should be seen as a red alarm. Bashir has now got the *casus belli* he has been looking for since July 9, 2011.

South Sudan now faces a clear and present danger, which could only be thwarted if the warring parties embrace genuine and lasting peace. And, for peace and reconciliation to be achieved, every South Sudanese who is committed to the country's sovereignty and territorial integrity must have a role to play, regardless of social status, regional, ethnic or party affiliation.

What is to be done?

Even before the outbreak of violence late last year, developments in South Sudan were being monitored with deep concern at home, and by the international community, as indicators for a potential conflict were discernible, even to casual observers; others predicted that we were shuffling towards a failed-state status; that our weakest points were our institutions that would not absorb jolting political or social upheavals; that the sense of entitlement in some sections of the society, especially among the former freedom fighters, was disenfranchising others; that lack of accountability was breeding a culture of impunity; or the huge gap between the haves and have-nots would create dissent, and so forth.

From a nationalistic perspective, however, we saw the authors of these observations as prophets of doom. We would have done better to do introspective work, critically examining our institutions, their performance and our own conscience, and act to avert the disaster that was about to explode. We responded by repudiating those warnings and went to sleep, ostrich-like, with our heads deep in the sand.

Paradoxically, this writer was one of the voices that used to dismiss those observers issuing dire predictions. He had two reasons: one, as a sub-national entity in the 1970s and early 1980s we, in the Regional Government of Southern Sudan, evolved and ran a relatively efficient and effective bureaucracy — far superior than systems operating in many independent African countries, mostly in the west of the continent. At that time the Southern Regional Government had very few financial and human resources. Two, we had — and still have — the capacity to manage a modern state, if our civil service was to be staffed with competent managers of unquestioned probity, and free from control and excessive abuse of office by the power elite.

When the dreaded implosion did arrive, on the night of December 15-16, 2013, almost everyone, beginning with the country's senior clergymen, the regional and international community — Igad, African Union, EU and the UN — did not hesitate to call the conflict what it is: a dangerous and worrying crisis with the potential for ethnic polarisation and self-destruction. Hoping that it was not too late, friends of South Sudan urged the parties in the conflict to stop fighting and to opt for peaceful means at the earliest possible opportunity.

These bodies, together with South Sudanese civil society organisations at home and in the diaspora, have been — and are still — appealing for peace and reconciliation. Since then, these groups have been contributing, each in their own ways, towards ending the war through a negotiated settlement.

Journalists as partners in the peace and reconciliation process
The international news media, especially the Qatari Aljazeera and the BBC World Service, radio and television, have satisfactorily played their traditional role of providing to the public at home and abroad the much needed impartial information. It is mainly from these channels that even our own citizens are getting the information about their own country.

Because of the weak, substandard and gagged national news media, some electronic media operated outside the country have filled the news deficit. Some of these websites attract a comparatively wide readership. Furthermore, unlike the domestic media outlets, these websites enjoy what appears to be an unfettered level of freedom to publish almost all ranges of opinions with virtually no editorial intervention.

Welcomed as that freedom appears, it is the reason why, unfortunately, some critics are uncomfortable with it: it could be abused by some individuals who prefer emotional outbursts over cool and persuasive arguments. Enjoying absolute free reign, these writers often express unconcealed antagonisms against certain public institutions, groups of people and individuals. Although bias is a trait that is in almost all people, its blatant forms, sometimes contents amounting to incitement, are capable of marring even a cogently argued piece, and consequently they will put off readers looking for objective information. That this aberration is common in these media organisations is another source of anxiety.

Despite these criticisms, one should not ignore the commendable, if courageous work of some of my colleagues in journalism, and other peers operating at home or abroad who write responsibly – as citizens first and journalists or academics second. This time it is patriotism that is being tested, not professions. And it is from that prism where I approach the problem of war and peace in South Sudan. I have carved a role for myself and don't need permission from anyone or any organisation for that.

During these trying times, media practitioners from South Sudan can no longer afford to be bystanders, or to treat their job as "business as usual". The vacuum created by their continued role as reporters or commentators, instead of taking sides with the peace and reconciliation camp, is now increasingly being exploited by warmongers. These elements, who are mostly ethnic chauvinists – few as they may be – are very active in the diaspora where they are using hate speech and divisive communication through the social media.

Communication along those lines does not help the cause of peace and reconciliation; it hurts and hardens feelings across ethnic and political divides. What South Sudan now needs urgently is peace and national healing, not pouring of more salt into the deep wounds of our own making.

Doing one's small bit

As a result of this thinking, I will be publishing articles on my personal role and capacity as a journalist, in the service of peace and reconciliation. This is the first instalment out of several articles that will follow. Most of them are reports punctuated with reflection on issues of nation building, how absent institutions could be built, and existing fragile ones be strengthened.

The role of individual journalists in the promotion of peace and reconciliation should be the starting point from a personal viewpoint.

At first, I begin with narratives of what I have been doing in my personal capacity during the last three and half months.

The first of these engagements began with a lecture at places such as Sydney University's Centre for Peace and Conflict Studies, Australia, in February this year. This was later followed in March when I addressed a very successful church-sponsored event, organised by young South Sudanese students in Sydney to raise funds for the benefit of IDPs at home.

I must admit that, in all the public talks, my emphasis has been and continues to be on the need for all South Sudanese, wherever they are, to seek means to promote dialogue for achieving peace and reconciliation. By this approach I studiously skip the chronology of the tragic events and their root causes. I think the right and most qualified people to do that job for objective understanding of the conflict and for history should be political analysts and social commentators. South Sudan has many of these experts, especially in academia.

This is a conscious and deliberate omission: blame games and the identification of culprits, perceived or real, tend to be subjective and can further polarise parties and their sympathisers. Ideally, anyone engaged in creating an environment conducive to peace and reconciliation should avoid – as far as possible – the temptation to apportion blame to parties in the conflict. They instead must strive to build common ground and consider what is acceptable to the opponents. One can't work to reconcile quarrelling parties while, at the same time, sitting on a judgement seat. These are separate offices. This choice of silence on causes – and who are to be held accountable for the crisis – does not in any way condone criminal acts committed by the parties in the conflict.

These accounts and analyses form suitable ingredients for memoirists, historians, political scientists and human rights bodies, not for publication by persons or organisations engaged in ongoing efforts to end a conflict. Nevertheless, I am convinced all the parties have contributed to the mess in one way or another. The time will come for publication of specific roles and details some individual played to escalate or even explode the situation.

Price of working for peace

Working for peace is not only a thankless endeavour; it sometimes carries risks to the peace advocates themselves. For example, in early 2014, an Australian academic and peace activist, Patricia Garcia, who is a friend of

South Sudanese people organised a workshop at Parramatta, Sydney. The objective of the meeting was to discuss the role the South Sudanese diaspora, especially women, would play to mobilise the public for peace. The South Sudanese who went to the meeting were drawn from South Sudan's various linguistic groups. I went with my wife and our youngest daughter, then a high school student. The forum examined ways in which communities in the diaspora would begin the process among themselves, before they could reach out to fellow South Sudanese in the other Australian states, North America and finally home, all with the message of reconciliation. Unknown to Garcia and some of us was the motive of some young men who had come purportedly to take part in the exchange of views. A few days later, we learned to our chagrin that they were there to report – more accurately to fabricate and distort – the proceedings to authorities in Juba.

When the workshop ended, those fellows had secretly collected the attendance papers carrying the names and contacts of the participants. That data was sent to Juba. A few days later we were shocked by a video that had been recorded by one of those young men. Talking in a very poor English and rambling with statements which lacked logic or an iota of common sense, the producer began making a childish description of Garcia, the facilitator, before he claimed one former chairman of one of SPLM chapters in Australia, who hails from Equatoria, of trying to organise the "killing" of Dinka. The young man, who I was later told spent his early years in Khartoum during the war, raised questions about my presence in a meeting which he claimed was a plot by the Equatorians against the "Dinkas" in his words.

The author of those outrageous and outlandish allegations then circulated that defamatory stuff through social media. Most of us were genuinely shocked and alarmed by the degree of malice, falsehood and recklessness of the video maker.

Published in Juba Monitor, *May 11, 2014.*

[On receiving the offending video, which one of my colleagues who was present at the workshop sent me, I began consulting legal opinion with a view of taking the young man who had made and widely circulated the false and damaging accusation, to court. I was consulting for advice about what to do with the chaps who had stolen and sent to Juba attendance papers. Most of my friends agreed that the video was offensive in the extreme, and defamatory. Those who had seen the video and said they knew the maker of the message, expressed their sincere sympathy towards me. However, they advised me not to pursue justice through court. They appear – in my view – to believe that the young man did not deserve to engage in legal tussle with "respectable" persons lest they gave him decency they said he is devoid of. His profile, they said, was enough to make any person ignore him. His data: a dropout from a university in New South Wales; has been involved with saying and writing abusive statements against community leaders from his home area in Lakes, South Sudan; that he was reared in Khartoum during the war before he migrated to Australia through Egypt; that despite being able-bodied youth he has never worked to earn money. I later learned that soon after making the damaging video he flew to Juba where he was hoping to collect payment for his pro-government activities in Australia. When nothing was forthcoming from the government, he left Juba to join the anti-government rebels of the SPLM/A-IO. The latest information I heard about him in late 2016 was that he was back in Juba, apparently disappointed with the rebels. Meanwhile his colleagues who collected and sent to Juba the contacts of those who attended the workshop have learned that their "secret" action has come to light.

Putting aside the laughable and cruel attack on me and some of my compatriots working for reconciliation among communities of South Sudan abroad, the relevant question to ask is: is there any chance for successful peace and reconciliation among South Sudanese in the diaspora and at home, in the face of constant attempts by some people to widen divisions and fan ethnic antagonisms and mutual distrust?

During my time abroad for the last three months, I have been pleasantly surprised to discover that the majority of South Sudanese living there yearn for urgent and unconditional return of peace, and to that end they are prepared to do whatever it takes to reconcile as communities and as a nation.

It is a stand that is anchored in courage as some of people campaigning for peace are among those mourning their loved ones, killed during the last four and half months of fratricidal savagery.]

Reform should begin from the SPLM Extraordinary Convention Itself

The holding of the SPLM extraordinary convention that began on Friday last week, appears to have been done in a rush, almost a day after the parties had finalised the share of cabinet posts in the future government of national unity. The peace partners have a lot to do. Now they have to attend the meetings of the convention which require full-time attention. This is hardly time for a convention that should include all factions of the divided party. However, since the three wings – the SPLM in government, its rivals in the armed opposition and the former detainees – attended and their representatives spoke at the gathering, the organisers could claim the occasion is inclusive. Suspicion about the motives, the timing and the speed of the holding the gathering persist, nonetheless.

Signs of opening up?

Another point the SPLM in government, who are the organisers of the convention, will put out in their defence is that the occasion – which was broadcast live on the national TV channel, SSTV – has enabled the public to follow the proceedings and make their own judgement of everything that was going on at Freedom Hall, whether words or actions. Coupled with that is the presence of two high-profile guests representing the African National Congress, ANC, and the Tanzanian Chama Cha Mapinduzi, CCM, as well as foreign diplomats accredited to South Sudan. To that end, critics of the SPLM affiliated to government could be tempted to think that at long last the party managers and their allies in the executive branch and outside have embraced the path of openness, a norm for which the SPLM has been deficient through its long history – a generation plus.

Personality cult: revival of bad old habits

Although South Sudan is constitutionally a multi-party democracy, the manner in which the convention was conceived and staged by its apparatchiks tells another story; the audience were treated to an entrée reminiscent of the one-party state official functions in the less developed world of the 1970s through 1990s.

Some of the performances were so vulgar that even the object(s) of the veneration must have been embarrassed. Let's face it; Chairman Salva Kiir, for whom songs have been composed and sung in his praise, has better things he can be justly proud of than the authors of the cult of personality ever care to think. Except for the deniers who are bent on rewriting the history of the struggle under the SPLM/A, General Salva Kiir is not only on record as one of the top founding leaders of the movement, but also, according to what late Joseph Oduho told this writer in mid-1984, "without Salva [Kiir] and me, John [Garang] would not have been the leader [of the SPLM/A]". Oduho, who was referring to the vote taken a year earlier, during the contest between Akuot Atem Mayen and Samuel Gai Tut on the one hand and John Garang on the other, Joseph Oduho and then Captain Salva Kiir voted for Garang against Akuot Atem.

Other worthy credentials for the man who is now the head of South Sudanese state include being one of the few senior officers in leadership echelon of the SPLM/A known for humility, less interested in courting praise or being photogenic; for most of the time during the struggle, he lived a life of near-sacrifice, within the scarce means available to the guerrillas; the only member of the leadership who turned down a house in the Ethiopian capital Addis Ababa in 1990, rented and paid for in advance- without his knowledge- for him by a political ally of the movement; and finally, his patient stewardship of the process leading to impendence on July 2011.

The minions, who are trying to put a halo on him by distorting history, are doing him a disservice. These overzealous image-builders have taken advantage of the fact that most of the members of their audience were people less knowledgeable of the history of the SPLM/A early days, the audience are presumed to have no other versions. The authors of the clumsily-crafted and poorly-presented script have forgotten that many eyewitnesses of the events being distorted are still around, and must have watched the narrative with silent disbelief. History is not a close relative of gossip or hearsay; it can be distorted, but hardly erased.

It is reasonable to say that the crude enactment the public watched last Friday of praise for the leader of the party of liberation is a carryover from the cult of personality that Radio SPLA doled out during the years of the struggle. At the training centres, just to give an example, recruits composed and sang war and revolutionary songs which served as morale-booster and as a way the future soldiers expressed themselves, defined their enemies, the friends of the struggle and often in praise of their leaders.

Unfortunately, many of the songs of praise that were later to become the stuff of broadcasts concentrated on the SPLM/A founding leader, John Garang. Serious concern was expressed both within and from outside the movement, that songs of praise and Marhum Dut Kat's *Al Q'aid ma' el-thuwaar*, or the leader with the revolutionaries, an Arabic language programme on the clandestine station, were promoting a personality cult, especially of the SPLM/A chief. Commander Alfred Lado Gore, then head of the ideology branch, was one member who feared that the propaganda machine of the movement was slowly sliding into hero-worship culture. I shared this view but was unable to prevent it happening: Garang was the real spokesman of the SPLM/A.

The SPLA does not belong to the SPLM

Like most policy statements, the SPLA is a national army and not a militia of the ruling party, the SPLM. This is what the constitution states, and what senior officers, such as the former chief of staff, General James Hoth, have said publicly. The official position is that the two bodies, which in the past acted like conjoined twins, were separate entities serving the people in different and specified ways.

But do the organisers of the convention know these constitutional job descriptions? It appears they don't, otherwise why did the military band have to play at every interlude during the convention? Since the function had a national significance, the band playing the national anthem at the start would be appreciated and pardoned. But throughout the proceedings the band was acting as a backup ensemble to rally the party faithful. That was unacceptable; the SPLA is not a unit of the SPLM anymore. Roles changed after the guerrillas became a government more than a decade ago.

As if that was not in bad taste enough, one of the speakers began his angry and boring statement, delivered in a hoarse voice: "SPLM *hakuma bitana*,

SPLA *hakuma bitana*", a jingle that was crafted during the war time by Cdr James Wani Igga, the current Vice-President.

At that time, this piece, which was popular to the soldiers and civilians alike, made some sense. Rendered to English it goes: SPLM is our government and the SPLA is our government. Since the insurgents did not have a conventional government most of its members consoled themselves with "the government under trees". This refrain became redundant after the formation of the government of national unity, following the CPA in June 2005. The song's proper place is in national archives and war museums, which, unfortunately have yet to be built.

"We shall never, never surrender", which the same speaker rammed down the throats of his colleagues, was also completely out of tune. Unless this writer is mistaken, the gathering is a groundwork for reunification of the party, reconciliation and peace, not war. And with that assumption, one then begins to wonder about the purpose of militaristic utterances would serve on a peace platform. Who are "we" as opposed to the unnamed "them/they?" "Surrender" implies a war situation. Which armed conflict is the speaker talking about? Past, current or future?

Blaming our woes on weak institutions

During his speech, the Chairman of the SPLM, Salva Kiir, cited weak institutions as one of the factors responsible for the problems besetting the country and its people. True, weak institutions not only fail to deliver solutions or prevent problems from occurring; in fact, weak, inefficient, ineffective or absent public institutions can create problems where there were none.

In our situation, the leadership of a unified SPLM must take practical steps to effectively distance the army from the political; there is too much involvement of the men and women in uniform in matters that are political. This should begin now, starting with the delineation of roles. For example, during the first day of the convention, several speakers were addressing the leader of the party as President [of the Republic]. That was incorrect as he wears many hats: Head of State (president) and, in that capacity, the commander-in-chief of the armed forces, even if he were to be a civilian; chancellor of all public universities. At the party function he is Mr Chairman, or Comrade Chairman, with each form of role and function at hand to determine the status and relevant honorific of the leader.

In many countries of the world, members of regular forces and civil servants are prohibited by law to engage in politics. Of course, that does not mean they cannot vote for a party of their choice, but they should refrain from acts or making utterances that are clearly political, and therefore partisan. In South Sudan, most members of the armed forces, police, prison service and wildlife think that, because they were part of the SPLM, and because of their role in the liberation struggle, they have the right to take part in affairs that are not part of their mission. No wonder a police NCO, who was a former SPLA soldier, once bashed a journalist in the run-up to the referendum because the latter had said he knew some people might vote for unity.

Changing perceptions and stereotypes

South Sudan, like any human society, is inhabited by people who have different worldviews and perceptions about other people, including fellow citizens. Because of the antagonism conflicts generate, the "wall in our heads" gets stronger, thicker and higher every time we quarrel with others. In that context we have constructs such as "Garang Boys", "New Sudan Council of Churches Mafia", "NCP-South", "Hijackers-Plus", "ONC" (standing for Opportunistic Newcomers) and so forth.

These names, which logicians call an empty category, have found their way into everyday discourse and political lexicography to the extent that they have lives of their own, and they refuse to go away whether we like it or not. Derogatory as these labels are, they are a symptom of a deeper social malaise: division and its attendant mutual distrust, hatred and discord. Since no society can wish away these ideas that are fixed in the minds of its members, as it is difficult to vanquish negative ideas people hold of others including fellow citizens by a fiat from on-high (the only way for a nation engaged in restoring and rebuilding lasting peace), it is imperative that individuals should make their judgement of others on the basis of their deeds and words, instead of the blanket demonisation of groups or communities for the wrongs, real or suspected, of some of their members.

A successful implementation of a peace process happens when all the parties behave rationally and delink themselves from herd mentality and stereotypes as the weapons in propaganda warfare, in which truth becomes the first victim, according the ancient Greek playwright, Aeschylus.

South Sudanese peace partners should do better by heeding the wise pieces of advice given by several speakers, notably the weighty and measured words from South African statesman, the deputy leader of the ANC, Comrade Cyril Ramaphosa, a true pan- Africanist and revolutionary. We ignore their sincere counsel at our own risk. For us to reject such priceless and valuable admonition would amount to an African adage: "*Acï wëlke nyɔ̈ɔ̈k*" (nyook), meaning the speaker has given useful advice to someone who is unworthy of these words of wisdom. The other alternative meaning is that the advice given would be squandered and disregarded by the recipient.

The people of South Sudan deserve help, moral as well as material, from friends all over the world because they – South Sudanese – contrary to the bad press we have received, are capable of incorporating such assistance into "South Sudanese solutions to South Sudanese problems".

The dawn of the Addis Ababa Agreement of 1972: a recollection (1)

The talks that led to the peace accord signed on March 3, 1972, by the government of President Nimeiri and the political wing of the Southern rebels in the Ethiopian capital Addis Ababa was a closed door affair. The World Council of Churches that mediated the talks for the Sudanese enemies was one of the entities the Sudanese establishment frequently accused of backing the rebellion in the south of the country. The other alleged culprits included the State of Israel and "world imperialism", a reference to Western world especially US administration, UK, the former coloniser, and the Vatican. For that and other reasons, Sudan's state owned media deliberately said nothing about the progress of the negotiations. Even after the final text of the agreement had been signed, the government in Khartoum kept the public in the dark over the details and other related matters.

However, while the negotiations were going on in Ethiopia, members of educated class from Southern Sudan residing in Khartoum were keenly following the developments, in bits, at the venue by means of interpersonal contacts, and telex messages accessible to senior government functionaries and local journalists.

Southern Sudanese students in the capital city at the time, mainly at the University of Khartoum, were among the interest groups who kept track of the progress at the talks, particularly during the hours leading to the signing of the agreement. Although not unanimous in their stand, the majority of students within the nationalistic African National Front, ANF, viewed the grant of regional autonomy – as provided for by the June 9, 1969 Declaration – as falling short of the aspirations of what they thought was the wish of their people: complete separation and independence.

The students who opposed the terms of the agreement did not want the leadership of Southern Sudan Liberation Movement, SSLM, to sign it. But of course there were some students who, because of their association with the politicians within the Government of Sudan, were happy with the accord and pressed for its endorsement by the rebel leadership, as well as by the government whose delegation was led by a Southern cabinet member, Abel Alier, who was also vice-president of the whole country.

Despite the open opposition within the student body, the students who supported the agreement began to organise themselves to make the pact a reality. When the delegation of the government returned home, representatives of the students went to Khartoum airport to receive them. A banner written in a mangled Arabic by one of the students, who is now a senior minister in the Government of South Sudan (this was written in 2016, before that VIP was sacked), was shown on the state-controlled TV along with a small group of students shouting some slogans in Arabic for the benefit of their Northern audience.

Reactions to the agreement

The news of the agreement was received by the majority of Northern people with a mixture of shock and puzzlement; to some it was a sell-out to the rebels and their alleged foreign paymasters, while others viewed it angrily as a stepping stone towards secession of the South, an eventuality that nearly all

Northern Sudanese – regardless of their political alignments – equated with high treason.

Those attitudes came to the fore during a press conference that the government delegation held immediately after the news of the deal had been made public. Sitting next to the head of the government delegation, Abel Alier, Mansour Khaled, a member of the delegation, was asked by a local journalist to explain why the government had made concessions to the rebels who, in his view, had no military power to defeat the government. Dr Khaled, a suave diplomat and a lawyer with international credentials, agreed with the reporter: the government did not offer autonomy to the South because the Anya Nya insurgents had the capacity to defeat the government's armed forces, but for a different reason. As a foreign minister at the time he was speaking, Mansour Khaled knew what many Northern Sudanese did not know about the attitudes of African countries which viewed Sudan's successive governments dominated by Northerners as oppressing the people of Southern Sudan. The minister was referring indirectly to some sub-Saharan African countries where Christians were in the majority of the populations.

Some hardliners within Sudan's ruling class did not share the views of the liberal Mansour Khaled. For example, Major General Khaled Hassan Abbas, the regime's defence minister and a man who credited himself with capturing the almost impregnable Anya Nya headquarters of Owiny ki Bul about a year earlier, could not stomach what he perceived as a national humiliation. Sudan's armed forces were able to achieve their "feat" because the Ugandan government of Milton Obote allowed the Sudanese army to attack their enemies from the rear after being allowed passage through the Ugandan territory.

As a consequence, General Khaled Hassan Abbas went into self-exile in Egypt from where he returned a few years later, humbled by accepting the less prestigious health portfolio, after realising the sky did not come falling down over Sudan for making a deal with the "outlaws" as the rebels were known in the official circles. Babiker Awadalla, Nimeiri's first prime foreign affairs minister also left in a huff for Egypt, where he remained until his death. Awadalla never reconciled with Nimeiri.

SSLM leaders in Khartoum

After the signing of the agreement, Lagu and senior members of his party flew to Khartoum, following the government's grant of amnesty to the rebels and refugees, retroactive to 1955, the year the Torit in Equatoria mutiny, an event that signalled a resort to armed struggle by the people of Southern Sudan. While in Khartoum, Lagu and his team went to talk to the Southern students at the University of Khartoum. At this time there were over 300 students studying different disciplines at the country's only university (Cairo University, Khartoum branch was dismissed as an adult education centre). Lagu, who was accompanied by Joseph Oduho, Lawrence Wol Wol and Mading de Garang among others, was received at lecture theatre Room 102 of the Faculty of Arts. Nearly all the students from the South turned up to see the Anya Nya leaders, most of them known hitherto mostly through the media. As that part of the year – March – is always hot, none of the visiting VIPs wore a Western style suit; General Lagu sported a short-sleeved shirt over a matching pair of trousers.

They all talked about the need for peace and urged the Sudanese people to accept the accord as it was good for the country and its people. The "returnees" as they were known said very little, besides emphasising the need for people to support the peace agreement. Some of the listeners were disappointed.

Published in the Dawn *newspaper, Juba, December 3, 2015.*

The dawn of the Addis Ababa Agreement (2)

Nimeiri's tour of the three Southern provinces of Bahr el Ghazal, Equatoria and Upper Nile largely helped in convincing the populace there that the government was serious with the peace project. That understanding in turn translated into support for the president who by that time was facing serious opposition in his own Northern backyard. In 1970, for instance, his government fought a brief but bloody war with the conservative Ansar sect, the backbone of Ummah Party. And, barely a year later, the army crushed the communists, his former allies, following a failed- three-day long coup mounted by Major Hashim al Atta. In years to come, Nimeiri's erstwhile Anya Nya enemies, now integrated into the national army, became dependable allies in warding off various attempts to overthrow him and his regime.

Nimeiri therefore reaped huge peace dividends to the extent that there were calls in some parts of the world that the Sudanese leader be considered for a Nobel prize for peace as a result of ending the civil war in his country.

For a few fleeting years President Ja'afar Numayri appeared to be a truly national leader, embracing all Sudanese irrespective of ethnicity, cultures, lineage loyalties, and religion. He basked in an outpouring of international acclaim as a peacemaker in a war-torn country when, in 1972, there were very few in Africa. He relished the adulation and the rumors of a nomination for the Nobel Peace Prize.[35]

Aware of the man's unpredictability, the suggestion was met with scepticism by several observers of the Sudanese political scene.

Laying institutional foundation

After the ratification of the Addis Ababa Agreement on March 27, 1972, an interim High Executive Council, HEC, was formed to run the region for one-and-a-half years, leading to the holding of the first ever elections to a People's Regional Assembly. One of the priorities of the HEC was to expedite relief, repatriation, resettlement and rehabilitation of the citizens who had taken refuge in the neighbouring countries- Uganda, Zaire, now Democratic Republic of Congo, Central African Republic, Kenya and Ethiopia. A commission to take up that scheme was created and its head, Clement Mboro, former president of the Southern Front party was appointed. An adjunct, Special Fund, was set up to raise resources for the commission. The fund was placed under Peter Gatkuoth, a banker and a Southern Front member.

In its composition, HEC was a sort of coalition government, representing two main political groupings: "insiders" and "outsiders". The former

---

35 [1] Collins, Robert O., *A History of Modern Sudan*, p. 112., Cambridge University Press, 2008.

referred to politicians who were inside the country during the conflict while the latter consisted mainly of former Anya Nya leaders and people who were also known as returnees, meaning former exiles. The insiders were not, strictly speaking, a homogenous class as they represented two rival Southern political parties, namely Southern Front and Sudan African National Union, Sanu, which before the May 1969 coup d'état were the sole representatives of the people of Southern Sudan in the Khartoum-based Constituent Assembly.

The selection of commissioners – the nomenclature used by the agreement for ministers – was mindful of regional and ethnic, as well as political, diversity of Southern Sudan for which a balance had to be struck. In that regard, most of the cabinet seats went to Southern Front and SSLM while Sanu received two portfolios in government. Sanu was also given the post of commissioner of Bahr el Ghazal Province.

Some circles within Sanu took issue with what they saw as their Southern Front rivals having taken the lion's share of positions in the new setup. Perhaps that complaint was based on the fact that in the last parliament dissolved by Nimeiri in on assuming power by putsch, Sanu had 15 MPs against Southern Front's 10. However, that claim was oblivious of another fact: although Sanu had a larger representation relative to that of Southern Front, the former had MPs from Bahr el Ghazal and Upper Nile provinces, especially in districts that were predominantly Dinka speakers, and had no single legislator from Equatoria. Southern Front, on the other hand, drew its deputies from the three provinces and could claim to be more pan-Southern Sudanese than Sanu.

The decision, which was seen to have been ill-advised, was the appointment of Aggrey Jaden as director at the Ministry Housing and Public Works. While serving as an administrator – before rebelling against the Government of Sudan when he was a district commissioner, a fairly senior position at the time – Jaden was among senior civil servants from the South. In the bush, Aggrey Jaden once became leader of Sanu in exile. Seeing the appointment as a slight to him, he declined the post and continued to live in East Africa. He returned home in 1977, a sick and unhappy man. He lived his last days out of the public gaze and anonymously until he died, a couple of years afterwards.

One car, one office for the entire government
After taking oath of office, the council's members flew to Juba to take charge of their duties. The VIPs were accommodated at the historic Juba Hotel. That historical facility which should have been set aside as a heritage site has recently been destroyed in the name of development. For their workplace, the council had to operate in the boardroom formerly used by Equatoria provincial administration, a few metres across the road from the hotel. And there was only one station wagon car for the use of more than a dozen commissioners. Office spaces for ministries was another problem. That was solved when the Equatoria Province heads of departments gave up their office buildings and their governmental houses to the commissioners or ministers as they soon became known.

Despite the fact that Alier, Logali, or Toby Maduot – the head and members of the interim administration – had been in cabinet in Khartoum before, the new government lacked qualified staff to organise the council's weekly and extraordinary meetings, record and keep resolutions and oversee general administrative duties. Cleto Hassan Rial, then senior lecturer at the Institute of Public Administration in Khartoum, was transferred to Juba as the first secretary general to the cabinet. Several senior and middle ranking civil servants from the South who were working for the central government followed suit. And that was the beginning of the story of which future generations of South Sudanese could be proud, for the efficient and effective civil service organ, those pioneers evolved from early 1972 to 1983.

Slowly but surely, these dedicated civil servants began to train young entrants, most of them secondary school- leavers and university graduates. The motto then was that degrees and other paper qualifications were necessary requirements but not sufficient conditions for employment and productive performance in a bureaucracy. Both the greenhorns and their mentors accepted that everyone should learn – even from a junior – and that this was the way to go about the system. The idea that someone was too senior or too highly educated to learn or be taught the basics of civil service was dismissed as a myth. Time proved the wisdom of that message.

At the heart of the administrative system was the Ministry of Public Service which did not only process employment and training, locally or abroad. The ministry also oversaw transparent application of terms of service;

rights of all the employees – promotion, training, and the maintenance of discipline within the system. Public service also served as a protector and defender of public interests in form of discipline, making sure abuse of office and ineptitude were discouraged, and punished when detected.

To guarantee that people entering the public service were prepared to be competent and would in future discharge their duties diligently and responsibly, a mandatory probation period averaging two years had to be strictly observed before an official was eligible for any assignment involving making serious decisions in areas such as finance, or on matters affecting the welfare and progress of junior employees. Answerability to the system and to the public servant's own conscience was well-drilled into the staff – so much in fact, that direct and daily supervision over underlings became virtually unnecessary. And there was the job description in which everyone beginning with ministers down to clerical personnel knew where one's powers began and where they ended. In that way, the system provided protection to everyone within the bureaucracy; it also curbed potential abuse of power by occupants of powerful offices.

The dawn of the Addis Ababa Agreement (3)

Some people may still be surprised that the Sudan Communist Party, or SCP, shared similar views with Sudan's sectarian parties towards what was known as the Southern Question. Interestingly, the June 9 Declaration, the May regime's Southern policy, announced a few days after Nimeiri's assumption of power in 1969, was a brainchild of the SCP. The declaration admitted that cultural differences existed between North and South and that the South deserved the right to a regional autonomy within a united Sudan. There was a caveat: only socialists among Southern Sudanese should the ones to implement the policy. That ideological proviso was seen by many as a clever way of reneging on the declaration. That position raised several questions. For instance, would the Anya Nya, an important party to the conflict and with most of its leaders known for their anti-communist attitudes, be first converted into socialists before the grant of regional autonomy? Who would teach them socialism, where, and for how long? There was a suspicion within the circles of the Southern educated class that the person who might have influenced the inclusion of this condition was Joseph Garang Wel, a senior member of the SCP, and a Southerner who later became the first minister for Southern Affairs.

At the time of the signing of the Addis Ababa Agreement I was one of six students taking Political Philosophy as a paper at the Department of Philosophy, Faculty of Arts. Three of us were from the South. Philip Thon Leek, former governor of Jonglei and currently a member of the National Legislative Assembly in Juba, John Ruach Jal and myself, while the other three students were the late Katim Adlan, Mohammed Ali Guwei and Fatima Hamour. Those Northern colleagues were leading and active members of the SCP. A promising leader, Katim Adlan was seen at the time as a potential secretary general of the SCP. Katim Adlan Centre, the research body has been established in Khartoum in his honour.

During class discussion on contemporary ideological issues of the time, we from the South would question our communist colleagues why they were not championing the case of the South as a national question as would fit into Marxist-Leninist ideals. We told them that in the Soviet Union, the right of distinct cultural and racial groups to an autonomy was recognised under what was called the "nationality question". In their response, our communist colleagues were always evasive and very uncomfortable with the question itself. Ironically, our lecturer, a British Marxist and activist in his own right, Mr Robin Buckley, openly criticised the SCP for being indifferent to the plight of the people of Southern Sudan who in his view, were victims of socio-economic under-development and exploitation by the ruling Northern bourgeoisie.

Official media: from denigration to condescending brotherhood
Following the return of the Anya Nya leaders to Khartoum, the Government of Sudan ordered the state-owned media, mainly Radio Omdurman, to adopt the language of peace and to stop the aggressive and abusive tone that had characterised the war-time period. Within hours, editors, producers and presenters whose daily output consisted of hurling abuse at the "outlaws" and

their alleged foreign backers, especially Western organisations associated with the Christian Church, promptly changed gears and without scruples started talking of *Janoubna el habiib, Janoub el Watan,* and *akhwana el Janoubiin*, respectively: our beloved South, south of the Nation, and our Southern brothers.

And there was money to be made out of the changed situation; one of the Southerners in the three cities soon composed a song called *"Ana wa Akhui Malual"*, meaning I and my brother Malual, supposedly a Dinka man. The song was discordant by omission: no mention of other brothers such as Lado, Gatkuoth, Lohide or Odhong and so forth, was made to refer to other communities that constitute Southern Sudan.

It was amazing to listen to journalists who had gained notoriety for spewing venom against individuals branded as enemies of the state. All of a sudden, these hacks were now singing praise of the same persons without blushing or even a quiver in their tone. Years later, journalists who changed like weather vanes were dubbed by opponents of the Nimeiri regime as *al agalaam al majoora*, literally, "hired pens" [and microphones].

Despite their superficial contents, the lyrics emphasised that the peoples of South and North were brothers. The song, composed on the spur of the moment, sounded hollow and unconvincing, as what was needed was action, not words. That kind of suspicion, as will be seen later, turned out to have been well placed.

Nimeiri avoids meeting spoiler President Sadat of Egypt

The agreement between the Government of Sudan and its former insurgents was not a piece of bad news within many circles in the North only; Egyptian authorities were deeply worried by the developments taking place south of their border. It was in that context that the Egyptian leader, Mohammed Anwar el Sadat, requested his Sudanese counterpart, Jaafar Nimeiri, come for a short visit to Khartoum. Aware of the intentions of Sadat, Nimeiri told him to put his visit on hold as he was going on a tour of the South to explain the agreement. Seeing the futility of his plan, President Sadat altogether gave up the idea of going to Sudan on a sabotage mission. For Nimeiri and the Addis Ababa Agreement, a plot had been successfully disrupted. Although President Nimeiri was determined to thwart attempts at derailing the agreement, he and his advisers at the material moment were hatching their own schemes to divide Southern leaders.

On the night when the government held a banquet in honour of the Anya Nya leaders in Khartoum, SSLM leader General Joseph Lagu, learned that he was not going to head the interim High Executive Council. The task of the provisional Southern government was to implement the agreement; manage the resettlement of returnees; integrate the former guerrillas into the national army; prepare the region for its elections to its own legislature in about eighteen months' time, among others. The surprising and explosive news was that the ruling one-party Sudanese Socialist Union, SSU, had picked Abel Alier – the government's leader to the talks with the SSLM – as its candidate for the provisional chief executive of Southern Sudan.

Unofficial news filtering from the corridors of power at the time talked of a disappointed Lagu, and added that some Southern leaders intervened. The message from those unnamed leaders said the hurried announcement by Nimeiri and his advisers was meant to sow seeds of division and distrust among Southern Sudanese. Alier, those sources said, was a fellow Southerner who also had the interests of the region at heart just as Lagu and his colleagues; and that that particular time required someone who would be trusted by both the North and the South. Being a Southerner and someone who had been a member of government for more than three years, Northerners were bound to trust him more than Lagu, who had had led the military fight against the central government, formerly equated with the North. On that count, Lagu was requested to be patient and bide his time, the source added.

Despite that episode General Lagu went on air, using Radio Omdurman and his mastery of Juba Arabic, often replete with jests, and told his soldiers all over the South to remove all the landmines, wherever they had laid them. Peace had come and there was no need to kill anyone any more, Lagu said.

It is to be recalled that not all the rebel leaders had accepted the agreement. Aggrey Jaden and Gordon Muortat Mayen- each of whom had once headed the rebellion- were among the prominent "rejectionists" who argued that the agreement had fallen short of their objective: total independence for Southern Sudan.

The dawn of Addis Ababa Agreement: a recollection (4)

The establishment of the civil service and its institutions in Southern Sudan in 1972, owed its success largely to the number of former district and provincial administrators whom the Regional Government had deployed in Juba mostly to head ministries as directors. Those men had trained and worked directly or indirectly under the British colonial administration. They came from the class of the administrators who had formerly become the backbone of the country's bureaucracy, after the end of the Anglo-Egyptian condominium rule in 1956.

In addition to their role as accounting officers of their departments, directors often took time to train middle-ranking staff in office procedures; documentation of official correspondence; preparation and publication of periodic reports; handing over notes and the like. The top civil servants also made sure that official communication should be conducted in a grammatically correct, clear and formal- officialised- English, which the Addis Ababa Agreement recognised as the working language of the Southern Region. At the time any official who could type – learned at the lower clerical rung or by graduates of commercial schools – had an edge over colleagues who lacked the skills in high demand, as is the case with computer literacy today.

When I joined the civil service a couple of years later, the Ministry of Culture and Information sent me to Khartoum to proof-read and supervise the printing of the government's third volume of its *Annual Progress Report* for the preceding year. The document, which was produced yearly by the ministry contained reports on all the government's policies, phased plans, activities, projects and so forth. Each ministry had to compile the progress, or lack thereof, in area target projects. Those reports informed the public of what the government was doing and gave reasons for the schemes that had either failed to meet deadlines, or had totally failed to take off all together. In a way, the information contained in the reports provided a channel of communication between the government and the people; it was transparency at work.

Building physical infrastructures

The Regional Government did not have much money but that did not stop it from initiating the construction of important public utilities, since the buildings it had requisitioned from Equatoria Province were insufficient, and too small for a bureaucracy that was expanding rapidly every year. One of those projects was the construction of the region's public buildings, that included a ministerial complex and residential areas for ministers and directors- now occupied by ministers, some undersecretaries and generals in the regular forces!

Supervised by the ministry of housing and executed by a Yugoslav construction company those important structures that modernised the face of Juba of the day were completed within three years. They cost a little above 20 million Sudanese pounds. And they were a sensible and valuable investment for the people of Southern Sudan. Few people know that the seat of the National Legislative Assembly, which was part of those structures, is one of the most impressive parliament buildings in Africa or that J1, the current State House was not one of them but formerly a residence for the colonial governor of Equatoria Province. Also unknown is the fact that the first asphalted strip from the Juba airport to the roundabout in front of Central Equatoria State secretariat, formerly Equatoria provincial headquarters, then to ministries' complex was laid down for the first anniversary of the agreement in 1973.

Two armies which did not speak one language

"We as soldiers we understand one another" is a saying Sudanese army officers have been known to repeat when referring to how to end a civil war. By this they mean that the soldiers on the opposing sides feel and bear the full weight of fighting, unlike their civilian members from the political class, who sometimes appear to prefer a military solution to an armed conflict. At the end of the seventeen-year long civil war in 1972, both the former guerrilla fighters of Anya Nya and the officers and men from the Sudan armed forces metaphorically did not speak one language. Mutual distrust and, to some extent, disdain characterised their daily relations.

A photograph taken in Malakal soon after the agreement, showing the first meeting of Brig Yousif Ahmed Yousif, the officer commanding government forces in Upper Nile, with his Anya Nya counterpart Col Paul Awel Ruaai, was instructive. Col Awel does not get closer to the former for an embrace as was the case in the first meeting between General Lagu and General Nimeiri in Khartoum, but offers his hand, at an arm's length. That image is just one example of the figurative distance between members of the two forces that were going to be integrated into one force within a short time.

After the university closed following campus disturbances, students were sent home. I went to spend that break with a relative in Malakal. At that time Captain John Garang was at the army garrison east of the provincial capital. Most of the evenings he would pick me to spend time with him at the officers' mess. It was clear that officers from the Sudan armed forces kept their separate companies. I was surprised that this kind of segregation was also happening within the Anya Nya officers; some of them avoided socialising with fellow Anya Nya colleagues. Most of the time I went there it was Captain John Garang and his friend Major Stephen Madut Baak. One evening a onetime classmate of mine, who had become an Anya Nya captain was approaching, John and Stephen suddenly stopped talking: they did not want the captain to hear what they were talking about. The two officers did not trust a man who was supposed to be one of their comrades. Apparently they had their reasons for their suspicion. They did not, however, reveal the reason to me.

On another occasion I witnessed an ugly altercation between an Anya Nya captain and a 1st lieutenant from the Sudan armed forces, also a fellow Southern Sudanese. The captain was angry with the lieutenant for keeping a car assigned to him longer than was agreed. The lieutenant ignored the orders issued by the captain that his junior should apologise. "Captain! Captain!" he mocked him as he was driving off. I was stunned. However, it was common knowledge that officers who had attended Sudan's military college at Wadi Sayedna near Omdurman looked down on civilians, as well as their fellow soldiers who received their training elsewhere, including guerrilla warfare. This attitude gave birth to the claim that Wadi Sayedna was a *Masana' al Rujaal*, literally, a "factory that produces [brave and professional soldiers] men". That kind of chauvinism did offend women as well as male civilians and soldiers outside that particular military college. These attitudes were partly to account for the frictions that persisted throughout the life of the Addis Ababa Agreement and characterised relations between the former guerrillas of Anya Nya and their fellow soldiers who had attended Sudan's military college.

The dawn of the Addis Ababa Agreement: a recollection (5)

As we have seen in the foregoing paragraphs it was not surprising that mistrust between the two groups was going to be an adverse factor in the integration process. The first test for the former enemies was the March 1975 mutiny at Akobo garrison in Upper Nile, when soldiers from the absorbed Anya Nya forces killed their commander, Col Abel Chol, a Southerner from the old forces, along with several Northern soldiers. Commenting on the event, former head of the Regional Government, Abel Alier, in his book, *Southern Sudan: Too Many Agreements Dishonoured*, says "...the absorbed forces were a politicised group with a sharp ear for rumour-mongering, reinforced by their abiding suspicion of the old forces".

Malakal was the epicentre of activities generated by the mutiny in the nearby Akobo. Several military aircraft landed in Malakal and so did many senior government and military leaders. Tension in the town was very high as there was talk of a possible government military attack by air and infantry against the mutineers; that a counter attack was a likely response from the absorbed forces in Malakal. At that time, I was in Malakal, on my way to Juba to begin work as an employee of the Regional Ministry of Culture and Information.

Wisdom prevailed as use of force was ruled out. The situation gradually returned to normal after some of the mutineers had escaped into the bush for the second time.

A year afterwards, Anya Nya forces stationed at Kapoeta were on the verge of mutiny when they were told they would be transferred to Rumbek to the west, and their colleagues were there to replace them. Mr Abel Alier and General Joseph Lagu, the officer commanding all the forces in Southern Sudan, flew to Kapoeta where they managed to convince the absorbed Anya Nya soldiers to obey the order. General Lagu famously told his former soldiers that he had to sign the agreement because of their pressure to do so. He held aloft a piece of paper he said was one of the telegrams sent to him during the final days of the negotiation at Addis Ababa by the Anya Nya commanders in the field.

In Bahr el Ghazal, the killing of Brig Emmanuel Abuur Nhial by Captain Alfred Aguet, both former Anya Nya officers, followed a similar trend: the absorbed soldiers who had also been notified of a pending transfer, were suspicious of integration and were preparing to disobey the order.

I vividly remember the photograph of a handcuffed and dishevelled Captain Alfred Aguet, brought to the office of the *Nile Mirror*. This was from the office of the head of the Regional government, which had prepared the report we had to publish. The editor, the late Benjamin Warille was handed that photo with an accompanying story, written by someone high up within the government. The courier, who must have been a security officer, gave instruction that the story should not undergo the slightest form of editing. As features editor in charge of such stories I was supposed to go over the text but because of the order we had just heard, I simply gazed at the distress-rousing photo which, together with the typed story, I passed to the graphic designer. I had nothing to add or subtract; it was an unusual news story. For days on end, the sad image of Captain Aguet who was later sentenced to death by firing squad, haunted me despite the fact that he had no right to take the lives of others – Police Inspector Bullen Kucha a former elementary schoolmate of mine, and Major Jibril Abdalla Mabok.

Threats to the agreement were not confined to the former guerrillas of Anya Nya; Nimeiri's own enemies – and they were as numerous as their agendas for wanting to get him out of power – were determined to sabotage the accord by creating problems for him and his government.

Palestinian Black September members kill diplomats in Khartoum

One of these plots happened exactly a year after the establishment of the deal. While the country was preparing to mark the first anniversary of the agreement, which had been made a national day, March 3, armed members of the Palestinian Black September organisation struck. A function was taking place that night, at the Saudi embassy in Khartoum. The Saudi ambassador was the doyen of the foreign diplomats in the country, many of whom had turned up for this occasion. Since security was probably lax inside and outside the fenced compound the assailants were able to scale the wall of the ambassador's residence with ease. They entered the party area, where they began to slit the throats of their astonished and helpless victims. Among the dead guests were the American ambassador to Sudan and his deputy. The two US and other diplomats, one of them a European national of a Lebanese descent, were butchered there.

The ease with which the terrorists entered the fenced compound with high walls raised questions about the slack security. There was suspicion that the Palestinian killers had accomplices among local Sudanese. A couple of days later a lecturer in education at the University of Khartoum was picked up by the security organisation for investigation. He had just joined the university where his wife, a teaching assistant, taught Arabic poetry in second year. She had previously taught Arabic to me and colleagues. The lecturer was later released for what was said by his colleagues to be lack of evidence. The young holder of a PhD was known to be a sympathiser of B'ath, the pan-Arabist party whose objectives have always been the ultimate political, cultural and economic unity of all the Arab nations.

I was in Khartoum at the time. Students were preparing for final examinations. It was a crucial year: I was in third year and had to study very hard because students with the best results would be selected for honours class. I was hoping to excel in English which was my major. That part of the year is always very hot and dusty. That night was really nasty: very high temperatures and the haboob was blowing from the northwest. Even if there had been no exams to keep most students awake, the inclement weather was not conducive to cosy sleep.

Since most of the students were studying late, we were among the first to get the news of the carnage before it had been officially announced over state TV and radio stations, at Omdurman across the west bank of the Nile. The Saudi embassy, located in Khartoum, the seat of the government, was not far from the campus and our hostels.

What we didn't know that criminal acts were being committed several kilometres away from our hostels. it was towards morning hours that the news of the killings reached us through an unofficial channel.

While the Palestinians were committing their grisly deed in one of Khartoum's posh suburbs, Sudan's very important guest, the Ethiopian monarch, Emperor Haile Selassie was in Juba with President Nimeiri, where they had gone to join the leaders and people of Southern Sudan in their celebration of the day that meant peace and political empowerment for them. The news was received with both outrage and puzzlement. The logical questions people were asking themselves were: Who could be behind the atrocious act? And why?

Not long after the shock had barely sunk in, the bogeyman of the Arab world and indeed of the US, Col Muamar Gaddafi was named as the mastermind and paymaster behind the assassinations. The Libyan leader, who was against the agreement, was revealed to have planned the conspiracy to embarrass his archenemy, Nimeiri. This highlighted Gaddafi's hostility to both Nimeiri and the Addis Ababa Agreement. Nimeiri had declined to join Gaddafi's proposed union of Libya, Egypt and Sudan, a plan he had given some thought, because the South was openly against the merger that would make them second-class citizens of a federation whose ideology was Arabism and Islam.

Nimeiri swore he was going to make every day of the year black for all the members of the murderous Palestinian Black September gang. For his part, the American President Richard Nixon warned that those who accommodated terrorists would ultimately suffer from the actions of ungrateful guests of the Black September ilk. Believing the world had forgotten the March 3, 1973 slaying of the diplomats in Khartoum, the Government of Sudan set free the Black September murderers a couple of years afterwards.

Southern Sudan as an oasis of democracy in a dictatorship

Though it appeared the road to full and satisfactory implementation of the Addis Ababa Agreement was a bumpy one in several directions, the first ever legislature of Southern Sudan and its role shocked and disarmed doubters, while on the other hand, the performance of the lawmakers was embraced as a pleasant and welcomed development by well-wishers.

Historian Robert Collins has put it this way:

Many sceptics, both in the North and abroad, firmly believed that the southerners were quite incapable of effective governance, but when the Assembly's four-year term expired on 19 December 1977 its members could take pride that they had indeed been able to govern. Democracy was alive and well in southern Sudan. [36]

---

36 Collins, Robert O., *A History of Modern Sudan*, p. 115, Cambridge University Press, 2008.

Soon after taking their seats in the former Equatoria's provincial city council chambers, the MPs embarked on checking the activities of the government, whose probity they easily found wanting: there was a contract that went by the name of Tecma. The Tecma affair as it later became known, was a deal between some representatives of the Regional Government and a foreign road making company to asphalt streets in Juba. The contractors and their workers soon vanished as they had never existed before they had barely commenced what was a shoddy job anyway. Then there were scandals involving government officials alleged to have misappropriated money for school text books; another concerned tea from Tanzania.

The assembly wanted to probe the alleged corrupt sagas by senior government officials, but the speaker, Lumbari Ramba, supported the government at every turn, hindering investigation. A frustrated assembly instead turned to take issue with the speaker himself for allegedly compromising the independence and impartiality of his office. The government, as expected, came to the defence of the speaker. The assembly would not budge: the speaker must go. He had lost the confidence of the members as he was no longer an honest broker. The standoff between the executive and the legislature bore hallmarks of a serious crisis with a potential for instability within the regional setup.

However, the government, which had correctly read the public mood, gave in by allowing the speaker to resign. Nevertheless, the legislature, having scored a point, felt slighted when the former speaker was appointed minister for public service. The president reshuffled his government to weed out three of the ministers who had sided with their colleagues in the assembly. The ministers were Joseph Oduho, Housing, Ezboni Mondiri, Transport and Roads, and Toby Maduot, Culture and Information.

The President of the High Executive Council, Abel Alier, later wrote that constant criticisms of his administration by backbenchers in the People's Regional Assembly immediately stopped the moment those vocal critics had been given ministerial positions in government, or senior positions within the ruling Sudanese Socialist Union. That observation might have been correct to some extent, but overall some of their colleagues were driven by principles rather than by personal interests. For example, members such as Victoria Yaar Arol, the first Southern Sudanese woman to enter a legislature, and the first Southern female university graduate in the region's history, were doing their job of check and balance between the executive and the legislature.

Perhaps that round one – the sacking of the speaker – emboldened the lawmakers two years later to challenge the region's incumbent chief executive they had previously freely elected. In the elections of 1978, General Joseph Lagu, the former rebel chief, became the candidate of a group calling itself Wind of Change. The constituent members consisted of former Anya Nya leaders, Sanu, as well as independent personalities. Former Southern Front chairman, Clement Mboro was a heavyweight within the Wind of Change grouping. In a free and fair election, the Change camp garnered a majority in the People's Regional Assembly.

Lagu was elected and the sitting president, who respected the people's verdict, accepted defeat with grace. That was rare, almost a record, during those days of one-party state and military rule on the African continent. Paradoxically, Nimeiri and his Sudanese Socialist Union, SSU, who were no friends of the will of the people and their genuine participation to choose their own leaders, were not amused by the rising democratic tide south of the border.

Some analysts of the day believed the North and the one-party-cum-military rule under Nimeiri feared that the democratic virus from the Southern Region was potentially contagious, and therefore must be contained by any means necessary. At the time, however, there were other factors at play within the Southern polity that provided Khartoum with an ample opportunity to meddle in the affairs of the South. One of those combustible ingredients on the political landscape of Southern Region was the unethical methods of power struggle adopted by rival groups.

The role of the media in peace and reconciliation

Media role in South Sudan's conflict in need of redefinition

It is the height of arrogance for any media practitioner to claim that the news media are the single and most important institution in any society. What would members of judiciary, legislatures, executive or other interest groups under the umbrella of civil society organisations say about their role? Whether the media exercise power with or without responsibility, caring or not, independent or controlled by state, they are simply partners in the ordering of the society in which they operate. Neither are they the most important in this role.

Media practitioners must behave as public servants who should be accountable to the public through legislation and their own code of ethics and conduct, no less, no more.

With this understanding in mind, the role of the media in the search for peace and reconciliation should not be seen as a substitute for that of the parties in the conflict; that role has to be complementary to the domestic and external pressure on the parties to end the conflict through dialogue. Even though the parties clearly have shown open disregard to the appeals by civil society including national spiritual leaders and women's organisations, there is no reason for the media practitioners from South Sudan not to join – in their appeals for peace and reconciliation – the international community, consisting of Igad, AU, UN, EU or powerful nations such as the US administration. It makes us look bad that African leaders ignore local counsel, and instead hurry to patch up their differences to escape punitive acts by foreign powers.

Additional role for the media

It is common knowledge that some journalists in the developing parts of the world subscribe to the concept that the news media's role is static, concerned specifically with the traditional function of supplying the public with information, education and entertainment. Even within these categories, change has to be introduced to meet new and specific challenges that are peculiar to new states. For example, in recent years, the danger posed by abuse of electronic media, especially radio, has been noted with grave concern. How much freedom of expression can be allowed in social media is controversial even in the industrialised world.

Since this piece is concerned with the promotion of peace and reconciliation in South Sudan, I will confine myself to the specific role of our media practitioners.

Besides their conventional role in society as mentioned earlier, South Sudanese media journalists will have to strive to give prominence to news items and to report on acts and individuals doing or saying things that promote harmony. In other words, this is "good news journalism", as a friend who is an expert in communications has recently told me.

"Good news" journalism does not replace "bad news" journalism, since by definition news is usually bad to qualify as such. The two brands have to coexist, while reports of "positive events" and the actors behind them need to be given prominence. This sound as if one is encouraging propaganda by government or opposition. No. The following is an example of what I mean here.

In the fog of war and bitterness arising out of recriminations between rival factions, many people ignore small acts that show humanity, tolerance, generosity, sacrifices, bravery and patriotism, either by a whole community or by individuals. For example, when violence broke out in Juba, stories were later told of people from different communities giving protection to members from other communities who were targeted on ethnic lines; a Nuer hiding a Dinka and vice versa. And those who saved the lives of people speaking a language different to their own knew they were risking their own lives. This happened in Juba, Torit, Bor, Bentiu and so forth, from people speaking the same language as the attackers.

As far as I remember, none of these tales ever appeared in our media, despite the fact that the stories could qualify as news even by Western standards. True, these stories could not vie to capture headlines, but in an environment where the milk of human kindness is a rarity, they have to have a space in our news slots.

These apparently small and civilised deeds exonerate the entire society from being seen as having thrown humanity to the wind to embrace barbarity and the law of the jungle. Those accounts should have been published and given prominence they deserved.

Such stories are also a testimony that in every community there are evil as well as good people. It is within such conscientious individuals where peace advocates across the ethnic divide could be found, to spread love and forgiveness within the nation state.

Personally, I have recorded similar stories from observations and from stories I have heard of the heroic and selfless deeds of some of the unsung South Sudanese. These good people deserve to be acknowledged. Their actions and convictions are useful lessons to the youth from various ethnic communities, at home or in the diaspora. Some of these will be published in instalments in this paper.

Incitement and hate speech out of the media

The other way in which the media can work in the interest of peace and intra-communal harmony is a little controversial, since some critics will conclude that the "preventive therapy" is likely to contravene freedom of speech.

Recourse to abusive language, incitement to violence or hate speech is unacceptable to many rational people worldwide. However, prohibition of these forms of expression through legislation is opposed by some people who argue that such laws violate the right of people to free speech as enshrined in the article 19 of United Nations of the Universal Declaration of Human Rights of 1948.

This is not the place for discussing the pros and cons of this. Over the years some countries, have enacted laws that criminalise discrimination of what is called "protected group against being singled out for ridicule", for example, on the basis of race, religion, disability, gender or any other identity. In recent years, some countries have passed laws against hate speech.

As far as my proposals on a new approach to the use of media during war and other social upheavals are concerned, I am not calling on lawmakers to pass an anti-hate speech law at this time, since it could be abused to curtail genuine free speech.

What I ask – of my colleagues in the media in general and editors in particular – is to use extreme caution in making sure that this time they, and the whole country, do not publish divisive and hate-filled material in the media. They cannot afford to further fuel the already boiling cauldron of ethnic bitterness.

One is not asking too much here; common sense and sound judgement will save us untold problems from callous words, in print or soundbite. Two examples will help to illustrate the point I am making here.

Early in 2013, my colleague, Alfred Taban, received a news item from a cub reporter who had brought what, in the language of the trade, was certainly a good story but, from the moral and judgemental perspective, the news report could be summed in one word: outrage, with the perpetrators deserving to be branded as beastly.

I reproduce the story here for the benefit of those who didn't read it.

A man in his fifties had sex with a ten-year-old girl who as a result died soon afterwards. Like any other news story, it had to carry other details to make sense. And here is where the role of decision-making and new-processing report can make a huge difference.

The reporter had included the ethnic origin of the man. The reporter was absolutely justified in doing so, but the question here was: what was the relevance of the perpetrator's ethnic affiliation to the commission of a truly heinous crime?

Editors sometimes act as tyrants, and as far as sound judgement is concerned, there is nothing to complain about that. So Alfred the chief editor chopped off the sentence carrying the name of the man's "tribe". (This writer long ago outlawed the use of this word but in this book he reluctantly used the word).

There is no suggestion that if the additional information on the man was maintained there would have been trouble, but in a society where there is sensitivity about ethnicity, the background of the offender was best left out of the news story.

Free flow of information is a right, but information especially if an opinion is offensive and likely to create or exacerbate existing conflict that has racial, religious or ethnic overtones, then people managing news should take extra care. This is not a hypothesis: there are examples of the use of radio broadcasts that fuelled ethnic hatred and conflict in Rwanda in 1994; in Kenya during the post-election violence of 2007-8, and recently in our own country when according the report of the Unimiss- United Nations Mission in South Sudan- the rebels broadcast on the state FM radio station in Bentiu, urging the local people to rape and kill people from other ethnic communities and nationalities.

Published in Juba Monitor in 2014.

Current national tragedy: a possible satirist version

The violence that broke out in December 2013, and quickly morphed into a full-blown civil war, qualifies as a national tragedy. Whatever position one takes on the conflict, this fact is indisputable. The war has claimed thousands of lives on all sides of the divide; millions of citizens have been displaced from their homes and have taken refuge across the national borders, or as internally displaced persons; and a similar number of war-affected civilians are facing food shortages across the land.

Worst of all is the invisible wound: deep and increasing hatred based on ethnicity in a society where national cohesion was at best fragile. The ensuing environment of mutual intolerance has become the defining ideology of the opposing camps; a development in which citizens who oppose being dragged into the hate orbit are branded as enemies: a bipolar world where "you are either with us or with the enemy"; a world where independent thinking is viewed to be on the threshold of treason. Our society has reached a stage where, it would seem, some of our compatriots, also across the divide, regret that we have been "lumped together" with the "wrong people". Views such as these threaten our very existence as a nation born out of sacrifices by all the constituent nationalities of South Sudan and over a very long time.

Indeed, many people still believe that ending the bloodshed will usher in an era of peace, forgiveness, reconciliation and healing. However, given the depth of bitterness and when flexibility is mistaken for lack of resolve on both opposing sides; and given the strength of the desire for vengeance, national healing and genuine forgiveness will take a generation or even more. If that is not a tragedy, then what name would be apt enough to describe our current situation, where compatriots are tearing each other apart as a nation?

Various reactions to the catastrophe

We live in a time when disasters – natural or human-made – taking place anywhere in the world, are replayed live by television channels to people in their homes. Reports on the war in South Sudan have continued to shock viewers to this day. Now with social media, audience are almost being taken to the scene where the news is unfolding. These include images of corpses of elderly people, women and children, strewn in streets of towns after battles between government forces and rebels; views of burnt-out market places; of places of worship or hospitals, sanctuaries that have often been turned into killing zones; inside government offices where computers, files and documents had been deliberately destroyed. These are uncivilised acts which are repulsive to the conscience of many people, whether they are South Sudanese or foreigners. Because of the acts described above, the outside world these days views us- *all* South Sudanese- as modern day barbarians. Denial would not work: physical proofs exist.

It is important for readers to note the fact that persons bent on a blame game strenuously ignore: who are the culprits? While the parties in the conflict constantly exchange accusations for atrocities or responsibility for the violence and its consequences, South Sudanese, who are not associated with the warring camps are prone to think that the bad guys giving the country a bad name are the Government of South Sudan, the rebels of the SPLM-IO and the FDs, shortened form of former detainees, *only*. The "neutrals", unless they belong to the millions of *mwananchi,* Kiswahili for masses of the ordinary people, are kidding.

We, as members of the elite are all to blame, even if one has not remotely played any role at all before, during or even after the crisis: class membership (elite) means one is guilty by association. It is a fact that members of the generation who identify with the struggle for justice and eventual independence of South Sudan readily take pride in that role, regardless of actual input one might have made. By the same token, it makes no sense for one to brag for the achievements while at the same time shy away from the group's blunders. Proud legacies belong to generations, and so do debacles and defeats.

Two examples here will suffice to illustrate my point. While I was – together with many other Kenyan clients – watching TV news in a Nairobi hotel, in early 2014, the bulletin began with ghastly images of South Sudan's war. Those who knew I was from that hapless land began to throw insults, especially expletives, into the air. Someone loudly said, "These brutes!" Intuitively I understood that all the remarks were being directed at me. Should I have got up to protest that I was not part of the conflict? No way. Of course, I was not amused. The fact of the matter is that violent conflicts stoked by members of African power elites, Kenya included, as a result of power struggle, are not peculiar to South Sudan.

The second case was in Australia a few months after that event in Nairobi. I was walking to a train station near where I live when an elderly woman stopped me to say "Excuse me. Why do you people kill one another?" The lady had just watched a TV news programme on the war in South Sudan. I did not want to lie nor would it serve any purpose if I were to say "they", excluding myself, were responsible for the horrors she had just witnessed on her set. "It's a long and complicated story", I told her and sped off to catch my train.

The funny world of satire

As an undergraduate studying English Literature, and Linguistics, among others, my class was introduced to satire as a field of study. Miss J.L. Cook, the lecturer behind the scheme asked the students to define "satire" in Arabic. Seven of us from the South and who spoke about three different African languages were not "bothered" since she did not believe African cultures had such literary forms. It was "*sukhuriya*"; the answer came from the benches. So we began the study of Jonathan Swift's *Gulliver's Travels*. We had to read *A Modest Proposal,* also by Swift, as a reference. That introduction later led us to more exploration of the literary genre that included poet Alexander Pope and George Orwell of the *Animal Farm* and *1984* fame. (Orwell's satires have given us phrases such as "All animals are equal, but some animals are more equal than others" from *The Animal Farm*, an attack on the former Soviet communism, and "Big Brother is watching you" in *1984*, on loss of personal freedom in a totalitarian state).

In essence, a satire is a story or a fable that has two levels of interpretation; a literary version on the one hand and what one can call hidden layer or the true target on the other. A satire brings to the fore a glaring contradiction in a given situation or something too ridiculous to cause disbelief or laughter or both. Ancient Greeks postulated that, when people watch a tragedy being performed on stage, the act of witnessing a tragic event unfold before their eyes would create what is called *catharsis*, defined as "purification or cleansing – especially pity and fear – through art or any extreme change in emotion that results in renewal and restoration". In other words, there is healing through the arts.

The other role played by a satire is that when an artist exposes our own follies through a seemingly straight forward story we laugh at the object of caricature which could even be ourselves. And after we have laughed at the ridiculous or the outrageous we are actually healing ourselves of excess bitterness or our failure to understand the bizarre or mind-boggling acts of other people. Often, laughter at someone else or an idea may contain an element of malice, especially when the victim is an underdog, but all the same, it makes people feel good sometimes.

Things to laugh at

The armed conflict in our country, like its counterparts in other parts of the world, is full of paradoxes, some of which could form a rich mine for writers of satire. The former Croatian President Stipe Mesic's aphorism to the effect that, "wars are often waged by those who know each other well, at the expense of those who have never met" can apply to our own situation. "Those who have never met" are the ones who constitute the bulk of "our gallant forces" to their respective commands and who bear the brunt of fighting and other deprivations while their superiors rarely come under fire or get killed or wounded. Members of the top echelons on opposing sides in armed conflicts usually have three square meals a day, access better health facilities and sleep in safe and comfortable shelters, unlike their soldiers who rough it up in trenches, sometimes in the rain, with their clothes and their heads full of unpleasant lice.

And while war lasts, members of the political class – on both sides of the divide – are wont to appeal to the international community for relief assistance. Humanitarian assistance can – and has – saved millions of victims, especially of armed conflicts or natural disasters worldwide in recent years. But as Graham Hancock in his book *The Lords of Poverty* has noted, foreign aid, which accounted for $60bn in 1989, the year in which the book was released, has its own shortcoming: much of the funds allegedly go for the upkeep (and comfort) of their managers, and not to the targeted recipients in the developing world.

As expected the accusation rankled some aid agencies, do-gooders, as donors are known sarcastically, but this apparent hypocrisy can be a subject of laughter and at the expense of some aid workers or their local counterparts acting on behalf of the needy recipients of foreign donations. In the developing world in general, and Africa in particular, the rich nations of the North fund accommodation in expensive hotels and pay air tickets to warring parties to talk peace and end civil wars in their own countries. All these, and much more, are fertile grounds for playwrights, novelists or contrarian commentators to poke fun at the elites of the developing world.

Not yet the time for poking fun
Our situation since December 15-16, 2013, has been so distressful that it is not the time to laugh at all members of the elite, who are believed to be wholly or partially responsible for our woes and who may include the satirists themselves. Making fun- publicly-of alleged perpetrators now could be counter-productive, as that is likely to harden their positions, hence jeopardising the achievement of peace and reconciliation; making war – and anything associated with war – a subject of laughter will be in bad taste now, as families who have lost loved ones on both sides are grieving; and finally, any patriotic (not fond of the word "nationalist" as it is sometimes a synonym for "chauvinist") creative artists from South Sudan should resist at the moment any public portrayal of their society in a manner to "affirm" the "prediction" by some circles, who propagated the notion in the past that secession for the former region of Sudan would result in chaos. We, as a nation are in big trouble, no doubt, but it would be an unforgivable and grave mistake for any patriot to concede that the vote for nationhood was a

mistake, and that we are not capable of managing a modern state. That should be the work of a propagandist; it is not a job worthy of a self-respecting artist.

We have messed up our country, but we believe we are capable of running a modern state. The past is a witness for our potential as efficient, effective, diligent and responsible people. What is missing is: someone among us to show us the right way of running public offices. Competently. Responsibly. Humanely. Honestly.

Acknowledgements

This is an unconventional type of acknowledgement. The reader of these line will at the end appreciate why it has to be too long and virtually a story, instead of appearing as brief words of thanks to a few individuals who have helped in one way or another in the writing and production of these semi-autobiographical accounts.

A book like this one that doesn't involve research or interviewing individuals or people working for institutions is bound to have a limited number of persons to be thanked or acknowledged for their different contributions. However, since this is my first work to appear between two covers, I am bound to thank many individuals who have either mentored or encouraged me to reach the current level where I have prepared the book for publication. It has been a very long journey spanning more than four decades in which I have been writing mainly for the press. My writing has not been limited to newspaper articles edited by others; I have been an editor of several newspapers and magazines, an experience that largely helped to improve my editorial skills, which I sometimes apply outside journalism.

As a way of acknowledging the contributions of my mentors, whether they were schoolteachers, senior journalists or authors who inspired me to write professionally, I have honoured them in an essay appearing in this book. Sadly, many of them are not alive to read my homage to them. Mentioning them here in passing wouldn't be enough to express the debt of gratitude I owe them.

Since some of the pieces in this book were published in other periodicals, the editors deserve a big thank you. Several articles which are part of this work appeared over a long period in the past mainly in the Kenyan (*Daily Nation*, the *EastAfrican* and the *Standard*) and South Sudanese press. I am grateful to the editors of those publication. I thank my colleague, George Garang Deng Chol, former editor of the *SPLM/A Update*, which in the early 1990s carried my weekly column "Far Away from War". Dan Eiffe, former publisher of *Sudan Mirror* weekly and its editor, John Gachie, generously allowed me to express my stinging political views "Sudan: A Different Perspective on Issues" column without any kind of censorship.

Many thanks, Commander Dan and my friend John. In recent years nearly all newspapers based in Juba and three Arabic language dailies in Khartoum, have carried my writings. They and their editors are too many to be listed and acknowledged individually here. All the same, I am grateful to all of them. I regret that I am at the moment unable to mention and thank some of the papers that published my articles, some which have appeared here. In due course, I will make recompense by giving them their dues in the forthcoming books.

Although a sizeable number of South Sudanese journalists are decent men and women, I reserve special word of appreciation for Jacob J. Akol of the *Gurtong* website and magazine; Alfred Taban of *Juba Monitor*, and Victor Lugala. By choosing to stand with the people of South Sudan and not with any of the warring parties, these colleagues have given journalism a good name. I am proud of you comrades in pens. One of the pieces in this book discusses the potential difficulties and dangers which can befall a principled journalist. *Asante sana*, by your deeds, you have vindicated my erstwhile stand as a lone wolf on the issue.

As for my family members, friends and colleagues who have supported me in the production of this book, I should start first at home. My wife, Anna Abul Malual, popularly known to friends and family as Hanan, has been very instrumental in pleading with me to publish books out of the vast non-fiction material I have accumulated over the years. Although I am not a specialist in any particular field, she knows how passionate I am about cultural and social aspects of South Sudan, a subject on which I have extensively written over the years. And towards that end- reading and writing- she always makes sure that any property she rents must have a room set aside to provide a space and an environment that are conducive to study and writing. Without that understanding, it would have been difficult for me to execute my writing task that guaranteed concentration.

For their part, my children, now adults, have always been ready to help with my writing. When the diskettes containing the bulk of my published articles were found to have been corrupted, my daughter, Atong, typed some of them from the hard copies of the newspapers in which they had appeared. Both Dut, Deng Jr, Jido and Nancy, have often been on hand to teach me- even while they were in primary or high school- how to use any new computer program or fix a technical hitch affecting my laptop. I am thankful to them all.

I also appreciate the role of my family members in South Sudan and other parts of the world. They as always, have been unfailing in their constant support for me. My daughter, Nyanluak Sr and her husband, Majok Deng Adoor, and my son, Emmanuel Deng – Diktoor as he is known to us – are my closest family members living in South Sudan. In the US, my nephew Atem Aruei Yaak and his wife Akuol Kuany Ajang, have always remained very close to me wherever I may be based. Their frequent phone chats and uplifting wishes for good health and hope for return of peace to the bleeding motherland, serve to rekindle hope in me and a stimulus to keep on writing. Gabriel Alaak Garang, a lifelong friend who has maintained communication- which is perceived by some as "contraband" and therefore "treasonable"- with me since I left Juba in early 2014. I sincerely thank him for being the buddy to whom the phrase "a friend in need is a friend indeed" aptly applies. Writing about home of which one has no contact is to be reduced to the level of fiction writing.

Since some of the pieces in this book were published in other periodicals, their editors deserve a big Thankyou. Several articles which are part of this work appeared over a long period in the past mainly in the Kenyan (*Daily Nation*, the *EastAfrican* and the *Standard*) and South Sudanese press. I am grateful to the editors of those publication. Dan Eiffe, former publisher of *Sudan Mirror* weekly and its editor, John Gachie generously allowed me to express my stinging political views "Sudan: A Different Perspective on Issues" column. Many thanks, Commander Dan and my friend John. In recent years nearly all newspapers based in Juba and three Arabic language dailies in Khartoum, have carried my writings. They and their editors are too many to be listed and acknowledged individually here. All the same, I am grateful to all of them.

Since this book is mainly autobiographical, I shouldn't forget to thank individuals who contributed, in the past or recently, to the welfare of my family or my own, because dead people don't write. In that regard, I must register my sincere gratitude to Dr Lual A. Deng, the friend who got me out of a camp for the internally displaced persons, IDPs, in Equatoria in 1992 when he found a job for me in West Africa. It was that offer that enabled me to pursue family reunion while in Nairobi in transit to Abidjan, Cote d'Ivoire. A year later my efforts resulted in what could be called "release" and subsequent arrival in Kenya of my family from Nasir where they had been "stranded" for more than two years. It was while in Lodwar, Kenya, reunited with my wife and small children, I was able to write my weekly column, "Far Away from War". Some of those pieces are in this book. Many thanks "Sihyooni". This is what friends are for.

I was able to travel outside Southern Sudan after Cdr Chagai Atem Biar- related to me through marriage- had requested the then deputy leader of the SPLM/A and the head the movement's security organ, Cdr Salva Kiir, to release me. The request was readily approved. It was an act of kindness that I will always remember with gratitude, considering that there were individuals within the SPLM/A, who secretly but firmly opposed my trip for reasons that are best known to those "comrades".

At my base at the Central Coast, NSW, Danielle Habib and her husband Akuei Lual Lual Akuei, have been very kind to introduce me and my family to the multicultural society, resulting in making friends from whom I have learned a lot of important things. These exposures in turn have enriched my experience in cultural diversity. I am thankful to the couple for giving us this rare opportunity.

South Sudanese community in Australia represents true face of their cultures in various forms. Elders in particular although their number is very small, constitute what could be considered as custodians of our African societal personality and norms. Writers usually draw from such a pool by way of concepts, vocabulary and knowledge of oral history. Late Buup Athel Mach, a lady with crisp sharp memory, used to be one of my sources providing, usually accurate, information in regards to cultures and recent history of the society of Bor people. In general, I owe a debt of gratitude to her and the following elders from South Sudan living in Australia: Prof Martin Marial Takpiny and his wife Susan Ajak Simon Ngong; Madit Kon Chol; Abuk Gordon Apec Ayom; Adau Ajang Duot; Rachel Ayen Garang Dut; Aliet Ajak Thot; Apajok Kuoyo; Adual Jang; Agot Leek Deng, as well as others.

Some families and individuals in Australia who have morally supported this and other writing projects are many. It wouldn't be possible to record all their names here. The following are among the few of those friends: Ajang Chiman Ajang and wife Nyibol Kou; Chol Achuoth Ajang and wife Abuk Garang; Peter Garang Deng and wife Rebecca Athok Manyang; Samuel Diing Aruei Bol and wife Ayen Lul; Diing Bul Atem and wife Adhieu Nyuon Akoi; Atem Athian Atem and wife Apajok Deng Manyuon; Ajang Deng Biar and wife Mary Aduk Barach and their children; Akech Arok and wife Adhieu Kuoyo; Deng Tor Yong and wife Ishrak Gabriel Beriberi; Dau Akoi Jurkuch and wife Achol Garang Aguer; Deng Gabriel Dau and wife Susan Aduk Gideon Dau; Chol Abednego Achiek and wife Adhieu Gideon Dau; Deng Atipas Arok Biowei and wife Adau Thuch Dut; Mayom Deng Maketh and wife Nyakiir Deng Akuoch; Abraham Deng Malek and wife Ayen Deng Akuoch; Majok Gurech and wife Akuch Gaiyo Galuak; Biar Malual Atem and wife Akur Aguer Bior; Deng Biar Deng and wife Atiliu Manyok Diing; Ajang Reech Gak; Pageer Alaak Yuot; Kongor Maketh Gak; Awak Kongor Gak; Deng Ajang Duot; John Panrach Kuol; Kuol Garang Deng Majok; Aguer Tor Bior.

Family friends and former colleagues and co-workers who deserve Thankyou for their unfailing support and friendship include: Yaar Paul K. Awar; Kuir Deng Biar; Abeny Nai Kur; Agum Abdon Atem; Ayak Maketh Duk; Nyanwal Majier Gai; Akuot Jeroboam Machuor; Nyandeeng Kuir Aleu.

Some South Sudanese church congregations use vernacular languages in their services and even teach them. I benefit from these groups as I also write in the vernacular. I am grateful to Rev Samuel Khot Majok of St Mark Church, where I sometimes teach Dinka language to children and adults, Sydney; Rev Chol Awuol Yai of Canberra; Rev Anyang Manasseh Mach of Lutheran Church; Melbourne; Rev Martha Adau Kongor of St Mark Anglican Church, Perth, Lay Reader Arok Kuek Atem, Sydney; Rev Chol Majok Manyuon of Brisbane, Queensland; Marial Ayuel of Sydney.

SPLM chapters, especially those in New South Wales, NSW and Australian Capital Territory, ACT have always been working to unite all South Sudanese, and acting as a forum where communities celebrate national occasions as a way of remembering sacrifices made by South Sudanese over centuries in search of dignity and nationhood. Writers feed on such events. I am very pleased with and grateful to their patriotic leaders, among them Dr Matur Gorjok, the articulate current chair; previous chair, David Lokosang; members: Arou Job Adier; William Orule; Simon Winya, and Abraham Bol Malek of ACT chapter, among other comrades. They provide good example for youth to follow: harmony and unity of purpose.

Although beset by division and power struggle, the SPLM remains a political organisation which is part of our history and to some extent a creator, for better or for worse, of South Sudan's political consciousness, and above all, the mid-wife of our national independence. The NSW chapter should be a role model.

Community leaders play an important role in keeping alive the cultures of the people by occasional celebrations, which involve traditional dances, wrestling and singing. The current leaders deserve praise and support of all although they need to use the small entities they lead to be bricks in the larger edifice: national unity and nation building enterprise. At any rate, the efforts of many these leaders in bringing communities together are slowly bearing fruits. Thanks for that task go to: Kenyatta Dei Wal President: Federation of South Sudanese Associations in Victoria Inc FSSAV; Kot Monoah Chairperson of South Sudanese Community Association in Victoria Inc; Henry Leke of Kajo Kaji Community of NSW; Akuot Aciek Akuot Chairperson of South Sudanese Community In Western Australia Inc.; Emmanuel Kondok of South Sudan and other Marginalised Areas; Julius Clement of Equatoria Community of NSW; Mareng Bol; Karakon Athieu of (greater) Bor Community; Marial Ayom of Bor Community; Kuer Dau Apai; Twï Community of Australia, Nuul Mayen Deng, leader of Twich East Community Inc., NSW; Sunday Meshach Makuei; Mading Wade; Adeng Gaiyo Galuak; Adau Lual; Anne Atong Dimo among others.

I have realised that the columns I wrote in the 1990s and later in early 2000 attracted a lot of readers who became my loyal fans. Some of those readers have in person or via phone calls requested me to provide them with stories similar to those which appeared under the "Far Away from War" column. Happily, for them, I have included some of those articles in this book. Some of those fans are: Ajak Deng Chiengkou; Abul John Manyuon; Biar Ngang; Deng Lueth; Deng Abraham Chol Riaak; Arok Kongor Arok; Mabior Aguang Atem; Malith Mayom; Marial Isaac

Kot; Deng Garang Ager; Deng Dau Atem; Dor Akech Achiek; Dau Nyok; Duom Kuany Duom; Kiir Kedhekia Chol Aguer; Bul Geu Ayuel; Atem Mayen Bior; Abuoi Jook Alith; Mamer and Apajok Yaak; Ajang Jok Ajang; Dut Biar; Manyok Yaak; Deng Tor Deng; David Ajak Ajang; Manyok Kuany Deng; Yong Achuoth; Chol Akoi Jurkuch; Bol Akoi Nyuon; Garang Mayen; Manyok Kuany Deng; John Panrach Kuol; Chol Gak Manyuon; Biar Malual Atem; Chol Akoi Jurkuch; Yong Achuoth; Atem Aleu; Abul Dau Aruei; Deng and Aruei Bol Aruei.

With the production side of the book, Peter Lual Reech Deng, the founder and CEO of Africa World Books and his bold but welcome initiative to go into publishing, deserves a lot credit. I extend my appreciation to his team, especially Manyang Deng Biar and his wife Nyankiir for their generosity and hospitality in accommodating me on several occasions when I was visiting Perth, Western Australia, during launches of books published by the African World Books.

My editor, Rachel Kear, deserves all credit for making the book take form out of what was a jumble of writings on disparate topics, most of which had little in common except they were by one author. Rachel has brought order to what seemed a chaotic collection of articles, tackling issues with my often-lengthy sentences. As English is her mother tongue, I had the confidence when I first approached her that she was going to rescue me from the pitfalls most users of a foreign language are often prone to. My expectations have been well placed. Many thanks, Rachel. More material on its way to you. You have done me a favour I will not forget.

On the production side, I have a huge debt of gratitude to my son, Dut Atem and his company for designing the impressive cover. Dut has patiently been working with me in arranging the material before I sent it to the editor. In addition to all that, he has always been on hand with things IT, including introducing me – when he was a young boy – to thorough knowledge and effective use of Dinka fonts which I have been using for translation work for more than a decade now. Many thanks, Dut-Ayämkuëi, as your namesake and the family forebear was known.

I am grateful to Steve Barwick for the excellent artwork and his valuable technical advice he freely gave me during the final stages of the production of this book. *Shukran jazeelen*, Steve!

Of course, none of those individuals mentioned above has any role in the imperfections that readers will spot when they pass over the stories. None of these many people, too, bears any blame for what is not right with this book or be associated with some of my opinions that are likely to meet disapproval from some readers particularly those who will identify with the unnamed characters, the recipients of my seemingly uncharitable comments and judgement. As the author I take full responsibility for what may not be right in and with the book.

Jungle Chronicles

www.ingramcontent.com/pod-product-compliance
Lightning Source LLC
Chambersburg PA
CBHW020637300426
44112CB00007B/144